Gay Rights and the Mormon Church

GAY RIGHTS

AND THE

MORMON CHURCH

Intended Actions, Unintended Consequences

GORY A. PRINCE

House Man colophon

This is dedicated to the memory

of LGBT people within the Mormon tradition

who suffered and, in too many instances, died for lack of

a supportive community; but mostly it is dedicated to

the amazing LGBT people who still consider Mormonism

their tribe and to the hope that their futures will be

filled with joy, love, and fulfillment.

CONTENTS

PREFACE

Proposition 8 was the first cause of this book, although I did not comprehend it immediately. In November 2008, one week after the election that made Barack Obama the forty-fourth president of the United States and simultaneously embedded in the California Constitution a ban on same-sex marriage, I received an urgent phone call from Helen Whitney. I had worked with Helen on her 2007 *Frontline/American Experience* documentary for PBS, *The Mormons*. Her call came in response to an email from Andrew Solomon, a distinguished writer and one of Helen's best friends—and a gay activist. Having learned of the pivotal role that the Church of Jesus Christ of Latter-day Saints[1] had played in the passage of Prop 8, Andrew lashed out at Helen for having produced a documentary film that put the church in a favorable light. She asked that I help her to mend the rift.

After a virtual introduction from Helen, Andrew and I carried on an email correspondence for many months that gradually brought the temperature down and became the basis of a genuine and lasting friendship. Andrew became not only a friend but also a tutor and role model, sensitizing me for the first time to nuances of the lesbian, gay, bisexual, and transgender (LGBT) world. Our friendship eventually resulted in the publication of a wonderful interview in *Dialogue: A Journal of Mormon Thought*, but the thought of writing a book had not yet germinated.[2]

Another unplanned contact who became a lasting friend and further expanded my consciousness was Rick Jacobs, one of the most outspoken critics of the LDS Church during the Prop 8 campaign. But the most important event leading to the writing of this book occurred when Randall Thacker, the newly elected president of Affirmation: LGBT Mormons, Families & Friends, asked that I join Affirmation's board of directors. I accepted the invitation and served on the board for five years. Experiencing, secondhand, the challenges facing LGBT Mormons who are attempting to blend their homosexuality with their spiritual tribe convinced me of the need to place in historical perspective the church's long and uneven relationship with homosexuality, both among its own members and in the public square.

I have conducted more than one hundred interviews in the course of researching this book, many of them with non-LDS sources. Some were of LGBT church members who stayed, but many others were of LGBT people and allies who had left the church. I also have amassed a database of over fifty thousand pages. Hugo Olaiz, Carol Lynn Pearson, and David Combe were remarkably generous in sharing their own archival collections.

Particularly valuable has been my association with William Eskridge, the John A. Garver Professor of Jurisprudence at Yale Law School. Bill is acknowledged as one of the leading legal authorities in the world on LGBT issues. He played a crucial role in gaining access to the rich record of court documents in the pivotal Hawaiian lawsuit *Baehr v. Lewin* that played the same role for marriage equality that the Stonewall Riot of 1969 did for national LGBT awareness. Bill has also provided ongoing critique of the text of the book. His "trifecta" of being gay, non-LDS, and a legal expert has been invaluable in my quest to try to get the story right.

Although I have attempted to engage voices from all sides of the issues treated in this book, I have been frustrated by two groups. The first was lay Mormons who advocated for Proposition 8 with time and means (donating more than $20 million to the cause) and remained supportive of it since the election. Whether for "buyer's remorse" or other reasons, none were willing to go on the record and talk about their motivations and actions that helped propel Prop 8 to an unlikely victory.

The second was the LDS Church hierarchy. When I met with Michael Purdy of LDS Public Affairs in April 2015 and discussed the possibility of interviewing church officials for the book, he asked that I send him a formal proposal, which I did. Four months later he sent me the following in an email: "After discussion, the decision was made to not offer anyone directly affiliated with the Church to be interviewed."[3] The decision of church leaders not to participate necessarily means that their perspectives on the story are largely missing, except through documents in my database and secondhand accounts from other interviewees. Readers who see an imbalance in the narrative should understand that the church's absence was their decision, not mine.

I felt urgency with this book that I had not felt with my prior three. The topic was and is timely within American and Mormon society, but more important is the effect of the church's policies and doctrines on the every-day lives of its LGBT members and their families. Nothing is more important than human life, and too many LGBT Mormons have chosen suicide because life was no longer tolerable. If this book can save even one life, I will have been overcompensated.

INTRODUCTION

The Mormons were late to the battle. Although LGBT issues were first reflected in church policies in 1968 and announced nearly simultaneous to the 1969 Stonewall Riots that thrust gay rights on to the national stage, those policies looked inward and had no discernible effect nationally. Furthermore, in building its policies on the foundational assumption that homosexuality was a bad choice that could be unchosen, the church positioned itself within the mainstream of religious and secular thought in the United States. What the church did with—and to—its LGBT members hardly differed from the treatment given by other religious traditions and thus wasn't even a blip on the national radar.

In 1993, however, the Mormon Church "crossed the street." When a lawsuit in Hawaii, *Baehr v. Lewin*, appeared to set the stage for that state to become the first in the country to legalize same-sex marriage, the church entered the public square and became a potent force for preserving what was euphemistically called "traditional marriage." This was a problematic term given the major changes in the definition of marriage in prior decades that made questionable just what was being preserved and inescapably ironic in a church that, a century earlier, had gone to the mat to defend its practice of polygamy, a form of marriage so nontraditional that it had been termed one of the "twin relics of barbarism"—the other being slavery—and was a key issue driving the formation of the Republican Party.

Hawaii was a crucial turning point for the Mormon Church. In the first place, it marked the first time that the church effectively set aside its long-standing enmity toward Roman Catholicism, which had achieved near-canonical status when Mormon leader Bruce McConkie, in an encyclopedic and audacious book entitled *Mormon Doctrine*, referred to it as the "Church of the Devil...singled out, set apart, described, and designated as being 'most abominable above all other churches.'"[1] Since Hawaii, the two churches have come together on several occasions to pursue mutual interests, and institutional enmity has vanished. In the second place, the church quickly honed its political skills and became a significant force in circumventing the outcome of the lawsuit by facilitating the passage of an amendment to the state constitution that specifically outlawed same-sex marriage. Hawaii became the "playbook" that was used by the church in subsequent successful efforts in other states to thwart marriage equality.

Although the church was a significant force in Hawaii, its role barely registered nationally and then only momentarily. Church leader Gordon Hinckley, who later became church president, kept the church in the background, largely through the formation of a front organization, Hawaii's Future Today (HFT). And because public sentiment was still solidly against marriage equality—polling in Hawaii consistently put it at the mid–60 percent level—the efforts of the church resulted in the maintenance of the status quo, and there was no public backlash. Little attention was paid to the church's efforts when subsequent histories of the LGBT movement in the United States were published. Emboldened by their success in Hawaii, church leaders fought successfully in Alaska, California (Proposition 22), and other states to block marriage equality, in each instance playing an important, if not decisive, role while remaining largely invisible nationally.

Proposition 8, the California ballot initiative in 2008 that embedded one-man/one-woman marriage in the state constitution, changed the national LGBT landscape and the fortunes of the Mormon Church. A temporary setback for marriage equality, Prop 8 was a major turning point for LGBT rights. Although it represented a high-water mark for opponents of same-sex marriage, Prop 8 elicited a national backlash that caused the dominoes to begin to fall in the opposite direction, culminating in , the 2015 U.S. Supreme Court decision establishing marriage equality as the law of the land.

The death of church president Gordon Hinckley just weeks before the church's decision to jump into the Prop 8 fray resulted in the abandonment of Hinckley's counsel to remain in the background. Instead, the church essentially became the "point of the spear," with some reporters referring to Prop 8 as "the Mormon Proposition." Unlike Hawaii, where the church's actions preserved the status quo, Prop 8 took away the short-lived legalization of same-sex marriage in California. And the Mormon Church, because of its leadership role, became the target of an immediate, harsh, and sustained backlash. In dealing with the backlash, the church took the unprecedented move, less than a year after Prop 8, to give full-throated endorsement of proposed Salt Lake City ordinances that, for the first time in Utah history, extended to LGBT persons antidiscrimination protection for housing and employment. The nation noticed.

With the passage of time, historians have focused more on the post–Prop 8 world than on the initiative itself. Two important histories that focused on *Hollingsworth v. Perry*, the trial that challenged the constitutionality of Prop 8, are *Forcing the Spring: Inside the Fight for Marriage Equality*, written by Jo Becker, a *New York Times* reporter, and *Redeeming the Dream: The Case for Marriage Equality*, written by David Boies and Theodore B. Olson, who headed the legal team challenging the proposition. Since the Mormon Church had retreated to the sidelines in the aftermath of Prop 8 and was not a factor in the trial, both books mention it only in passing. The full role of the church in passing Prop 8 has never been chronicled.

In June 2013, the U.S. Supreme Court declined to hear an appeal of *Hollingsworth v. Perry*, thus legalizing same-sex marriage in California but leaving the issue open in other states. A ruling by federal judge Robert Shelby in December 2013, in a Utah case, *Kitchen v. Herbert*, challenging the church-supported Amendment 3 that outlawed same-sex marriage, once again thrust the Mormon Church into the national spotlight. And a clumsy press conference a year later, in which church leaders were widely perceived to be using religious liberty as a cloak to protect anti-LGBT discrimination,[2] resulted in another full-throated church endorsement of antidiscrimination, this time for statewide protection—thus far the only such legislation passed by any "red state" legislature. Again, the nation noticed.

Yet in spite of these instances where the church played a significant, if not decisive, role in the national LGBT scene, the details and nuances of its role have gone mostly unnoticed in published works. To bring to a broad audience this role is one of the principal goals of this book. It is a supplemental, rather than revisionist, history, filling in important gaps while leaving intact the larger national narrative written by other authors.

The other audience—and arguably the more important one—consists of LGBT Mormons and ex-Mormons and their families and friends. While they have been affected by the national debate, the deeper effect has been at the hands of their own church. The primacy of family in Mormon theology, as a unit that will endure into a postmortal existence, raises the stakes for LGBT children. By condemning their homosexuality as evil, self-inflicted, and impossible in postmortal existence, the church has opened the door to draconian behavior by parents, peers, and congregations. The alarming number of homeless LGBT teenagers in Utah, many of them from Mormon homes, is a jolting manifestation of such behavior. Even more alarming is the rise in teen suicides in Utah: the number has more than tripled in the past decade and is the highest per capita rate in the country for this age demographic.

Although there appears to be a shift that is taking place, wherein some families are electing to show solidarity with their LGBT children and leave the church en bloc, the needless tragedy in such cases merely shifts from the family to the church. It is my hope that this book will help these individuals by chronicling the church's attitudes and actions toward LGBT people, both Mormon and non-, and particularly by showing how those attitudes and actions were informed by now-discredited assumptions about the nature of homosexuality. Perhaps the church itself will benefit from a clearer understanding of how it got to where it is today.

While generally resistant to change, the church has, in fact, made several important changes relating to homosexuality. Openly gay youth can now serve proselytizing missions, something unimaginable not many years ago. Acknowledgment of a biological cause of homosexuality has been stated implicitly on the church website, and some church leaders acknowledge, in private, that they now accept the biological paradigm. Full acceptance of this paradigm will inevitably call for a systemic reevaluation of policies, practices, attitudes, and even doctrines regarding homosexuality that were built on the crumbling foundation of the behavioral paradigm. It is my hope that this book will accelerate such a process.

Because this book focuses on the story of the Mormon Church and its engagement in LGBT issues, it places disproportionately greater emphasis on some issues than other authors have given—such as the Hawaii lawsuit that brought the church into the public square, Proposition 22, Proposition 8, and Utah-centric issues such as Amendment 3, Salt Lake City ordinances, *Kitchen v. Herbert*, SB 296 (the statewide antidiscrimination law passed in 2015), and "the Policy" introduced by the church later that year in response to *Obergefell v. Hodges*—and less on major national episodes of unquestioned importance but where the church had little if any role. These include the Defense of Marriage Act (DOMA), *Hollingsworth v. Perry*, *Obergefell v. Hodges*, and, in general, the public national debate on LGBT issues.

The story of LGBT issues within Mormonism is not a microcosm of the national story, but it has been informed by that story and, at times, has also informed it. I do not attempt to give it a disproportionate role; rather, I hope to place it in its rightful, and often shifting, role on the national stage—a role that was sometimes dominant, sometimes recessive, and sometimes nonexistent.

A word about the internal organization of the book. There are many threads to the Mormon/LGBT narrative, and they do not come together to form a coherent tapestry. Some of these threads run in parallel without intersecting. For instance, attempted "cures" of homosexuality were not informed by, and did not inform, the church's foray into the political arena in Hawaii in 1993. To attempt to weave all threads into a chronological narrative would be artificial and would do violence to important elements of the story, and so I have written the chapters topically. While the chapters generally appear in chronological order, the chronologies often overlap, and I have written each chapter as an independent story rather than attempting to move forward chronologically with all threads simultaneously. I have given each chapter—each story—the amount of space that I felt was necessary to tell that story. In some cases the story is lengthy—particularly the chapters "Hawaii" and "Proposition 8"—while in others it is only a couple of pages.

ALTA CLUB

Four years earlier it would have been impossible to imagine two men, Rick Jacobs and Bill Evans, even in the same room, let alone breaking bread together. At that time they represented major organizations opposing each other in a bitter campaign to determine the future of marriage equality in California: respectively, the Courage Campaign and the Mormon Church.

My friendship with Rick, which had much to do with my decision to write this book, began in a most improbable way. In June 2010, while attending my first meeting of the National Advisory Council of the Johns Hopkins University School of Education, I met Eric Paquette, a vice president of Sony Entertainment. Eric worked in Los Angeles, and when I told him that I was speaking at a symposium at the University of Southern California the following week, he invited me to lunch.

Proposition 8 was still very much a topic of conversation in California at that time, and as we were discussing it Eric was surprised to learn that I, a Mormon, supported marriage equality. Later that day he sent me an email that said, "I want to introduce you to my very good friend Rick Jacobs who runs the Courage Campaign here in Los Angeles. I am not afraid to say that he is more responsible for pushing for progressive change and equality across California and the nation than anyone. He is a true hero and someone that I am proud to know." Two days later, the three of us met for dinner in Beverly Hills. Rick and I found that we had much in common, and we quickly became close friends.

A year later, while in Salt Lake City, I was introduced to Bill Evans, who had worked for three decades in the Public Affairs office of the LDS Church. Bill and I also became close friends. When I learned that Bill had been the church's point man, from the professional side, for Proposition 8, I mentioned my friendship with Rick. Bill stiffened and said, "Do you know who he is?" I told Bill that I was well aware of Rick's role but suggested that that was then and this was now and that I saw an opening for dialogue.

A year later, shortly after the November 2012 presidential election, Bill called me at my home in Maryland and said, "I sent a request up the ladder, and it has been approved. Would you and JaLynn [my wife], on behalf of the church, invite Rick Jacobs and his partner to attend the Mormon Tabernacle Choir Christmas Concert as VIP guests and fly out to host them?" I immediately called Rick, who quickly accepted the invitation.

I then called Jim Dabakis, whom I had met only a few months earlier. Jim, who is the only openly gay senator in the Utah Legislature, agreed to cosponsor a dinner of attendees, prior to the concert, at the Alta Club, a venerable institution only a block from the concert venue. He led the way in assembling a guest list that included Bill Evans, two other people from LDS Public Affairs, and a remarkable group of LGBT luminaries who also were VIP guests of the church: Chad Griffin, the new national director of the Human Rights Campaign (HRC); Dustin Lance Black, Academy Award–winning writer of the screenplay for *Milk*; Bruce Bastian, cofounder of Word-Perfect Corporation and a major philanthropist and LGBT activist; Trevor Southey, one of the greatest Mormon artists ever; Valerie Larabee, executive director of the Utah Pride Center; Brandie Balken, executive director of Equality Utah; Troy Williams, then a Salt Lake City radio personality and now executive director of Equality Utah; Erika Munson, founder and director of Mormons Building Bridges; and Rick Jacobs.

Much had changed since the bitter fight over Prop 8. The heated and widespread postelection backlash had caught church leaders by surprise, and they had worked ever since to improve the external image of the church. A year after the election, the church gave public support to Salt Lake City ordinances that forbade discrimination against LGBT people in housing and employment. During the 2012 election cycle, in a decision widely viewed by outsiders as an attempt to avoid any negative publicity that might affect adversely the presidential candidacy of Mitt Romney, the church withdrew completely from the political arena, even though four states—Maine, Maryland, Minnesota, and Washington—had ballot measures regarding marriage equality. (All four were decided in favor of marriage equality.) And finally, only a week before the dinner, the church had quietly launched a website, MormonsandGays.org, that was groundbreaking in acknowledging that "individuals do not choose to have [same-sex] attractions." Common ground for the church and the LGBT community had expanded, and the atmosphere in the room as guests assembled was upbeat.

We seated Rick and Bill next to each other, not knowing what the outcome would be. At the end of the dinner we found out. Jim stood up and said, "We have half an hour before we need to walk to the conference center for the concert. I'd like to call on several of you to express yourselves spontaneously." Trevor Southey, in earlier years, had been outspoken and bitter because of the church's policies, among them the counsel to marry a woman in order to "reorient" his homosexuality. Ultimately, the marriage failed and Trevor was excommunicated. Now, gaunt from the cancer that took his life three years later, he wept as he said, "Words cannot express how grateful I am for the changes that I have seen the church make in recent months." Lance Black also wept as he spoke of the possibility of rapprochement with his Mormon family. Rick Jacobs said, "Four years ago Bill Evans and I were enemies. Now, we are friends." Bill Evans responded, "Were it not for Proposition 8, this dinner could not have happened." And he was right: Prop 8 was indeed a catalyst, but the story is far deeper and more complex.

GENESIS

In the early morning hours of June 28, 1969, New York City police raided the Stonewall Inn, a popular gay bar in Greenwich Village. Police raids on gay bars had long been common in the city, and thus the police were surprised at a spontaneous show of resistance from the bar's patrons, which escalated to riots and protests spanning several days. While not the beginning of the gay rights movement in the United States,[1] the Stonewall Riots thrust the movement into the international spotlight.

Three months later, the Mormon Church effectively entered the public discourse on LGBT issues when senior apostle Spencer Kimball's book *The Miracle of Forgiveness* was published. Prior to *Miracle, homosexual* was a word rarely used within Mormonism, and when used at all it almost always referred (and still does) to men. *Lesbian, bisexual, transgender,* and *intersex* were essentially missing from the Mormon lexicon.[2] The first time *homosexual* appeared in the *Church Handbook of Instructions*[3]—the Mormon embodiment of canonical law that was first published in 1899—was 1968, and then it was part of a lengthy list of transgressions that might result in church disciplinary action. No explanations or guidelines accompanied its mention, and thus a single word inserted into an earlier list was all that defined official policy on LGBT issues after 138 years of the church's existence.

THE NATIONAL SCENE

Attitudes toward same-sex relationships in ancient societies—the word *homosexual* was not coined until the late nineteenth century—varied from acceptance to tolerance to condemnation. By the nineteenth century the colonization of much of the world by Christian European cultures pushed homosexuality into the closet, where it largely remained until Stonewall. Embedded attitudes treating it as a normal, albeit minority, expression of sexuality were gradually replaced by condemnation as clinicians, aided by ecclesiastics, came to view it as pathological.[4] This attitude was codified in 1952 when the American Psychiatric Association published the first edition of its *Diagnostic and Statistical Manual of Mental Disorders* (now universally abbreviated *DSM*). Public policy mirrored medical opinion, such that by 1960 private, consensual sex between same-sex partners was not only condemned as morally wrong but also defined as a criminal act in every state in the country. Social worker Dr. Caitlin Ryan painted a bleak verbal picture of the LGBT landscape that she experienced in that era, albeit one that was dissociated from localized thriving gay and lesbian cultures in other parts of the country in the 1950s and 1960s:

> Until Stonewall, we didn't have an organized LGBT community. We didn't have social institutions. We didn't have health institutions, recreational supports, faith-based settings that would welcome. There wasn't the foundation of a civil society for LGBT people. There was nowhere for them to fit in.... Everything about gay people, all the novels were tragic, all the media representations were distorted, the messages to young people were "Hide!" ... You would hide your identity, you would never discuss it, you would dress in certain ways, kids would pretend to be straight.... The sanctions for being gay were so extreme that nobody would come out.[5]

Although scientific research over the subsequent two decades increasingly challenged the *DSM* classification, resulting in the deletion in the 1973 edition of prior characterizations, the larger society continued to view homosexuality as aberrant, dangerous, even contagious—becoming, in a word, "homophobic." The 2016 massacre of forty-nine mostly LGBT persons in Pulse, an Orlando, Florida, gay bar, underscores the persistence, depth, and danger of homophobia in the United States.

The societal reaction to Stonewall and the *DSM* reclassification, among other factors, resulted in significant, albeit geographically variable, gains in public acceptance of LGBT persons, coupled with occasional local legal protection of their rights. Those protections, in turn, elicited a strong reaction from religiously motivated activists who were personified by Anita Bryant, a popular singer and runner-up for Miss America in 1959. Following the enactment in Dade County, Florida, of an LGBT antidiscrimination ordinance, Bryant led a successful campaign to invalidate the legislation through a county referendum that passed by more than a two-to-one margin. Emboldened by her success, she dominated the national anti-LGBT scene, helping to roll back LGBT protections in communities throughout the country by portraying homosexuals as continually proselytizing children to join their ranks.

Bryant's message resonated well in Utah. Barbara Smith, general president of the Relief Society (the women's organization within the LDS Church), sent her a laudatory telegram in 1977: "On behalf of the one million members of the Relief Society, we commend you for your courageous and effective efforts in combatting homosexuality and laws which would legitimize this insidious life style." The following month, Apostle Mark Petersen, in an editorial in the LDS Church–owned *Church News*, wrote, "Every right-thinking person will sustain Miss Bryant, a prayerful, upright citizen, for her stand. Righteous people everywhere also should look to their own neighborhoods to determine to what extent the 'gay' people have infiltrated their areas."[6]

Later the same year Spencer Kimball, now church president, stated in a press conference that Bryant was "'doing a great service' by attacking the homosexual rights movement.... 'We feel the homosexual program is not a natural and normal way of life.'"[7] In the two decades following Bryant's activities in Dade County, more than sixty jurisdictions across the country held referenda to dismantle gay-rights protections, with the large majority being approved by voters.

Amplifying the national pushback against LGBT rights was the acquired immunodeficiency syndrome epidemic in the United States. Introduced into the country in the mid-1970s through male homosexuals, AIDS became known as the "gay disease," even though in other parts of the world its transmission more frequently occurred through heterosexual intercourse or through shared needles among intravenous drug users. President Ronald Reagan turned his back on the epidemic for the first four years of his presidency, until his friend Rock Hudson became ill with AIDS in 1985. Moved by Hudson's illness, Reagan finally spoke publicly on AIDS, but by that time the epidemic was in its sixth year in the United States, and thousands had died from it. (In a tone that stood in contrast to increasing national empathy toward the AIDS epidemic, Mormon apostle and retired cardiac surgeon

Russell Nelson, who now [2019] presides over the LDS Church, publicly called AIDS "a plague fueled by a vocal few who exhibit greater concern for civil rights than for public health, a plague abetted by the immoral."[8] Decades later, as described in a later chapter, Nelson played a key role in one of the most divisive LGBT policies the church ever enacted.)

The enormous toll that AIDS took on the male homosexual population in the United States, coupled with the exemplary manner in which the LGBT community coalesced in response to the epidemic, gradually worked to destigmatize homosexuality and increase its acceptance within the larger society.

THE UTAH SCENE

The ripple effects of World War II continued for many years after the cessation of hostilities. Of the sixteen million people who served in the armed forces during the war, countless thousands were gay, albeit closeted, for being openly gay was justification for dishonorable discharge. Many, sheltered in the towns of their upbringing, did not become aware of their own homosexuality until they passed through the military induction process. Their exposure to the wide world that they had not previously experienced included in many cases awareness that big cities—particularly port cities such as New York, San Francisco, Los Angeles, and Seattle, which had a heavy military presence—were more gay tolerant than small towns and cities, and after the war those cities and others, including Salt Lake City, became congregating places for gay men in particular.[9]

In 1948 two straight business partners, Elvin Gerrard and Lee Caputo, opened the Radio City bar in Salt Lake City. It gradually evolved into a gay bar that is believed to have been the oldest in Utah. Nikki Boyer, onetime manager of the Sun Tavern, another Salt Lake City gay bar, recalled, "We had no rights, but we were rich in gay bars. . . . This is where we felt safe. It was the only place we felt safe."[10]

The safety that may have existed in the late 1940s and early 1950s eroded in the face of a wave of Cold War–driven hysteria over homosexuality. Upon becoming U.S. president in 1953, Dwight Eisenhower banned federal employment of homosexuals. A July 1953 article in the LDS Church–owned *Deseret News*, carrying the headline "107 Fired in State Department," underscored the determination of federal officials to purge government agencies of what Eisenhower's executive order called "sexual perversion." The challenges facing a young LGBT person in Utah at that time were daunting, as portrayed in an article in the *Salt Lake Tribune* in 2014:

> To a young homosexual awakening to his or her sexual orientation in Utah, there were no positive role models in the 1950s to which one could aspire. Society's predominant view of homosexuality was typified by the *Salt Lake Tribune* editorial board's opinion that it was a "social evil that must be fought." *The Idaho Statesman*, even more virulent, called homosexuals "monsters" to be crushed. Virtually all editors of newspapers along the Rocky Mountain region called homosexuality everything from "moral perversion" to a "cancerous growth." Children learned at an early age that to be called "queer" was about as demeaning as any name-calling could be.
>
> Homosexuals in Utah were virtually invisible because the concept of homosexuality was revolting to the general public who viewed it akin to a social disease. The archives of Utah's largest circulated newspaper, *Salt Lake Tribune*, revealed few articles on homosexuality from 1950 to 1959 and those were mostly in regards to criminal conduct and national security. The *Deseret News* [wholly owned by the church] was even less inclined to report on homosexuality as if the very mention of it might incline some to indulge in the practice. These few news reports would have been the only way in which a homosexual in the 1950s saw him or herself portrayed in the media.
>
> For Utah homosexuals of the 1950s it was mostly a time of quiet desperation. Sexually active homosexuals guarded their sexual identity closely without any institutional or community support. The legal system regarded them as sex offenders, perverts, molesters, deviants, unnatural, degenerates and security risks. All churches of the 1950s viewed homosexuals as immoral reprobates and sinners, while society described them in a whole catalog of disparaging names: queer, faggot, sissy, pansy, fruit, pretty boy, pervert, effeminate, tom-boy, lezzie, lesbo, dyke. It was a bleak time to be gay.[11]

The legal landscape in Utah became increasingly homophobic after the 1969 Stonewall Riots in New York City. A 1977 bill in the Utah Legislature outlawing homosexual marriages—this in the background of the ongoing national battle over the Equal Rights Amendment (ERA), which many held to be the first step toward marriage equality—passed in the Utah House of Representatives by a vote of seventy-one to three, without any floor debate. Later the same year, Democratic U.S. congressman Gunn McKay announced in a press conference, "I do not believe that the Gay's right to be free from discrimination is greater than the right to live and work in a community whose moral standards reject homosexual activity. People should not be compelled against their will to hire, rent to, or have their children taught by homosexuals."[12]

Public sentiment reflected the legal landscape. A poll conducted the same year by the *Salt Lake Tribune* showed that 75 percent of LDS respondents opposed equal rights for gay teachers or ministers (versus 64 percent of non-LDS respondents), and 62 percent favored discrimination against gays in business and government (versus 38 percent of non-LDS).[13] The majorities among LDS respondents paralleled, in turn, the developing gay-unfriendly attitudes and policies of their church.

THE LDS CHURCH SCENE

The policies and attitudes of the LDS Church and its members toward homosexuality have been shaped by three basic tenets: it is a grievous *sin* that requires *punishment* by the church (often excommunication in earlier times) and is *caused* by a conscious choice of the LGBT individual rather than being biologically determined.

SIN

In the early 1950s, when U.S. government hysteria over communism spilled over into hysteria over homosexuality, particularly in the State Department, former undersecretary of state—and now First Presidency counselor—J. Reuben Clark Jr. lashed out at homosexuality at a time when the word was rarely heard from a Mormon pulpit. Speaking to the annual conference of the Relief Society in 1952, he condemned "the person who teaches or condones the crimes for which Sodom and Gomorrah were destroyed—we have coined a softer name for them than came from old; we now speak of homosexuality." Two years later he broadened his audience by condemning "that filthy crime of homosexuality" during the semiannual church General Conference.[14]

Church president David O. McKay, while never addressing the issue publicly, made it clear in private that he and Clark were of one mind on the subject. Ernest Wilkinson, president of Brigham Young University (BYU), wrote that in a meeting with senior apostles, "I was informed that President McKay, in one of the temple meetings, had said that in his view homosexuality was worse than immorality, that it is a filthy and unnatural habit."[15]

In the same time frame, Bruce McConkie, an LDS General Authority by virtue of his membership in the First Council of Seventy, published an encyclopedic book with the audacious title *Mormon Doctrine*, which many church members then and now consider to represent the official doctrines of the church, even though it was never endorsed by the church, was criticized by other General Authorities, and now is out of print.[16] He listed "prostitution, and whoredoms...and homosexuality" among sins that "are condemned by divine edict and are among Lucifer's chief means of leading souls to hell."[17] What little downside remained was filled several years later by Apostle Mark Petersen who, in an editorial in the *Church News*, placed "homosexual offenses" next to murder in his hierarchy of sins.[18]

Although the initial mention of homosexuality in the *Church Handbook* was in the active sense—"Cases handled by church courts...include, but are not limited to: fornication, adultery, homo-sexual acts"[19]—the emphasis soon shifted to the passive. The subsequent edition of the *Church Handbook*, and the first published during the presidency of Spencer Kimball, listed homosexuality, rather than homosexual acts, as grounds for church court action.[20] For many years thereafter, *being* homosexual was cause for church disciplinary action, including excommunication, even if the person was celibate, and subsequent editions of the *Church Handbook* equated the passive sin of homosexuality with the active sins of adultery, fornication, and child molestation.[21]

The 1989 edition of the *General Handbook*, which was the first published after the death of Spencer Kimball, signaled a slightly softening approach by equating homosexual *relations* to adultery, fornication, and child molestation. A First Presidency circular letter two years later emphasized the shift by noting, "There is a distinction between immoral thoughts and feelings and participating in either immoral heterosexual or any homosexual behavior."[22] While homosexual "behavior"—generally considered to be sexual intercourse—remains highly placed among the hierarchy of Mormon sins, there has been an increasingly tolerant attitude toward LGBT church members who do not engage in such behavior or who are willing to discontinue it. The most visible evidence of such change is the fact that openly gay church members, whether celibate or repentant, can serve full-time proselytizing missions—something that would have been unimaginable during the Kimball years.[23]

While the official church policy remains one that accepts homosexuality as nonsinful if not acted upon, interpretation by lay leaders and family members sometimes differs. Anecdotal accounts of harsh treatment continue to be received, with none more poignant than that of Mitch Mayne, a gay church member who gained national prominence when his bishop called him to be his executive secretary. He wrote retrospectively, in an article published in a national magazine in 2012, "I mourned for my mom, who wanted so much to do the right thing and keep me safe and yet, without the resources to understand and support me, instead told me it would have been better for her if I had been born dead than gay."[24]

PUNISHMENT

Given that homosexuality was not even mentioned in church canonical law until 1968, it should not be surprising that there was no standardized church response either to homosexuality or to homosexual intercourse. The most frequent de facto response for well over a century was usually benign neglect,[25] although the attitude of some church leaders was hardly benign. For example, three years prior to the publication of the 1968 *Church Handbook*, church president David O. McKay told his counselors, "They [homosexuals] should be excommunicated without any doubt, that the homosexual has no right to membership in the Church.... I said I think they should be dealt with immediately if they are guilty."[26]

Although men at the top often had strong feelings about homosexuality, they gave discretion to local leaders over the nature and exercise of church discipline. For example, the 1983 *Church Handbook* stated, "Church courts *may* be convened to consider ... homosexuality," and options for local leaders ranged from acquittal to excommunication.[27] Only in the case of homosexual behavior on the part of members "holding a prominent church position" was a disciplinary council mandatory,[28] and even then local leaders had (and have) those same options.

Unofficial injuries can be more severe and damaging than the punishments administered by church disciplinary councils. These punishments continue to the present day, as noted by Mitch Mayne: "I have been told by Church leaders that I am unworthy of ever taking the Sacrament.[29] I have been told that I will never work with the youth of the Church. I have been told in meetings that it is because of people like me that the AIDS pandemic has come upon the Earth—that my sins are bringing punishment upon the wicked and the sinless alike."[30]

Tragically, the words and actions of family members and local church leaders sometimes result in the extreme act of self-punishment: suicide. This subject will be treated in a subsequent chapter.

CAUSE

For many decades the Mormon position with respect to cause has been informed by dogma rather than science, and even church leaders who today acknowledge a role of biology in determining sexual orientation (to whom the individual is sexually attracted) and gender identity (with what gender, anatomy notwithstanding, the individual identifies) do so with abundant caveats.

The earliest (1973) church-published guide for ecclesiastical leaders chided "professionally trained people" who differed among themselves in their opinions regarding the cause, whereas "the gospel makes the issue clear. Homosexuality...is learned behavior (not inborn)." General church officers, most notably Apostle Boyd Packer, were even more forceful in denouncing any notion of a biological basis. "There is a falsehood that some are born with an attraction to their own kind, with nothing they can do about it. They are just 'that way' and can only yield to those desires. That is a malicious and destructive lie. While it is a convincing idea to some, it is of the devil. No one is locked into that kind of life." To drive his point even deeper, Packer later gave a major address on homosexuality to the Brigham Young University student body that intentionally mentioned the word *homosexual* only once, and then as an adjective. "Please notice that I use it as an adjective, not as a noun; I reject it as a noun.... I accept that word as an adjective to describe a temporary condition. I reject it as a noun naming a permanent one." A later church-published guide reiterated Packer's insistence on the adjective: "Be careful not to label the person as homosexual or gay. Such labels can undermine the person's belief that change is possible and may communicate the mistaken notion that a man or woman is born with a homosexual identity that cannot be changed.... Although some struggle with unwanted homosexual thoughts and feelings, there is no conclusive evidence that anyone is born with a homosexual orientation."[31]

If, as these sources claimed, biology is not the cause, then what is? In a survey of forty-eight published statements by church leaders since 1879, when George Q. Cannon of the First Presidency, in a creative defense of plural marriage, implicated monogamy as the cause for the "crime against nature," Connell O'Donovan identified more than thirty purported causes of homosexuality, including contagion, Satanic influence, pornography, curiosity, and proselytizing. None was tempered by uncertainty.[32] Many restated societal conclusions that included "a domineering mother and a passive father,"[33] poor relationships with peers, unhealthy sexual attitudes in the home, and childhood experimentation.[34] Some were more creative, such as Boyd Packer's suggestion that the root cause was selfishness "in a very subtle form.... Every prescription against selfishness of any kind will bring some control of this disease."[35]

The aversion to a biological explanation of homosexuality is common among other conservative religious traditions, which justify their sin-based viewpoint by a highly selective reading of biblical verses,[36] but the Mormon construct is more nuanced. Packer, for one, began with the premise that homosexuality is inherently sinful and then used circular reasoning to conclude that a biological explanation would defy moral law: "Test it against moral law and you learn something very quickly. If a condition that draws both men and women into one of the ugliest and most debased of all physical performances is set and cannot be overcome, it would be a glaring exception to all moral law." Taking a similar tack, the First Presidency later wrote, "To believe that immoral behavior is inborn or hereditary is to deny that men have agency to choose between sin and righteousness.... It is inconceivable that—as some involved in homosexual behavior claim—he would permit some of his children to be born with desires and inclinations which would require behavior contrary to the eternal plan."[37]

Yet another explanation derives from the unique Latter-day Saint belief that one's identity, including gender, began prior to mortal birth—that is, spirit beings in a premortal state bore the identity that they would later have as physical personages—and will remain unaltered in a postmortal, resurrected state. Using again as a starting point the assumption that homosexuality is inherently sinful, this exercise in circular reasoning goes on to conclude that God is incapable of making a mistake that would place a person into a sinful state because of biological imprinting, and therefore there is no biological basis for homosexuality. Boyd Packer gave this explanation: "From our pre-mortal life we were directed into a physical body. There is no mismatching of bodies and spirits. Boys are to become men—masculine, manly men—ultimately to become husbands and fathers."[38]

In the aftermath of his 1978 BYU speech, Packer posited yet another cause of homosexuality. In a personal message to BYU president Dallin Oaks, he complained that the university newspaper, the *Daily Universe*, had given coverage to the speech: "I have already said that we can very foolishly cause things we are trying to prevent by talking too much about them."[39]

THE BIOLOGY OF HOMOSEXUALITY

Two caveats to get started. One is that this and subsequent sections will focus on the "LGB" portion of the LGBT world. That is, lesbian, gay, and bisexual, all of which refer to sexual orientation—the persons to whom one is sexually attracted. The flip side of the coin is gender identity, which is the gender with which a person self-identifies, independent of that person's anatomical sex. If the two match, one is called "cisgender." If they differ, one is "transgender." Transgender is an entirely different reality than LGB, one that science has yet to illuminate significantly. It will be treated in a subsequent chapter.

The other caveat is that this section will focus primarily on male homosexuality. This is not because lesbianism or bisexuality are any less important but rather because the nearly universal focus of—indeed, fixation on—LDS Church policies, procedures, and statements has been gay men.

PREVALENCE OF HOMOSEXUALITY

There a general consensus that between 3.5 percent and 5 percent of adults throughout the world self-identify as gay, lesbian, or bisexual. There is no persuasive evidence that the percentage has varied significantly across time or geography.

While not representing the majority within a given species, homosexuality is a common phenomenon within the animal kingdom—Apostle Boyd Packer's claims to the contrary notwithstanding when he said, without documentation, "Animals do not pair up with their own gender."[40] A well-documented study of sheep showed that, given a choice, 8 percent of

rams mated exclusively with other rams. Long-term same-sex pair bonding has been reported in ungulates and some birds. A standard reference
on the subject of homosexuality in animals, published in 1999, documents
homosexual behavior in nearly five hundred species of animals,[41] while an
estimate seven years later put the number at fifteen hundred—an astonish-
ingly broad array of species.

HOMOSEXUALITY IS COMPLEX

Seven decades ago, when Alfred Kinsey brought the study of human sexuality into the daylight, he placed it on a scale from 0 (completely heterosexual) to 6 (completely homosexual), with a score of 3 denoting bisexuality.
Although Kinsey's scale moved understanding forward in the short term, it
worked against it in the long term, for two reasons. First, it described only
one side of the coin: sexual orientation. It said nothing about gender identity. Second, by placing various embodiments of sexual orientation on a
single straight-line scale, it suggested that while different sexual orientations may vary from each other quantitatively, they were qualitatively the
same. But they are not. Indeed, male homosexuality is not simply the mir-
ror image of female homosexuality. A special issue of *National Geographic*
in January 2017, entitled "Gender Revolution," notes that Facebook offers
users fifty terms to characterize their sexuality. Rather than viewing sexuality linearly, one should imagine a multidimensional array—something like
a galaxy of stars with clusters in some locations, single stars in others, and
empty space in between. If you can construct that mental image, you have
some appreciation for the complexity of human sexuality in all of its flavors—
heterosexuality included—and can also appreciate that the search for a single basis of all homosexuality is as fruitless as the quest for the Holy Grail.

GENETICS

In attempting to shed light on the causes of homosexuality, I turn first to
genetics. In using that word, I refer to the sequences of nucleotides in DNA—
the beads on the string—that constitute the blueprint by which genes produce proteins. *Epigenetics*, treated subsequently, refers to the large variety
of mechanisms that control how the genes function.

Dean Hamer, a pioneer of the molecular biology of sexuality, didn't find
the gay gene he sought, but he did find that gay brothers had an increased
probability of sharing markers in the Xq28 region of the X chromosome.

While not identifying a single cause underlying male homosexuality, Hamer's work, which has been confirmed broadly by other laboratories, provided strong evidence for a contribution of Xq28 and, hence, for genetics. More recent studies have shown that an additional marker, this one on chromosome 8, is shared between homosexual brothers at a rate significantly higher than between straight brothers.

Before molecular biology came of age, family studies, wherein homosexuality clusters in certain families, and twinning studies pointed toward a significant, though not decisive, role of genetics. The twinning studies are particularly compelling. There are two types of twins. Identical twins have identical DNA sequences, while fraternal twins share variable percentages of DNA sequences with each other. If genetics were the only factor underlying homosexuality, one would expect 100 percent concordance among identical twins—that is, both twins would be either heterosexual or homosexual. If genetics were not a factor at all, one would expect the same concordance among fraternal twins as among identical twins, since fraternal twins develop in the same in utero environment.

In fact, the numbers fall between the two extremes. The concordance among identical twins is up to 60 percent, but among fraternal twins it is only about 15 percent. This is strong evidence that while genetics is a factor, it is not the only factor that determines sexual orientation. The other, and more dominant, factor is epigenetics.

EPIGENETICS

From the time the fertilized egg is implanted in the wall of the uterus until birth, the developing fetus is immersed—literally—in a sea of maternal factors that help to shape its development. Sometimes, epigenetics can take the fetus down a different pathway than the genetic code prescribes. There are two important examples of how epigenetics can shift sexual orientation toward homosexuality.

The first is the birth-order effect, which is seen only in males. It is estimated that 15 percent to 28 percent of gay men owe their sexual orientation to this effect. While the mechanism is not completely understood, it appears to be due to interactions between the male fetus and the maternal immune system that have increased consequences for each subsequent male birth. After the birth of one son, the likelihood of each subsequent son of the same biological mother being gay increases by 33 percent. If the likelihood of the first is 3 percent, then that of the second is 4 percent. The effect is additive, such that the seventh son would have a 17 percent chance of being gay. Daughters do not experience a similar phenomenon, nor is the effect on sons influenced by the number of older sisters. And the effect is true for only right-handed sons.

The other example is probably more important in causing homosexuality. It is called "epigenetically canalized sexual development." In plainer English, at a very early stage of fetal development, epigenetic factors that are not part of the DNA but can be passed from either parent to the fetus affect the way the "sex" of the fetal brain is imprinted. What that means is this: Testosterone is present in all developing fetuses, but in higher levels in the male. But in order for testosterone to exert its effect in imprinting maleness into the fetal brain, there must be a receptor for it within that brain. Generally, male fetuses have higher levels of testosterone *and* higher levels of testosterone receptors, while females have lower levels of testosterone *and* lower levels of testosterone receptors.

In some instances, however, there is a mismatch that is determined by an epigenetic factor inherited from a parent. This can result in male embryos with low levels of receptors, in which case testosterone cannot fully exert its masculinizing effect on the brain. Alternatively, female embryos can have high levels of receptors, in which case even the normally low testosterone levels that circulate within the blood of female fetuses are preferentially grabbed by those receptors and allowed to exert a masculinizing effect on their brains.

All of this brain imprinting occurs prenatally. At the time of puberty, when testosterone or estrogen levels begin to spike, the imprinted brain is impervious to their effect, notwithstanding the gender of the genitalia. In other words, a female with a fetal-masculinized brain will be sexually oriented toward women, while a male with a fetal-feminized brain will be sexually oriented toward men, hormones—and hormone therapy—notwithstanding.

Since these epigenetic factors are not necessarily inherited equally, one identical twin may be gay while the other is straight, in spite of their having identical DNA. Identical twins are not as identical as we once supposed.

The genesis of sexual orientation is an area of science that is undergoing much cutting-edge research, and it is certain that future discoveries will elucidate more examples of homosexuality being biologically determined, whether through genetics, epigenetics, or a combination. But the bottom line has already been written: homosexuals are, indeed, "born that way."

CHOICE

The contrary assertion that homosexuality is merely a choice, rather than a biological imprint, continues to be held by many, including members of the LDS Church hierarchy. Notwithstanding their fervor in defending this position, many data argue persuasively against it:

- While it is documented that homosexual behavior increases when the opposite sex is absent—think of prisons or unisex schools—such behavior is transient, and upon reentering the larger society these people resume their heterosexual orientation, never having completely abandoned it.
- Even in societies such as New Guinea, where adolescent male homosexual behavior is encouraged as a means to preserve female virginity until marriage, adult males show no higher incidence of homosexuality than those in nonpermissive cultures.
- The percentage of homosexual men in gay-tolerant societies such as Thailand and the Philippines is no higher than in gay-averse societies.
- Currently available scientific studies show little or no influence of education in determining sexual orientation.
- And finally, children raised by homosexual parents are no more likely to become homosexual than children raised by heterosexual parents.
- To quote a prominent expert, "No theories that attribute the development of homosexuality to non-biological causes have produced convincing data to support their interpretations. If *any* role of social and educational factors exists, that it so far has escaped a rigorous demonstration strongly suggests that these roles are severely limited."[42]

Biology notwithstanding, by proclaiming without reservation that homosexuality is a choice rather than a biological imprint, church leaders naturally concluded that the choice could and should be reversed—in other words, homosexuality could and should be "cured."

THE CURE, 1.0

Cure, as either a noun or a verb and generally used in reference to a disease, was the first imagery used by church leaders to describe the manner in which homosexuality should be approached. The *Bishop's Training Course and Self-Help Guide*, published in 1970, proclaimed, "Though many have been told it is incurable, that is not true." The same year, Spencer Kimball and Mark Petersen's pamphlet concluded with the promise, "REMEMBER: Homosexuality CAN be cured, if the battle is well organized and pursued vigorously and continuously." Kimball's second pamphlet on the subject, published in 1971, again employed the disease analogy: "Though [homosexuality] is like an octopus with numerous tentacles to drag you to your tragedy, the sin is curable and you may totally recover from its tentacles."[1]

Later pronouncements tended to back away from the disease-cure paradigm and employ other imagery: "an extremely difficult habit to change" (1973), a "behavior [that] can be conquered" (1975), and "problems [that] can be controlled and eventually overcome" (1992).[2] However, the consensus remained that homosexuality was a conscious choice in the opposite direction of the "natural" state of heterosexuality, and the earliest attempts at "curing the disease" focused on self-help. In essence, "You chose to be homosexual, so you can choose *not* to be homosexual."

Guidance from church leaders as to how to cure oneself of homosexuality has spanned a broad spectrum of suggestions. Apostle Mark Petersen, who counseled hundreds of gay men, advised one merely "to 'distract' himself with his music and other interests."[3] Petersen and Spencer Kimball, in their pamphlet *Hope for Transgressors*, advocated another kind of distraction, wherein *heterosexual* was substituted for *homosexual*. "There must be substitution. The person should purge out the evil and then fill his life with constructive positive activities and interests. He will throw away his pornographic materials and will have ceased reading articles about homosexuality and will substitute therefor the scriptures and worthy books and articles which will give the mind proper occupation."[4] LDS Welfare Services carried this theme a step further by advocating the substitution of avoidance for engagement—that is, "to flee from other gays, even if it contradicted their responsibility to 'guide those who stumbled' since 'a sympathetic effort to work with other homosexuals to "help" them is especially dangerous.'"[5]

Another strategy was to use the process of repentance. LDS Welfare Services counseled local leaders in 1973, "While it is an extremely difficult habit to change, homosexuality can be repented of as can any other deeply entrenched habit."[6] This counsel was explicitly endorsed by the First Presidency two years later: "There are many who have repented and become clean through repentance, prayer, self-discipline and loving support from others."[7] The problem with this approach was that it viewed *homosexuality* as the sin, as opposed to later church policy that accepted celibate homosexuality but condemned "homosexual acts." One gay church member summarized the frustration of many: "Mormons view homosexuality as a sin that can be overcome. I know of many gays, including myself, who prayed until their knees are bloody and their hearts broken and still can't change."[8]

In addition to praying, many LGBT members have attempted to rid themselves of their homosexuality by increasing the zealousness with which they practice their religion. Tom Christofferson, an openly gay church member whose high profile is due, in part, to that fact that his older brother Todd is a member of the Quorum of the Twelve Apostles, spoke for many in relating his own experience with hyperorthodoxy: "My approach to it was, 'If I do all the right things, if I do everything God tells me to do, then this will go away.' I really loved my time serving as a missionary, and came home and was quite surprised to discover that I was still gay. I thought the deal was, 'I'll go do the two years, and then when I come home it's all going to be perfect.'" Indeed, such frustrated efforts on a broad scale recently led the church to caution local leaders, "Avoid offering overly simplified responses, such as the idea that...missionary service will eliminate same-sex attraction." Robert Rees described the view from his position as congregational leader: "As a bishop of a singles' ward, I counseled with many gays who accepted the promise of prophets and they did everything—went on missions, went to the temple often, read the scriptures, etc., trying to prove to God that they were worthy of change. Often when change didn't come they blamed themselves for not being sufficiently righteous or diligent. This kind of experience has led many gays to attempt and many to succeed at suicide."[9]

But the most damaging and perhaps most pervasive approach to self-help derived from the belief that social role playing was the pathway out of homosexuality. Kimball and Petersen wrote, "The entrenched homosexual has generally and gradually moved all of his interests and affections to those of his own sex rather than to the opposite sex and herein is another step. When you feel he is ready, he should be encouraged to date and gradually move his life toward the normal." And the "normal" meant marriage to someone of the opposite sex. For decades, countless numbers of men have been counseled to marry a woman, with the implied or expressed promise that this would "cure" their homosexuality. The story of one family speaks for the experience of many: "Our grandson, when he came home from his mission, and the gal he married came home from her mission and they were married in the temple—it just didn't last. It couldn't last. He told her, before they married, that he was gay. They decided they could make a go of it, with the Lord's help. But it didn't work out." Tom Christofferson elaborated on the meaning of "didn't work out" through his own experience: "The next step of that was getting married, and a short marriage to a woman who certainly didn't deserve that situation of me not knowing how to be, and not being completely forthcoming or having any way of trying to warn her what she was getting into."[10]

While there are some success stories of "mixed-orientation marriages," the overall track record of such marriages has generally been dismal, often catastrophic, and sometimes lethal, best intentions notwithstanding.[11] The largest study of the subject showed a 51 percent divorce rate at the time of the survey completion, projections suggesting an eventual divorce rate of 69 percent, and the likelihood that successful mixed-orientation marriages involved a bisexual, rather than strictly homosexual, partner.[12] Claudia Bradshaw, an LGBT ally in St. George, Utah, spoke of a particularly tragic, failed marriage:

It's a wreckage that just keeps going downhill and downhill, and how much wreckage these families are going through and how hard it is for some of the children. I knew one man who had been a bishop and had eight children, and then came out later. He said, "I just found my true self. I just finally came out." He wanted to all those years, and he knew. He was married and doing all the stuff that they had told him to do, and he had eight children. The damage there was enormous when he came out. He and his wife divorced, and then the kids looked at him and said, "You hypocrite!" But he did what the church wanted him to do. So it's just been really fractured. They don't even want him to be around the grandchildren. It goes down for a generation or two here and how that's affected the families. The old faulty advice, "Tell him to go ahead and get married; he'll get over it," doesn't work, didn't work, and it has caused a lot of wreckage.[13]

T. J. O'Brien wrote in a similar vein:

What about these brothers and sisters who have been "cured" with prayer and fasting and are now happily married? I am personally aware of several dozen such individuals who were "cured" of same-sex desires and went on to marry and have children. Among them are personal friends and family members. Have they lived "happily ever after"? Perhaps in storybooks, but the "cure," many later admitted, was more of a "suppression" that they learned to live with for years. Same-sex feelings eventually surface, leaving families torn apart and emotionally scarred. Most of the marriages ended in divorce. Among these individuals were a bishop with eight children, a bishop's wife with four, a member of a high council with seven, and a mission president with six. For many following the marriage dissolution, a same-sex lover soon came into the picture.

A few have hung on, and to the outside observer their marriages look stable. One of these husbands confessed to me he wished he had never married, and another, an elders quorum president, confided that he enjoys his family but has had sexual intercourse with his wife about as often as he has had children. Even then, he candidly admitted, he has to "fantasize being with a man." Can this honestly be called a cure?[14]

As church leaders gradually became aware of the damage resulting from many mixed-orientation marriages, they began to speak out against them. The first high-placed leader to do so publicly was Gordon B. Hinckley, then a counselor in the First Presidency. In a General Conference address in 1987 he said, "Marriage should not be viewed as a therapeutic step to solve problems such as homosexual inclinations or practices." Five years thereafter, the policy was formalized for church leaders: "Marriage should not be viewed as a way to resolve homosexual problems. The lives of others should not be damaged by entering a marriage where such concerns exist. Encouraging members to cultivate heterosexual feelings as a way to resolve homosexual problems generally leads them to frustration and discouragement."[15]

Although this policy appears to be unambiguous, there continue to be instances where it is ignored. Ron Schow, a respected scholar of LDS–LGBT issues, reported, "We think maybe that's a thing of the past, but I know a young man who was just released from his mission a year ago [2012], and he has been counseled twice, by two different bishops, when he told them about his gay feelings, they both told him to go ahead and get married and not tell anybody."[16]

Recently, one of the most publicized LDS mixed-orientation marriages, that of Josh and Lolly Weed, came to an abrupt end. "For 15 years, the Mormon couple did everything their church advised. They were best friends. They prayed together, studied scriptures together, worshipped together, raised four daughters together. They even shared careers as marriage and family therapists." In their blog, *The Weed*, Josh came to terms with his own sexuality and the futility of having fought his identity for so long. "About three years ago, I finally saw how important it was to love myself, to truly love myself as a gay man." Lolly, rather than condemning him for having entered the marriage, was totally supportive. "You aren't just a broken straight person. Your gayness is a part of who you are. And your sexual orientation is beautiful. You are as God intended you to be."[17]

Focusing first on his own experience, Josh wrote critically of conflicting messages received over the years from LDS Church leaders:

> For people who are not gay or LGTBQ it might feel like church leaders should have room to express and explore opinions like this over time, even in General Conference, and that it's okay that sometimes those opinions aren't accurate in the long run.... These

shifting opinions and incorrect, often psychologically damaging utterances are more than a thought exercise. This is our lives. Our futures. Our hopes and dreams. And so when you get mixed messaging from leaders about something so personal and so relevant, eventually you realize you can't rely on those flimsy, topsy-turvy opinions to direct your life. You realize it rests upon you to get your own answers from God himself.[18]

And then he leveled a withering critique at the men behind the messages and the damage they had done to him and others:

This is what the church's current stance does to LGBTQIA people. It actually kills them. It fills them with self-loathing and internalized homophobia, and then provides little to no help when the psychosomatic symptoms set in, instead reacting to this unexpected by-product (after all, living the gospel isn't supposed to bring misery and death! It's supposed to bring immeasurable joy! Right?) with aphorisms like "have more faith," or "have an eternal perspective" or "be grateful." And the LGBTQIA person is left even further alone, now having been shamed by having it implied that their unhappiness and lack of health is their own fault because they aren't being righteous enough, or trying hard enough. And so, they try harder. And they get sicker. And the cycle continues. It is a sick, pathological spiral. Worst of all, and what amounts to the very crux of the problem: the church also deprives them—us— of attachment, and a natural, verified, studied reaction to attachment blockade is suicidality.[19]

In summary, the self-help approach to "curing" homosexuality has taken several forms over several decades, including distraction, substitution, repentance, hyperorthodoxy, and marriage. All had one thing in common: they rarely, if ever, worked. That set the stage for new approaches that employed outside intervention—the subject of chapter 10.

4

SPENCER KIMBALL AND *THE MIRACLE OF FORGIVENESS*

Spencer Kimball is the subject of an entire chapter because of his unique role in setting a dark tone respecting homosexuality, one that was accompanied by some of the harshest policies ever enacted by the church toward LGBT members.

Few in the church expected that Kimball would become church president, for ahead of him in the succession order was Harold B. Lee, who was younger and healthier than Kimball. President at the age of seventy-three—young by Mormon standards, for his three immediate predecessors had been seventy-five, seventy-eight, and ninety-three years old when they became president, and his successors have been seventy-eight, eighty-six, eighty-seven, eighty-five, eighty-one, and ninety-three—Lee was assumed to be the incumbent for as long as two decades. His unexpected death after only a year and a half in office stunned church members, who had to adjust quickly to the prospect of a very different kind of church president. Whereas Lee had been proactive in restructuring the entire church bureaucracy, Kimball had spent three decades in the Quorum of the Twelve as a defender of the status quo. Shortly after Lee's death, church historian Leonard Arrington wrote, "I was told this afternoon that President Kimball was a traditionalist, very conservative as to doctrine and as to procedures. A prediction was made that he would most likely choose Elders [Ezra Taft] Benson and [Mark E.] Petersen, as the senior members of the Quorum after him, to be his counselors. He has great compassion for ordinary persons and their problems, but his approach is that of a traditionalist rather than an innovator."[1]

The assessment proved to be wrong on all counts. Instead of choosing Benson and Petersen as counselors, he retained those of his predecessor, and although he had been a traditionalist as a follower, once he had to lead rather than follow he turned out to be the most innovative church president of the twentieth century—this in the face of heart disease requiring open-heart surgery and of cancer surgery that robbed him of much of his ability to speak. His innovations reached into many realms of Mormon life, but his most significant was to abolish the church policy that, for more than 120 years, had prohibited men of black African ancestry from being ordained to the church's lay priesthood.

While Kimball was progressive on some issues such as race, on matters of sexuality he took a hard-line approach that reached both inward—for example, the announcement in 1982 that "the First Presidency has interpreted oral sex as constituting an unnatural, impure or unholy practice,"[2] even within marriage—and outward, with the church's opposition to the proposed Equal Rights Amendment, opposition driven in part by fears that the ERA would open the door to same-sex marriage:

> Passage of the ERA would carry with it the risk of extending constitutional protection to immoral same-sex—lesbian and homosexual—marriages. The argument of a homosexual male, for example, would be: "If a woman can legally marry a man, then equal treatment demands that I be allowed to do the same." Under the ERA, states could be forced to legally recognize and protect such marriages. A result would be that any children brought to such a marriage by either partner or adopted by the couple could legally be raised in a homosexual home. While it cannot be stated with certainty whether this or any other consequence will result from the vague language of the amendment, the possibility cannot be avoided.[3]

Kimball's attitudes concerning sexuality were shaped by an assignment that he received in 1947, four years after his entry into the Quorum of the Twelve, to review cases of fornication, adultery, or homosexuality that had been referred to the First Presidency, and to make recommendations for church disciplinary action. The review process required Kimball to conduct "a constant stream of distressing interviews over the years." In 1959 he and fellow apostle Mark Petersen were given an added assignment "to counsel homosexuals" in response to what was perceived to be a growing problem within the church.[4]

In a private meeting at Brigham Young University in 1964, Kimball reflected on his gradually evolving view of homosexuality. Lumping together "'peeping toms,' exhibitionists, homosexuals, and perverts in other areas" as "deviates," he then took aim at homosexuality, employing the disease-cure paradigm described in the previous chapter. "Through the years, we have heard that homosexuality was an incurable disease but now many authorities agree that one is recoverable from its clutches.... We know such a disease is curable.... The cure for this malady lies in self mastery which is the fundamental basis of the whole gospel program."[5]

Five years after the BYU meeting and just a few months before the Stone-wall Riots thrust LGBT issues into the national scene, Kimball and Mark Petersen gave a formal report to the First Presidency of their eight-year-old assignment, during which time they had counseled more than one thousand individuals.[6] Church president David O. McKay "was greatly shocked and dismayed to learn of the extent of the penetration of this dreaded practice"—homosexuality—"which has spread even to the membership of the Church. Elder Kimball mentioned that this problem has grown all over the world, and that it has now come out in the open, whereas formerly it was undercover. Now, an effort is being made to make this perversion respectable." Sagging under an increasing caseload, Kimball and Petersen requested ten additional staffers.[7]

THE MIRACLE OF FORGIVENESS

At the time of his meeting with the First Presidency, Kimball was putting finishing touches on his first major book, *The Miracle of Forgiveness*. Kimball's son and biographer acknowledged the irony of the title: "Indeed, it was a book more on sin and repentance than on forgiveness."[8] The book devoted an entire chapter to male homosexuality but took a total pass on lesbianism, bisexuality, and transgenderism.[9] While generally reflective of common thinking of that era, the chapter's observations are jolting to today's reader:

- Masturbation "evolves often into mutual masturbation ... and then into total homosexuality."

- "The sin of homosexuality is equal to or greater than that of fornication or adultery."
- "Many have been misinformed...that 'God made them that way.' This is as untrue as any other of the diabolical lies Satan has concocted. It is blasphemy. Man is made in the image of God. Does the pervert think God to be 'that way'?"
- "Certainly it can be overcome, for there are numerous happy people who were once involved in its clutches and who have since completely transformed their lives. Therefore to those who say that this practice or any other evil is incurable, I respond: 'How can you say the door cannot be opened until your knuckles are bloody, till your head is bruised, till your muscles are sore? It can be done.'...Let this individual repent of his perversion, force himself to return to normal pursuits and interests and actions and friendships with the opposite sex, and this normal pattern can become natural again."[10]

Miracle became a best seller within Mormon circles, ultimately selling at least 1.6 million copies.[11] It was routinely given to embarking missionaries, but for those who knew or suspected that they were LGBT, it conveyed a message that turned out to be contrary to reality. John Gustav-Wrathall, president of Affirmation: LGBT Mormons, Families & Friends, spoke of the dilemma that it presented to him as a missionary in France and Switzerland: "I think that more than anything else, it was that book that put into my head that, 'If I live faithfully, if I pray, if I study the scriptures, if I serve my callings faithfully, if I serve a faithful mission, if I do all this stuff, then it will fix this. This will go away.' I think that was how I pretty much had it in my head that, 'Once I complete a faithful mission, then I'm going to be clear of this. Then I'll be able to marry and have kids.'"[12]

He was not alone in seeing in *Miracle* a promise from Kimball that increased righteousness, both during and after his mission, would change his sexual attraction. Erika Munson, founder of Mormons Building Bridges, summarized the implicit promise of the book: "If you pray hard enough, fast hard enough, and are a good enough Mormon, your sexual orientation will change or go away. [That] has caused incredible pain and has even cost lives."[13] Gustav-Wrathall described the devastation he experienced when the promise did not hold up:

I worked extrahard at the Missionary Training Center. I worked extrahard in the mission field. If we were supposed to be out tracting until 5:00 p.m., I wanted to be out until 6:00 p.m. I wanted to go the extra mile in everything I did, because I thought I just needed to work that much harder....

I had filled in all the boxes, I had done everything I was supposed to do, and not only did it not go away, it was worse than ever. I'm at BYU, and my sense of a same-sex attraction was that it was stronger than it had ever been.... That's why postmission becomes this shattering disappointment.... That was the beginning of the downward spiral at BYU. I had two more years at BYU, and by the end of my junior year I was ready to commit suicide. I just thought, "I can't do the rest of my life this way." The book set those expectations for me, and the book painted a picture of homosexuality that was so dark, that was so evil and terrible, that it literally felt to me like life or death—like I had to overcome this or I was the worst of the worst. The book made the penalty of failure seem that much larger, and then it set an expectation of being able to overcome this that was just impossible. So I think, in some ways, that that book contributed very directly to my suicidality.[14]

While Gustav-Wrathall did not act on his suicidal thoughts, other returned missionaries did. David Malstrom, who followed a similar pattern of hyperorthodox behavior and experienced similar devastation when it did not result in a change in his sexual orientation, wrote, "Finally I decided that I was not worthy of life, and after many hours of prayer, and searching President Kimball's book, I concluded that I must end my life. On May 1, 1985, I took an overdose of several different types of sleeping pills in an attempt to do just that. Fortunately, this attempt was unsuccessful, but for five days I was unconscious in intensive care."[15]

The harmful effects of *Miracle* were totally antithetical to the pastoral nature and the intent of its author. Allen Bergin, a BYU professor of psychology, was founding director of the university's Institute for Studies in Values and Human Behavior, and as such he had significant contact with Kimball on issues relating to homosexuality. "He said—this was when he was president; he was really old—but he said, 'If I could have a chance to rewrite that book, I would change my language.' He had learned that he had hurt people. He was so tender—the longer he was the prophet, the more tender he became and the more liberal he became in his views—or liberating or empathic."[16]

BEYOND MIRACLE

Several months after the publication of *Miracle*, the church published a pamphlet, *Hope for Transgressors*, written by Kimball and Mark Petersen, that reemphasized the book's assertion that homosexual orientation is chosen and that it can be unchosen. "If they will close the door to the intimate associations with their own sex and open it wide to that of the other sex, of course in total propriety, and then be patient and determined, gradually they can move their romantic interests where they belong. Marriage and normal life can follow."[17]

Coincident with the publication of the pamphlet was a letter from the First Presidency to all stake presidents and bishops that endorsed the special assignment of Kimball and Petersen. The letter concluded, "If additional assistance is required, it can be requested from President Spencer W. Kimball and Elder Mark E. Petersen who will send material and give counsel."[18]

A year after *Hope for Transgressors*, Kimball published a companion pamphlet, *New Horizons for Homosexuals*, in which he gave an apocalyptic warning to the world: "The world cannot survive through this ugly practice. Imagine if you can, the total race skidding down in this practice like Sodom did—no more marriages, no more children, no more family life— just one generation of gratification of lusts and the end." He reiterated the warning in a second edition of *New Horizons*, retitled *A Letter to a Friend*, which was published in 1978: "Homosexuality certainly is a leaky cistern. It means waste of power, an end to the family and to the civilization. One generation of it would depopulate the world leaving it a dry well as Peter described. (Read 2 Peter 2.)."[19]

Given Kimball's status as a senior apostle, *Miracle*'s status as the first quasi-official LDS book to deal directly with the subject of homosexuality, the First Presidency endorsement of his assignment, and the widespread distribution of his pamphlets, Kimball's assertions quickly achieved prominence. His ascension to the church presidency in 1973 elevated them even further, conferring ex post facto canonical status in the minds of many church members.

In the October 1974 General Conference, nine months after Kimball became church president, he made his first presidential statement about homosexuality: "Every form of homosexuality is sin."[20] Dustin Lance Black, a lapsed Mormon, recalled the effect of Kimball's words:

> It was really hard growing up. I knew I was gay. We'd go to church on Sundays, and beamed in every Sunday was President Kimball, the seer, the one who knows—who speaks the word directly for the Lord—and he would tell us how next to the sin of murder is the sin of impurity: homosexuality. When you're told from the age of 8 that you're criminal, you're wrong in God's eyes, that breaks your spirit. . . . You're told that you're here to do good in God's eyes. But then you're told your very nature is evil. It's very isolating. This thing that's inherent in you dooms you. So then, why is life worth living? It's a logical progression.[21]

Kimball's blanket condemnation, which did not differentiate between *being* homosexual and *acting* on one's homosexuality, set the stage for years of harsh, even predatory, treatment of gay church members.

THE MEMORANDUM

Prior to being called to the Quorum of the Twelve Apostles (the second-highest governing council in the LDS Church) in April 1984, Dallin Oaks had a distinguished career as a professor at the University of Chicago Law School, president of Brigham Young University, and justice on the Utah Supreme Court. Although other attorneys have been and currently are members of the Quorum, Oaks's unique experiences as law professor and jurist made him the go-to apostle on legal issues in general. Four months after his calling to the Quorum, and nearly a decade before the church entered the public square at the beginning of the same-sex marriage battle, Oaks wrote a memorandum, "Principles to Govern Possible Public Statement on Legislation Affecting Rights of Homosexuals." To a large degree, after more than three decades its recommendations still inform church action on LGBT legislation.

The purpose and audience of the memo were explicit in the introduction: "In time it may be desirable for the Church to make a public statement on proposed legislation affecting the rights of homosexuals.... This memorandum proposes general principles to guide those who prepare the text of a public statement if one is needed."[1]

He noted that LGBT activists were "skillfully appropriating the rhetoric and tactics of civil rights activists [to] present themselves as an oppressed minority who should be protected by antidiscrimination laws."[2] This was a key, and eventually decisive, point when battles moved from legislative to judicial venues. At issue was the legal doctrine of "protected classes." For instance, race, religion, and national origin had long had this classification within the United States, and legislation adversely affecting them could be challenged in court using the principle of "strict scrutiny"—meaning that the burden of proof was on the government to demonstrate a compelling public interest served by a law discriminatory to any of these classes, in order for the law to remain valid. If sexual preference and gender identity were not deemed protected classes, a discriminatory law could be defended by the lower standard of "rational basis," merely by showing a rational connection between its means and its goals. A decade before the first court trial on same-sex marriage would revolve around this point, Oaks saw the risk to the church's position on homosexuality of having the issue framed as civil rights, and thus more likely to invoke strict scrutiny, and he set the stage for a fundamental argument that church leaders have used to this day for many LGBT issues: they are *moral* rather than civil rights issues.

Oaks then focused on strategies for responding to three areas of legislation that he felt were likely to be at the forefront: decriminalization of sodomy or other homosexual acts; protection of LGBT people against discrimination in employment, housing, public accommodation, education, and credit; and legalization of same-sex marriage.

Decriminalization: Noting that laws against consensual adultery were rarely enforced, he raised a rhetorical question: "whether homosexual relations or conduct need to be *more* criminal than sexual relations or conduct between a man and a woman." He answered the question by saying, "Antisodomy statutes have been repealed in many states, and in others their enforcement is a dead letter because the detection of such crimes almost inevitably involves a violation of some constitutional right of privacy." He recommended inaction by the church on this issue. "I believe there is little to be gained by having the Church enter public debate and take a public position on an expansion or retention of the criminal law to cover illicit homosexual relations to a greater extent than illicit heterosexual relations. The law already covers the most grievous types of behavior that are enforceable, so any additional criminal penalties are likely to be marginal as a practical matter."[3]

One dimension that Oaks did not discuss, but that likely factored into his thinking, was that, unlike antidiscrimination and same-sex marriage legislation, this was a matter of criminal rather than civil law, and thus would have no effect on church policies allowing ecclesiastical punishment of members engaging in homosexual acts. Church leaders followed his recommendation and did not venture into defending or expanding antisodomy laws. (In *Lawrence v. Texas* in 2003, the U.S. Supreme Court struck down all remaining antisodomy laws throughout the country. The LDS Church attempted no intervention in the case.)

Antidiscrimination: The church had (and has) far more at stake with respect to antidiscrimination laws, for they can govern behavior of individual church members as well as the commercial activities of the institutional church, particularly in the arenas of housing, employment, and public accommodation (provision of goods and services). "Gay rights groups," he wrote, "are promoting laws that would preclude any consideration of 'sexual orientation or affectional preference' in decisions on employment and a variety of other matters."[4]

Oaks's first argument was that antidiscrimination laws are unnecessary because gays, in his view, were not victims of discrimination: "The gay rights groups present themselves as victims of intolerance against the *condition* of homosexuality and of broad-based discrimination against persons with that condition. However, there is little evidence of such intolerance or such broad-based discrimination."[5] (This assertion, doubtless shared by his ecclesiastical colleagues, later became a key point of contention in *Hollingsworth v. Perry*, the 2010 court case that invalidated California's Proposition 8. The court ruled in favor of the plaintiffs, in part because there was overwhelming evidence of such discrimination.)

His second argument focused on employment. Favoring some form of employment discrimination, Oaks suggested that there were two legislative approaches. One would allow blanket discrimination, but he cautioned against this approach. "The public will see the debate as a question of tolerance of persons who are different, like other minorities. Perceiving the issue in those terms, the public will vote for tolerance, and those who oppose may well be seen as unmerciful persecutors of the unfortunate."[6]

The second approach, which he favored, would carve out certain kinds of employment and make the case that LGBT persons in such jobs—and he did not differentiate between celibate and noncelibate—would pose an unacceptable risk to society. "If the legislative issue is posed in terms of whether the public has a right to exclude from certain kinds of employment persons who engage in (and will teach) *practices* the majority wish to exclude for the good of society (such as abnormal sexual practices that present demonstrable threats to youth, public health, and procreation), the gay rights proposal will lose." As an example, he wrote, "Parents who prefer and a society which prefers male-female marriages and procreation should be able to insist on teachers and youth leaders who will teach and demonstrate (or at least not contradict) those values."[7]

Oaks then went to a topic earlier articulated by Spencer Kimball and other church leaders: "Since public policy must obviously favor perpetuation of the nation and its people, laws should permit employers to exclude from key positions of influence those who would proselyte and promote the homosexual lifestyle."[8] Given the stable percentage of LGBT people in the population, which generally is conceded to be 5 percent or less, one may wonder whether Kimball, Petersen, Oaks, and other church leaders truly considered the possibility of a "gay takeover" of the planet and subsequent cessation of procreation to be a credible threat. Nonetheless, he was not alone within the LDS tradition in believing, without supportive documentation, that LGBT people proselytize to enlarge their ranks—indeed, that proselytizing is the *only* way they can perpetuate homosexuality.

Quick to defend laws allowing discrimination in employment, Oaks did not advocate extending such laws to other areas. "It should be noted that the arguments that would permit job discrimination against homosexuals in certain types of employment have no application to permit discrimination in credit, education (admissions), public accommodations, and housing. If there is a basis to approve discrimination in these areas against persons with the homosexual condition, it has yet to be suggested." (Oaks changed his mind on one key point sometime after writing the memorandum, for in 2015, in the midst of a heated legislative debate in Utah over proposed non-discrimination legislation, he vigorously argued against protections for LGBT persons in the arena of public accommodations.)[9]

He then turned his attention to strategies for opposing LGBT antidiscrimination legislation. "Total opposition (that is, opposition to all nondiscrimination legislation benefiting homosexuals) would look like a religious effort to use secular law to penalize one kind of sinner without comparable efforts to penalize persons guilty of other grievous sexual sins (adultery, for example)." The better strategy would be to propose "well-reasoned exceptions"—for example, "a youth-protection exception" in teaching and counseling jobs. "Such opposition should be explained, with careful emphasis on the bad effects of homosexual *practices* (not homosexuals) and the need—for the good of society—to protect youth from homosexual proselyt[iz]ing and role models among their teachers and counselors." If the exceptions could be worked out behind the scenes, the church "would not need to support the law—it could just refrain from opposing it."[10]

Same-Sex Marriage: The strongest message of the memorandum addressed same-sex marriage. Unlike criminal penalties, where Oaks advocated nonaction, and antidiscrimination legislation, where he advocated behind-the-scenes action where possible, he recommended full engagement by the church in the battle against same-sex marriage. Characterizing such marriages as "a devilish perversion of the procreative purposes of God and the earth life He has granted His children" and "wholly deviant to the procreative purpose of sexual relations...[and] the patriarchal family," he wrote that "the interests at stake in the proposed legalization of so-called homosexual marriages are sufficient to justify a formal Church position and significant efforts in opposition."[11]

He then recommended four talking points if church leaders elected to enter the public square and oppose same-sex marriage:

1. "We speak in defense of the family, which is the bulwark of society."
2. "The legal rights conferred on marriage partners are granted in consideration of the procreative purpose and effects of a marriage between a man and a woman. (Even marriages between men and women who are past the child-bearing years serve this procreative purpose, since they are role models for younger, child-bearing couples.)"
3. "Cohabitations between persons of the same sex do not meet the time-honored definition and purposes of 'marriage' and therefore should not qualify for the legal rights and privileges granted to marriage."
4. "One generation of homosexual 'marriages' would depopulate a nation, and, if sufficiently widespread, would extinguish its people. Our marriage laws should not abet national suicide."[12]

All four arguments (as well as others) were employed by other opponents of same-sex marriage, both inside and outside the LDS Church.

In a closing statement, Oaks pointed out an irony that the church could face in entering the same-sex marriage debate, which involved the role that the 1879 *Reynolds v. United States* Supreme Court decision had in defining marriage. In the final legal blow outlawing plural marriage among Mormons, "the Court defined marriage as a legal union between one man and one woman.... The modern relevance of the *Reynolds* opinion is in its reference to marriage as being between a *man* and a *woman*. The irony would arise if the Church used as an argument for outlawing homosexual marriages the decision that a century earlier outlawed polygamous marriages." (Indeed, the church, in an amicus brief under the name of its surrogate organization, Hawaii's Future Today, *did* cite *Reynolds* to bolster its view that "traditional marriage" must be maintained by outlawing same-sex marriage.)[13]

The Oaks memorandum was also significant beyond its legislative focus in that it appeared to be part of the process by which church leaders turned a corner from the Kimball years. (Kimball was alive but incapacitated when the memorandum was written.) In a section titled "The 'Condition' of Homosexuality vs. Homosexual Practices," Oaks quoted two passages from Kimball's writings and made editorial comments on each. To the passage, "Homosexuality can be cured if the battle is well organized and pursued vigorously and continuously," Oaks responded, "This obviously refers to the *condition* of sexual attraction to persons of the same sex." To the passage, "Homosexuality, like other serious sins, can be forgiven by the Church and the Lord if the repentance is total, all-inclusive, and continuous," he noted, "This obviously refers to the *practice* of sexual relations between persons of the same sex."[14] While one can see how he might parse Kimball's language in this manner in order to support the church's evolving policies, it is important to note that both rhetoric and actions during the Kimball administration viewed *homosexuality* as the sin, and even celibate homosexuals were subjected to excommunication.

HAWAII

The political tsunami began in Hawaii and swept east across the entire country. By the time its virtual waters receded, Congress and most state legislatures had constructed legal barriers to block the consequences of what
they saw as the inevitability of Hawaii becoming the first state to legalize
same-sex marriage.

The quest for marriage equality did not begin in Hawaii. Within two
years after Stonewall (1969), four lawsuits asserting a constitutional right
to same-sex marriage were filed in Kentucky, Minnesota, Washington,
and Wisconsin. The first began in the spring of 1970. Jack Baker and Mike
McConnell, who had met and fallen in love in Oklahoma, moved to Minnesota so Baker could attend law school. While attending religious services
at the University of Minnesota's Newman Center, they asked the Catholic
priest, William Hunt, "Do you feel that if two people give themselves in love
to each other and want to grow together with mutual understanding, that
Jesus would be open to such a union if the people were of the same sex?"
Hunt replied, "Yes, in my opinion, Christ would be open." Emboldened by
the response, they made wedding plans that were thwarted when they were
refused a license.

They then filed a lawsuit against the State of Minnesota and asked the
American Civil Liberties Union (ACLU) and the Kinsey Institute to assist
them. Both organizations declined, failing to see gay marriage in the early
1970s as a viable civil rights issue. The case was dismissed on summary
judgment in the district court, Minnesota Supreme Court, and U.S. Supreme
Court, with the latter seeing in it no "substantial federal question."[1]

Following Baker and McConnell's case, three same-sex couples—two lesbian and one gay—in Kentucky, Washington, and Wisconsin, respectively, filed similar lawsuits and experienced the same result.[2]

The ACLU's reluctance to advocate same-sex marriage is not surprising when viewed in historical context. Many LGBT activists were either averse or apathetic to marriage of any kind. However, as more and more LGBT people came out of the closet and pursued ordinary lives alongside their heterosexual friends and coworkers, many found marriage an appealing prospect. Some gay and lesbian individuals, who had been encouraged to pursue heterosexual marriages, found the stresses of such arrangements unmanageable. After divorcing, they often found a same-sex partner. Some of these partnerships included children from prior marriages and a corresponding wish to solidify their family relationship through marriage. Against this backdrop, several other factors were subtly shifting attitudes broadly at the grassroots level.

The AIDS epidemic, which exploded in the United States in the early 1980s and took a disproportionate toll among gay men, focused attention on medical rights taken for granted by married couples but inaccessible to others. William Eskridge, a national expert in LGBT law, noted, "That so many partners of people with AIDS were treated badly by hospitals and surviving relatives created a huge demand for domestic partnership and even marriage recognition among many gays who had never contemplated the matter before AIDS."[3]

Medical issues other than AIDS also highlighted the inequities suffered by the LGBT community. Nikki Boyer, a lesbian activist in Salt Lake City, recalled, "I was one of the people saying, 'Shut up! [Same-sex marriage] is not the issue to push for. Start with anti-discrimination laws." But her attitude changed with the death of her partner of more than twenty years. The medical examiner would not release the body to Boyer for a funeral "because I wasn't family." Her partner's mother, in her nineties and living in a nursing home, had to sign a waiver to give Boyer custody.[4]

Other shifts in attitude were generational, as noted by Andrew Sullivan in a pivotal 1989 article that both reported and shaped thinking.[5] He noted that the rebelliousness that characterized Stonewall and fueled the national coming out in its wake did not transfer to the next generation. While respectful of the rebellion itself and the rebellious attitudes of its pioneers, many younger gays and lesbians viewed the world differently. "A need to rebel has quietly ceded to a desire to belong. To be gay and to be bourgeois no longer seems such an absurd proposition. Certainly since AIDS, to be gay and to be responsible has become a necessity." The younger generation saw in marriage a venerable and beneficent institution that was more than the sum of parts offered by alternatives such as domestic partnerships and civil unions. Their motives were additive rather than subtractive—strong homosexual marriages and the families that they could raise would add to society's aggregate strength without degrading heterosexual marriages or the institution of marriage itself.

BAEHR V. LEWIN

Ninia Baehr and Genora Dancel, both in their late 20s and living in Hawaii, were introduced to each other by Baehr's mother. Romance quickly ensued—"I had been searching for Ms. Right," Baehr recalled, "and now I'd found her"— but not plans for marriage. When Baehr suffered an acute earache, however, a practical advantage of marriage became clear. Dancel, a television station engineer, said, "I wanted to get her on my insurance, but only married people can do that."[6]

Baehr and Dancel along with Joseph Melillo and Patrick Lagon, partners for thirteen years, and Tammy Rodrigues and Antoinette Pregil agreed in December 1990 to go together to the Hawaii Department of Health and apply for marriage licenses. Their request, to no one's surprise, was declined. In the company of Bill Woods, a local gay activist who had brought the three couples together, they then visited the local chapter of the ACLU, anticipating an offer of legal representation so that they could challenge in court Hawaii's ban on same-sex marriage. As had been the case in Minnesota two decades earlier, the ACLU declined to represent them. Kate Kendell, then an ACLU employee and now executive director of the National Center for Lesbian Rights, which also declined to get involved, reflected on the novelty—and implausibility—of such a lawsuit. "I thought the idea that same-sex couples would be marrying and those marriages would be recognized by the government was fanciful and not likely to happen anytime soon."[7] The Lambda Legal Defense Fund, the top LGBT legal organization in the country, similarly declined to represent the couples.

Finally, they turned to local attorney Daniel Foley, a former ACLU employee who had only one previous experience in a gay-rights lawsuit: a male cross-dressing pageant.[8] Foley filed a complaint in May 1991 in the Hawaii Circuit Court rather than federal court, anticipating a higher likelihood of success because a clause of the Hawaii Constitution banning sex-based discrimination appeared more favorable to LGBT rights than anything in the U.S. Constitution. Of the six plaintiffs, Baehr was the one whose name appeared first. The defendant was John C. Lewin, state health director. Four months later, Judge Robert Klein granted the state's motion for judgment on the pleadings and dismissed the complaint in *Baehr v. Lewin*.[9] The judge ruled the plaintiffs had failed to show that Hawaii could not constitutionally exclude their same-sex unions from civil marriage. Foley appealed the case to the Hawaii Supreme Court and this time secured the assistance of the ACLU and Lambda Legal.

THE HAWAII SUPREME COURT

A turning point in the case occurred when the Hawaii deputy attorney general Sonia Faust was questioned by one of the state's supreme court justices. "'OK. A male and a female walk in, and they're not married and they want a license; you give it to them. A male and a male walk in and want a license; you won't give it to them. You are discriminating against them.' 'Our position is that that is permissible discrimination,' Ms. Faust responded."[10]

In May 1993, the Hawaii Supreme Court ruled, in a plurality but not majority vote, that while there was no constitutional right to same-sex marriage, the denial of marriage licenses to same-sex couples constituted discrimination based on sex. (The morality of homosexuality was not addressed by the court.) It then remanded the case back to the lower court for trial, with the requirement that the legal standard of "strict scrutiny" be applied. Strict scrutiny is the most rigorous legal standard, and it shifted the burden of proof from the plaintiffs to the state. That is, rather than the plaintiffs having to prove in court that the law had unnecessarily harmed them, the State of Hawaii would have to demonstrate a compelling state interest that would be served by prohibiting same-sex couples from marrying. If not, by virtue of the Hawaii Constitution same-sex couples would have the right to be married in Hawaii.

Reaction within Hawaii was swift. Backed by a large majority of the population that opposed same-sex marriage, the state legislature passed a law in June 1994 reaffirming its desire to protect the status quo. Given the constitutional nature of the issue, however, few expected the law to survive a legal challenge. All eyes focused on the trial, which was postponed in order to allow third parties the opportunity to intervene.

A second response of the legislature to the supreme court decision was to create "a commission to study and make recommendations as to the recognition and extension of public benefits to same-sex marriages. . . . Two [of the eleven members] shall be representatives from the Catholic Church diocese; two shall be representatives from the Church of Latter-Day Saints." The two LDS representatives, appointed by the governor of Hawaii, had a short-lived tenure. In response to a legal challenge, a federal judge ruled that their presence on the commission violated the Establishment Clause of the U.S. Constitution. "The selection of particular denominations (e.g., the Latter-Day Saints and Catholics) for membership on the commission is likely to give rise to the perception of endorsement prohibited by the Supreme Court."[11] Nonetheless, the Mormons were in the game.

THE MORMONS ARE COMING

In January 1994, *Affinity*, the newsletter of Affirmation: LGBT Mormons, Families & Friends, published a report that "unsubstantiated rumors are circulating that the Mormon Church is quietly encouraging its members in Hawaii to get involved in the fight to perpetuate the ban." Less than a month later, the First Presidency gave credence to those rumors in a circular letter sent to local church leaders worldwide, with instructions that it be read during worship services: "We encourage members to appeal to legislators, judges, and other government officials to preserve the purposes and sanctity of marriage between a man and a woman, and to reject all efforts to give legal authorization or other official approval or support to marriages between persons of the same gender."[12]

Two months after the First Presidency letter was circulated, the church-owned *Deseret News* published an article that looked both backward and forward in acknowledging the church's activity in the public square—not only the battle over same-sex marriage but also larger LGBT issues. "In the mid-1970s, the Mormon Church launched an unprecedented campaign against the Equal Rights Amendment, saying its passage would promote lesbianism and degrade the American family"—an argument foreshadowing the battle over same-sex marriage. "Two decades later, the church is gearing up to fight another perceived threat to home and hearth: same-sex marriages."[13] Downplaying the extent to which the central church was thus far involved in Hawaii, the article went on to report, "Church spokesman Don LeFevre said that other than the February statement, church leaders have not involved themselves. . . . There are those, however, who believed that if church leaders are not conducting the campaign now, they will be."

One year later, the church role in the same-sex marriage battle shifted abruptly from low to high profile. As *Baehr v. Lewin* moved slowly toward a trial, church leaders became convinced that the State of Hawaii would be either unwilling or unable to mount the robust legal defense required to satisfy the demands of strict scrutiny and thus preserve marriage as a heterosexual-only institution. On February 23, 1995, against the wishes of the Hawaii director of health (the named defendant in the case), the church petitioned the court to intervene in the case—essentially to become a codefendant.[14]

The stated basis of the petition was the fear that local LDS bishops and stake presidents, who were licensed by the State of Hawaii to perform marriages, would be put at risk by a law that legalized same-sex marriage. Charles Goo, a stake president at BYU–Hawaii in Laie and one of the named petitioners, submitted in an affidavit:

> I am reasonably concerned that I will be asked to solemnize such marriages which, under the usages of the LDS Church I am prohibited from doing. If this should occur, I am reasonably fearful that I as a Stake President, as well as the other Stake Presidents of the LDS Church in the State of Hawaii could have my license to solemnize marriages revoked, and/or face claims and lawsuits for damages for alleged discrimination based upon sex by same gender couples for whom I, or any of the other Stake Presidents of the LDS Church in the State of Hawaii, refuse to solemnize.[15]

But in an accompanying document, church attorney James Sattler fleshed out, for the first time in a public forum, the deeper arguments for the church's opposition to same-sex marriage. The arguments were not unique to Mormonism, and indeed were common fare for opponents of same-sex marriage. Each carried a dire warning:

- Same-sex couples lack the parenting skills of heterosexual couples, and some of their children thus "will be condemned to a higher incidence of some social maladies such as substance abuse, poverty, and violence. Children will also suffer from sexual identity problems because they lack a traditional family role model."
- The state's interest in fostering procreation "will be severely undermined by the recognition of same-sex marriages."
- "The important state interest of upholding society's moral and ethical standards" would be undermined by giving same-sex couples access to marriage.[16]

One additional argument that earlier had been made clear by the church was articulated the following day, in a *Deseret News* article, by the church's highest-ranking official in Hawaii, regional representative Donald Hallstrom. Seeking a delicate balance that was and still is difficult to achieve, he said, "The church takes a moral stand against homosexuality but does not try to impede the civil rights of individuals. We do not see this as a civil-rights issue. We see it as a protection of traditional marriage." Legal scholar William Eskridge pointed out the significance of this statement: "The LDS Church was thus the first to set forth a coherent set of arguments against marriage equality grounded in a general moral theory of sexuality, gender and the law. (Catholics have such a theory but did not mobilize as soon as LDS, and of course soon piggybacked.) LDS was first on the ground and in airwaves with the moral and pragmatic and legal theories in support of traditional family values—all the other religions followed LDS's first moves."[17]

Sattler's arguments made it clear that the church's underlying concern was not over licensing to perform marriages—a specious argument totally unsupported by legal precedent and one quickly and completely rebuffed by the court. Instead, the church had little confidence that the state would be robust in its defense of the stated societal benefits of heterosexual-only marriage and no confidence that it would be willing to condemn homosexuality on moral grounds. Family is core to LDS beliefs and practices, and any threat to the LDS ideal of family, whether actual or contrived, would be attacked vigorously. Given the central authority structure of the church and the constant mantra of "Follow the Prophet," the church could be a formidable foe, as it wished to be in the court case.

In oral arguments before Judge Herbert Shimabukuro, counsel for both the State of Hawaii and the plaintiffs argued against the church's petition for intervention. Assistant Attorney General Steven Michaels said, "Both the Free Exercise Clause and the Religious Freedom Restoration Act, which provides very substantial additional statutory protection for that free choice by the LDS Church, would step in and we submit would block that kind of a situation." Daniel Foley, speaking on behalf of the plaintiffs, added, "This motion can be disposed of just on a plain reading of 572-12 of Hawaii Revised Statutes where it basically authorizes a licensee to perform a marriage. It doesn't require a licensee to solemnize any marriage. And in fact, the statute even makes it clear that any solemnization of marriage shall be according to the usages of that denomination or society and providing that the solemnization is in accordance with the rules and customs of that society." The judge agreed with Foley's reading of the statute. "I'm looking at Section 572-12, it's discretionary as to how the religious ministers, priests, and also of any religious denomination may or may not solemnize marriage according to the usage of such denomination or society."[18] Four weeks later the court denied the church's motion to intervene. Within hours the church appealed the matter to the Hawaii Supreme Court.[19]

On the same day the LDS Church first petitioned the court to intervene, it participated in a news conference with an unlikely ally in its fight to block same-sex marriage: the Roman Catholic Church. Decades earlier, when General Authority Bruce McConkie's book *Mormon Doctrine* had labeled the Catholic Church the "Church of the Devil,"[20] such an alliance would have been unthinkable for most Mormons. But times had changed, and now Donald Hallstrom flanked Father Marc Alexander, diocesan theologian for the Hawaii Catholic Conference, as Alexander announced that while the LDS Church sought to intervene as a codefendant, the Catholic Church in Hawaii would pursue the same goal through the filing of an amicus curiae, or friend-of-the-court brief.[21] (Not long thereafter, the two churches would form a surrogate organization and work together to press their case in the state legislature and directly to the voters.)

On January 23, 1996, the Hawaii Supreme Court issued its ruling on the appeal of the intervention petition. Noting that while Hawaii law *allowed* ministers to perform marriages, it did not *require* a minister to perform *any* marriage, whether in accordance with the faith tradition's beliefs and standards or not. Thus, no minister could be compelled by the state to perform a same-sex wedding. The court also dismissed the church's allegation that its officers who refused to perform same-sex marriages would be targets of credible civil lawsuits. "The mere chance that a non-meritorious lawsuit may be filed against a party seeking intervention does not create an interest requiring intervention in the present action."

The church's other pleas, advanced by James Sattler, were not addressed by the supreme court, which affirmed the order of the circuit court. William Eskridge, an advocate of same-sex marriage, nonetheless commended the church's unsuccessful attempt to introduce a novel argument. "Mormons have this great normative theory of the procreative eternal family. LDS lawyers in Hawaii were right to say they had a different theory to support the law. Denying intervention deprived the Hawaii trial of the great moral debate that could have occurred if LDS lawyers could have put on their witnesses."[22]

While awaiting the decision of the Hawaii Supreme Court on the appeal of the motion to intervene, the church embarked on two simultaneous missions. One was to enter the political arena and attempt to influence the Hawaii Legislature to amend the state constitution to outlaw same-sex marriage. The other was to codify, for the first time, the church's policy on what families are—and what they are not.

THE PROCLAMATION ON THE FAMILY

In both word and practice, family is foundational to the LDS Church. A central feature of LDS temples throughout the world, more than one hundred in number, is a rite where man and woman can be "sealed" to each other so that their marriage will transcend death, as will their familial relationship to their children. But until 1995, the LDS doctrine of family had never been codified.

The prior year, 1994, had been designated by the United Nations as the International Year of the Family. Conferences were held throughout the world. In an interview for a PBS documentary on the church, senior apostle Boyd Packer recalled the Cairo, Egypt, conference. "I read the proceedings of it and it was on the family, and in all the proceedings I couldn't find the word marriage, and as though those two didn't go together. . . . There was the thought that they were going to have such a meeting in Salt Lake City. And we thought if they are coming here for that kind of a convention we better issue, we better state our case and so made a Proclamation on the Family."[23]

According to Packer, drafting of the document occurred at the highest levels of the church hierarchy. As he recalled, "The members of the Twelve wrote that proclamation. It was considered word by word by the First Presidency and the Quorum of the Twelve."[24] Gordon B. Hinckley, the church president, introduced the Proclamation on the Family in the Relief Society (the women's auxiliary organization) General Conference on September 23, 1995, reading it aloud in its entirety. Although the document assigned traditional gender roles to men and women (men were to preside and provide; women were primarily to nurture children), apparently the male hierarchy did not believe it necessary to involve any women church leaders in its drafting.[25]

Homosexuality, though never mentioned by name in the proclamation, was a subtext throughout. The document defined marriage as being ordained of God and "between a man and a woman." The "sacred powers of procreation are to be employed only between man and woman, lawfully wedded as husband and wife." It warned that "the disintegration of the family will bring upon individuals, communities, and nations the calamities foretold by ancient and modern prophets." And it ended with a call to action, that "responsible citizens and officers of government everywhere" should promote measures, including constitutional amendments, "designed to maintain and strengthen the family."[26]

Lest there be any uncertainty in people's minds as to the link between the proclamation and the church's condemnation of same-sex marriage, Apostle M. Russell Ballard later drove home the point. "As a member of the Quorum of the Twelve Apostles, I participated in the process of drafting 'The Family: A Proclamation to the World.' ... We could see the people of the world wanting to define the family in ways contrary to God's eternal plan for the happiness of His children.... Gender is being confused, and gender roles are being repudiated. Same-gender marriage is being promoted in direct opposition to one of God's primary purposes—for His children to experience mortality."[27]

Written too late to be employed in the church's motion to intervene in *Baehr v. Lewin*, the proclamation was first used in the case in April 1997 as the introductory section of the church's brief of amicus curiae after the district court trial, which occurred September 10–20, 1996, while the case was being appealed to the Hawaii Supreme Court.[28] While it had no effect on the outcome of the trial, the proclamation quickly attained—and maintains—virtual canonical status within the church despite never having been presented to the church as revelation.[29]

What the proclamation and the church's intervention papers and briefs did accomplish was to articulate, in a manner not previously seen in marriage-equality lawsuits, the moral arguments against same-sex marriage. They argued that it would accelerate the deinstitutionalization of marriage, that role models for children must be gendered, and that homosexuality in general—and same-sex marriage in particular—were immoral. "Homosexual marriage is wrong, both from a moral and a social point of view. Its recognition will have grave consequences for every individual, for every family, for every community, for every state, and for American society."[30] Until then, government lawyers had not been making these arguments.

HAWAII'S FUTURE TODAY

Given the likelihood that *Baehr v. Lewin* would be decided in favor of the plaintiffs, the church shifted gears and began to focus on the legislative branch of government. In October 1995, one month after the Proclamation on the Family was unveiled, Loren Dunn, president of the North America West Area, began meetings in Hawaii to formulate a strategy. Dunn acted under the direction of the Public Affairs Committee and reported directly to its chair, Apostle Neal Maxwell. Donald Hallstrom, the highest-ranking church official residing in Hawaii, reported directly to Dunn.

Early meetings included four representatives from the church's legislative lobbyist, McNeil Wilson; Hallstrom; Francis DiLorenzo, bishop of the Roman Catholic Diocese of Honolulu; and Marc Alexander, the Catholic theologian present at the joint press conference earlier the same year. Hallstrom and DiLorenzo reported that Alexander and Jack Hoag, a prominent LDS businessman, agreed to cochair a Committee on Same-Gender Marriage, but all participants felt that in order to provide some cover from public scrutiny for the two churches, the chair of the committee needed to be someone "who is not visibly connected with either church." Other action items resulting from the meetings included a request to Lance Wickman, an LDS General Authority and the church's general counsel, to advise the group on how to structure the committee to meet the requirements of Hawaii law; an initiative to begin fund-raising for the committee, with emphasis on the mainland; and a forthcoming visit to Hawaii of Richard Wirthlin, a former pollster for the Ronald Reagan administration and future LDS General Authority, who would supervise polling on attitudes of Hawaii citizens toward same-sex marriage and advise the committee on strategy.[31]

In mid-November, coincident with Wirthlin's visit, Dunn chaired two days of strategy sessions with an expanded group that also included Hallstrom, Hoag, and Alexander. The official name of the political action group would be Hawaii's Future Today. The chair position was still vacant: "The coalition is looking for an articulate, middle-age mother who is neither Catholic nor L.D.S. as a chair but two have declined." In addition to keeping the two churches in the background, HFT's initial work with the Hawaii Legislature "will be done as quietly as possible." The legislative goal, in light of *Baehr v. Lewin*, was becoming clear: "We hear from all sources that this issue will recur and will only be put to bed with a [Hawaii] constitutional amendment."[32]

Within a week the chair position of HFT was filled, albeit not with the non-LDS, non-Catholic incumbent first envisioned. Instead, Debi Hartmann, an assistant professor of political science at Brigham Young University–Hawaii and active Latter-day Saint, agreed to chair the group. Hartmann was well connected politically, having served for six years (two years as chairwoman) as an elected member of the state board of education. Assisting HFT would be lobbyist Linda Rosehill, of whom Donald Hallstrom wrote to Loren Dunn, "Her background as a 'liberal democratic lobbyist' may appear conflicting with our position on this issue, however, we have had extensive discussion and time with her and are convinced her 'heart' is with us. In fact, her persona probably works in the Coalition's favor as it is easy for the group to be labeled as 'right-wing conservative.'"[33]

A STRATEGIC PLAN

In a report to the Public Affairs Committee at church headquarters, Dunn underscored what had become a national concern for those opposed to same-sex marriage. "It should be noted that no state legislature in the United States has passed a same-gender marriage bill, nor has the national Congress. Everyone is looking to Hawaii with the feeling that if it should be the first, it would cause a domino effect."[34] Dunn did not specify, nor was it generally comprehended at that point, exactly what the feared domino effect would be. Was it subsequent legislation in other states, or the Congress legalizing same-sex marriage, or the de facto "spread" of same-sex marriage as couples married in Hawaii returned to their states of residence and demanded, because of the Full Faith and Credit Clause of the U.S. Constitution, that their marriages be recognized?

A week later, Dunn reported to headquarters the results of Richard Wirthlin's polling in Hawaii. Sixty-three percent opposed legalizing same-sex marriage, a strong grassroots base of support for the church position. The church itself, however, polled negatively: on a scale of 0 (very unfavorable) to 100 (very favorable), it scored only 49, versus 57 for the Catholic Church. "This information suggests that the Church should maintain a very low visibility in this campaign.... A well-known tactic in political issue campaigns is to demonize the messenger if the issue itself cannot be demonized. It is most advisable to keep a formal distance between the Church and the Coalition involved in fighting the issue." Instead of opposing same-sex marriage publicly, the church would do far better to engage in a campaign extolling "family values."[35]

A final point of the report was to suggest a long-term strategy for Hawaii. Noting that the Hawaii attorney general had already committed to appealing a court decision favorable to Baehr et al., Dunn noted, "This gives us a minimum of two years' waiting time before another decision would be handed down. We should use this time wisely, perhaps to set the groundwork for a constitutional amendment—but even this, ultimately, will likely be appealed to the Supreme Court of the United States."[36]

Three days after Dunn's report, Hawaii's Commission on Sexual Orientation, from which the two Mormon and two Catholic members had been removed by court order, issued its final report. By a vote of five to two, it recommended that the legislature legalize same-sex marriage, with a backup recommendation that domestic partnerships be legalized if there was not sufficient support for the marriage proposal.[37] The report added another layer of urgency to the mission of Hawaii's Future Today.

In a year-end written communication to headquarters, Dunn advised Neal Maxwell of his attempts to give the church the appearance of being arm's length from the workings of HFT, while at the same time not ceding strong influence. "Don Hallstrom is working with me and is our on-site liaison with the coalition, principally Jack Hoag. In this way, we have distanced the Church from the coalition itself but still have input where necessary through our local source."[38]

CIVIL RIGHTS OR MORALITY?

Another piece of the strategic plan for Hawaii derived in part from the church's own history with civil rights and in part from its recent public statement. Having opposed racial civil rights for decades in the middle of the twentieth century, and having banned ordination of blacks to its lay priesthood for more than a century before reversing the policy in 1978,[39] the church was in a vulnerable public position with respect to anything that was portrayed as civil rights. And now, having stated earlier in 1995, "The church takes a moral stand against homosexuality but does not try to impede the civil rights of individuals,"[40] it would open itself to charges of hypocrisy if it fought against what the public considered a civil rights issue: same-sex marriage.

Its solution was to attempt to portray the issue as one of morality rather than civil rights. In January 1996, Loren Dunn wrote to Neal Maxwell, "What is currently most needed by national interests are . . . well researched and documented professional articles which intelligently counter the case for same-gender marriage, especially combating the 'civil right' argument." They immediately turned to a man who arguably was their most credible legal voice in the public square: Rex Lee. Lee had been the thirty-seventh solicitor general of the United States during the Reagan administration and was highly respected on both sides of the political aisle. He went on to become president of Brigham Young University, a position he held for over five years before resigning at the end of 1995 during the terminal stages of a lengthy struggle against cancer. Working from his hospital bed only five weeks before his death, Lee wrote an op-ed article that was circulated to Hawaii legislators and published in the *Honolulu Advertiser*. The article began with the sentence, "Same-sex marriage is not a constitutional civil rights issue."[41]

In late February, Donald Hallstrom reported to Dunn that Lee's arguments were persuasive. "At the end of the hearing, [Senate Judiciary Committee chairman Rey] Graulty delayed the voting until Monday, saying some of the committee members had become 'confused' as to the question of this being a civil rights issue and they wanted more time to ponder. This means the Rex Lee material had impact as previously they all clearly believed it was a civil rights issue." The impact, however, was incomplete. Two weeks later, Dunn wrote to Neal Maxwell, "In spite of Rex Lee's excellent brief, there are still some in the Senate who see this as a civil rights issue and if they don't address it in some other way, the courts will legalize same gender marriage which at this point neither House nor Senate want, nor do the public by a 71% majority."[42] In fact, same-sex marriage is a moral issue *and* a civil rights issue, and the choice of which label to use depends on the labeler. While the church has the right to speak in the public square on *political* issues so long as its remarks do not endorse *candidates* for public office, it has chosen to frame as *moral* issues those that it chooses to address publicly. Gay-rights organizations, on the other hand, see same-sex marriage as a *civil rights* issue—indeed, *the* civil rights issue of our times. While an appeal to the Hawaii courts on moral grounds would not prevail, morality was an important issue within the Hawaii Legislature.

THE HINCKLEY TOUCH

Gordon B. Hinckley was sustained as the fifteenth president of the LDS Church in March 1995. For six decades previously he had worked in the employment of the church, in both the bureaucratic and the ecclesiastical lines. Arguably the most skilled person in the hierarchy in public relations, he worked hard to raise the public image of the church during his thirteen-year tenure as president.

Hinckley's approach to managing the church's campaign against same-sex marriage involved a blend of high-profile and low-profile initiatives. To ensure that his own flock understood the depth of alliance that was being forged with the Roman Catholic Church, he met in early 1996 with Catholic bishop Francis DiLorenzo and Father Marc Alexander and directed that the church-owned *Deseret News* publish a story documenting the meeting. But once the church moved into the political arena, Hinckley insisted that it work as part of a coalition, rather than alone, and that wherever possible it keep a low profile. Loren Dunn explained to Neal Maxwell, "One reason I wanted us organized in Hawaii the way we are is because President Hinckley wanted it that way. A coalition is hard to attack and particularly a young mother [Debi Hartmann] who was Chair of the State Board of Education

(Chairman).... Our input to the coalition is through Don [Hallstrom] to Jack Hoag. The ideas are introduced but the Church is not visible."[43]

WORKING THE LEGISLATURE

With the trial phase of *Baehr v. Lewin* still months away, Hawaii's Future Today pursued the arduous process of shepherding legislation through the Hawaii Legislature. With some input from HFT, which met with House Speaker Joseph Souki prior to the 1996 legislative session,[44] the state house of representatives approved a constitutional amendment rejecting same-sex marriage by the required two-thirds majority. The problem for the church was the state senate. Loren Dunn reported to Neal Maxwell, "A two-thirds majority in the Senate would put the amendment before the people which would probably settle the court case before it got started," but by a four-to-three vote the senate's Judiciary Committee blocked it from a floor vote. Frustrated by the committee vote, Dunn suggested to Maxwell an alternative if private pressure did not prevail. "As we get down to crunch time, our demonstrators will be out literally twenty-four hours a day to bring this to the attention of the Senate."[45]

HFT's lobbying efforts were noted by the press. "The three leaders of Hawaii's Future Today are working the Senate everyday, trying to pick off one vote or another."[46] By contrast, church leaders managed to follow Gordon Hinckley's advice and keep the church in the background. At the end of April, Dunn reported on a statement presented to the Judiciary Committee in favor of the proposed constitutional amendment. While the statement was endorsed by many constitutional lawyers, it had been written by two church attorneys. "Neither the name of Lynn Wardle or Von Keetch appeared on the statement, nor was the Church mentioned, in keeping with our policy of not getting ahead of the coalition."[47]

Ultimately, the state senate failed to muster the two-thirds vote necessary to approve the proposed constitutional amendment, despite the fact that "HFT was there at every step, even literally being brought into the behind closed doors negotiating meetings."[48] The failure of the proposed amendment was widely viewed nationally as an almost certain victory for the legalization of same-sex marriage. "Alarm bells went off across the country, and within two weeks the Defense of Marriage Act was introduced in the United States Congress."[49]

In the 1996 elections, voters expressed their frustration at the legislature's inability to pass a constitutional amendment. In the September primary election, Rey Graulty, chairman of the Judiciary Committee, was defeated by political newcomer Norman Sakamoto, who ran on a pledge to support the amendment. The president of the senate barely escaped defeat. In the November general election the Republicans picked up four seats in the state house of representatives, defeating incumbents who had supported same-sex marriage. Those who retained their seats in the legislature took note of the strong signal from the voters.

At the end of the year, anticipating better results in the subsequent legislative session, Loren Dunn wrote to LDS apostle Henry Eyring, "The Lord has blessed the coalition because it has given Hawaiians who oppose HLM [homosexual and lesbian marriage] a voice and focus without the Church being singled out for attack by the opposition.... The coalition was able to neutralize the last legislature on this issue and even exerted influence that turned legislators out of office and affected the leadership of the State Senate.... We are now poised for a constitutional amendment in the State that could settle the issue once and for all."[50]

BAEHR V. LEWIN REVISITED

Having been denied standing as codefendant, the church could only watch from the sidelines as *Baehr v. Lewin* was finally tried in court. Foreshadowing *Hollingsworth v. Perry* fourteen years later—the legal challenge to California's Proposition 8 that received far more national attention—*Baehr* highlighted the weaknesses in the state's allegation that banning same-sex marriage served a compelling state interest. The court found that the state had "failed to establish or prove any adverse consequences to the public resulting from same-sex marriage...the need to protect traditional marriage as a fundamental structure in society...a causal link between allowing same-sex marriage and adverse effects upon the optimal development of children...[and that] the optimal development of children will be adversely affected by same-sex marriage."

Conversely, the court found "that the single most important factor in the development of a happy, healthy and well-adjusted child is the nurturing relationship between parent and child...[that] gay and lesbian parents and same-sex couples have the potential to raise children that are happy, healthy and well adjusted ... [and that] gay and lesbian parents and same-sex couples can be as fit and loving parents, as non-gay men and women and different sex couples." Indeed, the case was made both then and subsequently that LGBT couples already raising children would be validated by getting married and that society would strengthen such families by granting them status equal to that of any other families.

Citing a recent court case in the District of Columbia, the court got to the heart of the issue: "A mere feeling of distaste or even revulsion at what someone else is or does, simply because it offends majority values without causing concrete harm, cannot justify inherently discriminatory legislation against members of a constitutionally protected class."[51] The court therefore declared Hawaii Revised Statute 572-12 unconstitutional and void. The decision was immediately appealed to the Hawaii Supreme Court, and, pending appeal, the implementation of the decision was delayed.

A CONSTITUTIONAL AMENDMENT

The battle in Hawaii was far from over. Having lost their case in court, opponents of same-sex marriage still had one option. The day the court's decision was announced, Hawaii's Future Today issued a press release. "Despite Judge Chang's decision, the fact remains that the majority of Hawaii residents oppose the legalization of same-sex marriages. Thus, it remains the responsibility of the legislature to pass a constitutional amendment reaffirming that marriage is exclusively a union between one man and one woman."[52]

HFT immediately sprang into heightened action. Whereas during the prior legislative session it had focused on attempting to pass a constitutional amendment whose language had been drafted within the legislature, it now took the lead in writing new language. One week after the decision in *Baehr* was announced, a local law firm wrote to the firm of Kirton McConkie, the church's outside counsel in Salt Lake City, "Our office has been retained by Hawaii's Future Today ('HFT') to develop alternative language for a constitutional amendment that will, in effect, avoid judicially imposed same-sex marriage, answer most of the concerns of uncooperative legislators, and be constitutionally sound." A week later the church's own legal counsel, Lance Wickman, informed Neal Maxwell, "Von Keetch and Lynn Wardle of the BYU Law School are reviewing this proposed amendment, particularly in light of the recent *Romer* decision, to make sure that it does not run afoul of federal constitutional requirements."[53]

Proponents of an amendment got an unexpected boost in January 1997 from Ronald Moon, chief justice of the Hawaii Supreme Court. In his State of the Judiciary address to the legislature, Moon appeared to signal his disapproval of the lower court's decision in *Baehr*. "When deciding cases, judges often apply common law, statutory law, or constitutional law to new facts and circumstances. In so doing, we do not intend to usurp the legislative function. However, under our system of checks and balances, if we stray into legislative perogative [*sic*], the legislature has the ability to cure the trespass." The following day the *Honolulu Advertiser* noted, "Some lawmakers took that as a message that if they didn't like the recent state court decisions legalizing same-sex marriage in Hawai'i, the changes are up to them." Loren Dunn wrote to Neal Maxwell, "If this is true, it is a major statement and means we won't have to worry about the Hawaii Supreme Court second guessing the Legislature on passing this legislation. As was expected, it is in the hands of the Legislature and we see this as a good development."[54]

While the church's ideal outcome would have been a constitutional amendment with no strings attached, the political reality was that passage of an amendment would likely require the extension of some marriage-associated rights to LGBT couples. Indeed, Apostle Dallin Oaks, the predominant legal voice within the Quorum of the Twelve, had foreseen such a possibility more than a year earlier. Writing to Loren Dunn, he expressed the sentiment that legalization of domestic partnerships "would be unacceptable because this would give domestic partnerships a standing and effect equivalent to marriage for many purposes.... A more acceptable approach would be to have an enabling legislation to permit private parties to enter into private agreements that would grant some rights to a domestic partner that would otherwise be unavailable or difficult to establish." The rights acceptable to Oaks would include life and health insurance benefits, pension benefits, hospital and prison visitation, bereavement leave, power of attorney, and housing nondiscrimination.[55]

Early in 1997, Apostle M. Russell Ballard replaced Neal Maxwell in overseeing the church's activities in Hawaii. In a memorandum in February, Dunn brought Ballard up to date, giving particular emphasis to political horse trading. "Elder Oaks was the first to recognize that in the political process that in order to win this battle, there may have to be certain legal rights recognized for unmarried people such as hospital visitation so opponents in the legislation will come away with something. This is proving to be the case."[56]

The need for compromise was underscored by Hawaii's law concerning constitutional amendments. If an amendment passed both houses of the legislature by a two-thirds majority, it would then go directly to the voters, who had to approve it by only a simple majority. By contrast, if either house of the legislature passed it by a simple majority but fell short of the two-thirds vote, it would be returned to the legislature during the subsequent legislative session, where it would again have to pass by at least a simple majority prior to going to the voters. Proamendment strategists were averse to extending the process by a full year, and thus the push for the two-thirds vote, even though it required compromise.

The proposal for a constitutional amendment fared much better in the 1997 legislative session. This was due, in part, to the results of the November 1996 election and in part because of more acceptable language in the new proposed amendment—language that included input not only by Hawaii's Future Today but also by other church surrogates. In April, Dunn wrote to Ballard, "Jack Hoag of the coalition has made arrangements so Lynn Wardle of B.Y.U. and David Coolidge[57] have direct input to Terrance Tom on the language being discussed. Tom is Chairman of the House Judiciary Committee and a conference committee member.... Thanks to our input, the language of the Amendment has greatly improved."[58]

A week later, Dunn reported to Ballard that both houses of the legislature had come to an agreement on two bills. HB 117, a proposed constitutional amendment, read simply, "The Legislature shall have the power to reserve marriage to opposite-sex couples." HB 118 extended to couples who could not marry about sixty benefits afforded to married couples, without labeling their relationship a domestic partnership. "Hawaii's Future Today (HFT) was always focused on a clean, strong constitutional amendment and was not supportive of 118. However, HFT recognized 117, especially in any acceptable form, would not become reality without 118.... Some may focus on 118 and suggest failure; however, we believe what has occurred will set back the opposition's movement significantly, both in Hawaii and nationally."[59]

Later in April, both houses of the legislature passed HB 118 by margins well in excess of the two-thirds required for a proposed constitutional amendment to go to the voters: twenty-four to zero in the senate and forty-four to six in the house. HB 117 passed by similar margins. Dunn wrote to Ballard, "Our satisfaction is only tempered by the existence of 118; however, we know there would be no constitutional amendment without it."[60] As problematic as HB 118 was, it was less so due to the efforts of BYU law professor Lynn Wardle, as noted by Dunn. "The coalition did not like H.B. 118 or any effort to give support to SGM [same-gender marriage], but recognized without 118 there would be no 117 and the courts would rule. Through intense Hawaii's Future Today lobbying and the input of B.Y.U. constitutional scholar, Lynn D. Wardle, the Senate version of 118 was completely altered."[61]

APPEALING TO THE VOTERS

The final step in ratifying HB 117 was a popular vote in the November 1998 general election with a simple majority approving it. Even though polling had consistently shown that a large majority of Hawaiian voters was against same-sex marriage, church leaders braced themselves for a pitched and expensive campaign to ensure passage of the amendment.

A memorandum to the Public Affairs Committee in Salt Lake City, dated July 1, 1997, candidly acknowledged prior and future direct support by church headquarters: "The Church structure has been used to rally support for HFT and will be used to educate the electorate about voting and to get out the vote come November 1998." It then projected the need to raise $400,000 to fund the campaign—an amount far greater than what had been necessary to move the amendment through the legislature.[62] Plans to support a new "super coalition" were approved by the First Presidency and Quorum of the Twelve, and a letter from the North America West Area Presidency to church members in Hawaii was sent in mid-October. Fund-raising assignments would be given to stake presidents in Hawaii during a training session in early November.[63]

The new political action organization, Save Traditional Marriage '98 (STM), was formed to raise money and push for passage of the amendment. Announced publicly in early November 1997, it included on its steering committee Jack Hoag, the LDS vice chairman of Hawaii's Future Today.[64] Linda Rosehill, the lobbyist retained by Hawaii's Future Today, served the same function with STM.

In the summer of 1998, the amendment campaign heated up. STM went to the mainland to videotape an endorsement from Reggie White, who transitioned from a Hall of Fame career in the National Football League to fundamentalist Christian minister. White's recent Wisconsin sermon had attracted widespread criticism for its racist portrayals of Asians, Hispanics, and blacks, but Rosehill defended the decision to turn to him because he "cares about Hawaii's future."[65] Amendment supporters launched an intensive voter registration and volunteer recruitment drive and were rewarded by an early-August poll showing that 70 percent of voters opposed same-sex marriage.[66]

In mid-August, a challenge to the state Campaign Spending Commission resulted in an unanticipated decision that radically changed the funding dynamics of the campaign, though not the ultimate outcome. Bill Woods, the initiator of *Baehr*, accused STM of violating the $1,000-per-donor limit on campaign contributions. Instead of mandating that STM give back money that exceeded that limit, the attorney general ruled the spending limit unconstitutional, thus opening the floodgates to large contributors. The two largest almost canceled each other out: the Human Rights Campaign, headquartered in Washington, DC, contributed $985,000 to defeat the amendment, while the LDS Church contributed $600,000 out of general church funds to pass it.[67]

STM led the way in proamendment television commercials that appealed to the heart more than the head—a strategy similar to that used successfully a decade later in California to pass Proposition 8. Jennifer Diesman of Rosehill and Associates, which produced the commercials, said, "In the first ad we have a boy"—unidentified in the ad, but Linda Rosehill's eight-year-old son[68]—"reading from the book 'Daddy's Wedding,' which shows a picture of two men kissing as they get married. The ad says, 'If you don't think homosexual marriage will affect you, how do you think it will affect your children?' The second ad began this Monday. A man and a woman in wedding attire are running toward each other, and he runs past her into the arms of a man." The Reverend Joan Ishibashi complained that the ads "appeal to our deepest prejudices. We urge them to stop their campaign of intolerance."[69]

Antiamendment forces escalated the verbal warfare when they brought abortion into the discussion. One of the most liberal states in the country on social issues, Hawaii, in 1970, had been the first to legalize abortion. In a thirteen-second television spot sponsored by Protect Our Constitution/ Human Rights Campaign, "Dr. Jennifer Frank says she is 'frightened' that groups advocating a 'yes' vote on the ballot measure that would give the

Legislature the power to limit marriage to one man and one woman also 'intend to repeal abortion laws—taking away a woman's right to choose.'"[70]

A strategic issue that both sides had to address was a paradox within the ratification process. That is, a yes vote on the amendment was actually a no vote on same-sex marriage. A Mason-Dixon poll taken in the fall showed that 73 percent of voters "found the wording of the measure confusing."[71] The proamendment side also had to contend with a Hawaii law that stipulated that passage of an amendment required at least 50 percent of *all ballots cast*, not just of all votes respecting the issue. In other words, ballots that were blank on the issue were counted as no votes.[72]

Save Traditional Marriage's emotional pitch of the amendment being a referendum on same-sex marriage easily prevailed over the opposition's attempt to frame the issue within a civil rights context: 69 percent of voters approved the amendment. David Smith, a senior strategist with the Human Rights Campaign, acknowledged that STM waged the better campaign. "They had an easy, emotional message. We had a complex, technical message about government and civil rights: If this (denying marriage to gays) can be done to us, discrimination can also happen to you."[73]

Almost a year elapsed before the court stepped back in. "On December 9, 1999, the court finally issued a four-page summary disposition signed by three justices (Justices Moon, Levinson, Nakayama) and one judge (Chief Judge Burns, sitting in for Justice Klein, who had earlier recused himself). The court announced it was taking 'judicial notice' of the Marriage Amendment. It then announced that in light of the passage of the Marriage Amendment, the case was moot. It reversed the circuit court's decision and directed it to enter judgment for the State."[74] Hawaii was not the first domino to fall.

BACKLASH, 1.0

The 1993 decision of the Hawaii Supreme Court to remand *Baehr v. Lewin* for trial created an atmosphere of urgency, even paranoia, throughout the country. State after state as well as the U.S. Congress, in quick succession, enacted legislation both to block the performance of same-sex marriage within jurisdictions and to erect a barrier to the recognition of such marriages performed elsewhere. The LDS Church stood alone in the breadth and depth of its involvement in the legislative process at the state level.

UTAH: LEADING OUT

The U.S. Constitution states, "Full faith and credit shall be given in each state to the public acts, records and judicial proceedings of every other state." As the legal battle in Hawaii raged, Roger Hunt, a state legislator from South Dakota, expressed the fear of many legislators and voters: "Unless a state explicitly declares an exception, it may be obligated to give full faith and credit to a marriage entered into by two people of the same gender in another state."[1] While many states began to consider such legislation, Utah acted first. Given the First Presidency mandate of a year earlier "encourag[ing] members to appeal to legislators, judges, and other government officials,"[2] and given the fact that the large majority of the Utah Legislature at the time was LDS, no further urging by the church was needed. Drafted by BYU law professor Lynn Wardle, who was simultaneously working with the church in Hawaii, a law forbidding recognition of same-sex marriages performed elsewhere was passed by a near-unanimous vote in the final hour of the legislative session early in 1995.[3]

DOMA

Shortly after the Hawaii Legislature failed to pass a constitutional amendment outlawing same-sex marriage during the 1996 session, the U.S. Congress erected a federal firewall against the likely outcome that it would be legalized in Hawaii after *Baehr v. Lewin* went to trial later that year. The House of Representatives report of HR 3396, the Defense of Marriage Act, explicitly connected the dots between Hawaii and DOMA: "H.R. 3396 is a response to a very particular development in the State of Hawaii....The state courts in Hawaii appear to be on the verge of requiring that State to issue marriage licenses to same-sex couples."[4] DOMA defined marriage, for federal purposes, as being solely between one man and one woman, thus allowing the federal government to deny benefits to same-sex couples even if they were married legally. It also allowed states to ignore the Full Faith and Credit Clause of the U.S. Constitution and refuse to recognize same-sex marriages performed in other states.

Although the LDS Church had no role in the passage of DOMA, a sidebar story is of interest. As DOMA was being debated, Senator Harry Reid (D-NV) made no secret of his opposition to it. A local LDS Church leader in Nevada, irritated at Reid's public stance, wrote him a letter to the effect, "We might have to look into your activities if you continue to oppose this." Reid forwarded the letter to church headquarters and said, "What are you going to do about this?" Within a day, two officials traveled from Salt Lake to Las Vegas to inform the local leader, "The church is not going to tell Harry Reid how to vote."[5]

A NATIONAL GAME PLAN

In April 1998, LDS Church spokesman Don LeFevre told a reporter from the *Advocate*, a national LGBT magazine, that "homosexuality 'isn't really an issue' and is rarely mentioned at church headquarters in Salt Lake." One month later, an internal memorandum suggested otherwise. Written by Arthur S. Anderson, a member of the Same-Gender Marriage Advisory Committee who also had been active in Hawaii's Future Today, it was a blueprint for church involvement in the legislative process in more than half the states in the country. "At the last meeting," it began, "it was proposed that we design an instruction manual that would help the contact people in the 20 remaining states to organize a coalition." The end goal was to direct the organization of an "active coalition... in all states where there is not an adequate law in place that defines marriage as a contract between one man and one woman and that states that so-called marriages of people of the same sex will not be legally recognized if performed within the state or in other jurisdictions."[6]

The memorandum outlined the steps to be taken in each state, once a church representative was appointed. After determining the legislative need, be it "a law passed by the legislature, a change in the state constitution, the defeat of proposed legislation to legalize same-sex marriage, etc.," local leaders were to conduct a public opinion survey to guide strategy, organize a coalition, and begin raising funds to carry out the strategic plan.

Acting on information provided by the SGM committee, Public Affairs served a command-and-control function, meeting periodically to receive reports from the field and direct subsequent activities. For several states no activity was recommended other than to monitor any proposed legislative initiatives. For others, particularly Alaska, Nebraska, Nevada, and California, church involvement was important and even decisive.

ALASKA

Three years after Ninia Baehr and her coplaintiffs filed their lawsuit in Hawaii, Jay Brause and Gene Dugan applied to the Alaska Bureau of Vital Statistics for a marriage license. Upon being denied the license, they filed a complaint alleging that the prohibition against same-sex marriage violated the Alaska Constitution's guarantee of the right to privacy and equal protection. In his decision in February 1998, superior court judge Peter Michaelski wrote, "It is not enough to say that 'marriage is marriage' and accept without any scrutiny the law before the court. It is the duty of the court to do more than merely assume that marriage is only, and must only be, what most are familiar with." After citing *Baehr v. Lewin*, he came to the same basic conclusion as the Hawaii case: "Government intrusion into the choice of a life partner encroaches on the intimate personal decisions of the individual. This the Constitution does not allow unless the state can show a compelling interest 'necessitating the abridgement of the... constitutionally protected right.'" In other words, as had been the case in Hawaii, strict scrutiny applied, and the burden of proof shifted to the government to show the compelling state interest that was served by outlawing same-sex marriage.[7]

In contrast to the thunder of media attention that *Baehr* triggered, *Brause* was a faint echo. Nonetheless, since the referendum on the Hawaii constitutional amendment was still months away, some, including the LDS Church, looked to Alaska as a second floodgate that might open. Ten days after Judge Michaelski's decision, BYU law professor Lynn Wardle, who had been a key figure in Hawaii, testified before the Alaska Senate Judiciary Committee in support of "a proposed state constitutional amendment that says that a marriage to be valid in Alaska 'may exist only between one man and one woman.'"[8]

The measure was placed on the ballot for the November 1998 election. In September the church donated $500,000 to the campaign to pass the amendment. Whereas in Hawaii the church's $600,000 donation was more than offset by the Human Rights Campaign, in Alaska no major donor stepped up on the other side of the issue. Indeed, the church donation was five times as large as the entire budget of Alaskans for Civil Rights—No on 2, the group opposing the amendment. It also represented nearly 80 percent of the entire budget of the Alaska Family Coalition that was promoting the amendment. A spokeswoman for Alaskans for Civil Rights vented her anger publicly. "It's outrageous that a group based in Utah would flood our state with money to try to purchase a change to our constitution. We absolutely know we don't need religious leaders from Outside spending $500,000 to tell us what to do with our constitution—and our private lives."[9]

The amendment was approved by a 68 percent majority—the same as the Hawaii vote that occurred on the same day.

NEBRASKA

In the legislative session of 1998, Nebraska's unicameral legislature—the only one-house legislature in the country—initiated work on legislation to prohibit same-sex marriage. At a meeting of the SGM Committee in February in Salt Lake City, it was reported that the church's point man in Nebraska, Robert Valentine, planned "to wait until after the final reading, probably in April and see if pressure is needed. If so, they would contact members in the four stakes in Nebraska . . . to help put pressure on wavering legislators."[10]

Mormon support notwithstanding, the bill failed to pass during the 1998 session, and so the alternative of a voter initiative was pursued. Initiative 416, characterized as "the country's most sweeping effort to bar gay unions, a proposed amendment to the state Constitution that not only bans gay marriages but also declares same-sex civil unions and domestic partnerships invalid,"[11] was on the ballot for the 2000 general election. Unlike the elections two years earlier in Hawaii and Alaska, the church did not make a large monetary contribution. An article in the *Deseret News* explained, "Coalitions opposed to legalizing same-sex marriage in both Alaska and Hawaii received $500,000 and $600,000, respectively, from the LDS Church, but the move was criticized by opponents who accused the church of trying to influence the outcome of the election through large contributions.... This time, it appears the church has worked through grassroots channels." The grassroots efforts of church members in Nebraska were substantial. Placing the measure on the ballot required a statewide campaign to collect petition signatures. About one-fourth of the petition drive's 3,200 volunteers were church members, and they collected about one-half of the 160,000 signatures.[12]

Initiative 416 was approved by 70 percent of voters, virtually the same majority as in Hawaii and Alaska. The boots-on-the-ground approach in Nebraska became the model for subsequent LDS Church forays into the same-sex marriage political arena. From that point forward, "sweat equity" and financial support coming directly from church members replaced large checks from headquarters.

NEVADA

As in Nebraska, Nevada citizens employed the initiative process to place a constitutional amendment on the ballot. The Coalition for the Protection of Marriage was "heavily supported by the Church of Jesus Christ of Latter-day Saints, whose members were central to anti-gay marriage efforts in Hawaii and Alaska, and most recently, in California."[13] Getting Question #2 on the ballot required a minimum of 44,009 petition signatures, and church members played a key role in collecting them. A Las Vegas newspaper reported, "During the original petition drive to get Question #2 on the ballot many of the signatures were collected by individuals making use of their church (or 'Ward' [congregation]) directories and existing social venues. 'I was attending the singles ward at the University,' commented Jacki Keys, ... 'and the bishop would encourage us to walk the streets for the "Coalition for the Protection of Marriage.""'[14]

The Nevada Constitution requires two ballot votes for citizen-initiated constitutional amendments. Voters approved Question #2 in 2000 by 69.6 percent and in 2002 by 67 percent.

CALIFORNIA

California, a blue state with a long history of social progressivism, became and remained the focus of attention in the marriage-equality battle as the twentieth century drew to a close. LDS Church involvement in the same-sex marriage battle began early in 1996, when Assemblyman William J. "Pete" Knight authored Assembly Bill 1982, which would prohibit California from recognizing same-sex marriages legalized in other states. A letter from the North American West Area Presidency that was read to all LDS congregations in the state said, "Any effort that members, acting as individual citizens, can make to contact their own legislators in support of this measure would be in harmony with the Church's Proclamation on the Family."[15]

Writing later in the year, Loren Dunn suggested to Apostle Neal Maxwell an alternative strategy if the bill failed to become law. "If the legislation dies on the floor of the California Senate, one alternative would be to organize an initiative to bring the issue before the people of California in a general election. Judging from past initiatives, it would take about $1 million to get the necessary signatures to get the initiative on the ballot and another $2–3 million to help insure its passage."[16] After being amended in the California Senate Judiciary Committee, the bill failed to pass.

In 1997, at the beginning of the next legislative session, Marlin Jensen, a member of the LDS Public Affairs Committee, made an overture to the Catholic Church concerning a possible political alliance in California. Although the Hawaii case had not yet run its course, the Mormon-Catholic alliance in that state had been mutually beneficial. Jensen wrote to Loren Dunn, "I spoke today with Monsignor William Fry, Undersecretary to the National Catholic Conference on Bishops. He immediately put in a call to Bishop Cummins in Oakland, and has paved the way for you to contact Bishop Cummins and arrange for an audience to speak with him concerning HLM." A day later, Jensen conveyed encouraging information to a broader audience of church leaders. "Elder Richard Wirthlin's survey indicates passage of an anti-HLM referendum is feasible. Elders Dunn and Wirthlin will meet soon with Catholic leaders in California to assess the possibility of forming a coalition."[17]

Less than a week after receiving Jensen's letter, Dunn reported progress to Russell Ballard, who had replaced Neal Maxwell as the apostle in charge of Public Affairs. "Bishop DiLorenzo, in Hawaii, has contacted Bishop [John] Cummins about our coming to see him regarding HLM.... With your approval, we will start preliminary discussions with Bishop Cummins, the same that we did with Bishop DiLorenzo in Hawaii." Ballard approved, and within the month Dunn reported back on his meeting with Cummins. The report contained three important points. First, the prospect of getting "anti-HLM" legislation through both houses of the California Legislature "appears virtually impossible at present. There is a consensus that a referendum [ballot initiative] is the only route." Second, a survey conducted by Richard Wirthlin showed the public image of the Catholic Church in California to be better than that of the LDS Church—the same as in Hawaii. "In other words, if we get into this [coalition], they are the ones with which to join." And finally, he had "a cordial visit" with Bishop Cummins, chairman of the Catholic Bishops Conference in California. "They are prepared to join with us on this issue. Bishop Cummins told us the California Catholic Bishops are united in their opposition to H.L.M."[18]

The political climate in California differed from that in other battleground states of Hawaii, Alaska, Nebraska, and Nevada, where anti-same-sex marriage legislation ultimately passed by wide margins. In early March, Lynn Wardle wrote to his colleagues about a new field poll that showed Californians to be "increasingly tolerant of gay rights, though they remain opposed to same-sex marriages." While two-thirds favored some kind of domestic-partnership benefits, 56 percent were opposed to same-sex marriage. Underscoring his church's resolve to counter the trend of increased acceptance of same-sex marriage, LDS president Gordon Hinckley said to the World Forum of Silicon Valley that "his church will do all it can to stop the recognition of same-sex marriage in the United States." A week later, Loren Dunn reported to Russell Ballard, "Richard Wirthlin and I have been doing some work in California in order to develop names that could head a coalition established by ourselves and the Catholic Church."[19]

During the 1997 legislative session, Pete Knight, now in the state senate, sponsored another bill, this one to block California from recognizing same-sex marriages performed elsewhere. It also died. Lynn Wardle, who had been flown to Sacramento by Knight to testify in favor of the bill, wrote to Dunn, "It appears that it will not be possible to get non-recognition legislation through the legislature. So perhaps this has laid the foundation to proceed with an initiative."[20]

Within three weeks it appeared that the foundation was being laid. LDS pollster Gary Lawrence wrote to the California Defense of Marriage Leadership Group, "From the focus group findings and after numerous discussions with legal experts such as Prof. Lynn Wardle of BYU to distill and polish the concept, the initiative language we propose submitting to the Attorney General for ballot title and summary is: 'Only marriage between one man and one woman is valid or recognized in California.'"[21] The following month, Apostle Robert Hales conveyed to Russell Ballard the essence of a telephone conversation with Dunn in which they discussed plans to move forward with signature gathering in order to place an initiative on the ballot, "options to raise monies locally from our interested Church members and the California community for the name gathering and the subsequent campaign," and "the development, composition and LDS interaction with the 'California Family Values Coalition.'"[22]

In early July, Marlin Jensen, Loren Dunn, and Richard Wirthlin recommended to the Public Affairs Committee that the church join the effort to place an initiative on the ballot for the June 1998 primary election. They acknowledged that such a commitment would be expensive in both time and money "and may expose the Church to unfavorable publicity." On the other hand, several factors aligned to favor the commitment: "a supportive Governor, the advantages of a June ballot, the existing level of public support, and the momentum of the fledgling coalition.... To wait would, in our opinion, reduce the probability of winning so severely that a future initiative would be very unlikely." Specific recommendations included "using the priesthood structure to gather a major portion (70 percent) of the [seven hundred thousand] required signatures" and raising up to $2 million of the $10 million estimated total cost.[23]

Two factors operated independently to delay the proposed initiative. On the church front there was pushback. A somewhat exasperated Dunn wrote to Hales in mid-July, "As you know, the Public Affairs Committee targeted ten states (it has been enlarged to a great many more, as you are aware) to make sure that there are appropriate laws in place that could deal with same-gender marriage.... California was one of those target states.... We were also told that President [James] Faust[24] said we cannot lose California." Something had changed, however, and Dunn did not appear to understand the basis of the change. "Suddenly, we are in the position of defending ourselves with the Public Affairs Committee for something they asked us to do in the first place. We didn't buy this fight, but as you know, we see a reason to be there." Three months later, Dunn wrote to Jensen, "My understanding, if it is correct, is that the First Presidency and Twelve want to stand back and watch this matter."[25]

The other factor was a decision within Senator Knight's office to target the primary election of 2000, rather than 1998, in part to see the outcome of the Hawaii election. The stage was set for Proposition 22.

PROPOSITION 22

The point man in California state senator Pete Knight's office was Andrew Pugno. As he and Knight contemplated a strategy for a statewide initiative, Pugno reached out to BYU professor Lynn Wardle. "[Pugno] wondered whether, in light of how the Alaska Superior Court had interpreted the privacy position of the Alaska Constitution, I thought an Initiative Petition amending the state constitution would be wiser than an ordinary legislative change by Initiative petition."[1] Wardle replied that a constitutional amendment would be a better safeguard against same-sex marriage, but that it would also be a more daunting objective. Pugno appeared to lean toward an amendment, but eventually he and Knight settled on an initiative to change the state law.

Whereas LDS Church leaders in the fall of 1997 had backed away from involvement in an initiative, at the end of 1998 they did an about-face. In December Neal Maxwell "conveyed the decision of the First Presidency and Quorum of the Twelve that the Church may participate in the coalition of supporting the California initiative." The decision came with strings attached. First, as had been the intent in Hawaii—a Mormon, Debi Hartmann, wound up chairing Hawaii's Future Today after two non-Mormons declined the job—any coalition should be chaired by a non-Mormon, and LDS Church headquarters should remain in the background. Second, the financing model would be that of Nebraska and Nevada rather than Hawaii and Alaska. "Maximize monetary contributions from California members. Don't convey the impression that the church will step in if local efforts to provide financing fail."[2]

Given the nod, three LDS General Authorities—Marlin Jensen, Cecil Samuelson, and Richard Wirthlin—moved quickly. At the end of February they reported to the Public Affairs Committee that they had formed a coalition and that Wirthlin would serve on its executive committee. The Catholic Church in California was "committed but is considering the scope of its support for the campaign." Ned Dolejsi, executive director of the California Catholic Conference, "appears sympathetic to our position." As far as financing was concerned, "the impression has been conveyed to the coalition that the Church carried Hawaii and Alaska and it is now time for others to step up financially."[3]

In late May, a letter signed by the North America West Area Presidency was read aloud in all priesthood and Relief Society meetings in California. Under the heading "Preserving Traditional Marriage," it solicited the support of church members to pass what would become Proposition 22. Recipients were told that the initiative "provides a clear and significant moral choice" on which the church's position "is unequivocal." Then, the call to action: "We ask you to do all you can by donating your means and time to assure a successful vote. Marriage between a man and a woman is ordained of God, and is essential to His eternal plan. It is imperative for us to give our best effort to preserve what our Father in Heaven has put in place." Noting that "a broad-based coalition" was being formed, the letter concluded, "As details about the coalition become available, we will provide you with information on how you might become involved."[4]

Simultaneous with the area-presidency letter was one from Douglas L. Callister to California stake (diocese) presidents concerning fund-raising. "No undue pressure of any type should be applied" to members, and no fund-raising was to occur "on church property, through use of Church letterhead, or by virtue of general announcement in Church meetings." Finally, "experience shows that it is generally more successful to begin with the more affluent members, suggesting an appropriate contribution and thereafter extend the invitation to those of lesser means."[5]

Although the ban on "undue pressure" appears to have been honored generally, indirect pressure came in the form of quotas assigned to some wards (congregations) and stakes. One stake was given a goal of $37,500,[6] while a ward in a different stake was assigned a goal of $4,000.[7] In some instances, letters from local church leaders to members "contained appeals for specific amounts, which some local church leaders say went too far."[8]

While the large majority of church members responded positively to the call to action, as they did later with Proposition 8, there was pushback, including from some Mormons who voiced their complaints from afar. Gary Watts, a Utah physician, wrote to Cecil Samuelson, a fellow physician and friend and signatory to the area-presidency letter, "How are church members with gay children or gay siblings to respond? Millie and I have two gay children who are among the finest individuals I know. Are we supposed to donate our means and time to assure our two gay children that they are to be denied the very same rights as our four straight children?"[9]

Others protested with their feet. "With Prop 22 there were, across the cultural hall, all these signs to put up on people's lawns to oppose gay marriage and to pass 22. When church let out, people went through the cultural hall and someone would hand them a sign. They handed our son a sign—we felt so lucky to get him to come out to church—and he said, 'Hell no!' He left, and he never went to church again."[10]

Reports of church involvement soon appeared in the press. An article in the *San Francisco Chronicle* quoted a church spokesman in Utah as saying the letter read in church meetings "should be considered as 'inspired and coming from the Lord. . . . But it's up to the members as to how to proceed. . . . Nobody is going to be disciplined.'"[11] The article made clear a key point: "The Mormons had nothing to do with getting this initiative qualified for the ballot." Although there had been talk prior to Prop 22 that there would be a coalition, actual church involvement did not begin until after the measure had qualified to be on the ballot.

The article also emphasized another point: "One fear of the gay rights community is the church's instruction to donate 'means' to the campaign. That would essentially hide the source of financing for the initiative, since individual Mormon donors would not be required to cite their religion on disclosure forms." One report estimated that half the pro–Prop 22 contributions came from Mormons, but unlike Prop 8, where the evolved power of the Internet allowed documentation of contributions, it was an undocumented estimate.[12]

Public criticism of the church's role was sufficiently strong that church president Gordon Hinckley chose to address it during the October 1999 General Conference. "I have time to discuss one other question: 'Why does the Church become involved in issues that come before the legislature and the electorate?' I hasten to add that we deal only with those legislative matters which are of a strictly moral nature or which directly affect the welfare of the Church. . . . We regard it as not only our right but our duty to oppose those forces which we feel undermine the moral fiber of society." He noted that in past campaigns as well as Prop 22, the church had worked within coalitions that included other faith traditions. Then he lashed out strongly at same-sex marriage. "There is no justification to redefine what marriage is. Such is not our right, and those who try will find themselves answerable to God.... We believe that defending this sacred institution by working to preserve traditional marriage lies clearly within our religious and constitutional prerogatives. Indeed, we are compelled by our doctrine to speak out."[13]

Spurred on by Hinckley's remarks, church members redoubled their efforts. According to one published account in late January 2000, five weeks before the election, "The Mormons have been going door to door every weekend for three months." Another report stated, "Local leaders were instructed to tell members it was important that they 'support the prophet on this issue' and that their response to the call to support the Knight Initiative [Prop 22] was a test of their 'faith and willingness to follow the prophet.'"[14]

Although the Prop 22 campaign had a higher profile nationally than prior same-sex marriage campaigns in other states, the outcome was never in doubt. Kate Kendell, executive director of the National Center for Lesbian Rights, headquartered in San Francisco, said, "It was *obvious* Prop 22 was going to pass. Even our own polling showed that. Everyone doing any sort of polling could tell, 'Why should we put resources into this? We're not going to go all-in on something that we think we aren't going to win.'"[15]

The final vote in favor, 61.4 percent, was a decisive victory, although less than the margins of victory in Hawaii, Alaska, Nebraska, and Nevada. One church member recalled the reaction of his coreligionists: "It was like they won the football game. They defeated Satan, and they were so grateful that the Lord blessed them."[16]

STUART MATIS

Inseparably linked to Proposition 22 is the story of Stuart Matis. Of him, former LDS bishop Robert Rees wrote, "This is the best the Church produces." His friend Bruce Fey said of him, "He was a devout Latter Day Saint. He had a testimony. He was as clean cut as they come. He was a leader. He was one of those kids that did everything right. He was popular at school and a leader there as well. He went on to serve a mission in Italy, graduate from BYU and land a job at one of the big six consulting firms right out of college.... I viewed him as an example of righteousness personified."[17]

But Matis was gay, and even though he remained celibate, his homosexuality plunged him into a vortex of irreconcilable extremes. "Stuart never acted on his homosexuality," Fey continued, "and he tried for decades to overcome it. He was stuck between two worlds: the world of a devout Latter Saint and the world of someone who is gay. Those worlds were incompatible. He could not be fully one or the other in good conscience and he was both. That incongruity tore him apart."[18]

In a letter to the editor of *BYU NewsNet* published four days before his death and two weeks before Prop 22 was approved by California voters, Matis described his tortured path through life. "My first same-sex attraction occurred when I was seven, and for the next 25 years, I have never been attracted to women. I realized the significance of my sexuality when I was around thirteen, and for the next two decades, I traveled down a tortuous path of internalized homophobia, immense self-hatred, depression and suicidal thoughts." His response was that of many young, gay Mormons: "calluses on my knees, frequent trips to the temple, fast and devotion to my mission and church callings."[19]

Author Carol Lynn Pearson, whose marriage to a gay man who died of AIDS made her particularly sensitized to homosexuality within Mormonism, wrote, "[Matis] wept as night after night he prayed until morning, begging and pleading with a God he knew could help him if he was only worthy enough. As a child he would deny himself a favorite television program as punishment for a homosexual thought, or he wouldn't allow himself to attend a friend's birthday party." His mother wrote, "Stuart's entire life was spent striving for perfection. He reasoned that if he were perfect, then he would find God's approval. His efforts became a never-ending cycle: effort—perceived failure—effort—perceived failure. The harder Stuart strove for perfection, the more he hated himself.... He believed that he not only could change, but should change."[20] But nothing worked.

After coming out at age thirty-one, one year before his death, he approached his father and his bishop for help. "Each gave me a blessing inspired by the spirit that proclaimed that I was indeed gay and that I would remain gay." In the aftermath of those blessings, a letter to the editor by a BYU student was particularly devastating to him. "The author compared my friends and me to murderers, Satanists, prostitutes, pedophiles and partakers of bestiality. Imagine having to live with this rhetoric constantly being spewed at you."[21]

In a lengthy letter to his cousin Clay, written weeks prior to Matis's death, he described the effect that the Prop 22 campaign had had on him. "I'll tell you that the events surrounding this initiative have been painfully difficult for me to endure. Last July, I read online that the Church had instructed the Bishops to read a letter imploring the members to give of their time and money to support this initiative. I almost went into a panic attack. I cried for hours in my room, and I could do very little to console the grief of hearing this news." And he knew he was not alone in his agony. "The Church has no idea that as I type this letter, there are surely boys and girls on their calloused knees imploring God to free them from this pain. They hate themselves. They retire to bed with their finger pointed to their head in the form of a gun.... They are afraid of their parents. They are afraid of their bishop. They are afraid of their friends. They have nowhere to go but to lay on their floors curled in a ball and weep themselves to sleep." And then he addressed Prop 22 directly: "On the night of March 7th, many California couples will retire to their beds thrilled that they helped pass the Knight Initiative. What they don't realize is that in the next room, their son or daughter is lying in bed crying and could very well one day be a victim of society's homophobia. The Knight Initiative will certainly save no family. It is codified hatred."[22]

On the morning of February 25, 2000, Matis left a letter on his bed. He then drove to a Mormon chapel in Los Altos, California, where Apostle Jeffrey Holland was scheduled to speak to missionaries later in the day. On the steps of the chapel, after pinning a note to his shirt that said, "Do not resuscitate," Matis shot himself in the head.

His suicide was widely publicized, and the question of whether it was linked to Prop 22 quickly emerged as a story line. Five days after his death, a reporter called the Matis home. "'Our son's death had no relationship to Prop. 22 whatsoever,' said a woman who answered the phone at Matis' home Wednesday but would not identify herself and refused further comment other than to add: 'We feel invaded at a very private time of our life.'" But another Mormon woman, who had corresponded with Matis and who had spoken with his mother the previous day, disagreed. "His suicide note spoke clearly of his struggle, particularly the last few months while watching the battle regarding Prop. 22. He hoped that his death would become a catalyst for fruitful education of the members and leaders of the LDS church regarding the homosexuality and the homophobia that exists in the church and society. His death was his final statement on the need for change."[23]

In the aftermath of Matis's death, Deseret Book, the church's publishing company, approached his parents, Fred and Marilyn Matis, and asked if they would collaborate on a book.[24] They agreed. In 2004, after the manuscript had been "fully vetted by members of the Twelve,"[25] *In Quiet Desperation: Understanding the Challenge of Same-Gender Attraction* was published. While the parents declined in the book to link their son's suicide to Prop 22, a radio interview of Marilyn the same year told a different story. "He had been suicidal for years. And that last year of his life, we knew that entire year it was a battle to keep him alive. And he came to us the week or a few days before he did take his life, and at that time he told us that he had the gun and that it was in a safe place and not to look for it, that he could get it when he [needed] it. What pushed him over the top, actually, was Proposition 22."[26]

AMENDMENT 3

Utah probably didn't need Amendment 3. A law passed in 1977 had out-lawed homosexual marriage within the state, and in 1995, while Hawaii was struggling to settle the issue, a law was passed prohibiting the recognition within Utah of same-sex marriages performed elsewhere. However, in the years since the passage of Hawaii's constitutional amendment outlawing same-sex marriage, developments in Vermont and Massachusetts renewed concerns in Utah among opponents of same-sex marriage.

In Vermont a court case by three same-sex couples resulted in a decision by the Vermont Supreme Court that same-sex couples were entitled to "the same benefits and protections afforded by Vermont law to married opposite-sex couples,"[1] although the decision did not mandate same-sex marriage. The legislature responded early in 2000 by passing a law creating the cat-egory of civil unions, which gave same-sex couples the same legal rights and obligations as married couples but denied them the label of marriage.

In Massachusetts the Supreme Judicial Court ruled in an appeal of *Goodridge v. Department of Public Health* that the state's ban on same-sex marriage was unconstitutional. Despite objections by Mormon governor Mitt Romney, the state moved quickly toward legalizing same-sex marriage, and in the spring of 2004 it became the first state in the country to do so.

The renewed worry that the Full Faith and Credit Clause of the U.S. Con-stitution might require Utah to recognize Vermont same-sex civil unions or Massachusetts same-sex marriages motivated Utah state representative (and active Latter-day Saint) LaVar Christensen to construct yet another fire-wall, in the form of an amendment to the Utah Constitution. The proposed amendment consisted of two sentences. The first was similar to California's

Prop 22: "Marriage consists only of the legal union between a man and a woman." The second responded to the challenge of Vermont's civil union law: "No other domestic union, however denominated, may be recognized as a marriage or given the same or substantially equivalent legal effect."

Christensen's actions came at a time (2004) when about a dozen states were enacting laws or constitutional amendments to block same-sex marriage and when Republican strategist Karl Rove successfully used same-sex marriage as a wedge issue in the reelection campaign of George W. Bush. Yet in spite of requests from several states for support, the church, which only two years earlier had joined the coalition backing Nevada's constitutional amendment banning gay marriage, retreated to the sidelines. Troy Williams, who became executive director of Equality Utah in 2014, recalled, "My understanding is that LaVar and [state senator Chris] Buttars kind of went rogue, without the church's sanction of Amendment 3." Church spokesman Dale Bills conveyed the church's ambivalence, even apathy, by saying, "The church has taken no position regarding the proposed state gay marriage amendment."[2]

Approved by the legislature, the amendment moved to the ballot in the November 2004 election. In a move unique in Utah history, it did so without first being considered by the Utah Constitutional Revision Commission. An editorial in a Salt Lake City LGBT publication urged defeat of the amendment for that and one other important reason: "The Amendment also prevents the granting of even basic rights and protections to gay and lesbian couples and families, such as hospital visitation rights, medical decision-making rights, domestic partner health insurance benefits, inheritance rights, or tax and pension benefits." So overreaching was the amendment that it would deny rights even to heterosexual couples living together in either common-law marriages or other forms of domestic relationships.[3]

Despite the silence from their church, 68 percent of Mormons polled in the state said they would support both parts of the amendment—a sharp contrast to the minority support given by other religious groups.[4] Early in July the church issued a statement that was prefaced by an unusual disclaimer: "This is a statement of principle in anticipation of the expected debate over same-gender marriage. It is not an endorsement of any specific amendment." The statement itself read, "The Church of Jesus Christ of Latter-day Saints favors a constitutional amendment preserving marriage as the lawful union of a man and a woman."[5] Clearly sidestepping an endorsement of Amendment 3, the statement appeared to address the possibility of an amendment to the U.S. Constitution, coming just days before a U.S. Senate vote on the issue.[6] But no further explanation was given by the church, other than to say that it had not been involved in any way in the drafting of Amendment 3.[7] Michael Otterson, a church spokesman, said, "We don't want to get into the fray."[8]

As the election approached and ratification of the amendment seemed ensured, an unusual coalition stepped forward to condemn it: all three candidates for the office of Utah attorney general. They did so in a rare joint statement: "Because proposed Amendment 3 goes far beyond simply defining marriage, and would prove unnecessarily hurtful to many Utahns and their families, we oppose the amendment." The campaign manager of one of the candidates added, "This thing is so flawed, it's difficult to find an attorney practicing in Utah who thinks it's a good thing. It just creates a mess."[9]

The continued silence of the church led to speculation that was voiced in an article in the *Salt Lake Tribune*: "Mormon leaders' relative silence since that short news release has led some to speculate that perhaps church officials are uncomfortable with Utah lawmakers' attempts to define marriage. Others say church leaders—who have nearly monolithic religious and political power in a state where about two-thirds of residents are members—don't have to do anything else. And church officials, so far, refuse to say much more."[10]

In mid-October, just weeks before the election, the church issued a statement that appeared to endorse Amendment 3. Entitled "First President Statement on Same-Gender Marriage," it ended with the statement, "The Church accordingly favors measures that define marriage as the union of a man and a woman and that do not confer legal status on any other sexual relationship." An article in the church-owned *Deseret News* acknowledged the common perception that it was a de facto endorsement. "While the latest statement did not specifically endorse Amendment 3, some observers said the statement is akin to approval of the marriage measure that will be on Utah's Nov. 2 ballot."[11] Church spokesman Michael Purdy declined to elaborate on the church's statement.[12]

To no one's surprise, Amendment 3 passed overwhelmingly, with nearly a two-thirds vote. Gayle Ruzicka, president of the profamily Utah Eagle Forum, triumphantly announced, "That is a legacy that will live forever."[13] Contrary to Ruzicka's proclamation, the legacy that lived forever was not the permanence of Amendment 3 but rather its role in accelerating the national legalization of same-sex marriage less than a decade later in a lawsuit that took the country by surprise, *Kitchen v. Herbert*.

BUCKLEY JEPPSON

At the same time Amendment 3 was moving toward ratification, Buckley Jeppson, a Latter-day Saint living in Washington, DC, decided to get married to his partner, Mike Kessler. Earlier the same year (2004), Massachusetts became the first state to legalize same-sex marriage, but there was a caveat: Governor Mitt Romney invoked a 1913 statute that denied a Massachusetts marriage license to a couple from another state. Buckley and Mike chose Toronto, Canada, as the site for their marriage. (In June 2003, the Province of Ontario became the first jurisdiction in the Western Hemisphere to legalize same-sex marriage.) They were married on August 27, 2004.

For more than a year and a half few people knew or cared. Then his story attracted national attention and illustrated the challenges facing the LDS Church if it chooses to excommunicate same-sex couples who are legally married—a likelihood given a policy announcement late in 2015 that will be the subject of a later section.

Jeppson is a lifelong Mormon who served a proselytizing mission in South America, was married in the Los Angeles Temple, and was active in church callings, including being a bishop's counselor in two congregations. After his mixed-orientation marriage ended in divorce, he and Kessler, who was not LDS, attended church together, without fanfare. Jeppson, who had been out since 1997, said, "We tried to lay under the radar so that it wasn't going to be a big deal. I was not interested in creating a drama."[14] The drama came from his bishop.

New in the calling, the bishop decided that Jeppson's marriage was a serious affront to the order of the church, and he wanted to make a case out of it. However, since Jeppson was a high priest,[15] church law dictated that any disciplinary action toward him be initiated by the bishop's immediate superior, the stake president. The bishop pressed his case with the stake president, but nothing happened for several weeks. When the bishop persisted, the stake president contacted Jeppson and asked for a meeting.

From the first meeting it was clear to Jeppson that the stake president would rather have the matter disappear instead of having to convene a disciplinary council that would likely have resulted in excommunication. "At one point he told me he thought it would be a really good idea if I would just resign my membership and quietly go away and not cause any problems." After contemplating the situation, Jeppson informed the stake president at their next meeting that he would not resign. "I felt like I was at the edge of a cliff and I was asked to jump, or else be pushed. I didn't really find that to be a tenable choice—I was going to have to be pushed. So he said he would probably be convening a disciplinary council." That decision changed the tone. "Some time ago," Jeppson wrote to friends, "I made the decision to create as much noise as possible for the cause if the case develops further."[16]

He reached out to those friends in an attempt to determine if any similar cases might shed light on his own. "The first person I thought of was Lavina [Fielding Anderson] because of her organization of tracking ecclesiastical abuse [the Mormon Alliance].[17] I knew Lavina and had worked with her in publishing in Utah, so I contacted her and said, 'Do you know of any other case?'...She checked around a bit and came back and said, 'I don't think so. I hope it's OK, but I gave your name to a friend of mine who is a reporter for AP [Associated Press], and she'll probably contact you.'"[18]

The AP reporter, Jennifer Dobner, saw the case as unprecedented within the LDS Church and jumped on the story. She spoke several times with Jeppson, also with his bishop and stake president, but got little information from them. Once, when she called the bishop's home, his wife answered the phone. "[She] said the one thing reporters love to hear, which was, 'Well, I probably shouldn't say anything, but—.' And then she went on for an hour, giving everything she knew. Jennifer then had the validation of the story and sources and dates from the bishop's wife."

On March 15, 2006, Dobner's syndicated article was published in dozens of newspapers across the country, including the *New York Times* and *Washington Post*, and was the subject of many television news broadcasts. "Buckley Jeppson, 57, says he's been informed verbally by a senior church official that his life is incompatible with the doctrine of The Church of Jesus Christ of Latter-day Saints and that a disciplinary council will address the matter....It is believed that if Jeppson is excommunicated, it would be the first time a Mormon in a legal, same-sex marriage was punished by the church."[19]

After the article was published, silence ensued. No disciplinary council was held. In fact, members of the high council had never been notified of the possibility of one.[20] Jeppson recalled, "It never came up again. Once the article came out, that was it. There was nothing else." In a follow-up article five months later, *Salt Lake Tribune* reporter Peggy Fletcher Stack wrote, "Within a month after newspapers reported the threat to his membership, Jeppson's LDS bishop was called on a mission to Mexico and his stake president 'got quiet.' Since then, Jeppson has continued to do what he's always done—sit quietly on the back pew in his LDS inner city ward week after week and slip out without causing a ruckus."[21]

THE CURE, 2.0

An earlier section examined the self-help approach to "curing" oneself of homosexuality. It became increasingly clear, both in Mormon circles and elsewhere, that such an approach was not working. Gradually, an intervention-based approach emerged as an alternative. Generally called "reparative therapy" but sometimes going by other names such as "conversion therapy" or "sexual orientation change efforts (SOCE)," it implicitly acknowledged the futility of self-help approaches by introducing therapists to effect the "cure"—generally licensed psychiatrists and psychologists, but often unlicensed entrepreneurs. Acting as surrogates for the church, by referral from either LDS Social Services (later renamed LDS Family Services) or individual ecclesiastical leaders, therapists at Brigham Young University, private practitioners, and counselors at Evergreen, a church-endorsed but independent organization, employed a variety of reparative therapy techniques. At the time, all such therapies were within boundaries that represented conventional wisdom, but they were gradually disavowed by researchers and professional societies and ultimately outlawed in several states. The two most significant initiatives were various types of aversion therapy, most notably electrical shock,[1] which were used at BYU and by private practitioners to whom local church leaders often gave referrals, and more benign, but still problematic, reparative therapies encouraged by Evergreen.

AVERSION THERAPY

Over four decades have passed since electrical shock therapy was initially employed at Brigham Young University, yet at least three urban legends persist: First, *it was never practiced at BYU*. In spite of former BYU president Merrill Bateman insisting, "We have not been able to verify . . . that electric shock was ever used on gay and lesbian students at BYU,"[2] its use has been repeatedly documented, never more convincingly than in a doctoral dissertation written by the graduate student who used the technique on campus and under the direction of a BYU professor.[3] Second, *it involved connecting electrodes to male genitalia*. It did not, at least initially in the university-approved protocol. However, there is evidence that during the mid-1990s, in nonapproved protocols, electrodes were attached to male genitalia during treatment that occurred on the BYU campus as well as off-campus under supervision of BYU faculty.[4] And third, *suicides resulted from its use at BYU*. While there are several reports alleging this,[5] none has been accompanied by authoritative documentation.

Taking his lead from British therapists M. P. Feldman and M. J. MacCulloch, who more than a decade earlier had first reported "treating" homosexuality using electrical shock therapy, BYU graduate student Max McBride conducted university-approved research on campus that involved seventeen male subjects (fourteen completed the study). The purpose of his research was not to challenge the findings of the British researchers, whose "success rate for aversion therapy has been encouraging"—a reported 60 percent— but "to investigate only one treatment factor used in aversive conditioning of male homosexuality. The principal focus will be to determine whether the use of nude male and female pictures is a necessary requisite for successful treatment."[6] The subjects were responsible for collecting nude photographs from recent issues of *Playboy* and *Playgirl*.

The experimental design was simple. The subject had a pressure cuff placed around his penis to monitor sexual arousal and an electrode attached to his bicep. He then sat in front of a projection screen where photographs of nudes were projected. If he experienced sexual arousal from a photograph of a nude male, he would receive a shock in the bicep. A gradual increase of voltage upon repeated arousals was to serve as a negative-feedback stimulus that would, according to the hypothesis, "reorient" him from homosexual to heterosexual, whereupon photographs of nude females were supposed to elicit sexual arousal.

Two weeks after a series of treatments—the only follow-up interval measured—subjects "evaluated themselves as significantly less homosexual than heterosexual." McBride concluded, "This finding suggests that the type of

Behavior Therapy used in the present study was highly effective in changing subjective evaluation of sexual orientation." His enthusiasm for his own work notwithstanding, his research was highly problematic in design and findings, and it never resulted in a peer-reviewed journal article. But it did serve to earn him a PhD, to entrench the use of electrical shock therapy at BYU for several years, and to validate the biases of his dissertation adviser, Psychology Department chairman D. Eugene Thorne, who used similar procedures in his private clinical practice.[7]

For the subjects that McBride and others treated at BYU, however, the experience ranged from disappointing to catastrophic. On the disappointing end of the spectrum was Don Harryman, who attended BYU in the mid-1970s. "I was desperate to change my sexuality. A school counselor promised that aversion therapy would do the trick." At first, the therapy appeared to have worked. "I hadn't ever had sex [with a man] to begin with, and I just got used to not thinking about it. . . . Six months later, a new roommate moved in and I fell in love and was sexual with him within 24 hours. It was like the lights going on and me saying, 'Wow, this was all a sham!'"[8]

John Cameron bore deeper scars. "As a college student, Cameron volunteered for the experiment, conducted by then BYU-graduate student Max Ford McBride, hoping it would alter his same-sex attraction. Instead, the psychological and emotional wounds nearly crippled him, once leading him to contemplate suicide. . . . Over the course of his life, Cameron says he had tried to forget about the shock treatments and didn't want to talk about it, until he heard from a researcher that two men in the experiment had committed suicide."[9] Cameron wrote a play, *14*, whose title came from the number of subjects who completed treatment in McBride's experiment. In spite of the scars he bore, Cameron tried in his play to place the era in context. "I wanted to tell about it because I actually think they were trying to do a good thing with this [reparative therapy]. They were trying to help people. They were trying to help people out of sin, and that's what Church does. Not the best idea, but at that time did we know any better? No. We thought this was good cutting-edge work."[10]

Far worse was the experience of a man identified as David. Connell O'Donovan recalled his only meeting with him. "I spoke with him but he requested that I remain at least six feet in distance away from him. He then rolled up his shirtsleeves and showed me his arms. The deeply-scarred skin on the inside of his arms looked like raw hamburger and I almost vomited from the sight." David said that he had taken part in electrical shock therapy at BYU in 1977. Given the option of controlling the voltage that went to his arm upon being aroused by male pornography, and desperate to jettison his homosexuality, David intentionally ran the voltage up. "The results were badly burned arms and a complete inability to come physically close to any male without him emotionally breaking down from the trauma. His homosexual desires were as strong as ever but he was unable to touch another man even for a simple hug, he had no heterosexual desires whatsoever, and he was constantly on the verge of suicide."[11]

It is not clear how long electrical shock therapy was practiced at BYU. Physician Rob Killian places the date that it ceased no earlier than 1988, more than a decade after McBride's experiment. "I was offered electrical shock therapy in the Spencer W. Kimball Tower at BYU. ... There was an admission by BYU officials at some point in the past ten years that they had mistakenly said no electrical shock therapy occurred and they corrected themselves. ... I do know that the treatment was offered for longer than they admitted and that the practitioner eventually moved the service to a private address off of BYU campus and continued for some time offering this 'therapy.'"[12]

Lee Olson related his particularly painful experience upon being referred to a practitioner of electrical shock therapy in Salt Lake City. Upon having a sensor placed on his penis and electrodes on his arm, he was shown "a very graphic porno video of two or more men having sexual intercourse (and other activities). As I became excited and started to get an erection, the little ring around my penis would measure the slightest growth in circumference. This would then register on the device where the doctor sat, and he would hit me with a few seconds of volts." Unable to control the arousals, "I would be shocked again and again." The process continued for months. "I would go to this little room and allow myself to be tortured, all for the sake of change! The problem was that the doctor had to keep building up the voltage to get more effect. Like Skinner's rats, I got used to it to some degree. One day, after nearly two years, the charge was so intense that it kicked me out of my seat. I stood up, pulled off the electrodes, pulled off the little ring, and never went back! I was definitely not cured, just more messed up."[13]

Another man, who spoke anonymously, was offered electrical shock therapy by an unnamed BYU professor. The professor told him, "It will be applied to the genitals. It will go to a battery pack on your waist, and then a rheostat. Then, a line will go up your body, down your arm, to a place on your wrist where you will push a button to zap yourself when you think a bad thought or have a bad desire." He declined.

An alternative, but no less barbaric, form of aversion therapy involved the use of emetics (vomiting-inducing drugs). When Connell O'Donovan, at the age of fifteen (1976), confided to his bishop that he was gay, the bishop referred him to BYU for aversion therapy. "They explained to me that they would place a heparin lock in my wrist and hook an I.V. up to that, and I would be put in a room alone with a plethysmograph [sensor] on my penis that would measure my physical arousal so that when I got an erection they would know." Then, they explained, they would inject a drug that would induce vomiting. "I look back on that and think that I would have taken the electric-shock therapy had I known about it since I'm extremely phobic around vomiting." So extreme was his phobia that he declined treatment. "I told them I couldn't do it, and they gave me a 'shame' letter which I had to hand-carry back and give to my stake president telling him that I had refused to go through with the Lord's program for my cure."[14]

One man underwent emetic aversion therapy supervised by a BYU professor but administered off campus at the Provo Canyon Boys School in the mid-1980s. He agreed to tell his story upon condition of anonymity. Although he had never had a homosexual experience, he was instructed by the professor to "create a homoerotic story and then tape record and bring that with you. You may get a little bit sick, so bring a bowl and a washcloth with you." After being injected with an emetic drug, he was left alone in a room while the recording of the story was played back. The vomiting was severe and unremitting. "I was buckling at my waist because my muscles were so cramped I couldn't sit up straight. I got to the point where I was dry heaving because I had nothing left. I was wearing Levi's, and even the very cuff of the Levi's was soaked." The electrolytic imbalance caused by the vomiting was so extreme that he nearly died, yet the response of the professor was emotionless. "I'll just have to do a little bit less and continue the treatment." There was no continuation of the treatment.

Rob Killian, who as a BYU student had been offered electrical shock therapy, described a friend who submitted to emetic therapy in the office of a private practitioner. "He, the father of two children, loved his wife and wanted to be cured, wanted to finally be rid of the sexual urges that seemed to be driving him from a normal family life.... For eight months he would view homosexual pornography or discuss his sexual desires after taking the vomit-inducing drug called Ipecac. EIGHT MONTHS. He talks to this day of how much anger he holds over this failed treatment."[15]

The practice of emetic therapy continued to have quasi-official church sanction at least until the 1980s. Jake Zollinger, a clinical psychologist, recalled meeting another psychologist at a professional meeting. "He said, 'Could you drop by my office? I'm in private practice, and I want to talk to you about the research you've done on homosexuality.' I went by his office, and he said, 'I'm a clinical psychologist, and as far as I know, I'm the only one who is getting referrals from the General Authorities to do aversive therapy.' I said, 'Goodness gracious, in 1982? How do you feel about that?' He said, 'Well, I don't use shock.' 'What do you use?' 'Emetics to create nausea.'"[16]

EVERGREEN

In 1989 eleven Mormon men formed Evergreen International, an organization headquartered in Salt Lake City. Frustrated with other support groups, the founders "concluded there must be a solution other than destroying spiritual beliefs or denying sexual longings."[17] It held out its founders as proof of the feasibility of its mission: "Each member of Evergreen stands personally as a statement that it is possible to overcome homosexuality."[18] From the outset, it aligned itself with the LDS Church in sustaining "without reservation the standards and doctrines" of the church. It rested on a foundation of two beliefs: homosexuality is an "acquired condition," and while it "may have biological, developmental, and psychological causes," it "can be altered."[19] In other words, homosexuality is chosen, and, with help from Evergreen, it could be unchosen. Both statements reflected the near-universal beliefs of church leaders at the time.

Evergreen quickly became a go-to organization to which church leaders could refer LGBT members. Four years after its formation, Harold Brown, commissioner of LDS Social Services, in recommending it to a correspondent, endorsed its claim to be able to change people: "You inquired about visiting with someone who is familiar with changing sexual orientation. I mentioned the Evergreen organization. I am enclosing literature on their upcoming conference." While generally discreet about numbers, Evergreen's executive director said, in the fall of 2002, that the organization received "over 150 requests for help each month," 40 percent being from gay men who were married.[20]

Evergreen was never formally affiliated with the LDS Church and was careful to make that point clear on its website. However, the relationship between the two was cozy and often less than arm's length. "Our Board of Trustees usually includes one or more emeritus General Authorities and we continue to build relationships with Area Presidencies and other Church leaders. Upon request, we provide training to hundreds of stake and ward leaders each year. If your ward or stake would like our assistance, please contact us." At Evergreen's annual conference in 2006, Larry Richman, chairman of its board of trustees, said, "We maintain close relations with Church leaders and provide training to local leaders upon request.... We nurture and provide help to growth and accountability groups. We now have 34 active groups, with another 9 beginning to form. We are pleased to announce that we have recently reached an agreement with LDS Family Services to assist with many of these groups."[21]

Evergreen's annual conferences became quasi church gatherings. A newspaper article concerning its 2011 conference noted, "While the Mormon Church denies any affiliation with Evergreen, it hosts the group at the Joseph Smith Memorial Building at their headquarters in Salt Lake City and sends speakers and presenters to the events, including Jerry Harris, a counselor for LDS Family Services." Another report noted, "Its board of trustees usually includes one or more emeritus general authorities of the church and at least one such authority has spoken at the annual conference every year for the past decade." At the 2005 conference, James Mason, a former General Authority, director of the Centers for Disease Control, and assistant secretary for health for the U.S. Department of Health and Human Services, began his address to the conference with a ringing endorsement: "Congratulations to Evergreen International for sponsoring and organizing this 15th annual conference. It is an honor to be a member of its board. As you know, Evergreen sustains the doctrines and standards of the Church of Jesus Christ of Latter-day Saints without being affiliated with it." The General Authority assigned to speak at the 2011 conference, Jay Jensen, gave an equally glowing endorsement: "I love the Evergreen Constitutional Statement.... We like the way Evergreen faces."[22]

The conferences provided a forum wherein Evergreen and the church could reinforce each other's message concerning homosexuality. Regarding the underlying nature of homosexuality, Larry Richman, chair of Evergreen's board, channeled Boyd Packer's 1976 remarks by saying, "Today, we live in an evil world where Satan has captured the hearts, minds, and values of many people. His lie is that you are born gay." General Authority Bruce Hafen "told those assembled at a conference for Mormons trying to 'overcome' same-sex attraction that being gay is 'not in your DNA.'"[23]

With respect to the malleability of homosexuality, Evergreen's core belief that it is changeable was endorsed by General Authority guest speakers, none more strongly than James Mason in 2005: "President Spencer W. Kimball taught that homosexuality is curable and forgivable." Four years later, Bruce Hafen said, "Evidence that people have indeed changed threatens the political agenda of the activists, because actual change disproves their claim that homosexuality is a fixed condition that deserves the same legal protections as those fixed conditions like race and gender."[24]

While aligned with Evergreen's message, however, remarks of some of the LDS General Authorities did not keep pace with changing attitudes within the hierarchy. Hafen's remarks were particularly problematic and out of sync. Although they were posted on a church website, "an LDS Church spokesman declined to say whether Hafen was speaking on behalf of the church or whether his remarks represent a shift in the faith's views."[25] Concerned with the increasing divergence between Evergreen's message and that of the institutional church—remarks from General Authorities at Evergreen conferences notwithstanding—one observer sent a lengthy letter to Larry Crenshaw, commissioner of LDS Family Services, in 2011.[26] He noted that while the church had moved away from certitude that homosexuality was *not* inborn to a position that allowed for a genetic or biological basis, Evergreen insisted that it was a chosen orientation. While Evergreen continued to assert that there was a "high probability that therapy will help and feelings will diminish or change," the church position had moved to one acknowledging that "orientation is a core characteristic." While the church had moved to a position that no one—not parents, not self—was to blame for one's homosexuality, Evergreen continued to cling to "risk factors" including "family environment, distant fathers, molestation, poor peer bonding." And, perhaps most troubling, was the insistence by Evergreen that "with therapy and support heterosexual marriage is feasible/likely," while the official position of the church had long since moved to complete disavowal of mixed-orientation marriage as a means of addressing homosexuality.

Evergreen's persistent embrace of reparative therapy became increasingly problematic as conventional wisdom in the country changed and as troubling anecdotal reports surfaced. Particularly damning was a letter from a bishop of an LDS student congregation in Salt Lake City, sent to senior apostle Boyd Packer. After working with many homosexual returned missionaries, the bishop wrote, "I came to the painful realization that the 'reparative therapy' practiced by LDS Social Services and organizations such as Evergreen (whose board of directors I then served on) was not merely ineffective, it was terribly damaging. In every instance I found that this 'therapy' accomplished little more than driving these earnest brothers and sisters, desperate to believe that they would 'change,' deeper into self-loathing and despondency."[27] The bishop's outrage reached a boiling point when his own gay son attempted suicide. The attempt, said the son, "'wasn't [done] out of despair as much as it was [done] almost out of duty. It felt to me as if I was in this loop that I couldn't end. The church wanted me to change, and I couldn't get past that. And I couldn't change, and I couldn't get past that.... It was a quick resolution before doing the damage of falling into a life of sin. I believed too strongly in the church and the church's values, and I placed those above my own life.'"[28]

A damaging blow to the entire field of reparative therapy was a lengthy report in 2009 by the American Psychological Association Task Force on Appropriate Therapeutic Responses to Sexual Orientation.[29] A coauthor of the report was Lee Beckstead, a former Mormon whose doctoral dissertation at the University of Utah almost a decade earlier[30] had struggled with the concept of reparative therapy without coming to firm conclusions. The APA report's two key findings were that claims of reparative therapy's efficacy "are not supported" and that "there was some evidence to indicate that individuals experienced harm" from it.

Two events in the spring of 2012 portended ill for the fortunes of Evergreen as well as the entire field of reparative therapy. Early in April, Dr. A. Dean Byrd died of leukemia. A longtime employee of LDS Family Services, Byrd had also been president of the National Association for the Research and Therapy of Homosexuality, whose foundational belief was the efficacy of reparative therapy. A report by the Southern Poverty Law Center (SPLC) described it as the "main source of anti-gay 'junk science.'" A Salt Lake City LGBT periodical called Byrd "the foremost proponent of the so-called reparative therapy among Mormons."[31]

Later the same month, Dr. Robert Spitzer, whose earlier work had been foundational for those advocating reparative therapy, came out publicly to acknowledge the flaws in that work. His renunciation was stunning and was publicized nationally. He wrote, "I believe I owe the gay community an apology for my study making unproven claims of the efficacy of reparative therapy. I also apologize to any gay person who wasted time and energy undergoing some form of reparative therapy because they believed that I had proven that reparative therapy works with some 'highly motivated' individuals."[32]

Lawsuits in California against practitioners of reparative therapy were followed in the fall of 2012 by a California law outlawing it for people younger than eighteen years of age. Richard Ferré, a psychiatrist who consulted with the church on mental health issues, said, "When that happened, Family Services realized that they had no legal standing."[33] In 2012 the church pulled the plug on Evergreen, denying it access to the Joseph Smith Memorial Building for its annual conference and, for the first time in more than a decade, declining to assign a General Authority as a speaker.

In June 2013, Exodus International, a Christian-oriented group with a mission similar to Evergreen, shut its doors. Founded in 1976, it had consistently been one of the most vocal advocates of reparative therapy. In announcing its closing, Alan Chambers, who had presided over it for a dozen years, openly apologized "to the people who have been hurt by Exodus International. . . . I am sorry we promoted sexual orientation change efforts and reparative theories about sexual orientation that stigmatized parents." The apology came a year after Chambers admitted publicly that "99.9% of the people he had met who had endured such programs experienced no meaningful transformation in their sexual orientation, and he apologized for Exodus's erstwhile slogan of 'Change is Possible.'"[34]

At about the same time, David Pruden, president of Evergreen, approached another LDS-oriented support group, North Star, with a proposal that the two groups merge. "'There was some unnecessary competition between us,' [Jeff] Bennion [board chairman of North Star] told *The [Salt Lake] Tribune*. 'We were starting to step on each other's toes.'" In fact, there were two fundamental differences between the groups. As explained by Ron Schow, who had extensive contact with both, North Star does not "have a position on nature or nurture, or 'born that way,' and they do not have a position on whether people can change."[35] On New Year's Day 2014, a quarter century after it began, Evergreen closed its doors.

CONSEQUENCES

Even before some professional associations began to change their stance toward reparative therapy, individual Mormons complained about it. In 1995 physician Gary Watts, two of whose six children are homosexual, said in a public presentation, "It frustrates me to see the church align itself with fringe practitioners who still attempt to change orientation through 'reparative therapy' when their own professional organizations label such attempts as an 'abuse and misuse of psychiatry.' ... To date, there is no credible scientific evidence that supports the view that sexual orientation can change."[36] Professional groups such as the American Psychological Association, along with courts and legislatures, gradually came to condemn reparative therapy for two reasons. One was that when it was scrutinized scientifically, its claims of beneficial and permanent change in sexual orientation consistently came up short. The second was a growing list of case reports of adverse outcomes.

In 2014 Utah State University doctoral candidate John Dehlin began to publish a series of papers (and ultimately a doctoral dissertation)[37] based on a survey of more than sixteen hundred LDS homosexuals—the largest ever of that demographic. Three-fourths of the men who took the survey, and nearly one-half of the women, had attempted sexual orientation change efforts, "usually through multiple methods and across many years." Consistent with the APA report, Dehlin's research "support[ed] the conclusion that sexual orientation is highly resistant to explicit attempts at change and that SOCE are overwhelmingly reported to be either ineffective or damaging by participants."[38] Of particular note was that "zero open-ended narratives could be found indicating complete elimination of SSA [same-sex attraction] via SOCE and that only a small percentage of our sample (3.2%) indicated even slight changes in sexual orientation." In sharp contrast were reports of inefficacy or harm resulting from reparative therapy. Some "42% reported that their change-oriented therapy was not at all effective, and 37% found it to be moderately to severely harmful."[39]

A report by a U.S. government agency the following year matched Dehlin's findings. "None of the existing research supports the premise that mental or behavioral health interventions can alter gender identity or sexual orientation. Interventions aimed at a fixed outcome, such as gender conformity or heterosexual orientation, including those aimed at changing gender identity, gender expression, and sexual orientation are coercive, can be harmful, and should not be part of behavioral health treatment."[40]

BISEXUALITY: A HIDDEN EXPLANATION?

Almost absent from LDS discussions of homosexuality has been bisexuality. In the groundbreaking book *Sexual Behavior in the Human Male*, published in 1948, Alfred Kinsey and coauthors placed human sexuality on a linear scale of 0 (exclusively heterosexual) to 6 (exclusively homosexual). The midpoint on the scale, 3, was assigned to those who identified themselves as equally attracted to both sexes, or bisexual, with 2s and 4s, and 1s and 5s, respectively, indicating diminishing degrees of bisexual orientation.[41] Although subsequent research has shown that sexuality is a complex and multidimensional array rather than a two-dimensional line, bisexuality occupies a prominent position within that array.

Among reports of success of reparative therapy, the possibility that they represented merely the fluid redirection of people who were bisexual was rarely raised. However, one intriguing suggestion came out of a dissertation done at BYU in 1978. A meta-analysis of existing literature rather than the kind of original research generally demanded of doctoral work, it made the intriguing finding that 58 percent of 370 subjects who self-identified as "exclusively homosexual" showed no improvement from reparative therapy, whereas only 19 percent of 200 bisexual subjects did not experience improvement. Yet in reporting to the First Presidency, BYU officials cited the dissertation as documenting up to 60 percent success in "treatment of homosexuality," without mentioning the important caveat about bisexuality.[42]

Dr. William Bradshaw, who spent his entire career as a professor of biology at BYU, is arguably the foremost LDS expert on the biology of homosexuality and was involved in the design and analysis of John Dehlin's doctoral research. In attempting to define the best predictor of gay men's likelihood of maintaining affiliation with the church, he found to his surprise that "it's not doctrinal belief, it's not devotion, it's not activity." It is bisexuality. "It's very clear that those who have attempted mixed-orientation marriage and those few who have made a go of it are bisexual. They are in the middle of the continuum of orientation.... They are the ones who are able to remain closeted in their wards [congregations], who appear to be like every other traditional Mormon family, able to hide the fact that they have been wrestling with this duality of feelings."[43]

Allen Bergin, a clinical psychologist hired by Brigham Young University in the 1970s to head the newly created Institute for Studies in Values and Human Behavior, recently looked back after a long, distinguished career and gave a candid assessment of the decades during which there had been great expectations among many clinicians for reparative therapy. "At the moment, I see little evidence of permanent, positive change among exclusive gays, but much better long-term outcomes with bisexuals. Pretty sobering for one who used to be more optimistic."[44]

A CONSTITUTIONAL AMENDMENT

The Defense of Marriage Act, described in an earlier chapter, was drafted by Republicans in Congress as a firewall against the presumed legalization of same-sex marriage in Hawaii. But the timing of the legislation also served a political purpose: a wedge issue in a presidential election year. Faced with the likelihood of a veto-proof majority in both the House of Representatives and the Senate, the White House wrestled with how to respond. Press secretary Mike McCurry, in a 2014 interview, recalled the internal debate. "We were having political strategy meetings once a week. We'd go up and meet in the executive mansion on Wednesday nights. The president and vice president Gore were always there, and very often Tipper Gore and Hillary Clinton were there. And then there were all the senior staff people, all the people from the Democratic National Committee, and the people from the reelection campaign."[1]

Bill Clinton, who was nearing the end of his re-election campaign, had strong support from the national LGBT community and did not want to act in a way to alienate that constituency, but he was also confronted with polling data that showed that well in excess of 60 percent of the country was opposed to same-sex marriage. McCurry continued, "Clinton was very ambivalent about it. At least in all the discussions he kind of went back and forth, back and forth. You could tell his heart was not in signing DOMA." Finally, the discussion evolved to cast DOMA as a preventive measure for Clinton, in the hope of retaining the LGBT vote. "The argument that began to crystallize in the White House discussions went something like this: 'If we don't pass this legislation and provide some kind of federal protection for traditional marriage, there will then be a grassroots effort at the state level to pass a constitutional amendment.'"

The argument, though not embraced enthusiastically by Clinton, had merit, for there was talk in several states about an amendment to the U.S. Constitution that would ban same-sex marriage throughout the country. So Clinton tolerated DOMA as a way to ease pressure for such an amendment. McCurry continued, "I thought it was a bit of an artificial argument, and I think a lot of people in the White House did, too. I think maybe even Bill Clinton thought it was a bit artificial, but that's what he publicly articulated as his main reason for doing it." With that rationale, Clinton signed the legislation on September 21, 1996, with as low a profile as possible. McCurry concluded, "They gave me the assignment, 'You're going to announce tomorrow that the President signed DOMA'—in the dead of night, with no fanfare, no Rose Garden ceremony, no members of Congress standing around him. It was sort of slipping it under the door at the last minute."

Although voters in Hawaii ultimately circumvented the judicial system by passing a state constitutional amendment that outlawed same-sex marriage, and thus temporarily alleviated the acute angst that led to DOMA, there was lingering unease over the possibility of other judges in other states bringing about marriage equality through the courtroom rather than it occurring via the legislature or the ballot box. Michael O'Neill, former legal counsel for the U.S. Senate Judiciary Committee, recalled, "The concern was that judges would ultimately rule on the basis of the Equal Protection Clause and mandate same-sex marriage in contravention to the will of the people, and therefore they had to forestall it.... I think the concern was what ultimately happened, with respect to the Supreme Court."[2]

In 2002, six years after the passage of DOMA, the Alliance for Marriage, with assistance from a team that included Gerald Bradley of Notre Dame University, Robert George of Princeton University, and former Supreme Court nominee Robert Bork, whose contribution consisted mostly in lending his name to the effort, drafted language for the constitutional amendment that Clinton had feared: "Marriage in the United States shall consist only of the union of a man and a woman. Neither this Constitution or the constitution of any State, nor state or federal law, shall be construed to require that marital status or the legal incidents thereof be conferred upon unmarried couples or groups."[3] The bill never made it out of committee.

The following year, a bill with identical wording was introduced in the House by Representative Marilyn Musgrave (R-CO). It coincided with the legalization, by court order, of same-sex marriage in Massachusetts. Musgrave insisted, "If we're going to redefine marriage, let's let the American people, through their elected representatives, decide—not activist judges."[4] The bill, along with a similar one in the Senate the same year, died in committee.

A slightly revised version of the proposed amendment was introduced in both chambers of Congress in 2004. When the Senate bill got stuck in committee, Senator Wayne Allard (R-CO) reintroduced it and attempted to get a floor vote without committee action. After days of debate, a cloture motion failed by twelve votes, with six Republicans breaking ranks and voting with the Democrats.[5] In the House, the bill, for the first time, came up for a floor vote but failed by sixty-three votes to achieve the necessary two-thirds majority.[6] "There was an expectation from both sides of the aisle," O'Neill commented, "that this wasn't really going to go anywhere, that it was simply a political statement that people were making. . . . I think both sides saw it as [such] a move. I don't think Senator Allard, or anybody else that I can recall, really thought that it had any chance to actually go anywhere."[7]

The year 2006 represented the high-water mark for the proposed amendment. Opponents of same-sex marriage, imbued with a new sense of urgency in the wake of its legalization in Massachusetts, finally gained public support from a longtime ally: the LDS Church. Although the church had previously endorsed the idea of a constitutional amendment, it had not joined the public debate. Now, endorsement came from the highest level. The announcement of the church's support read, in part, "The Church of Jesus Christ of Latter-day Saints agrees with many other religious bodies and leaders that an amendment to the Constitution of the United States is necessary to protect and preserve the institution of marriage between a man and a woman."[8]

The same day as the church's announcement of support, LDS apostle (and later church president) Russell M. Nelson joined about fifty prominent Catholic, Protestant, and Jewish leaders in signing a petition in support of the amendment. The *New York Times* reported, "Organizers of the petition said it was in part an effort to revive the groundswell of opposition to same-sex marriage that helped bring many conservative voters to the polls in some pivotal states in 2004."[9]

While a floor vote in the House of Representatives was certain, the real action lay in the Senate, where Republicans had fallen short, in 2004, of ending a filibuster. One month after Nelson's endorsement, the First Presidency sent a letter to church leaders throughout the United States:

> We are informed that the United States Senate will on June 6, 2006, vote on an amendment to the Federal constitution designed to protect the traditional institution of marriage.
>
> We, as the First Presidency and the Quorum of the Twelve Apostles, have repeatedly set forth our position that the marriage of a man and a woman is the only acceptable marriage relationship....
>
> We urge our members to express themselves on this urgent matter to their elected representatives in the Senate.[10]

Shortly before the Senate vote, at least some, and perhaps all, local church leaders were instructed to read the First Presidency letter from the pulpit in Sunday worship services.[11]

While LDS legislators generally move in lockstep with a First Presidency directive, Senator Harry Reid (D-NV) signaled in advance his opposition to the amendment. In part, his objection was personal. Two neighbors in his Nevada neighborhood had become friends of himself and his family. While he never asked if they were gay, he presumed that they were and saw no reason for the government to dictate the terms of their relationship.[12] Because of Reid's high profile as Senate minority leader,[13] church leaders chose to make a public statement concerning his opposition, through a Public Affairs spokesman, Michael Otterson. "It's very important to recognize that elected officials are representatives of their constituents and are responsible to their constituents. Senator Reid or any other elected official does not represent the church. They are free to go anyway they choose."[14]

Four days prior to the Senate vote to end debate, an editorial in the *Salt Lake Tribune* took issue with the church decision to take a high-profile stand in favor of it: "Just three weeks ago, The Church of Jesus Christ of Latter-day Saints seemed content to state its principles on marriage and let it go at that. To press harder would only solidify 'misperceptions that the church hates gays. Nothing could be further from the truth,' a spokesman adamantly insisted. But what emerged from a leadership discussion in the temple just a week later was an 'incremental shift toward the tactical,' perhaps driven by perceptions the amendment had acquired fresh momentum."[15]

Two days before the vote, Apostle Russell Nelson "was among the religious leaders flanking President Bush at the White House, . . . urging Congress to amend the Constitution to ban gay marriage and stating that marriage between a man and woman is the will of God. It marks the first time since the church opposed the Equal Rights Amendment that leaders of the Church of Jesus Christ of Latter-day Saints have so outspokenly involved themselves in a constitutional fight."[16]

In the case of the Equal Rights Amendment, the LDS Church had been a major force in determining the outcome, which was to defeat ratification. This time, however, church leaders could only stand by and watch as the resolution to end debate in the Senate fell eleven votes short,[17] notwithstanding Apostle Nelson's plea that the amendment was needed "to protect our divine inheritance."[18]

In an anticlimactic move the following month, 236 members of the House of Representatives voted in favor of the amendment—9 more than in 2004 but still far short of the 290 votes needed for ratification.

Although the aftermath of the vote bore no resemblance to the backlash following Proposition 8 in California two years later, not all church members were quiescent. Gary Watts, a Utah physician, LDS Church member, and father of two LGBT children, wrote to four General Authorities:

> My "summer of discontent" began in May when the First Presidency decided to have a letter read in all of the United States wards and branches supporting the proposed amendment to the Constitution that would deny "marriage" to homosexuals and asking all members to write or call their representatives in Congress to support the amendment. I perceived that injunction as a direct attack on the civil rights of my gay children and gay people generally.
>
> That letter was buttressed by a second public announcement that the church had joined a group of conservative organizations called the "Religious Coalition for Marriage," a group that sent a letter to all elected congressmen urging their support for a constitutional amendment that was "for the exclusive union of *one* man and *one* woman." (A direct quote from that letter.) Elder Russell Nelson, just six weeks after having a second wife sealed him for

time and all eternity, shamelessly signed the document on behalf of the church. I still wonder if he understood the irony.[19]

A far different letter came from a church member in Nevada. Several weeks after the Senate vote, Harry Reid wrote to Nevada LDS bishops, explaining his position on the amendment. His letter elicited outrage from James Howard, a former president of the Las Vegas East Stake: "You chose your party's agenda over Nevadans', over your Prophet's wishes, and defied God in the process.... You have sold out for power and position. Whining about how offended you are that your 'Brethren' are not supportive of you anymore is not becoming of a leader of such high position. Justifying your weak stance in direct opposition to your Church's position is lame. You fear your party more than God."[20]

At the same time as the Nevada letter, Apostle (and attorney) Dallin Oaks defended the church's support of the failed amendment:

The time has come in our society when I see great wisdom and purpose in a United States Constitutional amendment declaring that marriage is between a man and a woman. There is nothing in that proposed amendment that requires a criminal prosecution or that directs the attorneys general to go out and round people up, but it declares a principle and it also creates a defensive barrier against those who would alter that traditional definition of marriage.

There are people who oppose a federal Constitutional amendment because they think that the law of family should be made by the states. I can see a legitimate argument there. I think it's mistaken, however, because the federal government, through the decisions of life-tenured federal judges, has already taken over that area. This Constitutional amendment is a defensive measure against those who would ignore the will of the states appropriately expressed and require, as a matter of federal law, the recognition of same-gender marriages—or the invalidation of state laws that require that marriage be between a man and a woman. In summary, the First Presidency has come out for an amendment (which may or may not be adopted) in support of the teaching function of the law. Such an amendment would be a very important expression of public policy, which would feed into or should feed into the decisions of judges across the length and breadth of the land.[21]

After the 2006 votes, the amendment to ban same-sex marriage was "mostly dead." Advocates in the House of Representatives reintroduced it in 2008, 2013, and 2015 but each time with diminished support—ninety-one, fifty-eight, and thirty cosponsors. It never made it out of committee. Having failed at the federal level, the LDS Church nonetheless was primed to jump in two years later at the state level, in the bellwether state of California.

DALLIN OAKS AND THE INTERVIEW

Among LDS General Authorities, the most durable paradigm about homosexuality has been that it is a chosen behavior. All earlier church policies
relating to homosexuality were built on that foundational belief, as were
most public attitudes throughout the country. While changes in policy—such
as allowing celibate gays and lesbians to serve proselytizing missions—do
not disturb the foundation, a change in the foundation could potentially
disrupt everything built upon it. It could also call into question the immu-
tability of LDS doctrine (despite the fact that a careful reading of doctrinal history shows that hardly any foundational doctrine has gone entirely
unchanged during the church's history).

In his 1984 memorandum, Dallin Oaks embraced uncritically the "behavioral paradigm" that accepted the sinner, upon condition of celibacy, while
condemning the sin. He referred approvingly to the distinction made in the
Roman Catholic Church, which tolerated "chaste homosexual inclination"
but condemned "active homosexual behavior."[1]

A decade later, in a seminal article in the church's magazine the *Ensign*,
Oaks still held the line on homosexuality being a behavioral choice rather
than a biological imprint. He rephrased a 1978 statement by fellow apostle
Boyd Packer ("I use it [homosexual] as an adjective, not as a noun; I repeat,
I accept that word as an adjective to describe a temporary condition. I reject
it as a noun naming a permanent one") by writing, "We should note that
the words *homosexual*, *lesbian*, and *gay* are adjectives to describe particular thoughts, feelings, or behaviors. We should refrain from using these
words as nouns to identify particular conditions or specific persons. Our religious doctrine dictates this usage. It is wrong to use these words to denote

the *condition*, because this implies that a person is consigned by birth to a circumstance in which he or she has no choice in respect to the critically important matter of sexual *behavior.*"[2]

Oaks then took a small step toward a modified position, one that acknowledged the possibility of biological input, while not relieving people of accountability. "Some kinds of feelings seem to be inborn.... All of us have some feelings we did not choose... but we do choose and will be accountable for the attitudes, priorities, behavior, and 'lifestyle' we engraft upon them."

While acknowledging a possible role of biology, Oaks dismissed out of hand the developing scientific consensus. "In contrast to our doctrinal approach, many persons approach the problems of same-sex attraction solely from the standpoint of current science. While I am not qualified as a scientist, with the aid of scientific literature and with the advice of qualified scientists and practitioners, I will attempt to refute the claim of some that scientific discoveries demonstrate that avowed homosexuals and lesbians were 'born that way.'" Oaks drew a fine line that separated biological *input* from biological *imprinting*. "The concept of *substantial heritability* should not be confused with the concept of *inevitable heritability*" (emphasis added).

He broke new ground, for a church publication, by referencing scientific studies of identical (monozygotic) twins. Noting that if one twin is gay, only half of the identical siblings "classified themselves as gay," he concluded, "If these studies show some inherited influence on whatever causes a man or woman to classify himself or herself as homosexual or lesbian, it is clear that this influence is not determinative." In other words, had there been 100 percent coincidence of homosexuality among identical twins, a "determinative" biological imprint would have been difficult to deny, but 50 percent coincidence left the door open to choice. Absent from his argument was the well-known finding that the coincidence of homosexuality in *fraternal* (dizygotic) twins was well less than half that in monozygotic—a clear indicator that DNA, though not totally determinative, cannot be removed from causality. Also absent was a discussion of *epigenetics*—that is, factors including the in utero interaction of maternal hormones and the developing fetus that affect the expression of genes, contribute to gender identity and sexual preference, and are independent of willful choice. Nonetheless, Oaks's *Ensign* article moved further toward a biological explanation of homosexuality than anything previously written by a member of the First Presidency or Quorum of the Twelve, even though it emphasized "the vital element of individual choice that we know to be a true principle of our mortal condition." In other words, while the church had begun to acknowledge *nature*, it still insisted that *nurture* was determinative.

THE INTERVIEW

In August 2006, a decade after the *Ensign* article was published, Oaks and Lance Wickman, who was the church's general counsel and a member of the First Quorum of Seventy, participated in an interview with the Public Affairs Department that revisited homosexuality and moved the needle. Ron Schow recalled, "Out of the blue that [interview] appeared on the church website. I don't know exactly how that happened, but that was an interesting dynamic that occurred there. In that interview there were some important things that really had not been the church position up until that time."[3]

The interview was posted, without announcement, on the Newsroom page of the church's website, lds.org.[4] Much of the interview consisted of restating prior church positions:

- The "homosexual lifestyle" is a sin. Oaks: "Over past years we have seen unrelenting pressure from advocates of [the homosexual] lifestyle to accept as normal what is not normal." Wickman: "Homosexual behavior is and will always remain before the Lord an abominable sin. Calling it something else by virtue of some political definition does not change that reality."
- Mixed-orientation marriage should not be viewed as a remedy. Oaks: "President Hinckley, faced with the fact that apparently some had believed it to be a remedy, and perhaps that some Church leaders had even counseled marriage as the remedy for these feelings, made this statement: 'Marriage should not be viewed as a therapeutic step to solve problems such as homosexual inclinations or practices.'"
- There is no double standard in demanding that gays and lesbians remain celibate throughout life. Oaks: "That is exactly the same thing we say to the many members who don't have the opportunity to marry. We expect celibacy of any person that is not married.... There are people with physical disabilities that prevent them from having any hope—in some cases any actual hope and

in other cases any practical hope—of marriage. The circumstance of being currently unable to marry, while tragic, is not unique."

- Same-sex marriage is nonnegotiable. Public Affairs: "If marriage is evolving, ought we to resist those kind of social changes?" Oaks: "That argument impresses me as something akin to the fact that if we agree that the patient is sick and getting sicker, we should therefore approve a *coup de grace*. The *coup de grace* which ends the patient's life altogether is quite equivalent to the drastic modification in the institution of marriage that would be brought on by same-gender marriage."
- The church supports an amendment to the U.S. Constitution. Oaks: "The time has come in our society when I see great wisdom and purpose in a United States Constitutional amendment declaring that marriage is between a man and a woman....It declares a principle and it also creates a defensive barrier against those who would alter that traditional definition of marriage."

But the interview also broke new ground in several important areas. On the cause of homosexuality it backed away from earlier insistence that it is simply a choice. Public Affairs: "You're saying the Church doesn't necessarily have a position on 'nurture or nature.'" Oaks: "The Church does not have a position on the causes of any of these susceptibilities or inclinations, including those related to same-gender attraction. Those are scientific questions—whether nature or nurture—those are things the Church doesn't have a position on."

Of greater importance, in that it had a direct effect on lives, was a shift in thinking regarding reparative therapy. While not making a wholesale condemnation, Oaks cast serious doubt on the efficacy of such an approach and attempted to distance the church from liability for past or future use of it. "The aversive therapies that have been used in connection with same-sex attraction have contained some serious abuses that have been recognized over time within the professions....We don't accept responsibility for those abuses."

While the interview broke progressive ground in two areas, in three others it did not. First, while Oaks urged parents of LGBT children to be loving toward them, he drew a hard line when it came to the treatment of partners of those children. Public Affairs: "At what point does showing that love cross the line into inadvertently endorsing behavior? If the son says, 'Well, if you love me, can I bring my partner to our home to visit? Can we come for holidays?'" Oaks: "I can imagine that in most circumstances the parents would say, 'Please don't do that. Don't put us into that position.'... I can also imagine some circumstances in which it might be possible to say, 'Yes, come, but don't expect to stay overnight. Don't expect to be a lengthy house guest. Don't expect us to take you out and introduce you to our friends, or to deal with you in a public situation that would imply our approval of your 'partnership.'"

Next, Oaks disapproved adoption by same-sex couples. "I cite the example of adoption simply because it has to do with the bearing and the rearing of children. Our teachings, even as expressed most recently in a very complete doctrinal sense in the Family Proclamation by living apostles and prophets, is that children deserve to be reared in a home with a father and a mother."

And finally, Wickman appeared to carve out a new doctrinal position that looked both backward and forward—premortal and postmortal existence. "Is this something I'm stuck with forever? What bearing does this have on eternal life? If I can somehow make it through this life, when I appear on the other side, what will I be like?... Gratefully, the answer is that same-gender attraction did not exist in the pre-earth life and neither will it exist in the next life."

The statement was particularly problematic for some. The Family Fellowship, an independent support group of LGBT people, family, and allies, saw it at variance with a passage from the Book of Mormon that states that the "same spirit which doth possess your bodies at the time that ye go out of this life, that same spirit will have power to possess your body in that eternal world." It raised the unanswered question as to whether a defining characteristic of that "same spirit" could be sexual orientation. Even more important for here-and-now living, as opposed to then-and-there supposition, "our greatest concern as parents is the implied suggestion here that those with homosexual orientation are fundamentally flawed and this shames our children rather than bringing them to God."[5]

GOD LOVETH HIS CHILDREN

Within the LDS Church hierarchy there is a world of difference between producing an interview and publishing a pamphlet. One year after the Oaks-Wickman interview, the church published a thin pamphlet entitled *God Loveth His Children*. However, the genesis of the pamphlet predated the interview by more than a decade, and the pathway to its publication was tortuous.

The new pamphlet was made necessary by continual changes in church policy that rendered earlier editions problematic. Gary Watts commented publicly on the three predecessors of *God Loveth His Children*. The first, published in 1973, "suggested that homosexuality"—as contrasted to homosexual acts—"was 'evil' and 'blamed parents for their children's homosexuality.'" The second, published a decade later, "de-emphasized the 'psycho-social causes' of homosexuality," and the third, published another decade thereafter, "eliminated parental blame altogether, pointing to the possibility of biological factors."[1]

FIRST ATTEMPT

By the late 1990s, work began on a fourth iteration that would better reflect the changing understanding of some senior church leaders. Since the church had long made it clear that homosexual behavior is sinful and requires repentance, continued emphasis on scriptures condemning homosexuality itself as sinful and evil might merely be alienating to LGBT church members as well as their families and friends. It also would ignore the science of causality of homosexuality and the evidence that supported the lack of choice underlying same-sex attraction.

Initially, a committee was organized under the direction of the Presiding Bishopric to reexamine these issues and produce a pamphlet that better reflected the changing views of the leaders. One view was provided by Dean Byrd, a psychologist and one of the strongest advocates in the church—and, indeed, the country—for reparative therapy.[2] Byrd stridently insisted that choice and not biology was determinative to the development of same-sex attraction, thus justifying his advocacy of reparative therapy. He had significant support from other members of the Quorum of the Twelve, particularly Boyd Packer.

Dr. Richard Ferré, a psychiatrist, was also appointed to the committee and presented counteropinion based on the emerging scientific consensus that biology played a determinative, if not *the* determinative, factor in homosexuality. Homosexuality, in his view, was the result of a combined influence of biology and experience that was determined at an early stage of development and was not a choice for the individual discovering his or her same-sex attraction.[3]

Apostle Dallin Oaks, who inclined more toward Ferré's viewpoint, was a central voice in directing the development of the new pamphlet. It is evident from his writings at the time, such as in his 1995 *Ensign* article "Same-Gender Attraction," that he was studying the science of homosexuality. His research included whether therapy could help homosexual individuals change their sexual orientation to become heterosexual. The references to the *Ensign* article include a significant number of scientific papers summarizing the then current understanding of sexual development and sexual orientation. Papers by R. C. Friedman and W. Byne, in particular, represented the conclusion that both biology and experience play a role in the development of gender and sexual orientation. In his article, Oaks quoted the opinion of Byne and coauthor B. Parsons: "It is imperative that clinicians and behavioral science begin to appreciate the complexities of sexual orientations and resist the urge to search for simplistic explanations, either psychosocial or biologic.... We propose an interactional model in which genes and hormones do not specify sexual orientation per se, but instead bias particular personality traits and thereby influence the manner in which an individual and his or her environment interact as sexual orientation and other personality characteristics unfold developmentally."[4] Conflicting points of view could not be resolved in this committee, and so it was discontinued.

SECOND ATTEMPT

The challenges of achieving a consensus led to the project being assigned to members of the Quorum of the Twelve and the Seventy, with Oaks central in directing the development of a pamphlet that could be supported by all of the church leadership. Individuals outside these quorums who previously had provided information through consultation were no longer called upon to be a part of this process.

The new committee worked for five years to produce *God Loveth His Children*. Much of its work involved building consensus within the Quorum of the Twelve. Ferré noted, "Every apostle had to read this and agree to it being published. It took a long time." Ron Schow reported, "We have been told, through our sources, that the Church Correlation Committee has never had anything that [required] more involvement from every apostle, until they finally got that so it could be published."[5]

THE PAMPHLET

A fundamental difference between the Oaks-Wickman interview and *God Loveth His Children* was the target audience. While the interview was primarily directed toward families, particularly parents dealing with a gay son or lesbian daughter, "*God Loveth His Children* was more directed to the individual, saying to them, 'This is what you can do if you choose to stay with the Church. We acknowledge that these feelings may not go away.' That was an important admission at that point."[6]

The basic message of the pamphlet was inclusiveness. "Notwithstanding your present same-gender attractions, you can be happy during this life, lead a morally clean life, perform meaningful service in the Church, enjoy full fellowship with your fellow Saints, and ultimately receive all the blessings of eternal life."[7]

On a doctrinal level, it stepped back from the bold statement of Lance Wickman in the prior year's interview that "same-gender attraction did not exist in the pre-earth life."[8] Not rebutting it directly, the pamphlet took a nuanced position: "You lived in [God's] presence before you were born on this earth. You cannot remember your premortal relationship with Him, but He does.... Many questions, however, including some related to same-gender attractions, must await a future answer, even in the next life."

With respect to the "cure" that earlier pronouncements and pamphlets had suggested or even promised, *God Loveth His Children* implicitly acknowledged a permanent imprint of homosexuality and shifted the focus to behavior. "Same-gender inclinations may be very powerful, but through faith in the Atonement you can receive the power to resist all improper conduct, keeping your life free from sin."

While progressive on some issues, the pamphlet did not change the church's position on same-sex marriage. "Heaven is organized by families, which require a man and a woman who together exercise their creative powers within the bounds the Lord has set. Same-gender relationships are inconsistent with this plan. Without both a husband and a wife there would be no eternal family and no opportunity to become like Heavenly Father." Acknowledging that in spite of their best efforts some "may not be free of this challenge in this life," it appeared to affirm Wickman's assertion that "same-gender attraction . . . [will not] exist in the next life" by stating, "As we follow Heavenly Father's plan, our bodies, feelings, and desires will be perfected in the next life so that every one of God's children may find joy in a family consisting of a husband, a wife, and children."

REACTION

Publication of the pamphlet evoked mixed responses. Within the more orthodox Mormon world, it was rightfully seen as a step forward due to its message of inclusiveness. In a letter to the editor of a Salt Lake City LGBT publication, a writer praised a shift in church attitudes. "The article further acknowledges that 'others may not be free of this challenge in this life.' In other words, the feelings of homosexuality do not go away in this life. This is an extraordinary change from decades of abusive, hurtful language that has been used to convince many of us that we should change to becoming heterosexual."[9]

Richard Ferré commented,

> The new pamphlet has provided a message of understanding and compassion to the families and individuals confronting the issue of same-sex attraction. It recognizes the present limits of science to establish causality for homosexuality and therefore avoids calling for 'change' therapy to provide a path to heterosexuality for

inclusion in the church. Furthermore, the pamphlet attempts to provide hope to families and individuals that they can be a part of the LDS community of believers and feel accepted in spite of the dilemma individuals with same-sex attraction face in remaining single in the LDS Church, which promotes family and marriage as central to the doctrine of salvation.[10]

But a drilling down to the details—which doubtless reflected the give-and-take process necessary to achieve a consensus within the Quorum of the Twelve—elicited a different message. Valerie Larabee, executive director of the Utah Pride Center, said it was "a step in the right direction but still will be hurtful to gay youths. . . . If your choice is to toe the line or be cast out of the only thing you know and the thing your parents live for, it can leave you desperate. It's why we have such a high suicide rate."[11] Gary Watts called it "incremental progress," but felt its negatives far outweighed its positives. "It implies that those who are able to change their orientation do so through faith and self-mastery, and are therefore superior to those who don't. 'If I'm a gay guy who's struggled for 10 years to change and can't, I'm going to ask: what's wrong with me? . . . [LDS leaders] are setting up an impossible situation for gays—either be celibate or change. Until they can figure out a way to sanction a faithful same-sex relationship, the problem will continue.'"[12]

WHAT ABOUT LESBIANS?

God Loveth His Children departed from its predecessors in important aspects noted in the previous chapter. However, it was in continuity with two of its three predecessors in making no mention of the word *lesbian*. Only the first pamphlet, published in 1973,[1] used the word, and then only twice. The spare references of any type to female homosexuality underscore the long-standing emphasis by the church on its male counterpart, sometimes to an absurd extreme.

Gender bias—or lack thereof—is easily quantifiable in each of the four pamphlets. The 1973 edition used male pronouns (such as *he* and *his*) and nouns (such as *men* and *males*) fifty-six times but female pronouns and nouns only fourteen—that is, male dominated by a four-to-one ratio.

The 1981 edition of the pamphlet[2] went to an extreme of using male pronouns and nouns two hundred times, while using female counterparts *only four times*—a fifty-to-one male bias. Although there is no public record of discussions about the imbalance, it is clear that the issue was discussed, because in the 1992 edition,[3] gendered pronouns and nouns almost completely disappeared, with only five uses each of *male* and *female*. Finally, the 2007 edition of *God Loveth His Children* was written in the second person—*you, yours*—and contained only two uses each of male and female nouns (*sons* and *daughters*) and no gendered pronouns.

While the male bias in official pamphlets gradually disappeared, there has never been an emphasis on lesbianism. Indeed, to a very large extent, lesbians have been absent from the church's radar screen. LDS psychologist Marybeth Raynes said:

For some reason parents of [LDS] gay and lesbian children don't advocate for their daughters the same way they do for their sons. Lesbian women in the church whom I've talked to sort of think the church is irrelevant. "We're second-class citizens to start with, since we don't have the priesthood, so this is sort of two-for-two. It doesn't mean spirituality or a connection to God is irrelevant; it's just that the structure doesn't work, so I'm out of here." And nobody goes after trying to get their stories.... I can name any number of lesbian LDS women, whether they have stayed or left, but nobody takes the time or interest to seek them out.[4]

The general focus of church leaders on male homosexuality, to the exclusion of lesbianism, is consistent with a misogyny that is apparent both on a broad scale, with the continual prohibition of ordination of women to the lay priesthood, and on a narrow one, recently (April 2017) demonstrated by a thirty-one-to-one ratio of male-to-female speakers during the General Conference weekend.[5]

There is no accurate way to determine the number of lesbians in the LDS Church, much less the number who have left the church. Neither is there any way of determining the ratio of gay LDS men to lesbian LDS women. Historically, both within and without the church, two women of postcollege age living together raised few eyebrows, while two men of the same age living together raised many. In other words, LDS lesbians tend to have a lower profile, often to the point of invisibility. Nonetheless, their stories are as laden with pain and rejection—and occasionally joy—as those of LDS gay men.

Many LDS lesbians lament their invisibility in comparison to their gay male coreligionists. Hermia Lyly wrote:

I was frustrated by how few people I could relate with on LDS LGBTQIA/SSA[6] websites. Nearly every personal profile or coming-out video featured a white man dressed in Sunday clothes sitting in a beautiful armchair and talking about how he knew he was gay since he was four or five years old. That wasn't me. I was a poor college student who had a hard time going to church, and didn't have any beautiful armchairs to sit in while someone interviewed me about my sexuality. Most importantly, I was not a man, and I didn't doubt my heterosexuality until my early twenties. How was

I supposed to relate to this crowd of men who had years of experience and confidence in their sexual attractions?

Where were the women? I scrolled through dozens of videos and profiles, but all I could find were straight women talking about their relationships with their gay husbands, fathers, brothers, uncles, sons, or grandsons. Stories of gay men were available at every click, but the stories of queer Mormon women were rare and difficult to find....

MormonsandGays.org, the LDS Church's official website regarding same-sex attraction, features 14 videos that focus on stories and viewpoints of specific individuals. Of these 14 videos, only 3 feature women. Only one of those 3 women [is] queer.[7]

Judith Mehr echoed Marybeth Raynes in attributing the invisibility to the culture of patriarchal domination within the church. "Women are the cows that produce the offspring. Men are the leaders and responsible for taking action to further the kingdom. This is more about misogyny than neglect of the lesbian as a sinful subclass."[8]

Maureen Davies, who came out to her parents at the age of forty-seven, wrote of her struggle to gain acceptance within her own family. "My parents were proud of me—but only part of me. They were proud of my work, my professional accomplishments and my college degree. It seemed they would forget or ignore the parts of me they were not proud of. When my mom saw me dressed up in business clothes ready to give a presentation to my medical technologist professional society, my second career, she looked so proud and said, 'I always wanted to have a son like you.'" Years later, in commemoration of her parents' fiftieth wedding anniversary, her sisters made a quilt that included one square for each of the nine siblings. "When I looked at the square for me, it only had my name. This quilt will get passed down for generations and is a representation that within one generation my relationship will be erased, yet my family and their church actively believe the genealogy records they keep are complete.... The church of my childhood and to which [my parents] dedicated their lives put a wedge between us."[9]

Others struggled to try to make themselves right with God and the church, only to meet with institutional rejection. One recalled, "I came to the conclusion that God would make me straight if I served a mission, and devoted 18 months of selfless service. In the end, I was denied after receiving a prompting from the Spirit to tell my Bishop that I was gay. At the end of the meeting I was stripped of my mission call, my temple recommend (I was set to enter the temple to receive my endowment only 3 days later), and was physically removed from the building."[10]

For some the struggle led to suicide, while others came close. Melissa Malcolm King described her near miss, with her rescue being due to a friend and to Affirmation:

> By 2013, I had planned my suicide out to a "T." I had my letter written out, I closed my bank account and mailed the funds in a money order to my sister. I decided life was no longer worth living and I didn't care if suicide equaled going to hell because I had been living in hell on earth....
>
> A church friend asked how I was doing the day I was supposed to kill myself. I told her about everything ... and I mentioned Affirmation. She sends me a link to the main page.... We talk a little longer and she sends me a link to something that Randall Thacker and Tina Richerson had written. I read their stories and cried and cried and cried some more. I wrote Tina and asked how I could join [Affirmation]. I watched videos and listened to Anna Empey read a poem, "We are all here." I cried and cried and cried and cried and prayed and gave thanks that there were other souls out there in pain and struggling.[11]

And for yet others, the struggle has led to personal victory. In the months following her realization that she was a lesbian, Laura Root prayed often for guidance. "One evening (and there were many) as I sobbed and pled with the Lord for guidance I felt an overwhelming calm, peace, and sense of love from Him. In that moment I imagined a host of angels surrounding me ready to shore me up. I knew then that Heavenly Father knew exactly who I was, gay and all, that I have always been this way, and that this fact was precisely what I was meant to learn and live with during my earthly probation."[12]

For Root, the victory came as she knelt in prayer at her couch. For Ellen Koester, it came as she prayed in an LDS temple.

I threw up my hands, in quiet desperation, and instead asked like this: "God...is it OK for me to be a lesbian?" And immediately after those words left my "mouth" I had an overwhelming feeling of warmth. Comfort. Assurance. Love.... I was stunned.... I went out on a limb and asked, "God, do you want me to be celibate? Do you want me to be alone?" No. A very clear no. But the Spirit continued...it testified, clear as day, that I needed to get married. That I needed to prepare to have a wife, and to have a family.[13]

Another for whom a very long and sometimes-bumpy road did lead to same-sex marriage with children, as well as continued church activity, is Barbara Graziano. Raised in an orthodox LDS home, Graziano as a preteen moved to Spain in 1970, when her father was the president of the first LDS mission in the country. Upon returning from Spain and showing talent as a tennis player, she received a full athletic scholarship to Brigham Young University. "When I went to BYU, some guy took me out. That was my first interaction with having an official date. I liked the feeling of being liked. It was the first time I had had any attention from a boy, and that actually felt good to think that a boy actually liked me. But I was very involved in tennis, and then that boy went on a mission."[14]

Within months, she married the only other man she ever dated, giving up her athletic scholarship in the process in order to "live a normal life." But it was not normal, even from the beginning. "On my wedding night, I bawled like a baby. I couldn't sleep, just cried and cried and cried. I was confused as to why I was crying, even then. I never heard of the names gay and lesbian, or if I ever heard of them, they were referred to in a negative way." Nonetheless, she played the role of mother, having her first of four children at the age of twenty-two. "I was determined to raise her as the church would say, the same way my parents had raised me. 'This is how it is. Follow the prophet. Black and white. This is how we live.'"

But attractions to women began even before her first child was born. "I started to have friendships with women, and I cared more about being around those girlfriends than around my husband. And yet, we got along great and didn't have a fight for years. We were best friends....But that's when I first remember having very attractive feelings towards friends, not even then considering that I was lesbian. I wanted to be with her, and if she touched my hands, I tingled. That kind of thing. It was weird that I didn't question it, but I didn't question it."

When her fourth child was two years old, Graziano finally came to the realization that she was a lesbian. "I said, 'I'm gay.' I was swimming one day when it hit me. I was swimming laps, and I was like, 'Oh, my gosh! I think that's it!' I had just turned forty. I had three surprise parties given for me, and for the first time I felt so loved, and I knew that I had to learn to love myself. I suddenly thought, 'I'm gay. That's what it is.'"

Despite the epiphany, she continued to live the conventional Mormon life for another decade, happy on the surface but miserable beneath. "I wasn't going to tell anyone, and then I ended up meeting a close friend, and we had a short relationship. It just sealed the deal. I thought, 'That's it. That's how I want to live my life. I can't possibly live it any other way.'" But it wasn't until just prior to her thirtieth wedding anniversary that she finally came out to her husband. "I came out to him and said, 'I need to live the life that I know will make me happy.' To be perfectly honest, that was the first time I could say, 'I know my Heavenly Father loves me.' It wasn't until I came out officially that I felt like I finally accepted myself and that I knew my God and my Savior loved me just how I was. . . . I don't think I've ever had a more spiritual experience."

After ending her first marriage, she remarried—this time to a woman who also had a child. Although disfellowshipped in the aftermath of the November 2015 church policy that declared same-sex couples apostates, Graziano continues to attend the Northern California congregation to which she has belonged for decades. "Prior to coming out, nobody knew I was living a depressed lifestyle, not knowing what to do that would be best. I finally came to the conclusion that I would come out. I've stayed here, and this community has been amazing. We're pretty lucky."

FROM THE MOUTHS OF BABES

The stories of LDS lesbians have been the stories of adult women, at least until one recent and notable "Testimony Meeting," the monthly Sunday worship service in which Mormons are given an open mike. In one Utah congregation in May 2017, a twelve-year-old girl named Savannah Kester stood at the pulpit and read a statement that she had written with the assistance of her mother.

I believe I was made the way I am, all parts of me, by my Heavenly parents. They did not mess up when they gave me brown eyes or that I was born bald. They did not mess up when they gave me freckles or when they made me to be gay. God loves me just this way, because I believe that he loves all of his creations. I do believe he made me this way on purpose. No part of me is a mistake. I do not choose to be this way and it is not a fad. I cannot make someone else gay, and being around me won't make anyone else this way. I believe that God wants us to treat each other with kindness, even if people are different. Especially if they are different....

I know I'm not a horrible sinner for being who I am. I believe God would tell me if I was wrong. I hope some day to go on dates, go to school dances, to hold hands, and to go off to college. I hope to find a partner and have a great job. I hope to get married and have a family. I know these dreams and wishes are good and right. I know I can have all of these things as a lesbian and be happy. I know that if God is there he knows I am perfect just the way that I am, and would never ask me to live my life alone or with someone I am not attracted to. I trust in him. He would want me to be happy. I want to be happy. I want to love myself and not feel ashamed for being me. I ask you...

And then the presiding officer cut the power to the microphone. Savannah, clearly baffled at the unexplained action, returned to her seat.

Shortly after a video of her remarks was posted online, Savannah's story attracted international attention. In an interview with the *New York Times*, Savannah gave her take on the killed microphone. "I think they did that because they didn't want my message. I don't want to be mean to them if this isn't true, but I felt like they were scared of me and what I was saying."[15] Neither the local leader nor church headquarters responded to a request from the *Times*, which obtained from Savannah the final sentences of her testimony—the words that she had been forbidden to speak to her congregation: "I had dreams of going to the temple and getting married, and was very sad when I found out that would never happen for me. Today I choose to find my joy outside of my old dreams from when I was little. I have new dreams and I know my earthly parents and my Heavenly parents love and accept me just the way I am. Amen."

PROPOSITION 8

IN RE MARRIAGE CASES

Shortly after the passage of Proposition 22 in California, remnants of the committee that had supported the proposition realized that proponents of same-sex marriage would work to overturn it by one of three strategies: ballot initiative, legislation, or lawsuit. The challenge came in the form of multiple lawsuits that were combined into a single action, *In re Marriage Cases*. In the spring of 2008, taking a page from *Baehr v. Lewin* in Hawaii, a four-to-three majority of the justices of the California Supreme Court declared sexual orientation a "suspect class" and thus applied the legal doctrine of strict scrutiny to the case. Since the state was not able to demonstrate a compelling public interest in excluding people from same-sex marriages, and since "the exclusion of same-sex couples from the designation of marriage clearly is not *necessary* in order to afford full protection to all of the rights and benefits that currently are enjoyed by married opposite-sex couples," on May 15, 2008, the court ruled that Proposition 22 was unconstitutional.[1]

Three weeks after announcing its decision, the court denied a request for rehearing and a request for a hold. On June 19, same-sex marriage became legal in California.

A CONSTITUTIONAL AMENDMENT

Opponents of same-sex marriage were prepared for the Supreme Court ruling. Indeed, a small committee that included Andrew Pugno, Senator Pete Knight's chief of staff, had been working on a plan for five years.

The Mormon Church was represented on the committee, albeit at a local level, without input from church headquarters. In 2003 Mark Jansson, who worked as a Public Affairs volunteer for the church in Sacramento, learned from a fellow church member of an organizing meeting. "He said, 'We ought to get ourselves involved and see what's going on.'" Also at the meeting was Ned Dolejsi, executive director of the California Catholic Conference. By the end of the first meeting, Jansson understood clearly its "end game." "We need to do something to develop an initiative, file, collect or buy signatures, and fund the thing because we can expect that the opposition will, indeed, attempt to overturn Prop 22."[2]

For the next four years, from 2003 to 2007, the committee worked successively on three potential initiatives that would embed in the California Constitution a ban on same-sex marriage. Jansson recalled, "We floated them singularly, in a chain. We were making stabs in the dark to see what kind of reaction we would get from the public, and what kind of support we might be able to glean from those with money." The first two iterations were pushed by groups wanting to turn the clock back to a time prior to the legalization in California of civil unions and domestic partnerships. Gary Lawrence, a consultant to the committee (and a Mormon), persuaded members against overreaching, and the third iteration of the initiative consisted of the exact language of Proposition 22, the only difference being that it was to be a constitutional amendment instead of the state law that Prop 22 was.

QUALIFYING FOR THE BALLOT

There is a higher bar for qualifying a California constitutional amendment initiative than for changing a state law, which in part had been the reason that anti-same-sex marriage forces in 2000 drafted Prop 22 as a law. However, when the court declared Prop 22 unconstitutional, the smoothest road to a new law banning same-sex marriage was an amendment initiative. Qualifying the initiative for the ballot required gathering signatures of 700,000 registered voters. Mark Jansson recalled, "We knew, at the time, that the best we could possibly hope for was about a 30 percent volunteer initiative success." The rest of the signatures would have to be purchased. "There are a number of organizations, and that's all they do. You come to them with an initiative, and they will go out and collect the signatures. They charge anywhere from $1.75 to $2.50 a piece for them, and in some cases it was as high as $4 or $5, depending on the campaign."

The initial fund-raising for qualifying the initiative came through the efforts of the Roman Catholic Church. Salvatore Cordileone, then an assistant bishop in San Diego and later archbishop of San Francisco, persuaded two local hoteliers to contribute several hundred thousand dollars each. That money was matched by the National Organization for Marriage, bringing the early total to about $800,000. According to Jansson, "Our focus at that time was to raise whatever money we could, and we solicited from anybody and everybody we could. We crossed every religious boundary, every religious wall we could find, and sought money to help get this done. We raised about $1.5 million to fund the project through the initiative filing."

Although 700,000 signatures were required to qualify the initiative, the goal was 1.2 million signatures. "The counties individually go in and compare signatures with the voting rolls. There are about one hundred counties in the state, and each one of the signatures that was collected would have to be submitted to the county in which it was signed. They would verify and then report back." Many signatures would not be authenticated, hence the need for overshooting the required number.

The window for collecting signatures extended from the middle of November 2007 to the end of March 2008. "We ultimately ended up qualifying, and the word back on the whole process was not only did we qualify, but we had the highest percentage of qualified signatures on any ballot initiative that had ever been turned in."

THE COALITION

Mormons and Catholics had worked together to outlaw same-sex marriage in Hawaii and again in California with Prop 22. In both instances the role of the LDS Church was crucial, in terms of money and ground game. In a meeting of the initiative committee, Ned Dolejsi said, "Except the Latter-day Saints are involved in this, it will fail." The problem for the committee was that church leaders were reticent to become involved again, largely because they had wound up carrying far more than their share of the load with Prop 22. One LDS Church official who asked not to be named said, "The representations made to the church for Prop 22 involvement were, in effect, 'Get involved. We'll carry our end of it and you carry yours, but we'll be in this thing together.' The truth was that we carried essentially all of it in Prop 22."

The LDS Church remained on the sidelines while the committee worked to qualify the measure for the ballot. Its sole activity in California during that time period was the filing of an amicus brief in the *In re Marriages Cases*, and it gave no public signal of intent to have deeper involvement. Although Mark Jansson was on the committee, he functioned solely as an independent citizen who happened to be LDS. "We had no contact, none whatsoever, with Salt Lake. There had not been as much as a whisper. There had not been as much as an inquiry. There had not been as much as a phone call."[3] Then George Niederauer wrote a letter.

Prior to rising to the rank of archbishop of San Francisco, Niederauer had served for more than a decade as the bishop of Utah, presiding over the state's two hundred thousand Catholics and building bridges to the LDS Church—and in particular to Thomas Monson, who at the time was a counselor in the First Presidency. Upon Niederauer's promotion, he was the recipient of high praise from Alexander Morrison, an LDS General Authority who had served with him on a community board. Morrison recalled, "His approach is something that transcends tolerance. It represents something higher, respect, understanding and acceptance."[4]

In May 2008, at a time when the initiative had qualified for the ballot and Prop 22 was about to be nullified by the court, the initiative committee discussed a strategy for bringing the LDS Church into the game. The consensus was that Archbishop Niederauer should be asked to write a letter to Thomas Monson, who months earlier had become church president, inviting the church to join the coalition to pass what was now known as Proposition 8. In December 2008, Niederauer published an essay in which he described writing the letter.

> Last May the staff of the [Catholic] Conference office informed me that leaders and members of the Church of Jesus Christ of Latter-day Saints (the Mormons) had given their support to the campaign for Proposition 22 in the year 2000, and were already considering an involvement in connection with Proposition 8. Accordingly, I was asked to contact leaders of the LDS Church whom I had come to know during my 11 years as Bishop of Salt Lake City, to ask them to cooperate again, in this election cycle. I did write to them and

they urged the members of their Church, especially those in California, to become involved.[5]

Receipt of Niederauer's letter immediately triggered the deployment of four church representatives—Elders Russell Ballard and Quentin Cook of the Quorum of the Twelve Apostles, Elder Whitney Clayton of the First Quorum of Seventy, and one officer from the Public Affairs Department—to California to conduct due diligence and make a recommendation to the First Presidency and Quorum of the Twelve. The group traveled around California for more than a week, met with officials of churches already part of the coalition, and returned to Utah with assurances that, unlike Prop 22, this time the Mormons would not be left to carry more than their share of the load.

Niederauer's letter was written in early June. The due-diligence group reported to the First Presidency and Quorum of the Twelve in mid-June, recommending formal church participation. Jansson reported, "You're talking about count the days on the fingers of one hand, minus some, and we have a letter that is issued and is out to the wards and stakes throughout California."[6]

The coalition made sense on three levels. First, it leveraged the considerable resources of the LDS Church. Gay-marriage activist Fred Karger, who became the church's most vocal critic as the campaign moved forward, spoke admiringly of the tools that the church brought to the battle. "They came in once it qualified, and then they put their operation into play. There is nothing like it in the world, as far as efficiency, and they were successful in doing everything they did."[7]

Second, by joining an already-formed coalition, the church would be able to operate as it had in Hawaii and earlier in California with Prop 22, as a key player but not as the point of the spear—or so it assumed. Looking back shortly after the election, Michael Otterson, managing director of the church's Public Affairs Department, told a reporter, "We were invited to join the coalition. We didn't unilaterally go into the battle.... Having Catholics, evangelicals and Jews in a coalition was exactly the right way to do it. We knew someone would make this a Mormon-versus-gays battle."[8]

And finally, the coalition of faith traditions "underscored a critical difference between the rival campaigns: Yes on 8 sought to marshal support among many religions, while the No on 8 campaign often put religion on the sidelines."[9]

THE LETTER

The First Presidency letter announcing the church's formal involvement in Prop 8 was dated June 20, 2008. It was leaked to the Internet the following day, more than a week prior to being read in all sacrament meetings (Sunday worship services) throughout the state of California. Under the title "Preserving Traditional Marriage and Strengthening Families," it began by tacitly disapproving the California Supreme Court decision the prior month that overturned what "California voters overwhelmingly approved." It then stated the church's core rationale for opposing same-sex marriage: "The Church's teachings and position on this moral issue are unequivocal. Marriage between a man and a woman is ordained of God, and the formation of families is central to the Creator's plan for His children. Children are entitled to be born within this bond of marriage."

The letter then issued to church members a call to action. "We ask that you do all you can to support the proposed constitutional amendment by donating of your means and time to assure that marriage in California is legally defined as being between a man and a woman. Our best efforts are required to preserve the sacred institution of marriage."[10]

Some church members, eager to join the Prop 8 battle, received the letter with enthusiasm. Others had very mixed feelings. Dean Criddle, president of the California Oakland Stake at the time, spoke of two leaders in his stake who preferred not to read the letter. One, a counselor to the bishop of a student congregation, had "a facility of speaking very fast, and he read that letter in record time." Another, a bishop who presided over a family congregation, "felt very, very conflicted. I sat on the stand next to him and asked, 'Bishop, are you going to read the letter, or is your counselor going to read it?' He said, 'Well, in bishopric meeting we decided maybe none of us would.' I said, 'Well, then give me time and I will read it.' He said, 'Oh, I'll do it,' and he stood and read the letter."[11]

For leaders and members, the letter quickly became a de facto loyalty test. Lance Wickman, the church's general counsel, later explained that supporting Prop 8 "was never meant to be a litmus test of faith." Morris Thurston, an attorney and former law partner of Wickman, asked Wickman during the Prop 8 campaign if he could remain a member in good standing while opposing the proposition. Wickman assured him he could, explaining that while the brethren regarded the question of same-sex marriage as a moral issue, Proposition 8 was being contested in the *political* arena, and the church did not require its members to vote uniformly in political campaigns. "I know Lance never felt, in his heart, that support of Prop 8 was a loyalty test, but this was never clarified at the time in any official pronouncement. There is no question that California members believed it was a loyalty test. The prophet had spoken; if you didn't follow the counsel of the prophet, your loyalty was suspect."[12]

THE RATIONALE

Church rationales for opposing same-sex marriage had existed even prior to *Baehr v. Lewin* in Hawaii, but they were updated and expanded as the church entered the Prop 8 fight. They were articulated during the summer of 2008 in a document posted on the church's LDS Newsroom website, "The Divine Institution of Marriage," and in a satellite broadcast to church leaders in California in October, "The Divine Institution of Marriage Broadcast," and can be grouped into two categories: marriage and religious liberty.

MARRIAGE

In the satellite broadcast, Apostle Quentin Cook cut to the chase: "Some ask what is wrong when marriage is granted to those of the same gender, as was done by the California Supreme Court. I've already stated one reason: it is contrary to God's plan."[13] While this rationale approached the subject on a philosophical basis, three others were put forward that focused on predicted outcomes if same-sex marriage were to become legal.

1. *The institution of marriage is crumbling, and it may be destroyed if same-sex marriage is legalized.* The first statement—that the institution of marriage is crumbling—is supported by increases in numbers of unmarried couples cohabiting, in numbers of children born out of wedlock, and in a steady increase, over several decades, in the rate of divorce, while the second is hypothetical. The "sexual revolution" of the 1960s and the national legalization of abortion in 1973 were major but not exclusive factors in gradual changes in marriage rates (down), divorce rates (up), premarital and extramarital sexual intercourse (up), extramarital cohabitation (up), age at marriage (up), abortions (up), and births out of wedlock (way up—"Since 1960, the proportion of children born out of wedlock

has soared from 5.3 percent to 38.5 percent [2006]"). "Divine Institution" stated that the legalization of same-sex marriage, which began in Massachusetts in 2004 and continued *In re Marriage Cases*, would further weaken the institution of marriage. "While it may be true that allowing single-sex unions will not immediately and directly affect all existing marriages, the real question is how it will affect society as a whole *over time*, including the rising generation and future generations."[14]

2.   *Misuse of procreative powers weakens the fabric of society.* A transcript of the satellite broadcast quotes Apostle Russell Ballard as saying, "There's no way that our Father's children—spirit children—can come to this Earth except through the bonds of marriage, of man to a woman."[15] Perhaps he intended to say that birth within the bonds of marriage is the *preferred* way, for the reality is that in many parts of our society *most* spirit children come to Earth outside the bonds of marriage. While births outside of marriage may weaken the fabric of society, it is hard to imagine how same-sex marriage would significantly weaken it further. In the first place, the entire LGBT population likely represents less than 5 percent of the total population, and in the second place, the relatively rare instances of birth to a same-sex couple (natural or artificial insemination by a sperm donor for a lesbian couple; natural or artificial insemination of a surrogate mother for a gay couple) would more likely occur within the bonds of marriage if same-sex marriage were available.

3.   *The primary purpose of marriage is rearing children, and same-sex couples are not adequately equipped to do so.* While rearing children is not the only purpose of marriage,[16] it clearly is an important purpose. "Divine Institution" concedes that not all opposite-sex married couples either desire or are capable of rearing children and gives them a free pass. But it then condemns same-sex couples who wish to rear children, charging that such couples are not capable of providing "the optimal environment for children to be protected, nurtured, and raised." While traditional marriage

> increases the likelihood that [the children] will be able to form a clear gender identity, . . . same-sex marriage likely will erode

the social identity, gender development, and moral character of children.... When marriage is undermined by gender confusion and by distortions of its God-given meaning, the rising generation of children and youth will find it increasingly difficult to develop their natural identity as a man or a woman. Some will find it more difficult to engage in wholesome courtships, form stable marriages, and raise yet another generation imbued with moral strength and purpose.[17]

Such grave outcomes were predicted widely among opponents of same-sex marriage, but they lacked sufficient supportive data to prove credible in courts of law when laws regarding anti-same-sex marriage were subsequently challenged. Indeed, recent (and ongoing) studies show that children fare at least as well with same-sex parents as with opposite-sex parents, particularly when the same-sex parents have solidified their commitment to each other and their children through marriage.[18]

RELIGIOUS LIBERTY

Six arguments were put forward suggesting that legalization of same-sex marriage would infringe on religious liberties of the church and its members.

1. *Interference with free exercise of religion.* Legalization of same-sex marriage could lead to infringement of "the constitutional rights of churches and their adherents to administer and practice their religion free from government interference."[19]

2. *Enforced nondiscrimination.* Church leaders saw same-sex marriage as the camel's-nose-under-the-tent and warned that if it became legal, "governments almost certainly will enforce a wide variety of other policies intended to ensure that there is no discrimination against same-sex couples. This may well place 'church and state on a collision course.'"[20] In other words, the church insisted on the right to exercise discrimination if it aligned with church doctrines and policies—an argument long used in earlier decades to justify discrimination against blacks. This argument would be repeated long after Prop 8, most notably in the midst of a heated debate in Utah on the passage of antidiscrimination legislation in 2015, wherein an unprecedented news conference involving three LDS apostles

elicited strong condemnation in the form of a *New York Times* editorial entitled "Mormon Church Wants Freedom to Discriminate."[21]

3. *Loss of tax-exempt status.* Loss of tax-exempt status would be a huge, and perhaps lethal, blow to many organizations, and church leaders worried out loud that legalization of same-sex marriage might lead to that outcome for the church. Apostle Quentin Cook, an attorney, said in the satellite broadcast, "Pressure will mount to revoke the tax exempt status of religious organizations and other charities that refuse to recognize same-sex marriages or open their facilities for the performance of such marriages. The argument will be that the government shouldn't subsidize discriminatory beliefs with tax exemptions." However, this was a hypothetical argument that went against the ruling of the Hawaii Supreme Court in 1996 assuring all parties that while the government *allowed* ministers to perform marriages, it could not *require* a minister to perform any kind of marriage—and thus could not penalize a church.[22] Likewise, the California Supreme Court in its decision overturning Prop 22 specifically stated that "affording same-sex couples the opportunity to obtain the designation of marriage will not impinge upon the religious freedom of any religious organization, official, or any other person; no religion will be required to change its religious policies or practices with regard to same-sex couples, and no religious officiant will be required to solemnize a marriage in contravention of his or her religious beliefs."[23]

4. *Loss of university accreditation.* Church leaders worried that church-owned universities—that is, the three campuses of Brigham Young University—could lose their accreditation if they failed to provide married housing for legally married same-sex couples or if they refused to allow same-sex couples to join campus clubs. Again, this was a hypothetical concern that did not square with the long history of flexibility accorded to church-owned colleges and universities—flexibility not extended to public institutions of higher education. Indeed, BYU had never been compelled to change either its on-campus or off-campus housing rules forbidding opposite-sex cohabitation or coeducational dormitories.

5. *Changes in school curricula.* Church leaders worried that if same-sex marriage were legalized, school curricula would undergo forced

change. "Unless Proposition 8 passes, children in public schools likely will be taught about same-sex marriages, and that such unions should be respected as the equal of traditional marriages." However, even before same-sex marriage was legal in California, the state's education code required age-appropriate instruction on respecting "marriage and committed relationships."[24] If church leaders wanted to force educators to denigrate same-sex relationships, that was not going to happen regardless of whether Prop 8 succeeded or failed.

6. *Ostracism.* In the years leading up to the 1978 revelation that abolished the ban on ordination of blacks to the priesthood, the church had been subjected to often-withering criticism of its policy and of the racism that many church members practiced—and justified—because of the policy. If same-sex marriage were legalized, then the gradually diminishing number of churches remaining opposed to it would likely be subjected to increased public criticism. "People inside of institutions with beliefs that oppose same sex marriage will increasingly be labeled as intolerant and subjected to legal penalties or social ostracism."[25] The way to escape ostracism, according to church leaders, was to turn back the clock and outlaw same-sex marriage in California by passing Prop 8.

The church's focus was on California, even though similar initiatives would be on the November ballot in Arizona and Florida. The reason was simple, as Michael Otterson, the church's director of Public Affairs, explained to the press: "If same-gender marriage is approved in California...other states will follow suit."[26] It was another attempt to keep the dominoes from falling.

LOGISTICS

It is doubtful that any religious tradition can match the LDS Church in its ability to mobilize its members. Almost since its founding in 1830, the church has employed a vast network of members who are assigned to visit other members in their homes each month. In the case of natural disasters, Hurricane Katrina being a prime example, church members using this network are often the first to respond, and they do so with enviable enthusiasm and efficiency. Thus, when the call came from the First Presidency to mobilize in support of Prop 8, the response was immediate and broad based.

On August 7, Gary Lawrence, the church's statewide supervisor of grassroots activities, laid out a sophisticated logistical plan for the campaign that "Elder Lance Wickman has aptly called the 'Gettysburg of the culture war.'"[27] Phase I was titled "Identification." Church members would mobilize on three "Walk Saturdays," August 16 and 23 and September 6, canvassing neighborhoods and recording which voters either favored Prop 8 or might lean in that direction. "The information will be used for the Get-Out-The-Vote (GOTV) efforts."

Of this effort Morris Thurston recalled,

> I remember reading some of the material: what you were to do was go door-to-door and ask people, "What do you think about gay marriage? Is it a good or a bad thing?" If they said, "I believe in it," you were just to thank them politely and go to the next door. If they said, "I'm not sure," you were to give them materials explaining why they should support Prop 8. If they said, "I do not believe in gay marriage," you were to take their names down and try to encourage them to get involved in the cause. On Election Day, you were to go back to these doors and inquire whether they had already voted and, if they hadn't, encourage them to do so.[28]

A document disseminated to church members in Yolo and Solano Counties drilled down to the logistics of the Phase I ground game. "We have been asked to contact over 58,000 registered voter households in Davis, Dixon, Esparto, Woodland, Winters and other portions of Yolo and northern Solano County.... To meet this objective we will require 40 people from each ward for each of the 3 Saturdays."[29] To broaden their reach, and perhaps to convey the impression that the canvassing campaign was not a Mormons-only activity, "we are encouraged to 'bring a friend' not of our faith, who is supportive of the initiative to walk or phone with us."

Phase II, "Advocacy and Persuasion," would involve recontacting "those who are in the Mushy Middle—Soft Yes, undecided, and Soft No voters. We will provide information and persuasive points for them to consider."[30]

Phase III, "Get Out the Vote," would have two parts: an ongoing effort to maintain contact with voters who intended to vote by mail and a mobilization effort on Election Day. "We will need 100,000 volunteers on November 4—about 5 per voting location."

RAISING THE MONEY

In the four years preceding Prop 8, twenty-four states had same-sex marriage issues on the ballot. The total amount of money spent by both sides on Prop 8—$85 million—was nearly triple the amount spent on those twenty-four campaigns *combined*.[31] It was also the most money spent on any social-issue campaign in the history of the United States.[32] A church prediction that Yes on 8 would "be outspent in the media by at least two to one"[33] proved highly exaggerated, but No on 8 supporters eventually raised 13 percent more money.[34]

The First Presidency letter asking church members to donate their means was followed by a rigorous fund-raising campaign. Every stake in California was given a financial quota, with the amount varying according to stake demographics. Stake presidents were contacted frequently to determine progress toward their quotas.[35] Although members were not supposed to be coerced to donate, and generally were not, some were subjected to intimidation, "such as saying that their souls would be in jeopardy if they didn't give."[36] When one congregational leader suggested that a tithe-of-a-tithe—1 percent of annual income—would be an appropriate donation, a member responded, "We don't have the funds to give that kind of money." The leader countered, "Well, we feel that you do, and we know the kinds of vacations that you have been taking."[37]

Others gave generously and voluntarily, sometimes at great sacrifice. One Sacramento family with five children between the ages of three and twelve and a stay-at-home mother donated $50,000. The mother told a reporter, "It was a decision we made very prayerfully and carefully. Was it an easy decision? No. But it was a clear decision, one that had so much potential to benefit our children and their children."[38]

FOLLOWING THE MONEY

The decision to ask church members to contribute money directly to the Yes on 8 campaign, rather than to have the church contribute as it had in Hawaii and Alaska, meant that independent tracking of the total donated by Mormons would be difficult, at best. Nonetheless, a church member, Nadine Hansen, devised a reverse-engineering strategy that resulted in an impressively accurate estimate.

Hansen accessed an open online register in the office of the California secretary of state that listed, on a daily basis, the names and cities of residence of all who donated $100 or more to Prop 8, this in compliance with state law. The list eventually included some 46,000 names. In order to make her survey manageable, she honed it down to 6,585 people who donated $1,000 or more.[39] Converting the data to her own spreadsheet, she then harnessed the power of the Internet to disseminate the spreadsheet throughout the state, asking that fellow Mormons identify LDS donors. Hansen recalled, "We continued to say, 'We are a neutral website. We are not taking a position on Prop 8. All we are doing is tracking the money, because we think that people have a right to know who is funding Proposition 8, and we want to see what the Mormon involvement is.' We never linked to anti-8 websites."[40]

Hansen's estimate of total Mormon contributions was almost dead even with that of the Yes on 8 campaign: approximately $20 million. This meant that at least half the total raised by the proponents of Prop 8 came from members of a church that accounted for only about 2 percent of the total state population. The campaign manager for No on 8, Steve Smith, remarked, "I don't think we have ever seen a single religion in the state . . . so significantly participate in one political campaign." Andrew Sullivan, a prominent gay writer, was more edgy in his assessment. "The main reason the ban on marriage rights for gay and lesbian couples has been able to finance a massive advertising campaign is that the LDS church is bankrolling the entire effort. . . . It's all legal, and totally within their democratic rights, but it is striking that one single religious grouping could invest so much in attempting to strip civil equality from gay couples." Even before the election, another writer noted that the Mormons were exposing themselves politically. "All of California's Catholic bishops have all come out in favor of the measure. So have many evangelical Christians and Orthodox Jews. Yet it is Mormons, who account for 2 percent of the state population, who are catching the most heat."[41]

DEPLOYING GROUND TROOPS

The church's ground game consisted of three parts: door-to-door canvassing, phone banks, and roadside demonstrations of support for Prop 8. All were accomplished with volunteer laborers whose numbers dwarfed those of other churches involved in the campaign. A postelection report in a Catholic publication noted, "Catholics make up 30 percent of California's population, compared to the 2 percent of the population who are Mormons.... Protect Marriage strategist Jeff Flint told the *New York Times* that Mormons made up 80 to 90 percent of the early volunteers who walked door-to-door in the campaign."[42]

Although Mormon grassroots participation far outweighed that of all other churches combined, church leaders attempted to minimize its profile, consistent with former church president Gordon Hinckley's counsel that the church be an active player but remain in the background. In the 2010 *Hollingsworth v. Perry* trial that challenged the constitutionality of Prop 8, plaintiff witness Gary Segura, a professor of political science at Stanford University, testified concerning church documents showing "plausible deniability or respectable distance between the church organization *per se* and the actual campaign."[43] Phone-bank volunteers were instructed to use only first names and not to identify themselves as LDS.[44] "When we went to our training meetings, they said, don't bring up the fact that you're Mormon. Don't wear white shirts and ties; don't look like missionaries. When you go out [canvassing], bring a non-member friend."[45]

Door-to-door canvassing: Canvassing began on Saturday, August 16. A reported fifteen to thirty thousand LDS volunteers knocked on doors on that day and two subsequent Saturdays, politely inquiring as to where residents stood on the issue of same-sex marriage. Volunteers placed each resident into one of five categories: yes, soft yes, undecided, soft no, and no. Those softly in favor of same-sex marriage and those undecided were designated for later follow-up contact and for get-out-the-vote efforts on Election Day.[46]

Phone banks: A satellite broadcast to church leaders and members throughout California on October 8 laid out the details of the telephone campaign. The key date would be October 27, when "the eight-day final calling list begins. Phone banks will be available for evening calling. Calling teams are also welcome to make calls from their homes. Calls will be both persuasive and 'get out the vote' in nature. Finally, the week of November 3. On November 3 we'll have all-day calling centers."[47] One church member recalled the effort within his congregation: "Our ward organized phone banks, so there were certain designated nights where you would go to certain people's houses, and everybody would call.... I think they had people go to people's houses because everybody would be there and you felt like you were part of it, so it made it easier for some people to call as a group."[48]

Roadside demonstrations: The final area of volunteer participation consisted of people standing along busy highways or intersections and holding placards advocating a Yes on 8 vote. Carol Lynn Pearson recorded that another church member "told me that 700 people from her daughter's stake in the LA area lined the Pacific Coast Highway last Saturday [October 27] holding Yes on 8 banners and signs. Apparently, numerous other stakes down there did the same." But not all church members were supportive. One woman recalled, "My daughters were in Young Women, and they would ask us to avoid certain areas of the town because they knew that the members would be standing on the corner protesting. Especially our oldest daughter, if we happened to be driving down the street and we saw the members, she would duck down in the car. I just remember one day driving and her doing that, it just made me cry."[49]

IN CHURCH

Church leaders in Salt Lake City intended to have local members participate in the Yes on 8 campaign of their free will, without coercion or stigmatization of those who chose not to participate. Many local leaders performed the delicate balancing act of fulfilling the congregations' quotas of money and hours without applying pressure and with particular deference to preserving the three-hour block of Sunday meetings as a time for worship and not for politicking. Dean Criddle, president of the California Oakland Stake, described the way he negotiated the campaign in his stake:

> We instructed our bishops that the three-hour block of worship services was not to be used for discussions of Proposition 8. Not for fund-raising, for sure; not for grassroots lobbying efforts, for sure. We didn't want any discussion of this political activity to invade the worship services. The worship services were for worship; they were not for direct or indirect political activity, including this.... The bishops were very supportive of that, although some of the local members were very critical. They felt the three-hour block was the time when people got together, and it should

have been used more fervently to stir up the troops. But that's not the way we felt.[50]

Criddle's stake, however, was an exception, and many reports during and after the campaign described co-opting of Sunday services to push Prop 8. These examples were typical:

- "I just walked out of the worst sacrament meeting in my entire life. . . . A high councilman came in and took ten minutes on the marriage thing. . . . Not participating is not an option, he said. . . . 'If you do not follow the church on this you do not follow Christ. We expect your time and your means.'"[51]
- "Three of the testimonies from today were lengthy discussions of Prop 8 topics covered included the need to help the amendment pass; the awful consequences for years to come if it doesn't pass; the joy of Prop 8 volunteer work; the idea of the depression about doing Prop 8 work is sent from Satan to try to block the work."[52]
- "It is mentioned in every meeting, donation sheets are passed around in RS [Relief Society] and there are pleas for donations and volunteers in the announcements as well as impromptu testimonies during classes. It is EVERYWHERE!!!! I can only imagine what we could do if we directed our efforts towards our local homeless population or something."[53]
- "For the last two months I have endured listening to the fear-mongering from the pulpit in my Southern California Sacrament Meeting, Stake Conference, Gospel Doctrine and in my High Priest group meetings; this in spite of our Stake President's instructions to 'not discuss this issue in our meetings.' . . . The message I'm getting is quite clear: if I do not support, campaign for, give money to and vote for prop 8, I do not sustain the brethren. Really? And if I disagree—they don't want to hear about it."[54]
- "I have a friend who told me she is going to attend the Presbyterian church until this is over so she can hear a lesson on Christ's love and feel the spirit instead of going to her ward where the talks are all about supporting Prop 8 and the sprit is gone. . . . In the Santa Monica singles ward, members were asked to stand up in Sacrament meeting to show who would vote for Prop 8. . . . In a Corona

Del Mar ward, individuals were called out into the hall and asked on the spot to commit 40-plus hours to walking and driving to support Prop 8 and asked exactly how much $ they would contribute. Members felt pressured into making commitments even when they did not want to."[55]

In some cases local leaders turned a dark corner and bullied, even threatened, members whose consciences went against support of Prop 8:

The scariest news came from my dear friend whose sister came to her home crying and shaking because a counselor from her Stake Presidency told the Elders Quorum and Relief Society that he is "going to help them find their testimony to support Prop 8." He went on to say that if you are against it, you are "aiding and abetting" and then gave what she and her husband called a fire and brimstone speech referencing Revelation 3:16 saying, "the Lord will spew out of his mouth those who oppose Prop 8 and they will be responsible for the sins of this generation." ... In another Southern California ward, the speaker told the congregation that this is comparable to the Great War in heaven and the wicked will be separated from the righteous in the church.[56]

Some members worried that failure to support Prop 8 might result in loss of their "temple recommend," the printed form attesting to personal worthiness that is required for entrance into any LDS temple. "I was so conflicted. I knew people that were gay, and I felt this action as a church was wrong. I was worried about the possible ramifications of voting against Prop 8, mainly in discipline, or having my temple recommend taken away."[57]

Others were overtly punished for failure to support Prop 8, such as a man who was released from his calling as high councilor:

I was on the high council, and I went to the stake president, President Crawford, and I told him, as the Prop 8 thing was getting going and the church was obviously getting very involved in it, "I think the Church wants to present a united front, and I'm not going to be part of that front as a member of this high council. You might find another calling for me somewhere." He said, "No, we can work around that. We'll work around it. We want you to stay." So I just went along with his advice on that. But then, after a month or so he called me in and said, "I just can't work around it anymore."[58]

For some, the activities in church meetings proved too much. One woman described a film shown in her congregation in mid-October that "used all the political tactics and deceptions other churches and political parties had been using. My husband and I sat stunned. We heard our leaders use the same arguments that more unscrupulous people had used to deny a minority the freedom of choice they deserved. On that day my husband, who had recently been a high councilor, walked out of the building, never to return."[59]

"SIX CONSEQUENCES"

One item that was showcased in church meetings was titled "Six Consequences the Coalition Has Identified If Proposition 8 Fails." Although it bore no authorship, Gary Lawrence, who headed the grassroots efforts for the church in California, wrote it.[60] Lawrence's close working relationship with John Dalton, who, as the church's area representative, directed California Prop 8 activities from the ecclesiastical side, resulted in Dalton circulating the document to all stake presidents in California, with instructions to use its talking points during the three-hour block of Sunday meetings. Some, like Dean Criddle, simply declined to do so. "I contacted my area authority and said, 'Look, we resolved not to talk about Proposition 8 at all during the three-hour block. Even if we did, I couldn't possible use these as talking points, and here is why.' He said, 'Well, you should do what you think is right.' So we simply didn't use them." But most discussed the document at one point or another, generally with receptive audiences. At times, however, it intensified the pain of church members who did not support Prop 8. One woman recalled, "They brought out that 'Six Consequences' document and read it, word for word. I remember taking notes, because I just couldn't believe what I was hearing. I pretty much cried throughout the whole meeting."[61]

Shortly after reading "Six Consequences," attorney and church member Morris Thurston decided to respond. "As I read what he wrote, it was clear to me that most of the so-called consequences were legal consequences, and they were just plain wrong.... I just felt like something had to be done, and since this was well within my area of expertise, why not go ahead and research it, and do something about it." Two months before Election Day, Thurston sent his point-by-point rebuttal to local and general church authorities and posted it on the Internet.[62]

Consequence 1: Children in public schools will have to be taught that same-sex marriage is just as good as traditional marriage. "No provision of the Education Code requires any teacher to teach that same-sex marriage is 'just as good' as traditional marriage. Teachers are to teach respect for marriage and committed relationships, and Proposition 8 will not change this law."

Consequence 2: Churches may be sued over their tax-exempt status if they refuse to allow same-sex marriage ceremonies in their religious buildings open to the public. This conclusion was based on a misrepresentation of a New Jersey case—at a time when New Jersey did not allow same-sex marriage—in which a Methodist organization had taken advantage of a state law granting a real estate tax exemption for a seaside pavilion that was dedicated for public use. The organization wanted to prohibit a gay commitment ceremony in the pavilion. "The New Jersey real estate commission ruled that if OGCMA [Ocean Grove Camp Meeting Association] intended to claim a property tax exemption for a building open to the public, they could not discriminate." The case did not involve the overall tax-exempt status of the Methodist Church, but merely whether the pavilion could avoid paying property taxes.

Consequence 3: Religious adoption agencies will be challenged by government agencies to give up their long-held right to place children only in homes with both a mother and a father. This cited case involved Catholic Charities in Boston, which, unlike LDS Family Services, accepted public money and was under contract with the State of Massachusetts—thus, an agent of the state. It *voluntarily* ceased providing adoption services in Massachusetts rather than arrange an adoption to a same-sex couple. Because it did not accept public money for its adoption services, LDS Family Services has never been compelled—and cannot be compelled—to place adopted children with same-sex parents.

Consequence 4: Religions that sponsor private schools with married student housing may be required to provide housing for same-sex couples, even if counter to church doctrine, or risk lawsuits over tax exemptions and related benefits. The cited case involved Yeshiva University in New York, which is chartered as a *nonsectarian* institution. By contrast, the courts have given wide exemptions to church-owned universities to enact policies consistent with their doctrines. "The gay marriage problem will not arise at BYU and other Church universities because engaging in homosexual activity is a violation of the honor code and is a basis for expulsion from the University."

Consequence 5: Ministers who preach against same-sex marriages may be sued for hate speech and risk government fines. The cited case was in Canada, which has much greater restrictions on public speech than the United States. Furthermore, it did not involve a minister. "This would never be an issue in the United States because we have far more liberal freedom of speech and religion laws than does Canada. There have been no hate speech lawsuits in Massachusetts, which has been a gay marriage state for four years."

Consequence 6: It will cost you money. This change in the definition of marriage will bring a cascade of lawsuits, including some already lost. "The change in the definition of marriage will not bring a 'cascade of lawsuits' because heterosexual and homosexual registered domestic partners already have all the rights of married couples in California."

Within weeks following Thurston's rebuttal, a group of fifty-nine constitutional and family-law scholars from most of the law schools in California, as well as the *Los Angeles Times* editorial board, published similar refutations of these legal arguments.[63] Nevertheless, there was no church response to Thurston's rebuttal, and "Six Consequences" continued to circulate.

LATE TO THE GAME

The No on 8 campaign was late to arrive. In part this was due to a sense of apathy within much of the LGBT community—apathy that derived both from an unbroken chain of electoral defeats across the country for LGBT rights, including marriage equality, and from general indifference toward marriage. Rick Jacobs, founder of the Courage Campaign, a California political action organization, said, "We lost all those states, and we kept losing.... Nobody cared about the issue because nobody thought it was possible. People just didn't care about marriage. I think if you had done a survey of self-identifying LGBT people in 2007, people would have said, 'It's not my issue. It doesn't matter.' Very few people had been pushing for this." George W. Bush effectively used same-sex marriage as a wedge issue in his 2004 reelection campaign because the majority of Americans still strongly opposed it. Jacobs continued, "There was absolutely no uprising after 2004. Zero. Think about that! Not one! There was no mass mobilization, no fight, no 'This is terrible.' It didn't happen. We just lost."[64]

But one thing had changed since 2004, and that was the court decision that invalidated Proposition 22. That decision opened the door to same-sex marriage in California, and before Prop 8 slammed the door shut, some sixteen thousand same-sex couples had been legally married in the state. So even though the wording of Prop 8 was identical to that of Prop 22, and even though Prop 22 had passed by a margin of 23 percent, something was different. Clifford Rosky, a law professor specializing in LGBT legal issues, said, "There was a sense of taking something away that had been given. That is always a little bit sharper."[65]

Mobilizing opposition to Prop 8 was an uphill struggle, in part because of the head start by the Yes on 8 group, which before the court decision had quietly worked for months to qualify the ballot initiative. A British newspaper, in an article published several weeks before the election, commented on the lead. "No on Eight, the group leading the battle against Proposition 8, admitted it had been caught off-guard by the size of the anti-gay-marriage advertising campaign, funded by $30M of donations." Because of the strategy employed by the LDS Church, with individual members writing checks to Protect Marriage, it took weeks for No on 8 to recognize the strategic advantage, both in money and logistics, that the Mormons had brought to the campaign. Bruce Bastian, a former Mormon who eventually donated $1 million to the No on 8 campaign, said, "I made phone calls to everybody I knew and said, 'This is really serious, people.' 'Oh, Prop 8 will *never* pass in California. We have good polling.' I said, 'No, you need to pay attention to this, because the [Mormon] Church is going to put their money and their resources and their little army of people on the ground. This is a serious thing.'"[66]

Even when No on 8 workers belatedly learned of the extent of Mormon backing of Prop 8, they were slow to react, in part because of reluctance to take on the church openly. Rick Jacobs recalled, "It became really clear to us by mid- to late September that that was where a lot of the money was coming from and that that was where a lot of the foot soldiers were coming from. The anti–Prop 8 campaign said, 'We do not wish to take that on head-on. We don't want to call out the church. We think that's bad for the campaign.' . . . So we—the Courage Campaign—said to our side, the anti–Prop 8 campaign, 'We're going to take this on.' They said, 'Be our guests.' And so we did."[67] With militant language, Jacobs named names. "Those speaking in the name of their God and prophets, led principally by out-of-state Mormons and joined by evangelical Christians, have made the removal of my rights a holy war for the new century."[68]

Eventually, No on 8 raised about $5 million more than Yes on 8. However, the way the Yes on 8 campaign spent its money, combined with its strong ground game anchored by LDS volunteers, overcame the monetary imbalance.

THE ADVERTISING CAMPAIGNS

The most expensive part of any political campaign is television advertising. While both sides of the Prop 8 issue spent heavily on TV spots, the No on 8 side acknowledged that Yes on 8 was far more effective in its ads. Kate Kendell, executive director of the National Center for Lesbian Rights, conceded, "As soon as Frank Schubert's first ad hit, around what kids are going to be taught in schools, we started dropping like a stone. Our support was a mile wide and an inch deep."

Frank Schubert was a principal with Schubert Flint Public Affairs, which handled the advertising campaign for Yes on 8. While No on 8 ads played to the mind, Schubert targeted the hearts—and the fears—of

voters. Three ads, in particular, were highly effective in motivating voters to approve Prop 8.

Gavin Newsom: San Francisco mayor Gavin Newsom, whose 2004 offi-
ciating at multiple same-sex ceremonies had no legal validity but attracted
national press coverage, jumped into the fray again in 2008 in the immediate aftermath of the court decision striking down Prop 22. The *Wall Street
Journal* reported in late October that the Yes on 8 campaign had "been running a television ad for several weeks that shows San Francisco Mayor Gavin
Newsom delivering a boisterous response to a throng of supporters after the
state Supreme Court ruling. 'The door's wide open now. It's going to happen, whether you like it or not,' the Democratic mayor says loudly. 'Gavin
Newsom has been a great player on our team,' said Sonja Eddings Brown,
spokeswoman for Protect Marriage California, a group that has been leading the 'Yes on 8' campaign."[69]

The Wirthlins: Joseph "Robb" Wirthlin and his wife, Robin, introduced
themselves, in a Yes on 8 television ad, "as the unwitting parents of a boy
who was read the gay-friendly book *King and King* in his Massachusetts
classroom. The Wirthlins claimed in several interviews to be unintentional
players in the debate. They became the embodiment of the traditional family
for Yes on 8 and appeared in a $2 million ad campaign central to the propo-
nent's argument that Prop 8 was needed to protect California schoolchil-
dren from being taught about same-sex marriage."[70] After the ad had run
for some time, the Wirthlins took a weeklong bus tour through California
to reinforce their message.

Two aspects of the Wirthlins' story did not become widely known
until after the election. One was that they were not "unintentional players." Indeed, they were members of a political organization that was pushing for an amendment to the Massachusetts Constitution to ban same-sex
marriage.[71] A published report stated that they had moved into the community "in order to become actively involved in the issue and to join [David]
Parker in filing a lawsuit to enforce parental rights to approve all materials used in the education of their son"—a lawsuit that they filed only weeks
after moving into the school district.[72]

The other aspect was that Robb Wirthlin was the grandnephew of LDS
General Authority and principal Prop 8 strategist Richard Wirthlin and
grandson of LDS apostle Joseph Wirthlin.

The Lesbian Wedding: With no apparent awareness of the gift they were handing to the Yes on 8 campaign, two lesbian women asked that Mayor Gavin Newsom officiate at their wedding—this time, unlike 2004, a legally valid ceremony. One of the women, a schoolteacher, invited the young children in her class to attend the wedding. Mark Jansson, who since 2003 had been on the planning committee for what became Prop 8, described the reaction from the Yes on 8 camp:

> Gavin Newsom presided at the wedding, and it was front-page San Francisco Chronicle. It broke the next day in the Chronicle, and Paul Cobb and Glen Greener were having breakfast in Oakland. Paul opened the newspaper, read the front headline, and turned around and handed it to Glen Greener and said, "You just got a gift from God." Glen Greener said, "You're kidding me." Paul said, "No. Do you know what they've just done? These guys have just shot themselves in the foot by including a school and a schoolteacher in this, which flies in the face of everything they have been trying to tell the public about what they weren't going to do." We made hay out of that ad and just said basically, "Hey, folks, here is what is going on." ... It was one of the dumbest blunders that they committed during the campaign. There were a couple of them, but that was the biggest one. We were down seventeen points in the polls the week before that ad broke. We moved from seventeen points down to six points ahead by late October as a result of that ad, as a result of that article, as a result of everything that we did to capitalize on what they had said and what they had done in the advertising that they were running.[73]

By contrast, only one ad opposing Prop 8—and it did not come from the No on 8 campaign—was memorable, and it came out way too late to have any effect on the election. The ad, "Home Invasion," which was produced by the Courage Campaign at a total cost of $800 and filmed in the home of Rick Jacobs, began with a knock on the door. A legally married lesbian couple opened the door, whereupon two actors playing the part of Mormon missionaries said, "We're here to take away your rights," barged into the house, pulled the wedding rings off the women's fingers, and riffled through their drawers until they found—and shredded—their wedding license. As they left the house, one missionary said, "That was too easy," to which the other replied, "What should we ban next?"[74]

Reaction to the ad was immediate and fierce. Maggie Gallagher, president of the National Organization for Marriage, wrote, "Go see the ad 'Home Invasion' online. Judge for yourself. But while you're doing it, I'm going to ask you: Imagine that instead of Mormons, the ad featured two guys in yarmulkes and accused Jews of donating too much money for a cause they believed in. This was a truly vile and outrageous attempt to win a political election by exciting religious hatred against a minority faith community." Even the Mormon Church, which had attempted to maintain a low profile during the campaign, complained to the No on 8 campaign, asking that they take down the ad, which had amassed hundreds of thousands of views on YouTube. Rick Jacobs recalled, "The anti–Prop 8 campaign said the truth, which was, 'It's not our ad. We don't control it.'"[75]

Leaders of the Courage Campaign did not expect the ad to make a difference in the election, for it was already apparent to them that Prop 8 would be approved by voters. Instead, the purpose of the ad was to send a message to church leadership—and church members—in Salt Lake City. "It was important that people understand that a church had taken a position on something that affected lots and lots of people in California. That was the whole thing we did.... I think every television station in Salt Lake City ran that ad for free. Now again, if you think about it, nobody in Salt Lake City was voting on Prop 8, but we wanted to make a point."[76]

THE LOYAL OPPOSITION

Particularly within the United States, Mormons constitute a population that is overwhelmingly unquestioning and obedient in response to statements from the church hierarchy. The First Presidency letter in June was unambiguous in requesting the support of church members, to the point where some local leaders considered it a to be a loyalty test, even though top leadership denied such intent. Gary Lawrence, who directed the grassroots Yes on 8 efforts, "compared opponents of Proposition 8 to those who sided with Lucifer against Jesus in the pre-mortal existence."[77] A bishop in Southern California said that "the people who wouldn't get behind Proposition 8 were like the wicked and foolish people in Noah's day and would meet a similar fate."[78] A bishop in Northern California "spoke of 'severe punishments' that would befall those who didn't follow the prophet, suggesting that those who were opposed to Proposition 8 might suffer dire consequences."[79] And an editorial in the *Daily Universe*, the campus newspaper of Brigham Young University, noted that "'active Mormons' know that when the prophet speaks, the debate is over. No matter how diligently someone reads their Scriptures, attend church or pays a full tithe, unless they sustain President [Thomas] Monson, his counselors and the other 12 apostles, they are not 'active Mormons.'"[80]

Nonetheless, even though there was enormous peer pressure to conform to and support Prop 8, some church members raised their voices in opposition, either privately or publicly. Some remained active church members, while for others the church support of Prop 8 was the last straw that led to temporary or permanent separation.

Perhaps the highest-profile LDS supporter of No on 8 was Barbara Young, convert to Mormonism from a Christian church background, ardent supporter of LGBT rights, sister of an openly gay (and not LDS) man, and wife of National Football League Hall of Famer Steve Young. Upon learning that the First Presidency letter was to be read in all worship services on June 29, she appealed to her bishop. "I am writing to beg you not to read the political letter that the Presidency has asked you to read in our most sacred meeting, Sacrament. The letter will be destructive and divisive. Families will be torn apart, wards will be taking sides, and many young men and women will feel cut out from their family and church, feeling they have no alternative but to end their life."[81] The bishop nonetheless read the letter publicly.

Young then proceeded to contribute money, time, and yard space to the No on 8 campaign. Speaking several years later upon being honored by the Human Rights Campaign for her efforts, she recalled:

There were, it felt like, maybe a dozen of us who were shouting from the top of our lungs, "Please don't do this! You don't know what you are doing! You are dividing families, LGBT kids are being cast from their homes, and, worst of all, you are killing our LGBT brothers and sisters, especially our youth."

We shouted. We screamed. We ran around teaching everyone we came in contact with. We spoke to reporters. We wrote op-eds. We countered the arguments for Prop 8 with mass emails and handouts. A few started groups and forums where compassionate Mormons could find others who felt like we did.

We gathered at homes and parks. We strategized. We came up with plans. We worked to the bone, trying to make others see the true nature of Prop 8. But our voices weren't strong enough.

There were many who, in confidence, let us know that they felt the same way we did; but they were afraid, so they decided to stay silent....

But soon after [the election], this beautiful, Mormon gay young man approached me, with tears in his eyes, and said, "Just when I felt all the people around me were against me, when it got so dark I no longer wanted to live, hearing what you did and said was like a candle in the darkness, and it lit up my whole world." In that moment, I knew it was all worth it.[82]

Young received no pushback from church officials, either local or at headquarters. Neither did Senate Majority Leader Harry Reid, a devout Mormon who was openly supportive of same-sex marriage and in private told presiding church officers that "they were about to make a terrible mistake."[83] But other church members with lower public profiles received either unofficial shunning from fellow church members or varying levels of official disapproval and sanction for their expressions of opposition to Prop 8.

Robert Rees, who two decades earlier had served as bishop of a singles congregation in Los Angeles and had made a special effort to create a welcoming atmosphere for LGBT members, wrote an op-ed column for the *Salt Lake Tribune*, published a week after the First Presidency letter was read publicly, in which he suggested that members follow their consciences regarding Prop 8 rather than having the letter serve "as a test of their willingness to 'follow the brethren.'" While he was in Salt Lake City attending a mission reunion, he was informed by his stake president, via email, that he had been released from his calling as a high councilor. Furthermore, his stake president informed the bishops' council and the high council—but not Rees directly—that he was "forbidden from speaking, teaching, praying or bearing your testimony." Three months after the Prop 8 election, Rees wrote to a friend, "I just found out that the direction to take action against me came from Church headquarters."[84]

In one family in California, one man was released from the high council because he "supported gay marriage in the meetings," his wife was released from her teaching job in the Relief Society after she "decided to wear a rainbow ribbon on her dress (at church)," missionaries who had rented a room from the family were told to vacate the premises after a call from church headquarters because the family "was quoted as saying they were saddened by the church's position on this issue," and a family car was disfigured while parked in the church parking lot "because they have a No on Prop 8 sticker on their car."[85]

A most intriguing example of opposition from within began in Nebraska. Andrew Callahan, an LDS high priest, decided in the week following the reading of the First Presidency letter to gather voices of dissident Mormons on a new website, "Signing for Something"—a play on words referencing a book published by prior church president Gordon B. Hinckley, *Standing for Something*. "We started up with no budget, no advertising, nothing; just spreading it essentially by word-of-mouth among dissident Mormons. . . . By July 4th, Signing for Something went live. It was really not getting much notice."[86] To stir the pot, Callahan began to send letters, under a pseudonym, to midlevel church leaders such as stake presidents, temple presidents, and mission presidents: "Dear President So-and-so: We are a group of people who are organizing in opposition to the First Presidency. You have been recommended to us, and you probably know who recommended you. We'd like for you to join our ranks."

Unwittingly, church leaders in Salt Lake City helped to propagate Callahan's movement. After receiving many forwarded copies of Callahan's letter, the Public Affairs Department sent a response to local church leaders throughout the United States:

> A person using the name "Dale Callahan" is currently conducting an extensive letter-writing campaign to priesthood leaders, members, and missionaries. In the letters, he denounces California Proposition 8, which is an amendment to the California Constitution defining marriage as between "a man and a woman." He urges Californians to vote "no" on the proposition. We are not certain if this is a former member of the Church by the name of Dale Callahan or someone merely using that name.

Church members should be made aware that Dale Callahan is not affiliated with the Church and does not speak for the Church in any way. His communications should be disregarded.[87]

On the strength of the church letter, traffic to Signing for Something skyrocketed. "This was like the 'bean in the ear' concept: you don't tell a child not to put a bean in his ear, because what's the first thing that kid's going to do? Put the bean in his ear. Well, after those letters were read in Sacrament Meetings, Relief Society meetings, priesthood meetings all over the country, people Googled this guy Callahan, and traffic on our website went up about sixfold after the first weekend, and then it doubled again the next weekend."[88]

As Callahan's role became known, he was threatened with the most severe punishment possible by the church: excommunication. "On September 11, 2008, my bishop, Bryan Woodbury of Clay Center, Nebraska visited me stating that he was there by assignment of higher authorities in the church." Upon declining the suggestion by the bishop that he resign his church membership, Callahan was informed that he would be subjected to a disciplinary council. "Bishop Woodbury stated that the reasons for the excommunication would be that I am 'going in a different direction' from the church, and I am in 'opposition' to the Mormon Church." Perhaps because the matter went public, church leaders stepped back. In late September, Callahan received a letter from his stake president: "We have decided to defer your disciplinary council to a later date given this politically charged election season. We feel that a more measured and considered discussion can be held at a date sometime in November."[89] That discussion never happened.

POLLING VERSUS POLLS

Polling throughout the summer and early fall generally showed the No on 8 side to be winning, at times by as much as 17 percent, a margin that probably worked against the effort to defeat the proposition. Kate Kendell recalled, "As we were trying to raise money to defeat Prop 8, all people said was, 'Oh, but it's going to lose.' 'No! This is way too early to say that.'"[90]

Throughout October the margin diminished, although polling done in late October still showed Prop 8 losing by 3 to 5 percent. Then one of the polls showed a substantial shift in public opinion. "The last Field Poll, conducted a week before the election, showed that weekly churchgoers increased their support in the final week from 72% to 84%. Catholic support increased from 44% to 64%—a jump that accounted for 6% of the total California electorate and equivalent to the state's entire African American population combined."[91]

On November 4, 2008, California lived up to its reputation as a reliable blue state as far as the presidential race was concerned, with Barack Obama—who opposed same-sex marriage—receiving 61 percent of the votes cast. But Proposition 8 passed by nearly five percentage points.

POSTELECTION ANALYSIS

Although the Mormons were late to the game, their extraordinary contributions to the Yes on 8 campaign, both monetary and logistical, led some to equate "Prop 8" with "Mormon."[92] In the immediate aftermath of the election, a *New York Times* editorial reinforced that narrative: "The most notable defeat for fairness was in California, where right-wing forces led by the Mormon Church poured tens of millions of dollars into the campaign for Proposition 8—a measure to enshrine bigotry in the state's Constitution by preventing people of the same sex from marrying."[93]

Another *New York Times* article, published a week later on the newspaper's front page with the provocative title "Mormons Tipped Scale in Ban on Gay Marriage," quoted Jeff Flint, a strategist with Protect Marriage, saying that the Mormons provided "80 percent to 90 percent of the early volunteers who walked door-to-door in election precincts." The article also documented a crucial Mormon role late in the election cycle, at a time when chief Yes on 8 strategist Frank Schubert said, "We're going to lose this campaign if we don't get more money." Alan Ashton, grandson of former LDS church president David O. McKay, responded with a personal contribution of $1 million. Protect Marriage estimated "as much as half of the nearly $40 million raised on behalf of the measure was contributed by Mormons."[94]

Opponents of Prop 8 freely acknowledged the crucial role that the Mormon Church had played. Kate Kendell, a former Mormon who knew the church from the inside, described its involvement as "massive and absolutely crucial to the result.... There is no doubt that had the church remained neutral, Prop 8 would have been defeated.... You essentially have a built-in field campaign, the likes of which are unparalleled. And it's all free and utterly dependable."[95] Another commentator seconded Kendell's observation by contrasting Mormon mobilization to that of the other faith traditions. "Catholics make a practice of ignoring their bishops, and evangelicals are a disparate flock, but Mormons believe that the head of their church is a prophet of God—and tend to act accordingly."[96]

Yet some felt the Mormons and their church actually received disproportionate credit—and blame. According to Frank Schubert, "We had the support of virtually the entire faith community in California. Prop 8 didn't win because of the Mormons. It won because we created superior advertising that defined the issues on our terms; because we built a diverse coalition; and, most importantly, because we activated that coalition at the grassroots level in a way that had never before been done."[97] Indeed, while Mormons provided ground troops and materiel, the field generals, non-Mormons Frank Schubert and Jeff Flint, masterminded the political campaign.

Many who supported Prop 8 used the argument that "liberal judges" were thwarting the will of the people, pointing out that Prop 22 had passed by a margin of more than 2.7 million votes yet was overturned by a margin of 1 vote in the California Supreme Court. This argument was addressed by the editorial board of the *Los Angeles Times* in the immediate aftermath of the election, which noted, "If the U.S. Supreme Court's landmark 1954 ruling in *Brown v. Board of Education* had been submitted to a national referendum, swaths of this country probably still would have legally segregated schools."[98]

LDS Church leaders had seen in Hawaii a danger if the public perceived the same-sex marriage battle to be one of civil rights, and so they consistently framed the issue as one of morality rather than civil rights. Similarly, Protect Marriage framed Prop 8 as being about something other than two individuals involved in a committed gay relationship. Schubert and Flint, in a magazine article published after the election, wrote, "We decided to withhold criticism of the same-sex couples who were getting married (after all, they were simply taking advantage of the rights the Court had granted them). . . . [We] recognized that passing Proposition 8 would depend on our ability to convince voters that same-sex marriage had broader implications for Californians."[99] Those implications, both real and contrived, became the message of Yes on 8, and the campaign remained tightly focused on its message through Election Day.

Calculating a hard-core base of support of only about 40 percent that needed to be expanded by a broader message, Protect Marriage began to warn the public that "gay marriage was not simply 'live and let live'—that there would be consequences if gay marriage were to be permanently legalized." To do so required a reverse psychology of going negative with a "Yes" campaign. "As far as we know, this strategic approach has never before been used by a Yes campaign." If voters were convinced that they—and, more important, their children—would be adversely affected by the defeat of Prop 8, they likely would vote for self-protection rather than civil rights.

After probing "long and hard in countless focus groups and surveys to explore reactions to a variety of consequences our issue experts identified," Protect Marriage settled on three hot-button issues where legalization of same-sex marriage could be portrayed as having an adverse outcome for the straight population: religious freedom would be abridged, individual freedom of expression would be curtailed, and children would be indoctrinated with a gay-is-as-good-as-straight message. The greatest traction came from the save-the-children message. "We ran an ad featuring a young Hispanic girl coming home from school, explaining how she had learned in class that a prince could marry another prince, and she could marry a princess! This ad was based on the actual experience in Massachusetts, the only state in the nation where gay marriage had been legalized long enough to see how it would be handled by the public school system." Following that was the Wirthlin ad and subsequent bus tour.

But, as pointed out earlier, the most effective ad by Yes on 8 was the misappropriation of video footage from the private wedding ceremony of two lesbians, one of whom invited her students. There is no evidence that any of the parents of the children involved had any problem with their children attending the wedding ceremony, and attendance was voluntary. The Yes on 8 forces, as Schubert recalled, then twisted the private affair into what he mislabeled as "the most ill-considered publicity stunt ever mounted in an initiative campaign."

But advertising was only one part of the Yes on 8 campaign. "We set ambitious goals: to conduct a statewide Voter ID canvass of every voter; to distribute 1.25 million yard signs and an equal number of bumper strips; to have our volunteers re-contact every undecided, soft yes and soft no voter; and to have 100,000 volunteers, five per voting precinct, working on Election Day to make sure every identified Yes on 8 voter would vote. All of these goals, and more, were achieved." Indeed, it was the ground game that ulti-mately differentiated Yes on 8 from No on 8. William Eskridge, a legal scholar specializing in LGBT issues, noted, "The truth is that No on 8 ran the same kind of campaign that was traditional for supporting/opposing initiatives: heavy on advertising and slogans. . . . Yes on 8 ran a campaign much like a presidential campaign generally"[100]—that is, concentrating on the ground game of mobilizing voters by one-on-one contact.

And No on 8 had been asleep at the wheel. "In July, when the Mormon Church was beginning to build its organizing machine—signing up volun-teers, raising money, spreading the word—key members of the No on 8 lead-ership were literally absent. [Geoff] Kors [of Equality California and chair of the No on 8 executive committee] took a 2½-week vacation. [Lorri] Jean [chief executive of the Los Angeles Gay & Lesbian Center] went to Alaska for the month." No on 8 was slow to realize the significance of the LDS Church entry into the battle, "was slow to raise money, ran weak and confusing ads, and failed to put together a grass-roots operation to get out the vote. . . . The field operation consisted of volunteers phone-banking from 135 call centers across the state, an effort that didn't begin ramping up until mid-October. 'They had no ground game,' says a leading Democratic consultant. 'They thought they could win this thing by slapping some ads together. It was the height of naiveté.'"[101] And on Election Day, Yes on 8 had a nine-to-one advan-tage in volunteers working the precincts and getting out the vote, many, if not most of them, Mormons.

The most remarkable achievement of Yes on 8 was convincing minority voters—"the very groups who continue to struggle for their own basic rights"—to vote heavily in favor of Prop 8. "Blacks who cast an overwhelming 95 per-cent of their ballots for the man who would become the first black president in the nation's history, refused equality to their gay and lesbian children by a margin of 70–30. 'Blacks,' said ABC News Polling Director Gary Langer, 'can be said to have put it [Proposition 8] over the top. Hypothetically, had no blacks voted we compute a vote of 50–50.'"[102]

Most LGBT persons were stunned or angered at the outcome of the elec-tion, but a few saw a thin silver lining. One, who asked not to be identified, said, "In a sense, Proposition 8 was the LGBT community's Pearl Harbor. It awakened a sleeping giant." Rick Jacobs, founder of the Courage Campaign, was even more enthusiastic in invoking the law of unintended consequences. "The best thing that has happened to the modern LGBT movement is Prop

8. The very best thing. It was the most cathartic event since Stonewall, and people like myself were too young to remember Stonewall.... [Before Prop 8] people who got involved were people who could give money, but there wasn't a politicization of LGBT people until Prop 8."[103]

BACKLASH, 2.0

The backlash against Prop 8 was swift, intense, sustained, and, many felt, focused disproportionately on the LDS Church. One church official, who spoke on condition of anonymity, said, "I don't think anyone thought through the consequences. They really didn't anticipate the backlash, and they were not prepared for it. It hurt us, and it really hurt us with the young people."

If one takes Prop 22 as a benchmark, it becomes apparent how it was that the church was caught so off-guard by the reaction to Prop 8. Prop 22 had passed by a double-digit margin, and since it preserved the status quo in California, its passage had the feeling of "no harm, no foul." There simply was no significant backlash. Since the wording of Prop 8 was identical to Prop 22, what could go wrong?

Plenty, as it turned out. Society had changed significantly in eight years, and even though the majority of Americans still opposed same-sex marriage, the size of the majority was continually shrinking. In California it had essentially disappeared. More important from the worldview of the LGBT population was that a constitutional right that had been extended to them by the state supreme court had suddenly been revoked by popular vote, albeit not until thousands of same-sex couples had been legally married. Even the status of those marriages was made uncertain by the passage of Prop 8, for anti-same-sex marriage activists attempted, though unsuccessfully, to have them nullified in the aftermath of the election.

And there was one other difference this time: the Mormons, who had kept in the background in prior campaigns because of the public relations savvy of Gordon Hinckley, were now the public face of Prop 8. Troy Williams, who later became executive director of Equality Utah, said of the church leadership, "I think they were stunned at the negative backlash that they received from Prop 8. What they didn't realize is that America likes gay people more than it likes Mormons. And it knows gay people more than it knows Mormons." When the leaders began to realize the extent of the damage, they also began to appreciate that Prop 8 had been a bridge too far. Bruce Bastian, a former Mormon and the largest individual donor to No on 8, recalled, "I've sat down with church PR people, and I think it was generally accepted that it was a mistake.... It backfired on them much more than they had ever imagined. Their new membership drive went down—they started to get fewer new members than they had in the past. Their tithing rolls went down."[1]

DEMONSTRATIONS

Within hours after the results of the election were announced, people took to the streets to vent their anger at the outcome. The Courage Campaign's Rick Jacobs recalled, "They didn't know what to do. They didn't know where to go. There were marches down Sunset Boulevard, people just spontaneously marching.... They didn't know where they were going or why. I joined them at one point. There were no leaders. It was just a spontaneous anger. 'We want to march,' and they did. Thousands of people."[2]

The following day, many people found a focal point for their anger: the Mormon Church. A British newspaper reported, "More than 2,000 gay rights protesters marched on a Mormon temple in Los Angeles on Thursday, throwing the church and its followers on to the front line of the battle over California's decision to ban same-sex marriage.... For the Mormon Church, it threatens a PR nightmare." However, what might have been an unruly, even out-of-control, situation in Los Angeles and elsewhere turned out to be remarkably uneventful. One church member who supported same-sex marriage called the temple president to see what damages had been inflicted and whether he could help repair them. "He told me there had only been about $100 in damages and then spent a few minutes telling me that he felt that overall the protestors had been very well behaved and there had only been a very few people who were problems." One week later the temple was closed for a day when an envelope containing white powder, which police quickly determined was harmless, was delivered.[3]

Within a week after the election, similar peaceful protests occurred around Mormon temples in Salt Lake City, Oakland, and New York City. The largest, in Salt Lake City, drew between two and five thousand people who carried signs and marched around the perimeter of Temple Square. Troy Williams was one of the marchers. "We knew where the money came from, and we were embarrassed and shamed by it. Here there was this beautiful moment in history where the first African-American president was elected, and yet gay America was just struck in the gut. It was devastating, and we were angry. We circled the temple, they shut the gates, and we just marched around and around."[4]

BOYCOTTS

Less than a week after the election, the editor of americablog.com, which had nearly one million monthly readers, called for a boycott that would punish Mormons indirectly—although not the church—by targeting Utah attractions. "He is calling for skiers to choose any state but Utah and for Hollywood actors and directors to pull out of the Sundance Film Festival."[5]

The following day, J. Willard Marriott Jr., chief executive officer (CEO) of Marriott International, Inc., and an active and prominent Mormon, moved proactively to avoid any boycott of the corporation:

> Some might conclude given my family's membership in the Mormon Church that our company supported the recent ballot initiative to ban same sex marriage in California. This is simply untrue.... Neither I, nor the company, contributed to the campaign to pass Proposition 8....
>
> I am very careful about separating my personal faith and beliefs from how we run our business....
>
> We were among the first in our industry to offer domestic partner benefits, and we've earned a perfect 100% score on the Human Rights Campaign's Corporate Equality Index for two years in a row.[6]

Gay activist Fred Karger waited three months to launch a boycott of Garff Automotive Group, headquartered in Salt Lake City. He did so upon learning that Katharine Garff, wife of the company's CEO, had made a personal contribution of $100,000 to the Yes on 8 campaign.[7] The boycott was short-lived and ill targeted. John Garff, Katharine's son, "said the company has gay and lesbian employees, has a zero tolerance policy for harassment and discrimination in the workplace and offers a benefits package that is favorable to those in same-sex partnerships. In Utah, the automotive group is also a longtime contributor to the Human Rights Campaign, a gay rights advocacy and education organization."[8]

The primary function of the demonstrations and boycotts was to vent short-term angst, and although many were alarmed that significant damage to body and property might ensue, the total disruption proved to be minor. A 2009 report from the office of the California attorney general documenting hate crimes during 2008 gave useful context. Of a total of some 1,400 such crimes within the state, 304 were anti-LGBT, 184 anti-Jewish, and only 75 anti-Mormon.[9]

EFFECT ON CHURCH MEMBERS

More problematic in magnitude and duration was the effect of Prop 8 on church members. For some, the challenge began even before the election, as people began to realize the extent of church involvement. Three weeks after the First Presidency letter was read publicly, LDS author Carol Lynn Pearson spoke with a friend who was "very, very upset at what the church is doing around this amendment business." The friend said her gay son had had his name removed from church records eight years earlier. Two gay nephews had committed suicide. "She told me she went in to see [her bishop] and told him how deeply upset she is, that she will not be able to support the effort of the ward around this, that she will not be able to pay tithing until after November if she thinks any of her money is going to this effort."[10]

For others, it took time for the full ramifications of Prop 8 to sink in. Emily Rampton was a student at San Diego State University during the campaign. "In 2008, when we heard the letter read in church, I was a little taken aback, but after listening to my family talk about it—and we had already gone through Prop 22—I took it very seriously that we needed to get involved and help with this. Basically, I was thinking that it was a revelation. 'It's important to God, so it's important to me.'"[11] So she jumped in, participating in phone banks, going on bike rides with signs on her body, and standing on street corners while holding signs in support of Prop 8.

We were really proud of ourselves. We stood there and tried to be civil and logical, and we believed our sources were good.... It's hard for me to go back to that time, because I feel so different about it now, but I really think that at the time I felt that this was God wanted, and that the world's way was different than God's way. I believed we didn't understand the calamity that would happen if gay marriage became legal, and we needed to fight against it. I remember being told, at the Institute of Religion, that this was a separation of the wheat and the tares, and being proud of myself that I was on the right side, and that members of the church who were not a part of Prop 8's efforts were somehow fooled by Satan and were not doing the right things, and were not on the right side.

Emily's attitude began to change two years later. "A friend messaged me something, and I don't even remember now exactly what it was. It was something like, 'Brigham Young said this. Did you know that?' I was about to go online and research and say, 'No, that's just not true. That's the anti-Mormon.' So I went online and learned that it was true, and that really bothered me. So then I just went down the rabbit hole, learning the history of my own church." After spending time reading of history, she turned her attention to gay Mormons. "I learned that in previous times in our church we thought that even just being gay was terrible. That was a change, and I thought if they could change in the past, they could change in the future. Then I had this moment when I realized, 'Oh, my gosh! I was so wrong!' Then, I started getting angry."

A different kind of "buyer's remorse" affected those with family members who were gay. Wendy Montgomery, who later cofounded Mama Dragons, a group of LDS mothers in support of their gay children, was initially a supporter of Prop 8. "The news had pictures of picketing the temple and people crying, and I remember having a moment where I thought, 'Why are they so upset? Don't they know that this is wrong? Don't they know that they can't have marriage? Marriage is for us. Marriage is for straight people.'"[12] But unbeknownst to her at the time, Wendy's preteenage son had been wrestling with his identity while his parents were carrying Yes on 8 signs. She later reflected,

I've done a lot of stupid things in my life, but if I could have just one do-over, it would be for that. I have such shame and regret over that, and the pain that I caused my son. He was nine, turning ten through all of this with Prop 8. He didn't know he was gay at that point. . . . When he realized he was gay, he remembered Prop 8. He remembered the sign we had in our yard. It was talked about so much in church. They passed out yard signs and bumper stickers in Gospel Doctrine class. You signed up for your route if you went walking. Some of the most atrocious things I have ever heard about gay people were in that time period. I sat there silently; I don't think I ever said anything negative about gay people, but I didn't defend them.[13]

In addition to hurting individuals, Prop 8 divided LDS families. Brandie Balken, who later became executive director of Equality Utah, said, "Right after that election we had Thanksgiving and Christmas, and I can't tell you how many friends I had that didn't want to go home, that didn't go home, that didn't invite their families to their homes because there was really no room at all for conversation. It seemed like so many of our doors had just been completely shut. There was no wiggle room; there was no opportunity for dialogue; there was no opportunity for any kind of commonality post-Prop 8."[14]

Michael Chipman described the disaster within his own family. "When Prop 8 happened, it was the worst fight I have ever had with my parents—screaming, swearing. I never swore at my parents until that day. It was bad and violent. . . . I said to my dad, 'So do you support me or do you support the Church on this?' He said, 'Well, if it comes down to it, I have to support the Church.' I said, 'Fine. Then you have a church, and you've lost your son.'"[15]

While Chipman had previously left the nest, other LGBT Mormons found that when their parents chose to support the church, they simultaneously decided to expel their adolescent children from home. Stephanie Pappas, a director of Equality Utah, said, "It was so sad, because families were literally being torn apart. Parents were torn between loving their children and loving their church. . . . We knew of young adults who were banished from their households. People were in such turmoil about 'How do I adhere to what the Church is saying?' . . . So there was a rash of homeless youth that were coming out of homes."[16]

For many, the pain was so intense that their response was to resign their membership. One high-profile resignation came from Matthew Lawrence, the gay son of the church's grassroots director for Prop 8, Gary Lawrence. Matthew said, "I love my family so much, but it's hard to not take this personally. We had a brief falling-out over Prop 22, but that got mended. But two anti-gay initiatives in eight years, it's impossible not to feel attacked." A point of no return was when his father had said publicly that "opponents of Prop 8 are akin to Lucifer's followers in the pre-existence."[17]

The LDS Church does not release information about resigned memberships, and so it is not possible to know the magnitude of hemorrhage in the aftermath of Prop 8. However, reports from two sources suggest that it was significant. Nikki Boyer, a lesbian activist and former Mormon residing in Salt Lake City, said, "I know of literally hundreds of people who had their names removed." Wendy Montgomery, who resided in California at the time of Prop 8, put the number of personal acquaintances who resigned their memberships at three to four hundred—"either I have met them through Facebook or they are in our community."[18]

LOST JOBS

A small number of people who suffered in the aftermath of Prop 8 were neither LGBT nor opponents of the initiative. Instead, they were devout LDS Church members whose well-intentioned financial contributions to Yes on 8 resulted in lost jobs, albeit by voluntary resignation rather than dismissal.

Marjorie Christofferson was a floor manager at El Coyote Café in Los Angeles and daughter of the restaurant's owner. Many of El Coyote's employees and clientele were LGBT, and when they learned that she had contributed $100 to support Prop 8, they were furious. "Hundreds of protesters converged on El Coyote on Beverly Boulevard on Wednesday night, and the picketing got so heated that LAPD officers in riot gear had to be called."[19] In spite of the restaurant manager's offer to make two $5,000 contributions, one to the Los Angeles Gay & Lesbian Center and the other to the Lambda Legal Defense fund,[20] protests continued. A month after the election, Christofferson resigned.[21]

Scott Eckern was the artistic director of the California Musical Theater in Sacramento, the state's largest nonprofit musical theater company. When gay and lesbian artists learned from public campaign records that he had contributed $1,000 to support Prop 8, they threatened a boycott of the theater. Jeffrey Seller, a producer of *Avenue Q*, which was scheduled to be part of the theater's 2008–9 season, said, "That a man who makes his living exclusively through the musical theater could do something so hurtful to the community that forms his livelihood is a punch in the stomach."[22] A week after the election, Eckern resigned, saying, "I am leaving California Musical Theater after prayerful consideration to protect the organization and to help the healing in the local theater-going and creative community."[23]

Richard Raddon was director of the Los Angeles Film Festival. A week after the Prop 8 election, his contribution of $1,500 in favor of the measure became public knowledge. Despite a unanimous vote of confidence from the festival's board, which included Don Cheadle, Forest Whitaker, Lionsgate president Tom Ortenberg, and Fox Searchlight president Peter Rice, Raddon resigned his position.

COMING TO THE CHURCH'S DEFENSE

Jeff Flint, who with Frank Schubert directed the Yes on 8 advertising campaign, called out those who were critical of the LDS Church in the aftermath of the election. "I am appalled at the level of Mormon-bashing that went on during the Proposition 8 campaign and continues to this day. If this activity were directed against any other church, if someone put up a website that targeted Jews or Catholics in a similar fashion for the mere act of participating in a political campaign, it would be widely and rightfully condemned."[24]

Also quick to defend the LDS Church was its principal partner in the Yes on 8 campaign, the Roman Catholic Church. Three days after the election, Bishop William Weigand, head of the Diocese of Sacramento, issued a formal statement:

> Catholics stand in solidarity with our Mormon brothers and sisters in support of traditional marriage.... The ProtectMarriage coalition, which led the successful campaign to pass Proposition 8, was an historic alliance of people from every faith and ethnicity. LDS were included—but so were Catholics and Jews, Evangelicals and Orthodox, African-Americans and Latinos, Asians and Anglos. Bigoted attacks on Mormons for the part they played in our coalition are shameful and ignore the reality that Mormon voters were only a small part of the groundswell that supported Proposition 8.

I personally decry the bigotry recently exhibited towards the members of the Church of Jesus Christ of Latter-day Saints.[25]

Also on board were prominent evangelical Christians who had been part of the Yes on 8 coalition. More than four thousand people, including Charles Colson of Prison Fellowship, James Dobson of Focus on the Family, Tony Perkins of the Family Research Council, and Richard Land of the Southern Baptist Convention, signed an online petition thanking the LDS Church for its support of Prop 8.[26] And a full-page advertisement in the *New York Times*, sponsored by the Becket Fund for Religious Liberty, decried the "'violence and intimidation' directed toward the [Mormon] Church because of its support of Proposition 8."[27]

An unlikely group intent on preserving religious liberty also stepped forward to defend the LDS Church. Three days after the election, the American Civil Liberties Union issued the following statement:

> As an organization long dedicated to protecting and promoting religious liberties and equal rights, even when those rights appear to be in tension with one another, the ACLU of Utah asserts that it is misleading and inaccurate to claim that recognition of same-sex marriage by the state of California in some way infringes on the religious liberty of the LDS Church or any other religious institution.
>
> State recognition of same-sex marriage in no way requires a church or religious institution to recognize or even perform such ceremonies. Legalizing same-sex marriage in California never would require the LDS Church to perform same-sex marriages in its temples against its religious principles—just as Catholic priests never have been required to marry persons who are divorced and Orthodox rabbis have never been compelled to perform interfaith marriages. The ACLU would be the first to defend a religious institution from being forced by the government to perform a marriage ceremony in violation of its religious tenets.[28]

PUBLIC OPINION

As an organization that from its founding nearly two centuries ago has relied heavily upon converts for growth, the LDS Church is particularly sensitive to negative public opinion because of its dampening effect on the church's proselytizing program. As people began to process what had happened with Prop 8, the church's image soured. Jan Shipps, a Methodist scholar of Mormonism with a decades-long friendship with and admiration for Mormons, told the *Los Angeles Times*, "The backlash is going on all over the country. There are people who had a lot of respect for the Mormons who now say, 'Well, they're just like the Christian right.'"

The Christian Right had long been homophobic, and despite long-standing efforts by LDS Church leaders to distance themselves from charges of homophobia by insisting that they were only against same-sex marriage but were fine with other LGBT issues, the public thought differently. Clifford Rosky, a professor of law specializing in LGBT issues, spoke of the transition in public thinking that began with Prop 8. "You used to be able to be pro–gay rights but not pro–gay marriage. There was a space for a period of time. Bill Clinton was such a person. But that space evaporated, and they began to see that evaporate in 2008."[29]

Within the LGBT world of 2008, churches that refused to support same-sex marriage for their own congregants—and they constituted the vast majority of American faith traditions—were tolerated. But there were limits to the tolerance, and writer and LGBT activist Andrew Solomon described the line that the LDS Church crossed with Prop 8:

When the Mormon Church moved beyond not wishing to support the acceptance of gay people within the Mormon Church, and it became a matter of the Mormon Church trying to prevent anyone else from accepting gay unions, as happened most visibly in Proposition 8, it was very hard for me after that not to think of the Mormon Church as an evil organization without which the world, as I see it, would be better off. It was hard for me not to feel a real suspicion of anything that was attached in any way to Mormonism, because I thought that to insistently and so aggressively pursue those policies when there are people who are starving, there are people who are dying of AIDS, there are people who have no education, there are people who have no drinking water—I thought, "All of those resources? Really? So that people like John [Andrew's husband] and me can't have the kind of life that we have? Is that really the priority of a church?" I read the Old and New Testaments many times. I know there are those various lines that sort of get called in, but essentially I feel like the message is of love and mercy and turn the other cheek. All of that seems to be so central. I just thought how does that engage with financing Proposition 8 in California, to take away marriage rights where they have already been established? What is the harm that these people who are getting married are doing?[30]

A poll taken in 2008 by Gary Lawrence—the person who headed the Yes on 8 grassroots effort for the LDS Church—"found that for every American who expresses a strong liking for Mormons, four express a strong dislike. Among the traits widely ascribed to Mormons in the poll were 'narrow-minded' and 'controlling.'"[31] As public opinion turned increasingly negative, proselytizing suffered. Fred Sainz, vice president of communications for the Human Rights Campaign, later said, "Because the model of the LDS Church is different than an evangelical church or the Catholic Church—they have these missionaries and they are looking to grow their church—their brand was immediately going to take a hit. . . . I have heard anecdotally from church leadership that they started seeing its effect virtually immediately in the doors that were being slammed in the face of their missionaries—not just in the United States, but around the world." Kate Kendell, a former Mormon who genuinely mourned the sinking image of the church, explained, "The Mormon Church became synonymous with haters and anti-gay. It was something that the Church never, never should have done. The Church is not equipped, genetically, to be in that role. It is so contrary. It was hard for me to travel around and have people castigate the Mormon Church and lump them in as haters with everybody else. It was just so contrary to everything I ever knew, and it was contrary to what I believe the Church really stood for and really was."[32]

WE ARE THE VICTIMS

In response to the backlash, proponents of Prop 8, including the LDS Church, began to portray themselves as victims, an ironic and yet politically savvy strategy considering their victory in the election. Michael Otterson, a church spokesman, said, "It's very clear that we've been singled out."[33] Joe Solmonese, president of the Human Rights Campaign, recalled the irony. "Right after Prop 8 we did the 'Dr. Phil Show,' and we were on TV a lot. I felt like, 'Every single time I come up against these people, they are the victims.' I would have done the same thing if I were them. It was a pretty smart narrative to be running." Bruce Bastian's reaction was less sanguine. "When did the LDS Church become the victim? Is this the same church that conducted a national broadcast to Mormon chapels calling on members to organize and write checks to the Prop 8 campaign? The same church that donated more than half of the $40 million behind Prop 8, even though California Mormons represent just two percent of the state's population?"[34]

While there were incidents of intimidation and minor property damage to Mormons and their places of worship, most of the backlash against the church came in the form of verbal condemnation and threats of boycotts—activities that the *Deseret News* acknowledged to be "protected free speech." Rick Jacobs, director of the Courage Campaign, tried to achieve balance in commenting on the backlash. "The LDS Church or any other organization has every right to use its power to influence elections to any extent that is legal. What it doesn't have a right to do is claim persecution when other organizations do nothing but expose the church's forays into the political arena before a discerning public."[35]

The most overreaching claim of victimization came from Apostle Dallin Oaks. Speaking at BYU-Idaho several months after the election, he made a comparison that many found both inaccurate and offensive: "The anti-Mormon backlash after California voters overturned gay marriage last fall is similar to the intimidation of Southern blacks during the civil rights movement." Marc Solomon, of Equality California, responded vehemently, "Blacks were lynched and beaten and denied the right to vote by their government. To compare that to criticism of Mormon leaders for encouraging people to give vast amounts of money to take away rights of a small minority group is illogical and deeply offensive."[36]

PIVOT POINT

For all of the acrimony generated by Prop 8, its passage turned out to be a historic pivot point in three ways, with all three being examples of the Law of Unintended Consequences.

First, it was a wake-up call. At a postelection rally in Salt Lake City the week after the election, one activist "told the crowd she was grateful that the Church of Jesus Christ of Latter-day Saints had 'wakened our sleeping giant. We finally have a civil rights movement equal to that of the '50s and '60s.'"[37] A similar sentiment was voiced the following month at a rally in San Francisco: "Thank you, Mormon Church. You have done something we could never do. You have mobilized the greatest civil rights movement in the last forty years!"[38] The mobilization was broad based, as recounted by Rick Jacobs. "It not only galvanized a lot of people who didn't really care about it before that—gay people—but it also galvanized straight people. People said, 'Wait a minute, we don't like voting on people's rights.'"[39] Straight people began to look at their LGBT family members and neighbors in a different light. Brandie Balken said, "It took us some time to mourn and tend to our wounds, and then we began the process of looking at each other as community members, as family members, and beginning to figure out how we can build a future together."[40]

The awakening was not a passing fad. In the two months following the election, online membership in the Courage Campaign skyrocketed from 125,000 to 350,000 because of Prop 8.[41] In Utah the LGBT rights movement mushroomed. An Associated Press report six months after the election stated, "More people—of all sexual orientations—are turning out for community organizing meetings, want training as citizen lobbyists and showing up for events like the post-Prop. 8 election protest march around the Salt Lake City Mormon temple that drew an estimated 3,000."[42]

Nationally, the dominoes of marriage equality began to fall in a different direction. A report in late May 2009 described the changing national climate: "Since the passage of Proposition 8, gay marriage has gained momentum around the nation. Iowa, Maine and Vermont have joined Massachusetts and Connecticut in recognizing same-sex couples. Similar proposals are under way in New Hampshire and New York."[43]

The second pivot was a changed relationship between the LDS Church and the LGBT community. Where communication links had never previously been forged, in spite of multiple efforts, a durable and productive dialogue began in the aftermath of Prop 8. Brandie Balken said, "I profoundly believe that Prop 8 did more to open the dialogue between LDS and LGBT people than anyone could ever imagine. While it is seen by many as a great mistake, or one of the greatest tragedies, I think it truly has been an incredible tool for building understanding and building conversation." The Salt Lake City LGBT community, in an ironic acknowledgment of a new order, bestowed on church president Thomas Monson its Person of the Year Award, noting, "When new Church of Jesus Christ of Latter-day Saints President Thomas S. Monson signed the now-infamous letter urging California Mormons to 'do all you can' to support efforts to pass Proposition 8, he could not have anticipated the effect that signature would ultimately have.... As strange as it may seem, we at *Q Salt Lake* believe that Monson and the Mormon Church are somewhat responsible for this resurgence in U.S. gay rights activism now known as 'Stonewall 2.0.'"[44]

The third, and most subtle, unintended consequence of Prop 8 was to initiate national appreciation of the crucial role that organized religion played in the debate and the necessity of engaging religious leaders in the future. Sharon Groves, who later directed religious outreach for the Human Rights Campaign—a department that had not existed prior to Prop 8—said, "When our side looked at the result of that, one of the first things they did was to recognize that part of why we lost was because we had such an intractable, religion-is-the-enemy response. When we worked at all with clergy, which was the most progressive clergy in the country, they were just backdrop, what we called 'rent-a-collar.' You kind of Photoshop them, but no engagement. So there was a whole rethinking about, 'We can't do this if we are not actually engaging religious leaders.'"[45]

THE KISS

At the time of Prop 8, two openly gay people, Jackie Biskupski in the Utah House of Representatives and Scott McCoy in the Senate, served in the state legislature—the highest number ever. Although they were able to introduce gay-friendly legislation prior to 2008, including a bill to outlaw discrimination in employment and housing, it never got out of committee. But the aftermath of Prop 8 brought a glimmer of hope.

The day after the election, already stung by negative public opinion, church leaders tried to blunt charges of homophobia by restating from their August press release, "The Divine Institution of Marriage," that they did "not object to rights for same-sex couples regarding hospitalization and medical care, fair housing and employment rights, or probate rights, so long as these do not infringe on the integrity of the traditional family or the constitutional rights of churches." Mike Thompson, executive director of Equality Utah, and Cliff Rosky, the organization's legal counsel, were essentially licking their wounds from Prop 8 when they heard the church's statement. Rosky recalled, "When I saw that, I thought, 'Wow, this is a huge opportunity!' I called up Equality Utah and said, 'We have to use this statement.'" Stephanie Pappas, board chair of Equality, quickly convened a task force. "We basically went through the Church's position *verbatim*, 'We don't oppose this, we don't oppose that,' so then we said, 'OK, if you don't oppose it, let's twist it and say, Would you support, would you support, would you support?'"[1]

Five days after the church's announcement, Equality Utah held a press conference. State senator Scott McCoy said, "I take LDS church leaders at their word that they are not anti-gay and that they sincerely understand that gay and transgender individuals and their families are in need of certain legal protections and basic benefits.... I am hopeful that the LDS church will accept our invitation to heal our communities by bringing its considerable social and political influence to bear in support of laws that prevent discrimination." Will Carlson, manager of public policy for Equality, then announced five bills that they intended to introduce at the legislative session that would begin two months thereafter. Three came directly from the church statement: hospitalization and medical care, fair housing and employment rights, and probate rights. The fourth addressed domestic-partner rights, and the fifth called for the repeal of the second part of Amendment 3, the anti-gay-marriage amendment to the Utah Constitution that had been passed four years previously: "No other domestic union, however denominated, may be recognized as marriage or be given the same or substantially the same legal effect."[2] Together, the bills were known as the Common Ground Initiative.

In addition to publicizing their bills, officials from Equality contacted William Evans, the official within LDS Public Affairs who dealt with LGBT issues, asking for a church endorsement—that it "supports" rather than "does not object." Evans, who would have required consent from his ecclesiastical superiors, did not respond. Annoyed at the silence, Equality posted a counter on its website, which Brandie Balken, who later headed the organization, described. "[It said] 'We have reached out to the LDS Church about these basic protections that you said you supported, and it has been 49 days and there has been no response.' Then 50 days. Then 51 days."[3] More silence. After more than a hundred days, the counter was taken down. Still silence. One church official, who spoke on condition of anonymity, said, "It wasn't deliberate, really.... The [ecclesiastical leaders] were so traumatized by that post-Prop 8 experience that they just didn't want to deal with it."

The legislative session, which begins each year on the fourth Monday of January, opened with all five bills being introduced—and still with no response, positive, negative, or neutral, from the church. One, a "wrongful death amendment," considered to be the least controversial of the five, died in the Utah Senate Judiciary Committee the following day.[4] Three of the remaining four also died in committee. The other, which would have clarified Amendment 3, had been pulled by its sponsor, Representative Jackie Biskupski, early in the session in a fruitless attempt to give the other Common Ground bills a better chance of passing.[5]

The primary obstacle facing Equality Utah was the intransigence of powerful, vocal legislators who viewed the bills as a nose under the tent that would inevitably lead to the legalization of same-sex marriage if they were enacted into law in Utah. Representative LaVar Christensen, the sponsor of Amendment 3 four years earlier, spoke for many in saying, "Utah should not now adopt the package of same-sex marriage predecessors that have been imported from California and elsewhere. They are not harmless, spontaneous proposed innovations stemming from isolated injustices witnessed in Utah. No, they are pulled directly from a national same-sex partner advocacy agenda that Utah does not need and does not support." With characteristically brutal rhetoric, Christensen's senate colleague Chris Buttars said, "[LGBT persons] are the meanest buggers I've ever seen. They's [sic] just like the Moslems.... I believe that, internally, they are the greatest threat to America going down that I know of."[6]

Viewed in context, the failure of the Common Ground bills was not surprising. The large majority of all proposed bills die in committee, and those dealing with LGBT issues, particularly in 2008, faced an even more daunting challenge, for no red-state Republican legislature had ever passed a sexual orientation nondiscrimination law.

Although the bills failed, Common Ground achieved some traction. Cliff Rosky noted, "It was revolutionary, because instead of playing defense at the legislature, we played offense.... When people are saying, 'The Church is opposed to discrimination. Let's ban discrimination'—if they are going to say no to that, it's much harder to say yes to something that is affirmatively anti-gay." Indeed, legislators opposed to LGBT rights were now put on the defensive. "We noticed that in hearings, increasingly people would have to start off by saying, 'Before I explain why I oppose this bill, I need you to understand that I am opposed to discrimination. I don't discriminate, and some of my best friends are gay.' I thought, 'Well, this is progress.'"[7]

Even outside Utah, Common Ground began to change the conversation. Stephanie Pappas said, "The *New York Times* picked us up, the *Washington Post*—we were getting so much national press.... It set the tone nationally, and people were starting to use Common Ground as a common phrase throughout the nation."[8] But the one thing that it did not accomplish was to secure a dialogue between LGBT leaders and church officials.

THE KISS

In 2003 Salt Lake City and the LDS Church negotiated a controversial land swap that gave the church ownership of one block of Main Street that connected Temple Square with the city block containing the Church Administration Building, Church Office Building, Relief Society Building, and Joseph Smith Memorial Building. Deeda Seed, then a member of the Salt Lake City Council and not a member of the LDS Church, spoke of the concerns of people in the community that what had been a public thoroughfare would now be controlled by a church—concerns serious enough to elicit a lawsuit by the American Civil Liberties Union. "I was strongly advocating for it to be open in the way that parks are open. We were concerned that it really would become very privatized, and that they would have sort of enforcers out there chastising people for things."[9] Seed's concerns turned out to be legitimate.

After an outdoor concert on an early July evening in 2009, months after the Prop 8 election, Derek Jones and Matt Aune walked home hand in hand. Their route passed through Main Street Plaza, the one-block park that had once been part of Main Street. As they strolled through the park, a display of public affection between the two men occurred. Accounts of the display differed substantially. Aune said he gave Jones a peck on the cheek; church employees said their behavior crossed a line of impropriety. Almost immediately, several security guards employed by the church approached the two men, handcuffed both, wrestled Jones to the ground, and called the Salt Lake City Police Department. When the police officers arrived, they issued misdemeanor citations to the two men for allegedly trespassing.[10]

What became known simply as "the kiss" happened on a Thursday evening. The next morning, Seed read a report of the incident in the *Salt Lake Tribune*. "For me, it triggered everything. It was like, 'I cannot believe that this has happened. This is a violation of what I thought this easement and the Main Street Plaza was about.'... I was just horrified that this had happened, on multiple levels." Trained as a community organizer, she utilized Facebook—a relative newcomer to organizers—to get the word out that there would be a "kiss-in" on Sunday, just two days later. She invited "all people to bring their loved ones—husbands, wives, boyfriends, girlfriends, kids and even pets—to the downtown plaza between 9 a.m. and 10 a.m. and show their love with a smooch."[11] She didn't know how many people would show up or how she would identify sympathizers. "I made my older son cut little hearts out of pink construction paper. We handed them out, and what we were trying to say, symbolically, was that it's OK to love who you love and to show public affection, and we've just all got to get over this."[12]

Her hope was that the kiss-in would "lead to a meeting between church officials and leaders concerned about the incident."[13] Church officials went on the defensive, releasing a statement that "the incident had nothing to do with the couple being gay, but with crossing the line of public affection."[14]

According to a newspaper report, more than one hundred people showed up for the kiss-in. "Wearing bright red lipstick, Isabelle Warnas smiled and planted a big kiss on her husband's cheek, something she said she has done often under the spires of the LDS Church's Salt Lake Temple. 'Nobody has said a thing to us,' the 50-year-old Salt Lake City resident said. This time, though, they had an audience."[15]

Two series of events were spawned by the kiss-in. The first, played out in public, included a second kiss-in in Salt Lake City, organized by others, along with similar events in other cities, and national attention that reached a crescendo with a reenactment on *The Colbert Report*. Still playing defense after the first kiss-in, church officials alleged that Jones and Aune had been guilty of far more than a peck on the cheek. "They engaged in passionate kissing, groping, profane and lewd language and had obviously been using alcohol."[16]

The second kiss-in, staged on July 19, attracted more than two hundred protesters. It also attracted counterprotesters from a group called America Forever, and the two groups spent "about 20 minutes" shouting at each other.[17]

The public phase ended with a whimper. Videotape from security cameras at Main Street Plaza "lacked audio and did not show the now-famous kiss."[18] Citing "significant evidentiary issues," the Salt Lake City Prosecutor's Office dropped the charges against the two men.[19]

The second series of events was more prolonged and far more consequential. Initially played out under a mutual agreement of secrecy, its profile gradually emerged into the public arena. After the first kiss-in, Deeda Seed spoke with Jim Dabakis, who attended the event. "I said to Jim, 'If there is some way that we can all get together and talk, would you do it?' He said, 'Yes, but we've tried in the past and had absolutely no success, but sure.'"[20]

Seed turned to Carlton Christensen, a member of the Salt Lake City Council with whom she had worked when she was on the council. Although they came from different political perspectives, they had a mutually trusting relationship. "I was really honest with him when I called him. 'I'm beside myself with angst over what's happened in my community. This is just so wrong.' He listened to me and he explained a little bit of the perspective the church had. Then I said, 'Do you think there's a way that we could get people together to talk? Would that be possible?'" Without promising results, Christensen started making some phone calls. Seed thought a meeting with church Public Affairs personnel was unlikely, because "from the time I was on the city council—they would never say it this way, but I was their biggest pain in the ass." To her surprise, Christensen succeeded in arranging the meeting. "Carlton told me later that it was kind of a test case for them to see if I was serious, if asking for these conversations was a sincere expression of goodwill. I think they got that."

THE MEETINGS

As Jim Dabakis had told Deeda Seed at the first kiss-in, for years LGBT leaders in Utah had attempted to engage church leaders in dialogue but had been rebuffed consistently. No one had been more active in the attempt than Dabakis, an openly gay businessman and talk-show host who had converted to Mormonism as a child and served a full-time proselytizing mission for the church. In the mid-1990s, Dabakis was one of the founders, and chairman, of the first LGBT community center in Salt Lake City. In that capacity, he sent a letter to the president of the LDS Church. "'Look, we are all here in the same town. There ought to be areas that we can get together on.'. . . Within a few days a letter came back, signed by a guy I never heard of, a functionary named Bill Evans, who wrote back and said, 'President Hinckley has said this about so-called gays.' It wasn't a very complimentary thing. 'There is no reason to meet.' And that was it. That was our first brush with the Church."[21]

Several years later, then in the capacity of chairman of Equality Utah, Dabakis tried again. "I pulled out my pen, and I wrote a letter to the President of the Church: 'We're all under the same sun. There ought to be a way we can communicate.' Well, the answer came back as basically the same letter." Silence remained the status quo for several more years. "There was no discussion between the Church and the LGBT community. There was no talk. There was no channel, none, either internally, for LDS-LGBT people, or with the broader community. Nobody knew what went on or how it went on.... There was absolutely no dialogue. None."

The first kiss-in changed the equilibrium. In the meeting with Seed following the kiss-in, Bill Evans told Seed, "We want to do this." She then called Dabakis. "They want to do it. Do you have some leaders from the LGBT community that would be willing to participate? I think the way that we should think about this is that these are going to be baby steps, open conversation, just a chance to get to know each other and hear each other's perspectives."[22]

Dabakis proceeded to get buy-in from Brandie Balken, who had just become executive director of Equality Utah; Stephanie Pappas, chair of Equality; Valerie Larabee, executive director of the Utah Pride Center; and Jon Jepson, Salt Lake City Human Rights Commission member and a director of the Pride Center. The next step was to find a place to meet. Dabakis recalled his phone conversation with Bill Evans:

> I said, "Where do you want to meet?" He said, "Why don't you come down to the Joseph Smith Building?" I said, "Why don't you come down to the Pride Center coffee shop?" It was a joke, but there was no laughter from him. So I said, "Oh, that would be wrong on two grounds, wouldn't it?" Silence. So I said, "Look, I have an idea. Let's go to the home of my friends, Sam and Diane Stewart. They are as Mormon, tithe-paying people as you could ever want, and they've got a beautiful house that is in the Avenues. We'll go there and we'll talk. It's neutral territory." So Bill said, "OK." Then I said, "When do you want to meet? And by the way, I can't go to this alone. I'm out of these loops now. There are much smarter people than I am. I'm happy to go, but we need a group." He said, "OK. That's fine."[23]

The five LGBT leaders—who eventually came to be known as the "Gang of Five"—were joined by three men from LDS Public Affairs: Bill Evans, Michael Purdy, and John Taylor. Deeda Seed and Carlton Christensen also attended.[24] Prior to the meeting, none of the LGBT leaders had even met any of the men from the Public Affairs office. The meeting focused on two things. The first was simply getting to know each other. "Where are you

from? What is it exactly that you do? How did you get to this point in serving the community?" More substantive was the second component: "What
do you see happening in our community right now?" Balken recalled how
that conversation shifted to a different depth:

> There was almost complete agreement around the profound con-
> cern about how hurt our people were at that time. It wasn't just hap-
> pening to one side or the other. People were really wounded, and
> people were really struggling to relate to each other in a way that
> was safe. There was no parameter for conversation. It seemed like
> any time LDS and LGBT had any interface, it was just adding to the
> fire. It was more and more "othering" each other, which is a pro-
> found tragedy when we are sharing families, and we are sharing
> neighborhoods, and our kids go to the same schools, and we are
> working in the same office buildings. The tension and the wound-
> ing had gotten really significant. . . . We all had an equal investment
> in doing anything that we could to take care of our people, to lessen
> some of the wounding that was really all around us.
>
> There was also a discussion about how the national focus on
> the State of Utah wasn't really helping things. Nationally, people
> love the story of conflict between LDS and LGBT. They are hungry
> for it. What people don't want to hear is that Mormons are good
> parents who love their kids, who are working to understand this
> much like Catholics are, much like Evangelicals are. People want
> to paint Mormons as an extraordinarily difficult, secretive and hos-
> tile community. I don't think that's fair, and I don't think it's true.[25]

Interspersed among the public narrative were the personal stories
of the participants, stories that changed perceptions. "There had been
no personal face. They were just talking to themselves, reinforcing their
own ideas, and they had never really sat down before and listened to real
LGBT people tell their stories and tell their connection to the Church. It
affected them."[26]

The meeting lasted more than twice as long as scheduled. At the end,
the LGBT leaders asked if there was to be another meeting. Evans said yes.
When? A month? Two months? "No, we want to meet next week." And they did.

Prior to that meeting, the second kiss-in occurred. Evans, who had not attended the first one, called Dabakis and suggested that they attend. Both men got a taste of increasing animosity. "I'm standing there in my suit and Bill is standing next to me and we were talking, still somewhat awkwardly, and a car started going by. The passengers were screaming at us with profanities. They were assuming that I was part of the church group because I was standing there with a tie and a white shirt and it was Sunday. I started looking over at Bill, and they were screaming names at us."[27]

As the meetings continued, Balken noted, "It became an open and really pretty friendly space. It wasn't public. There was an unspoken agreement that we weren't going to go out and talk about what was happening there. It was just for us to explore, and if there were opportunities, then we could pursue them as community members with unique positions to better our community and to help out our people."[28]

Something else happened as a result of the meetings. Evans, who had been assigned to assist ecclesiastical officers during the Prop 8 battle, began to engage in conversations within the community. Balken said, "He started coming to a series of home visits with LGBT people, where he would go to people's homes and sit and talk with them as couples.... Bill has a much higher level of literacy than most people do around LGBT issues, because of the immense number of conversations he has been engaged in on these issues."[29]

Dabakis, in particular, saw the meetings as an opportunity to educate his counterparts.

In my opinion, they were clearly locked into the 1950s in their approach to homosexuality. The cadre of people that were whispering into the ear of senior church leaders were brought up, and their best academic research was from the 1960s and 1970s, and it simply had not changed. It was a time warp of misinformation—or at least, not up-to-date information. So you ended up with a church that was making a 1950s and 60s political statement externally, and internally you ended up with Social Services and Correlation and Curriculum and General Conference speeches that were devoid of the very latest in academic research and in anything that had to do with relevant data from the last 40 years. Subsequently, you ended up with a church that was completely out of touch, certainly with dealing with their own people.[30]

Dabakis began to bring LGBT leaders to the Public Affairs offices. "We were talking. There were serious discussions. And the Church was coming out, I think, with a new perspective and a new view.... We continued the discussions until, for some reason, the Church said, 'No more meetings. We can't meet anymore.'" Although the church officials gave no explanation, it had been clear to the LGBT leaders, since the first meeting, that they were operating under tight constraints from their ecclesiastical superiors. Stephanie Pappas recalled, "There was a way that they couldn't talk. Depending on how the individual man may have been feeling himself, he couldn't completely talk about that because he still was representing the Church.... I don't think there was ever a time when they weren't feeling as though they had to represent. But I do think those early conversations were part of what really helped get us where we are today."[31]

There was no question that the relationship between the kiss-in and the meetings was one of cause and effect. Troy Williams, who succeeded Brandie Balken as executive director of Equality Utah, spoke to the connection. "Bill Evans has said to me, 'Troy, the kiss-in's were the final straw. That's when we knew we had to talk.' Dabakis was always over here saying, 'We need to talk. We need to talk. We need to talk.' And they were ignoring him, ignoring him, ignoring him. And then all the angry marches happened; and then the kiss-in's happened."[32] With Deeda Seed and Carlton Christensen acting as catalysts, rapprochement had begun, even though it reached an unexpected, albeit temporary, halt.

"SLAM THE DOOR"

The Human Rights Campaign, with more than 1.5 million members, is the largest LGBT-focused civil rights organization in the United States. Unrelated to the Salt Lake City meetings but occurring simultaneously were discussions at the HRC headquarters in Washington, DC, that targeted the LDS Church. Several HRC personnel confirmed the nature of the discussion. One participant in that process, who asked not to be named, said, "They had decided one of the strategies they needed was to find somebody to vilify as a way to raise funding, to have a shriek message.... The plan was, 'Who should we go after for the maximum effect?' At the top of the list were the Mormons. They had even gone to the trouble of coming up with a 'Slam the Door' storyboard, which would have instructed people on how to slam the door on Mormon missionaries." The proposal was to have A-list Hollywood personalities put out a message that essentially said, "Hi! Mormons hate gay people. Look at what they did in Prop 8. So when those Mormons come to your door, *slam the door!* And sign our petition that you will slam the door on Mormons, because they are hateful." The threat was credible. "The Mormons think the war is over. 'Hey, we are reaching out. We are doing stuff.' But the war hasn't even begun." Ironically, "Slam the Door" turned out to be the opportunity to reopen the stalled talks with church leaders.

Jim Dabakis, knowing of "Slam the Door," approached his contacts in Public Affairs and held out an olive branch that might avert a public relations nightmare: get out in front of a proposed Salt Lake City antidiscrimination ordinance. Joe Solmonese, president of HRC at the time, later recalled an intermediary asking for delay in implementing "Slam the Door." "He would say, 'I know you want to take a 2-by-4 to the church today and do X. Would you stand down? Would you step back and give us a little bit of space to make Y happen?' We always were willing to do it because I always got the sense from him that it was to the benefit of something good potentially happening for people in Utah."[33] The church accepted Dabakis's proposal, and "Slam the Door" was never launched.

THE ORDINANCES

Until 2009, throughout the state of Utah it was legal for an employer to fire an employee, or a landlord to evict a resident, merely because of his or her sexual orientation. Midway through the year, the Utah Labor Commission released a survey highlighting more than three hundred cases of such discrimination in the Salt Lake City area alone.[34] "One of these people, Candace Metzler, is a transgender woman who said she was fired after transitioning at work, and who lived on the streets for a year before finding another job."[35]

While the Utah Legislature was (and remains) overwhelmingly Republican, conservative, and Mormon, Salt Lake City contains a different and far more progressive demographic. During the summer of 2009, coincident in timing with the ongoing meetings of the Gang of Five but entirely unrelated to them, Salt Lake City mayor Ralph Becker proposed city legislation that would outlaw discrimination in employment and housing on the basis of sexual orientation. David Clark, Speaker of the Utah House of Representatives, signaled widespread antipathy toward the proposed legislation. Referring to the summary rejection of the Common Ground Initiative earlier in the year, he said, "I don't anticipate there's any more of an appetite to pass it now." And if the Salt Lake City ordinances were to pass, state legislators threatened to "shred it" by enacting nullifying statewide legislation.[36]

Although the city and the state were set to wage war that, if carried to an end point, would result in the state preserving the legality of discriminating against LGBT people, the LDS Church was in a position to broker peace. In the past, the church, in an attempt to distance itself from charges of homophobia, had said it "did not oppose" antidiscrimination legislation. That gave cover to legislators who *did oppose* such legislation. If, however, the church came out with a public statement of "we *support*," it might be a game changer at the state level. Days before the scheduled public hearing on the nondiscrimination ordinances, LDS Public Affairs officials, having received approval from ecclesiastical superiors, drafted a statement of support. Jim Dabakis described the events that unfolded the day of the hearing:

> They called me and asked if I could get the Gang of Five to meet over at the Stewart's. I said, "OK. But I'm not going to get everybody together if you're going to be against it." ... So I gathered everybody over at the Stewart's. I said, "Is this going to be good news?" They said, "Just get everybody there." So we got everybody there. We met at 4 or 5 o'clock, and the city council meeting was at 6. They had greased the wheels to have their guy, Michael Otterson, speak first at the public hearing.[37]

Brandie Balken was stunned by the news she heard at the meeting. "They said, 'First we want to say that we know that the intention of these meetings was not this, and that this was never requested. But we wanted to let you know that we have the intention of releasing a public statement in support of passage of these ordinances this evening, and we wanted you to be aware of that before you walked in.'"[38]

Clifford Rosky, legal counsel for Equality Utah, attended the city council meeting that evening in order to testify in behalf of passing the ordinance, but unlike Balken, he was unprepared for the course of events, even though he knew, from having canvassed the council members, that it would pass unanimously.

> I was writing down my talking points, waiting for my turn, and I write down, "This is not about marriage. This is about the right to earn a living and keep a roof over your head." Whenever we said, "We want to ban employment discrimination," they would talk about the story from Mormon scripture where the camel pokes its nose under the tent. It was their version of the slippery slope. "First this, and then marriage." So I wrote, "It is not about marriage." I'm sitting there, and this guy gets up, who I don't know, and he says, "I am Michael Otterson. I am the official spokesperson for the Church of Jesus Christ of Latter-day Saints. All across America, people are having a debate about morality, but that's not what we are here to talk about tonight. We are here to talk about the right to earn a living and keep a roof over your head. The Church supports this ordinance because it is fair and reasonable, and it does not do violence to the institution of marriage." I thought, "Did you steal my notes?"[39]

On two levels the church announcement was unremarkable. First, the ordinance would have passed even without a church endorsement. And second, the church conceded no turf by making the announcement. As Otterson pointed out, the ordinance contained a cutout that exempted religious organizations.

But the symbolic effect of the announcement was, in the words of the *New York Times*, "a thunderclap that would resonate across the state and in the overwhelmingly Mormon legislature, where even subtle shifts in church positions on social issues can swing votes and sentiments."[40]

Others who were closer to the scene thought differently. A spokesman for the conservative Sutherland Institute called the legislation "unsound in principle, clarity, and effect. . . . Homosexual activists seeking to redefine the meaning of marriage—as well as activist courts seeking to do the same— do not view these types of ordinances singly or in isolation but as a pattern of public opinion to justify radical changes to law as we saw in California." He concluded with a "call on the Utah State Legislature to overturn these local ordinances on the basis of sound public policy."[41]

The threat of legislative reversal was thwarted both by the church's shift to a statement of support, rather than nonopposition, and by a compromise within the legislature as the new session began in January 2010—a compromise of sufficient significance that it was reported in the *New York Times*. "Utah lawmakers will not consider a law that would ban discrimination against gay men and lesbians in the workplace and in housing, and will instead spend the next year studying the issue, key lawmakers said Friday. In exchange, opponents of gay-rights legislation will drop any effort to prevent local governments from passing their own nondiscrimination laws this legislative session."[42]

Some LGBT leaders viewed the concession as a sellout, but Clifford Rosky saw it as a tactical concession that would enable a strategic goal. "We sort of quietly agreed—it was not an easy thing to do—to stand down for one year, but not permanently. But we knew if the Salt Lake City ordinance were able to go into effect and people could see that the sky doesn't fall when you protect LGBT people, that that would be a huge gain, and it would build momentum in other cities and counties, and ultimately for the state. And that's what happened."[43] Not only did the sky not fall, but other municipalities within Utah—nearly two dozen—contacted Equality Utah to get copies of the Salt Lake City ordinance so that they could pass similar ones.[44]

While statewide antidiscrimination legislation was not proposed in 2010, it was in 2011, 2012, and 2013. In 2014, as detailed in a subsequent section, another truce was declared. Finally, in 2015 discrimination in employment and housing was outlawed throughout the state—but not until another, and even more decisive, intervention by the LDS Church.

RAPPROCHEMENT

The positive momentum that began with "the kiss" and reached a crescendo with the passage of the Salt Lake City ordinance continued. Jim Dabakis said, "The dialogue has never been closed off again. We have had a good working relationship. As issues come up, sometimes we just don't agree on stuff, but there is always a dialogue." Other LGBT leaders and luminaries, who began to meet with church officials at the church headquarters rather than on neutral ground, included Dustin Lance Black, a former Mormon who won an Academy Award for the screenplay of *Milk*; Rick Jacobs, founder of the Courage Campaign; and Joe Solmonese, president of the Human Rights

Campaign. The meetings began to make a difference, as noted by Dabakis: "Sometimes there have been strong differences of opinion, but a lot of times not. A lot of times, both sides begin to see each other, and as crisis has broken out, these channels have been very helpful."[45]

The most visible symbol of change involved the annual Christmas concert of the Mormon Tabernacle Choir. The hottest attraction in town, the two-night event draws requests for hundreds of thousands of tickets but can accommodate fewer than fifty thousand guests. In December 2009, the Gang of Five and their partners were invited to sit in the VIP section, along with their counterparts from Public Affairs. The group met in the lobby of the Joseph Smith Memorial Building and then walked together to the Conference Center for the concert, crossing through Main Street Plaza along the way. One of the Public Affairs employees, in a signal that a new era had arrived, said, "If anybody wants to kiss, it's OK."[46]

As they took their seats, Jim Dabakis noticed that Michael Waddoups, president of the Utah Senate, was sitting next to him. "He said, 'Why are you here?' I said, 'I'm here as part of the homosexual delegation that has been invited by the First Presidency as special guests.' He just looked over me, and then grabbed his program and his wife's hand. So we were starting to make changes."[47]

HOLLINGSWORTH V. PERRY

When proponents of same-sex marriage challenged Proposition 22 in court, they turned to the state court system, alleging that the proposition violated the California Constitution. When the California Supreme Court overturned Prop 22, opponents of same-sex marriage initiated Prop 8, which amended the state constitution. To challenge Prop 8, same-sex-marriage advocates had to turn to the federal court system, on the ground that the proposition violated the U.S. Constitution.

There were some advocates of same-sex marriage who pushed back at the idea of such a lawsuit. Rick Jacobs, founder of the Courage Campaign, critiqued that strategy:

> They were saying that if it got to the Supreme Court too soon, we would lose. There is a theory that has been set forth that we have to win elections in ten states, in the legislatures in ten states and in courts in ten states on the issue of marriage equality before we go to the Supreme Court. And let's face it, if you've got 30 or 40 years it's a great idea. I have another view of this, which is that I don't understand why any minority wants to subject itself to having its rights voted on by a majority. That usually doesn't work out well for the minority.[1]

One who agreed with Jacobs's view, actor and director Rob Reiner, cofounded the American Foundation for Equal Rights to support the legal challenge to Prop 8. In May 2009, an unusual legal team headed by David Boies and Ted Olson—unusual because the two had been on opposite sides in *Bush v. Gore*, which ultimately decided the 2000 presidential election—filed a federal lawsuit on behalf of Kristin Perry and Sandra Stier, who had been denied a marriage license in Alameda County, and Paul Katami and Jeffrey Zarrillo, who had been denied a license in Los Angeles County. That the liberal Boies would agree to support the cause of marriage equality was not surprising, but Olson, a conservative icon, surprised many by joining the team, arguing that "California's ban is 'utterly without justification' and stigmatizes gay men and lesbians as 'second-class and unworthy.'" Signaling their commitment to the principals involved, both Boies and Olson agreed to waive part of their fees.[2]

The named defendants included California governor Arnold Schwarzenegger and attorney general Jerry Brown, both of whom refused to defend Prop 8 in court because they believed that it violated the U.S. Constitution. In the absence of a state official to defend Prop 8, ProtectMarriage.com, the sponsor of Prop 8 during the initiative campaign, petitioned the court to become the defendant, and Judge Vaughn Walker, of the U.S. District Court for the Northern District of California, granted the petition. Dennis Hollingsworth of ProtectMarriage.com became a named defendant, whereupon *Perry v. Schwarzenegger* became known as *Hollingsworth v. Perry*. Judge Walker ruled that the case would involve a full public trial with evidence, expert witnesses, examination, and cross-examination to address specific issues that previously had played out largely on the airwaves, with the two sides talking past each other.

Whereas the LDS Church had a major role in the Prop 8 campaign, it remained on the sidelines for the trial. It did not petition the court to become a codefendant, unlike its action in Hawaii nearly two decades earlier; instead, it limited its role to coauthorship of one of dozens of amicus briefs filed with the court. However, it had much at stake in the trial. In spite of objections from defense attorneys, testimony would be presented in open court that portrayed the church in an unfavorable light. Furthermore, all of the rationales that the church had employed in its long campaign against same-sex marriage would play out in court, in full public view and under intense cross-examination. These rationales did not fare well under such scrutiny.

Much of the action in a court trial occurs in private and outside the courtroom. Particularly important are the depositions of witnesses. Conducted with attorneys from both sides present, they consist of probing,

on-the-record questioning by attorneys of the opposing side, and any testimony given during a deposition may be used in the courtroom phase of the
trial. In many cases, the outcome of the trial is effectively predetermined
during the pretrial phase. In the case of *Hollingsworth v. Perry*, the deposition process was devastating to the defense. Rick Jacobs, who live-blogged
from the courtroom during the entire trial phase, said, "By the time the
trial began [the defense] had only two witnesses, because the other ones
had been destroyed in depositions."[3] Both of those witnesses proved to be
disadvantageous to the defense. By contrast, the plaintiff team presented
eight lay witnesses (including the four plaintiffs) and nine expert witnesses.

The trial began on January 11, 2010, and lasted for sixteen days. On January 20, evidence of LDS Church involvement was presented. One courtroom
blogger wrote, "This is perhaps the most explosive bit of all, from a document between the LDS Church and the campaign: 'With respect to Prop. 8
campaign, key talking points will come from campaign, but cautious, strategic, not to take the lead so as to provide plausible deniability or respectable distance so as not to show that church is directly involved.'" Another
wrote, "We learned that over 20,000 Mormons were out door-knocking on
the final few weekends.... We learned that Mormon/LDS Church leaders
were powerful in the structure throughout the campaign. Of course, that
was no real surprise.... Rarely do you get word from a prophet ordering volunteers to show up. And rarely do you see an organization so religious completely subsume a campaign."[4]

But the large majority of courtroom time was devoted to detailed examination of questions that had been central to the marriage equality debate
for years. Judge Walker deliberated for six months and then issued a 136-
page ruling that included three parts: "Credibility Determinations," "Findings of Fact," and "Conclusions of Law."

All nine expert witnesses for the plaintiffs were accepted by the court,
but the two expert witnesses for the defendants were problematic at best
and in some instances counterproductive to the cause of the proponents of
Prop 8. Under cross-examination, one of the defense experts, David Blankenhorn, said he believed the principle of human dignity applied to gay
and lesbian Americans and that "we would be *more* American on the day
we permitted same-sex marriage than we were on the day before." He also
acknowledged that the well-being of children raised by same-sex couples
would improve if they were allowed to marry.[5]

Counsel for the plaintiffs objected to Blankenhorn's qualifications as an expert witness, and although Walker permitted him to testify, the judge ultimately concluded, "Blankenhorn lacks the qualifications to offer opinion testimony and, in any event, failed to provide cogent testimony in support of proponents' factual assertions....The court now determines that Blankenhorn's testimony constitutes inadmissible opinion testimony that should be given essentially no weight."[6]

The other witness for the defendants, Kenneth Miller, was a professor of government at Claremont McKenna College. He was called to testify that gays and lesbians had strong political support in California. In discounting Miller's testimony, Judge Walker wrote, "The court concludes that, while Miller has significant experience with politics generally, he is not sufficiently familiar with gay and lesbian politics specifically to offer opinions on gay and lesbian political power....The court finds that Miller's opinions on gay and lesbian political power are entitled to little weight and only to the extent they are amply supported by reliable evidence."

Walker then proceeded to outline eighty "Findings of Fact," based on the evidence presented at trial, that included the following:

- On the roles of church and state in marriage: "Marriage in the United States has always been a civil matter. Civil authorities may permit religious leaders to solemnize marriages but not to determine who may enter or leave a civil marriage. Religious leaders may determine independently whether to recognize a civil marriage or divorce but that recognition or lack thereof has no effect on the relationship under state law."
- On the effect of changes to the definition of marriage that were claimed to be detrimental to it: "Eliminating gender and race restrictions in marriage has not deprived the institution of marriage of its vitality."
- On the current legal definition of marriage: "Marriage is the state recognition and approval of a couple's choice to live with each other, to remain committed to one another and to form a household based on their own feelings about one another and to join in an economic partnership and support one another and any dependents."
- On the purposes of the state in licensing and fostering marriage: "Facilitating governance and public order by organizing individuals

into cohesive family units.... Developing a realm of liberty, intimacy and free decision-making by spouses.... Creating stable households.... Legitimating children.... Assigning individuals to care for one another and thus limiting the public's liability to care for the vulnerable.... Facilitating property ownership."

- On the nature of homosexuality and the possibility of changing sexual orientation: "Individuals do not generally choose their sexual orientation. No credible evidence supports a finding that an individual may, through conscious decision, therapeutic intervention or any other method, change his or her sexual orientation."

- On the ability of same-sex couples to form a successful marital union: "Same-sex couples are identical to opposite-sex couples in the characteristics relevant to the ability to form successful marital unions."

- On the benefits of marriage to same-sex couples: "Same-sex couples receive the same tangible and intangible benefits from marriage that opposite-sex couples receive."

- On the effect of same-sex marriage on heterosexual marriage: "Permitting same-sex couples to marry will not affect the number of opposite-sex couples who marry, divorce, cohabit, have children outside of marriage or otherwise affect the stability of opposite-sex marriages."

- On the suitability of an LGBT person to be a parent: "The sexual orientation of an individual does not determine whether that individual can be a good parent."

- On the welfare of children raised by same-sex parents: "Children raised by gay or lesbian parents are as likely as children raised by heterosexual parents to be healthy, successful and well-adjusted. The research supporting this conclusion is accepted beyond serious debate in the field of developmental psychology.... Children do not need to be raised by a male parent and a female parent to be well-adjusted, and having both a male and a female parent does not increase the likelihood that a child will be well-adjusted."

- On the effect of religious claims on LGBT people: "Religious beliefs that gay and lesbian relationships are sinful or inferior to heterosexual relationships harm gays and lesbians."

Walker then wrote his "Conclusions of Law" arising out of the facts he had found, which included the following:

- "Plaintiffs challenge Proposition 8 under the Due Process and Equal Protection Clauses of the Fourteenth Amendment. Each challenge is independently meritorious, as Proposition 8 both unconstitutionally burdens the exercise of the fundamental right to marry and creates an irrational classification on the basis of sexual orientation."
- "The evidence shows that the movement of marriage away from a gendered institution and toward an institution free from state-mandated gender roles reflects an evolution in the understanding of gender rather than a change in marriage. The evidence did not show any historical purpose for excluding same-sex couples from marriage, as states have never required spouses to have an ability or willingness to procreate in order to marry. Rather, the exclusion exists as an artifact of a time when the genders were seen as having distinct roles in society and in marriage. That time has passed.... Gender no longer forms an essential part of marriage; marriage under law is a union of equals."
- "Proposition 8 cannot withstand any level of scrutiny under the Equal Protection Clause, as excluding same-sex couples from marriage is simply not rationally related to a legitimate state interest."
- "The evidence at trial regarding the campaign to pass Proposition 8 uncloaks the most likely explanation for its passage: a desire to advance the belief that opposite-sex couples are morally superior to same-sex couples."
- "Moral disapproval alone is an improper basis on which to deny rights to gay men and lesbians.... Because Proposition 8 disadvantages gays and lesbians without any rational justification, Proposition 8 violates the Equal Protection Clause of the Fourteenth Amendment."

Judge Walker's decision that Prop 8 violated the U.S. Constitution was immediately appealed to the Ninth Circuit Court of Appeals. Same-sex marriage remained illegal in California pending the appeal.

In the immediate aftermath of the decision, the LDS Church signaled both its disapproval and its determination to continue to fight against the legalization of same-sex marriage. "California voters have twice been given the opportunity to vote on the definition of marriage in their state and both times have determined that marriage should be recognized as only between a man and a woman. We agree.... We recognize that this decision represents only the opening of a vigorous debate in the courts over the rights of the people to define and protect this most fundamental institution—marriage."[7]

On February 7, the Ninth Circuit upheld Judge Walker's decision, by a two-to-one vote. The dissenting vote came from N. Randy Smith, a Mormon from Logan, Utah, whose undergraduate and law degrees came from Brigham Young University. Setting aside Walker's findings of fact without adding supporting evidence of his own, Smith wrote that "allowing gays and lesbians to marry would weaken the status of marriage for heterosexuals and result in increased heterosexual cohabitation and therefore 'less stable circumstances for children.'"[8]

Once again, the defendants requested and were granted a stay of judgment in order to appeal to the U.S. Supreme Court. The Supreme Court heard the case in March 2013. In June of the same year it chose to sidestep the findings of Judge Walker and the Ninth Circuit Court. Instead, it ruled on the narrow issue of legal standing of the defendants:

> We have never before upheld the standing of a private party to defend the constitutionality of a state statute when state officials have chosen not to. We decline to do so for the first time here. Because petitioners have not satisfied their burden to demonstrate standing to appeal the judgment of the District Court, the Ninth Circuit was without jurisdiction to consider the appeal. The judgment of the Ninth Circuit is vacated, and the case is remanded with instructions to dismiss the appeal for lack of jurisdiction.[9]

Thus, Judge Walker's decision was upheld, and same-sex marriage once again became legal in California. Since the decision of the Ninth Circuit was vacated, the outcome affected only California rather than the other states within the Ninth Circuit. The question of national legalization would be decided another day.

THREE MEN, TWO MESSAGES

BOYD PACKER

No LDS Church leader was more vocal and more consistent in condemning homosexuality than Boyd Packer. Called to the Quorum of the Twelve Apostles at the relatively young age of forty-five, he spent another forty-five years in the Quorum. For more than two decades prior to his death in 2015, he presided over it. As a result of the change in church governance following the death in 1970 of church president David O. McKay, with nearly all church departments being directed by the Quorum of the Twelve instead of the First Presidency, the president of the Quorum was effectively the church's prime minister—the head of church government—while the church president was the head of state. Highly skilled in using the tools of power, Packer at times was arguably the most powerful officer in the church.

In a General Conference address in October 1976—three years into the presidency of Spencer Kimball, a dark era for LGBT church members—Packer lashed out at male homosexual activity, without using the word *homosexual.* "I am hesitant to even mention it, for it is not pleasant. It must be labeled as major transgression. . . . There are some circumstances in which young men may be tempted to handle one another, to have contact with one another physically in unusual ways. . . . If you are ever approached to participate in anything like that, it is time to vigorously resist."[1]

One who vigorously resisted was a missionary in the New England States Mission, over which Packer presided in the mid-1960s, whose companion apparently had made some sort of homosexual advance. He "said he had something to confess. I was very worried because he just could not get himself to tell me what he had done. After patient encouragement he finally blurted out, 'I hit my companion.' 'Oh, is that all,' I said in great relief. 'But I floored him,' he said. After learning a little more, my response was, 'Well, thanks. Somebody had to do it, and it wouldn't be well for a General Authority to solve the problem that way.'" While he concluded the narrative of the episode with a mild disclaimer—"I am not recommending that course to you but I am not omitting it. You must protect yourself"—the story opened the door to violent responses to homosexuality within LDS circles.

Packer then laid down his credo regarding homosexuality and held the line on it for the rest of his life: "There is a falsehood that some are born with an attraction to their own kind, with nothing they can do about it. They are just 'that way' and can only yield to those desires. That is a malicious and destructive lie. While it is a convincing idea to some, it is of the devil. No one is locked into that kind of life."[2] His 1976 General Conference address was published by the church the same year in pamphlet form and remained an overt endorsement of violent homophobia for four decades until it was taken out of print in 2016.[3]

A year and a half after giving the sermon, Packer was assigned by church president Spencer Kimball to address the topic again, this time at Brigham Young University. Kimball's son and biographer wrote, "Feeling inadequate, Elder Packer first responded, 'President, I just couldn't do it.' But after soul-searching he concluded he could not refuse 'an assignment from the prophet' and gave a very direct talk."[4]

This time, as noted in an earlier chapter, he used the "*H* word," albeit with a heavy disclaimer. "I accept that word as an adjective to describe a temporary condition. I reject it as a noun naming a permanent one."[5] He then proceeded to elaborate on the theme of his earlier 1976 General Conference address.

To the question of cause, his answer was unequivocal. "Is this tendency impossible to change? Is it preset at the time of birth and locked in? Do you just have to live with it? . . . Is perversion like that? The answer is a conclusive *no!*" He then dismissed science out of hand, utilizing a prefix—*so-called*—that he frequently employed to delegitimize things with which he disagreed. "Some so-called experts, and many of those who have yielded to the practice, teach that it is congenital and incurable and that one just has to learn to live with it. . . . Much of the so-called scientific literature concludes that there really is not much that can be done about it. . . . It is not unchangeable. It is not locked in."

Packer then applied circular logic to make his case for homosexuality being a choice rather than a biological imprint. "Test it against moral law and you learn something very quickly. If a condition that draws both men and women into one of the ugliest and most debased of all physical performances is set and cannot be overcome, it would be a glaring exception to all moral law." And if not biology, then what? "Have you explored the possibility that the cause, when found, will turn out to be a very typical form of selfishness—selfishness in a very subtle form? ... Every prescription against selfishness of any kind will bring some control of this disease."

As with the sermon two years earlier, the BYU speech was published by the church as a pamphlet, *To the One*, that was widely distributed to local church leaders for decades, thus giving it semicanonical status.

Packer's next high-profile foray into the debate on homosexuality did not occur for another fifteen years, a period during which feminists and, to use his term, "so-called intellectuals" were a greater focus of his attention. From the late 1970s through the early 1980s the LDS Church was a major force in defeating the Equal Rights Amendment to the U.S. Constitution.[6] As the amendment was going down to defeat, Packer worked with senior apostles Ezra Taft Benson and Mark Petersen to counter the growing influence of Mormon intellectuals. Their first step was to disassemble the History Division, the history-writing component of the LDS Church Historical Department that since its formation in 1972 had been publishing articles and books that challenged their view that all church history should be devotional. By 1993 Packer turned his attention and became the prime mover in trying to silence intellectuals who were not employed by the church. He ordered several stake presidents to take disciplinary action against six intellectuals, and in September 1993 five of them were excommunicated and the sixth disfellowshipped. The purge of the "September Six" sent a chill throughout the Mormon intellectual community and garnered national attention.[7]

In the run-up to the September Six, the Hawaii Supreme Court ruling in *Baehr v. Lewin*, which seemed to presage the legalization of same-sex marriage, sent a shock wave throughout the country. Thirteen days after the ruling, Packer spoke to the All-Church Coordinating Council and issued a stern warning: "There are three areas where members of the Church, influenced by social and political unrest, are being caught up and led away. I chose these three because they have made major invasions into the membership of the Church. In each, the temptation is for us to turn about and face the wrong way, and it is hard to resist, for doing it seems so reasonable and right." The three areas were those in which he had had a personal stake reaching back to 1976: "The dangers I speak of come from the gay-lesbian movement, the feminist movement (both of which are relatively new), and the ever-present challenge from the so-called scholars or intellectuals."[8]

While Packer did not have the high-profile role in the church's political involvement in same-sex marriage initiatives and laws that other church leaders did, his condemnation of homosexuality and his insistence that it was choice, and not biology, did not waver. In a General Conference address in October 2000 he said, "Pressure is put upon legislatures to legalize unnatural conduct. They can never make right that which is forbidden in the laws of God. . . . Some think that God created them with overpowering, unnatural desires, that they are trapped and not responsible. That is not true. It cannot be true." Four years later, in an address to the BYU-sponsored J. Reuben Clark Law Society, he said, "I know of nothing in the history of the Church or in the history of the world to compare with our present circumstances. Nothing happened in Sodom and Gomorrah which exceeds the wickedness and depravity which surrounds us now." In a 2006 interview with documentary filmmaker Helen Whitney, he reiterated his statement from 1978: "I don't accept the word homosexual as a noun; I accept it as an adjective." When asked by Whitney if mounting scientific evidence of a biological basis for homosexuality would influence the church's thinking, he responded, "I don't think so. That you could make the same case for child molesters. Tendency, pressures, I was born that way. Morality is morality."[9]

MARLIN JENSEN

The latter months of 2010 were tumultuous for the LDS Church. The Prop 8 victory against same-sex marriage was short-lived, with Judge Vaughn Walker's decision overturning it coming less than two years later. Although other states had legalized same-sex marriage in the interim, with three states and the District of Columbia doing so in 2009, California was still regarded as the bellwether of the nation: "As California goes, so goes the country." The enormous investment of the church and its members in the Prop 8 battle appeared to be for naught.

Also of concern was the continuing damage to some church members from the Prop 8 battle. Particularly in California, LGBT members as well as their families and friends had suffered deep wounds that were slow to heal. The month after Walker's decision was handed down, Marlin Jensen, who earlier had headed the church's Homosexual and Lesbian Marriage Committee, was assigned to preside over the semiannual conference of the California Oakland Stake. Dean Criddle, president of the stake, recalled the reaction when he and other stake leaders heard of the assignment. "We, as a stake presidency, looked at ourselves and said, 'This certainly is not random.' We seized the opportunity."[10]

When Criddle called Jensen to work out details for the conference, Jensen was receptive to an unusual proposal. "'If you're really interested in making a difference at this moment in time, there is a cross-section of my stake that still feels deeply wounded over this Proposition 8 episode. In my judgment, where you could make the most difference would be having an intimate meeting with a selected group of those people, identified by the bishops, who are continuing to feel anguish over that experience.' [Jensen] said, 'Do you really think that would be helpful?' [I replied] 'Absolutely,' [and he responded] 'OK.'"

Criddle worked with the bishops in his stake to compile a list of about 120 people. "Invitations went out, and I don't think there was a single person who declined the invitation to come. So that was the group, along with the bishops, a member of the stake presidency and the Relief Society president." He then worked out the format with Jensen. "'If you are willing to listen to peoples' stories, that would really be a great gift, just listening.' Elder Jensen said, 'Let's take half the time to listen to these stories. You open the meeting. You know who these people are, so let's have more or less an open mike, but call on people who you think will be responsible and genuine. I'd like to listen to their lived experience, and then I'll have a few concluding remarks.'"

As Criddle opened the meeting early on a Sunday morning, he said, "There are lots of people who would like to speak. I'm going to be very disciplined here. If anyone speaks for more than three minutes, I'm going to stand up right here in front, where everybody can see, and wave my hands. Then, it's time for you to stop." But in three minutes, people were able to relate their experiences in sometimes gritty, emotional language. "They were telling stories about receiving electric shock therapy at BYU, about being cut off by family members, all contact. Just difficult, horrible things. There was not a dry eye in the room while this was happening, [including]

Elder Jensen. He was facing the congregation as people stood up, one at a time, and he was weeping openly, along with just about everybody else."

Then, it was Jensen's turn. After relating some of his own experiences he made an extraordinary statement:

> I have very limited authority. I'm called a General Authority, but the scope of my authority is a sliver. But I do have some authority, by assignment, when it comes to stake conferences. So that's what brings me here today. You have to understand that in this narrow scope of limited authority, almost on a personal level, I want to apologize to all you people for what you had to endure over these years. I just feel like I need to give you my own, personal apology. It's not up to me to apologize for the church, but I just feel that that's what I should do today.[11]

Some reported Jensen as having apologized for the church's involvement in Prop 8 or for Prop 8 itself. Carol Lynn Pearson, who was at the meeting, quickly corrected the misunderstanding. "There was never a statement suggesting that Elder Jensen felt the Church's support of Proposition 8 was an error or that he was apologizing for that event." Joanna Brooks, writing in *Religion Dispatches*, put the meeting into context. "It was not, to be sure, an apology for Proposition 8 itself. It was not a renunciation of Mormon doctrine on homosexuality. But it was a significant acknowledgment of the experience of gay Mormons and their allies, an instance of dialogue between Church leadership and membership. It was, in short, a reason for hope."[12]

CANONIZING THE PROCLAMATION ON THE FAMILY

While it is not known if there was a direct cause-and-effect relationship between Jensen's remarks in Oakland and Boyd Packer's General Conference address one week later, a church official who spoke on condition of anonymity said that Packer was well aware of what had happened and was not pleased. On October 3, Packer delivered an address that appeared to be an attempt to dispel any thoughts that the church might be softening its stance on LGBT issues—and then some.

Lashing out against those who saw homosexuality as inborn, as he had done in previous years, he asserted, "Not so! Why would our Heavenly

Father do that to anyone? Remember he is our father."[13] But he also broke new ground—or tried to, as he attempted to canonize the Proclamation on the Family. After noting that the proclamation was fifteen years old, he said, "It qualifies, according to the definition, as a revelation, and, uh, it would do well that members of the Church to read and follow."[14] Packer was fastidious in preparing his General Conference addresses. He even recorded each address prior to the conference so that it could be broadcast without interruption if there was any disruption in the meeting. To read the text of his actual words, which included an uncharacteristic *uh* and a grammatical error—"it would do well that members of the Church to read"—suggests that he inserted the sentence impromptu. Certainly, it caught his colleagues off-guard.

Reaction to Packer's address was immediate. One writer linked Marlin Jensen's apology to Packer's retrenchment. "A statement from Mormon leader Boyd K. Packer reaffirms the Church of Jesus Christ of Latter-day Saints' opposition to marriage equality, which a recent apology from another Mormon leader seemed to soften.... Last month Marlin K. Jensen, the church's historian and a prominent member of the general authorities leadership hierarchy, told a group of Mormons gathered in Oakland, Calif., that he was sorry for the pain caused by the church's substantial involvement in the Proposition 8 campaign."[15] Another, Kristine Haglund, editor of *Dialogue: A Journal of Mormon Thought,* called it "a last volley in what President Packer sees as the last great battle of his life."[16]

The harshest words came from the Human Rights Campaign, which issued a formal statement the following day:

> The Human Rights Campaign (HRC), the nation's largest civil rights organization dedicated to lesbian, gay, bisexual and transgender (LGBT) equality, today called on Boyd K. Packer, the president of the Mormon Church's Quorum of Twelve Apostles, to correct statements he made yesterday calling same-sex attraction 'impure and unnatural,' claiming that it can be corrected and characterizing same-sex marriage as immoral....
>
> "Words have consequences, particularly when they come from a faith leader. This is exactly the kind of statement that can lead some kids to bully and others to commit suicide," said Joe Solmonese, president of HRC. "When a faith leader tells gay people that they are a mistake because God would never have made them that

way and they don't deserve love, it sends a very powerful message that violence and/or discrimination against LGBT people is acceptable. It also emotionally devastates those who are LGBT or may be struggling with their sexual orientation or gender identify. His words were not only inaccurate, they were also dangerous."[17]

No less dramatic was the reaction within the hierarchy. A church official who spoke on condition of anonymity said that the day after Packer made his remarks, he was summoned to a one-on-one meeting with church president Thomas Monson that lasted nearly one hour. Shortly thereafter, the most problematic portions of the speech were changed or removed. For instance, "Not so! Why would our Heavenly Father do that to anyone? Remember he is our father" was changed to "Not so! Remember, God is our Heavenly Father." And the entire sentence by which Packer attempted to canonize the Proclamation on the Family was removed from the official transcript, without explanation.[18] The *Deseret News*, while detailing some of the changes, attempted to downplay their significance.

> The official text of the October general conference address by President Boyd K. Packer, president of the LDS Church's Quorum of the Twelve Apostles, was posted online Friday afternoon with acknowledged amendments, but not the type or magnitude of revisions gay-rights activists have called for in protests and petitions since the talk was given Sunday.
>
> "The Monday following every general conference, each speaker has the opportunity to make any edits necessary to clarify differences between what was written and what was delivered or to clarify the speaker's intent," said Scott Trotter, spokesman for The Church of Jesus Christ of Latter-day Saints. "President Packer has simply clarified his intent."[19]

News of the editing did little to quell the backlash. Four days after Packer's address, a crowd estimated at two to three thousand by the *Deseret News* (and forty-five hundred by *Q Salt Lake*) surrounded Temple Square in silent protest.[20] Paul Guequierre, spokesman for the Human Rights Campaign, said, "It's still a hateful message that [Packer has] conveyed. We're calling on Elder Packer to make it right. We want him to speak to the kids across the country who are struggling with their own identities... [and] tell them they are loved just the way they are."[21] HRC president Joe Solmonese added, "Elder Packer and the church must immediately and fully correct the factual record. Sexual orientation and gender identity is an immutable characteristic of being human and, no matter how hard you pray, that won't change."[22]

The HRC turned up the heat further by collecting 150,000 signatures for a petition "asking the Church to withdraw statements made by President Boyd K. Packer about same-sex attraction, which he said was unnatural and with enough faith can be overcome,"[23] and Solmonese, along with leaders of Utah's LGBT community, delivered them in person to church headquarters.[24]

DIETER UCHTDORF

Neither Boyd Packer nor the church responded to HRC's demand of an apology. However, three weeks after Packer's address, Dieter Uchtdorf spoke by satellite broadcast to two hundred thousand Utah Mormons and struck a tone similar to that of Marlin Jensen. As second counselor to Thomas Monson, Uchtdorf sat in the highest governing council of the church, the First Presidency. Charismatic and arguably the most popular speaker in the entire church, he commanded enormous moral authority.

The *Salt Lake Tribune* noted that Uchtdorf's basic message, "God loves all his children... may not seem significant, [but] the messenger was." While Uchtdorf made no mention of Packer in his remarks, there was no question in the mind of the reporter as to how to connect the dots between the two men. "The gentle tone and emphasis of Uchtdorf's remarks—spoken at the Conference Center in downtown Salt Lake City and beamed to dozens of church buildings—came in the wake of an earlier speech by Boyd K. Packer, senior member of the LDS Quorum of the Twelve Apostles."[25]

On one key issue, the cause of homosexuality, Uchtdorf distanced himself from Packer—and laid down a line on behalf of the church that implicitly dismissed Packer's teachings over the prior three decades. He "reiterated the church's position that it doesn't know the cause of homosexuality and that it doesn't matter. 'Many questions in life, however, including some related to same-gender attractions, must await a future answer, even in the next life,' Uchtdorf said. 'Until then, the truth is, God loves all his children, and because he loves us, we can trust him and keep his commandments.'"[26]

BRIDGES TO SOMEWHERE

Beginning in 2010, bridges began to be constructed between the church and LGBT-focused organizations, on a level never before seen. While the organizations were not connected to each other or coordinated in their engagement of the church, they all found the "soil" of church's willingness to engage to be fertile as never before.

HUMAN RIGHTS CAMPAIGN

At the time the meetings with the Gang of Five were happening, the Human Rights Campaign was ready to go to war against the LDS Church. The stand-down brokered by Jim Dabakis resulted in an uneasy peace that was shattered by Boyd Packer's 2010 General Conference address. Although conditions were ripe for all-out conflict, HRC's peaceful petition to the church, signed by 150,000 people, proved to be the opening to a changed relationship with the church.

Joe Solmonese, president of HRC, had made inroads among Roman Catholics by realizing that "lay Catholics sort of make their own rules, and they are much more willing to buck authority.... You could speak directly to Catholics and sort of sidestep the leadership of the Catholic Church." But the Mormons were different, and it took him a while to recognize the difference. The change began when he and Bruce Bastian, a former Mormon and a generous supporter of HRC, attended Carol Lynn Pearson's play *Facing East*, which tells the story of LDS parents of a gay son who committed suicide and their encounter with his partner at the grave site. "It was incredibly moving, but when I walked out I said to Bruce, 'I have a hundred questions. I just don't get it.' He really taught me a lot about the LDS Church, and about how a parent in the Church would react to their child. I thought, 'The path with the LDS Church is very different. The only sort of conversation for us to have is with the leadership of the Church.'"[1]

As Solmonese prepared to fly to Salt Lake City to deliver the petitions to LDS Church headquarters, he received a phone call from church officials. They said, "We understand you're coming. We understand you're bringing news crews. We understand you're bringing boxes of petitions. Here's how this is going to work. Go to this corner, stand here, somebody will come out, somebody will take them."[2] The handoff was peaceful and respectful, and it opened a door to a subsequent meeting in Salt Lake City. Solmonese recalled,

> I think because of the way we conducted ourselves around the delivering of the petitions, we were able to get a meeting with what most people thought were an impressive group of church leaders. [Our group included] Bruce [Bastian] and Jim Dabakis and Sharon Groves and Fred Sainz and me....
>
> Sharon, who really hadn't said very much, had the right profile and the right presence in the room. She said, "Is there a way that you can look at us and see that contained within our agenda, as it were, is this commitment to believe that young people shouldn't live in environments where the things going on around them encourage them to take their own lives? Can you put aside all of your own history and, at the very least, respect that that is a part of our agenda and a part of our work, and that it would be reasonable for you to recognize and respect that, and to see if there is a place that we could find some common ground to have a conversation about that?" She said it just like that, and it was like all of the energy in the room changed.... It was this moment where I think she respected them and characterized the nature of our work in a way that they were able to find common ground with us. To my way of thinking, it was the conversation that opened up the door for them to be able to say, "If we are going to work with anybody, these are people that we could work with. If we are ever going to find common ground, these are people we could find some common ground with. It may only ever be around this issue

of young people and homelessness and teen suicide, but that is
what it will be."[3]

MORMONS BUILDING BRIDGES

Erika Munson, a stay-at-home mother of five children, had no familial connection to LGBT issues. Instead, her motivation was social justice. "My
church has taught me that Jesus Christ's message of unconditional love for
others brings great happiness. My support for the gay community and my
commitment to the church have long coexisted but I have been frustrated by
an inability to bring these two groups together."[4] Her response was to march.

Salt Lake City hosts two major parades each year. The largest and oldest is the "Days of '47 Parade," which celebrates the entrance of Mormon
pioneers into the Salt Lake Valley on July 24, 1847. The parade has been an
annual affair since 1849. The Utah Pride Parade began in 1990. The 2012
Pride Parade occurred just days after public announcement of the formation of Mormons Building Bridges, organized by Munson.

Shortly after Munson arranged for Mormons Building Bridges to participate in the parade (and was assigned the number 80 spot at the back of
the parade), she approached Troy Williams, an LGBT activist who now is
executive director of Equality Utah. "She wanted my advice, and this was a
scary thing to do.... We met at the Pride Center and she pitched this idea to
me: 'We are going to come in our church clothes, and we are going to sing
hymns on the parade route.'...I was terrified at this idea. I was worried
about how our crowd would treat them, because there was so much anger."[5]

Williams contacted the parade's grand marshal, Dustin Lance Black.
"He said, 'Troy, let's put them at the front of the parade with us.' I was going
to drive him in the first car. The lights went on. I thought, 'This is it!'" With
a celebrity leading the parade and Mormons Building Bridges right behind,
Williams had the potential for national publicity. "We called up the *New
York Times*, CNN, everybody. We said, 'This will be the most subversive
thing we will ever do!'"

Munson sent out word via social media, asking that Mormons who
wished to show support for the LGBT community show up in their Sunday
best—the parade was on a Sunday—and march. She made it clear that there
was no political agenda, no call for church support of marriage equality.

"We are faithful Latter-day Saints dedicated to sharing a message of love and acceptance to the LGBT community. We seek to build bridges of understanding and respect after many years of strife and heartbreak. We want our gay brothers and sisters to feel welcome in our congregations and safe in our pews."[6]

Given the late entry of Mormons Building Bridges into the parade, Munson expected to attract only one hundred marchers. However, "about ten minutes before parade start time, marcher Clair Barrus of Draper, Utah, counted about 475 members of the Mormons Building Bridges delegation, ranging in age from toddlers to senior citizens." One sign said, "LDS Love LGBT." Another said, "Sorry We're Late." Troy Williams watched as he drove the lead car. "It was the beginning of a truth-and-reconciliation moment. We were bawling as I watched them marching so stoically behind us. I knew I was experiencing history—it was changing the game. I thought, 'Things will never again be the same after this.'"[7]

People noticed. A lot of people, including a reporter for the *New York Times*. "Mormons marched in a gay pride parade on Sunday, holding signs that read 'God Loves His Children' in a unique display of support from believers of a religious tradition that has long opposed homosexuality."[8] A week later, another article in the same newspaper highlighted the possibilities for the new organization:

> If it succeeds in creating a sense that gay Mormons are welcome in the church, Mormons Building Bridges may eventually bring about important shifts in the church's relationship to its gay members and its involvement in anti-gay politics. Gay Mormons have left the church in droves. One route Mormons Building Bridges might take would be to work to stop and even reverse that trend with a vigorous public campaign that assures gay Mormons they belong in church. Were gay Mormons to become a sizable and visible presence in church wards across the country, perhaps the church will take notice and adjust accordingly.[9]

Smaller groups representing Mormons Building Bridges marched in other Pride Parades across the country. At the end of the year, the group received the *Salt Lake Tribune*'s Utahns of the Year award.[10] It has marched in the Salt Lake City Pride Parade each year since 2012. It also has applied each year to join the Days of '47 Parade and has been turned down each year.

FAMILY ACCEPTANCE PROJECT

At the same time Erika Munson was creating Mormons Building Bridges, Caitlin Ryan was putting finishing touches on a booklet that introduced a jolting reality into the Mormon community. Dr. Ryan, a clinical social worker at San Francisco State University, started the Family Acceptance Project in 2002 in an effort to improve—and save—the lives of LGBT youth by educating their families.

Ryan's research looked past the contentious issues of the causes and morality of homosexuality and instead focused on family behaviors and how they influenced the lives of LGBT children. Her results were groundbreaking and stunning: LGBT children with supportive families had one-eighth the rate of attempted suicide of those with unsupportive families, one-sixth the incidence of depression, one-third the rate of illegal drug use, and one-third the rate of HIV infection.[11]

Wanting to tailor the message to specific faith traditions, Ryan turned first to the Mormons. "I saw a qualitative difference in Mormon LGBT homeless youth, compared to the others. It affected me on a feeling level, because I felt that they were in great despair, and I felt that there was something that was different about their loss of a future—about having ended up out of home, ended up on the street, ended up away from their families—that there was another element to it, and I was really trying to understand that." That element, paradoxically, was the strong LDS emphasis on the family, particularly the possibility of family as an eternal unit. "As I learned more about the culture of the Mormon world and Mormon families, I realized that what I was seeing was a multi-dimensional level of rejection. It was the rejection by their family, the rejection by their church and their culture, and the rejection for eternity because they would lose their family and all of those connections for eternity.... If you were a Mormon and you were gay, there was not a place for you."[12]

Prior to the Prop 8 campaign in 2008, Ryan and her coauthor, Robert Rees, a former LDS bishop, met with LDS General Authority Bruce Porter. "He looked at all of the research, all of my charts, all of our findings. He was really fascinated by them. I went over all of the rejecting behaviors that we had identified in our research and shown how they related to serious health risks. He said, 'Well, we would not want any of our families to be engaging in any of these behaviors.' I thought, 'That's great!' Because if we now know that the Church would not be supporting any of these rejecting behaviors, that's a great place to start." The hang-up was with the accepting behaviors. While agreeing with most of them, Porter pushed back against one: "Supporting your child by welcoming LGBT friends and partners to the home." In doing this, he echoed the earlier pronouncement by Dallin Oaks.

Using Porter's comments as a guide, Ryan and Rees worked for several years on an LDS version of *Supportive Families, Healthy Children*. In 2011 she and Rees met with church officials and presented them with a draft version of the booklet. "What happened was in the meetings they said that they really needed more time to learn about it.... They asked me if I would consider working with the Church to potentially put out a church version of the publication. I said to them, 'I would be happy to discuss that with you. That means going to the Correlation Committee and so forth?' They said, 'Yes.' I said, 'Yes, I'd be happy to discuss that with you.'" But the discussion never happened. "They did not respond after that meeting."

Absent endorsement from the church, Ryan and Rees proceeded to publish the LDS version of the booklet in June 2012. An article in the *Deseret News* suggested a reason for the lack of endorsement. The article quoted Ty Mansfield, a marriage and family therapist and openly gay Mormon in a mixed-orientation marriage, who "expressed concern that the way the pamphlet is framed 'is unhelpful and may even do subtle harm. The pamphlet's assumption of a predetermined and rubber-stamped "LGBT" identity is problematic.'"[13] In other words, neither Mansfield nor the church was yet willing to acknowledge that homosexuality is biological.

While the church did not endorse Ryan's work, many Latter-day Saints did. Wendy Montgomery, whose son came out shortly after the Prop 8 campaign, said, "This book gave me hope when I couldn't find it anywhere, and I have looked harder than at any other time in my life. I wasn't sleeping, I wasn't eating. I was researching everything, and I started with the Church, because that was what had always given me answers before. I read every single word that was ever written, that I could find, about homosexuality in the Church, and all of it was devastating to me. It was the darkest place I had ever been in my life. Ever. When I found her work, it felt like sunshine."[14]

Montgomery felt strongly that Ryan and Rees's booklet needed "to be in the hands of every bishop and every stake president. We were given an Evergreen pamphlet that is horrible. This is what needs to be given." But when she attempted to spread the message to a broader base of church members, she hit a wall. Reacting to a request to use a church building in California to talk about the pamphlet and show an accompanying film, *Families Are Forever*, produced by Ryan and featuring the Montgomery family, Apostle Boyd Packer responded, "There will be no talk of the Montgomerys' story, and there will be no talk of the Family Acceptance Project in any of our church buildings."[15]

AFFIRMATION

In 1977 a group of gay LDS students organized Affirmation/GMU (Gay Mormons United). An article in the *Advocate*, a national LGBT magazine, said, "The organizers have worked slowly and carefully to assure that their group is able to survive the hostility that the L.D.S. church has traditionally shown toward gay people." Affirmation's first director, S. Matthew Price, explained, "Before organizing ourselves, we were a small, close-knit group on the campus of Brigham Young University. But after hearing about all the suicides taking place, we decided it was time for us to come out."[16]

An early newsletter of Affirmation, which called Mormon gays "the most oppressed and guilt-laden group, as well as the most misunderstood, within the Church," summed up the organization's mission: "To provide a positive and supportive atmosphere where LDS gays and Lesbians can meet each other, discuss issues of importance; to help lessen the paranoia and guilt, fear and self-oppression that LDS homosexuals experience via programs, activities, projects, mutual edification socially, emotionally, as well as religiously." Animosity toward the church characterized the organization, as recalled by Buckley Jeppson. "I was the membership secretary for years. I went through those years of horrific antagonism. The activism and the yelling and the screeching were just unbearable."[17]

In 1982 Paul Mortensen, one of Affirmation's founders, tried to put a positive spin on the group's efforts. "We want to change the church rather than leave it. We don't want to throw out everything just because they're wrong on this one point." In words that proved prophetic, he foresaw "an end to automatic excommunication of gays, and more integration of openly gay people into the church."[18] But despite periodic attempts to engage the church hierarchy in dialogue, Affirmation leaders were consistently rebuffed.

When Thomas Monson became church president in early 2008, the group's leaders tried once again, requesting what the *Los Angeles Times* called "an unprecedented meeting"[19] with Monson and his counselors:

> We extend to you an olive branch, a symbol of peace.... We would like to open a dialog with you to work together to find better ways to counsel and to support those Church members who are homosexual, as well as their family members and their Priesthood leaders.... Although there are many areas of hurt and disagreement that have separated us, there are many more areas on which we can find agreement and, in so doing, become a blessing in the lives of many of the Saints, both straight and gay.[20]

The request was bumped down to the sub–General Authority level to Fred Riley, commissioner of LDS Family Services. Nonetheless, David Melson, an Affirmation officer, said, "We're pleased the church is opening up the possibility for dialogue. Affirmation has tried 5 or 6 times over the past 31 years to meet with church leaders."[21]

The meeting—the first ever between Affirmation officers and any arm of the church—was scheduled for August 2008. But three weeks prior to the appointed date—and in the heat of battle over Proposition 8—the church backed out. When Affirmation publicized the news, the church responded testily, "The issues surrounding same gender attraction deserve careful attention not public posturing. It appears from Affirmation's actions today that it has opted for a public rather than a private exchange."[22] The meeting was never rescheduled.

In late 2012, just months after the strides forward of Mormons Building Bridges and the Family Acceptance Project, Randall Thacker was elected president of Affirmation. Things began to change quickly, and not just because of Thacker. John Gustav-Wrathall, Thacker's successor in 2015, noted,

> Affirmation became more willing to open up a dialogue with the Church because quite a few of us also realized that we needed to engage with our faith and come to terms with our sexual orientation or gender identity in a space where we could affirm that you

can be both LGBT and Mormon, that you shouldn't have to leave
one or the other aspect of yourself at the door. A number of us were
starting to coalesce through social media between 2005 and 2010,
and then the Affirmation conference at Kirtland, Ohio, where we
had an incredible devotional in the Kirtland Temple became a kind
of turning point for Affirmation. A lot of us were determined to
claim our faith without compromising what we had learned about
ourselves in the process of coming out and coming to terms with
being L, G, B or T.[23]

One of Thacker's first initiatives was to request a meeting with Bill Evans
in LDS Public Affairs. Evans accepted the invitation, the meeting with officials in Public Affairs was not postponed this time, and the relationship
between the two organizations changed. Alan Blodgett, the church's former
chief financial officer, who later came out, praised the change. "I have been
astounded, and pleased at the change that has taken place in the Affirmation organization since Thacker took over. Before him, Affirmation leaders
thought of the organization as an activist group in opposition to the church
and its leaders. Affirmation was in decline and consideration was given to
disbanding the group. With Thacker and his associates, the appeal has been
to those who wish to hold on to their faith, and they work toward reconcile-
ment with the church."[24]

Accompanying Affirmation's qualitative changes in 2012 have been
ongoing quantitative changes. Gustav-Wrathall reports "a quadrupling in
conference attendance, hundreds of straight family and allies attending conference, unprecedented numbers of LGBT youth/teens attending, unprecedented financial growth, . . . [and] new chapters in a dozen countries."[25]

MAMA DRAGONS

A more recently formed group is focused on protecting LGBT children rather
than building a bridge to institutional Mormonism. Formed in 2014 by eight
LDS mothers of LGBT children via a Facebook message group, by the end
of 2017 the Mama Dragons had more than seventeen hundred members.

A 2015 article described the activities of the group: "The Dragons open
their homes to gay Mormons fleeing their families for fear of retribution
or shunning. They invite lesbian, gay, bisexual and transgender kids over

for dinner on holidays or anytime the young people feel lonely or, some-times, suicidal.... On two occasions, several Mamas traveled together to funerals to support mothers of young gay Mormons who took their lives." One of the cofounders, Wendy Montgomery, made it more personal. "I am a Mama Dragon. For my son, and for every other gay, lesbian or transgen-der child out there who needs me. I will fight for you, love you and breathe fire for you. Because that is what the God I believe in has asked me to do."[26]

MORMONSANDGAYS.ORG

In late December 2012, newly elected Affirmation president Randall Thacker met with members of the church's Public Affairs Department. What otherwise might have been a perfunctory getting-to-know-you meeting instead went in a different direction because of what had happened two weeks earlier: the unveiling by the church of a new website, MormonsandGays.org. Thacker reported to his board, "They were great. Asked lots, and lots, and lots of questions and listened spectacularly. They want lots of ideas about how to show members how to build more inclusiveness, including ways to enhance *mormonsandgays.org*. They want us to feel comfortable coming to them with ideas and suggestions."[1]

According to one internal source who asked not to be identified, the website had been in development for three years—which meant work had begun during the Prop 8 backlash. The official announcement by the church began, "In an effort to encourage understanding and civil conversation about same-sex attraction, The Church of Jesus Christ of Latter-day Saints has launched the website 'Love One Another: A Discussion on Same-Sex Attraction.'"[2]

The website was truly groundbreaking in several ways:

- The name itself, by using *Gays* as a noun, broke with the decades-old insistence by Boyd Packer that *homosexual* and its synonyms were adjectives indicating a temporary status rather than nouns indicating a permanent one.
- "Even though individuals do not choose to have such attractions, they do choose how to respond to them." This reversed the statements of many church leaders over many decades, including church

presidents, who insisted that people choose to have same-sex attraction.

- "Attraction to those of the same sex, however, should not be viewed as a disease or illness." This reversed statements by previous church leaders, such as one by Spencer Kimball: "Through the years, we have heard that homosexuality was an incurable disease but now many authorities agree that one is recoverable from its clutches.... We know such a disease is curable."[3]
- "No one fully knows the roots of same-sex attraction." While using the qualifying adverb *fully*, the statement effectively undermined dozens of church leaders who, for over a century, were unambiguous in their pronouncements of the causes—and cures—of homosexuality.
- "Unlike in times past, the Church does not necessarily advise those with same-sex attraction to marry those of the opposite sex." This statement was important because it acknowledged, by implication, that its leaders' past advice may have been erroneous, something the church seldom does. It was also a much-needed reassurance to those who did not want to—or were not able to—venture into a mixed-orientation marriage.

What the website did not include was any change in the church's position on same-sex marriage or homosexual intimacy. Indeed, the church restated its prior position, but added, "What is changing—and what needs to change—is to help church members respond sensitively and thoughtfully when they encounter same-sex attraction in their own families, among other church members or elsewhere." Without specifically mentioning Caitlin Ryan's work, the church was endorsing her findings.

A major focus of the website was to assist LGBT Church members in staying and to welcome back those who had left. Apostle Todd Christofferson, in a video clip on the website, said, "When people have those [same-sex] desires and attractions our attitude is, 'Stay with us.'"

Missing from the website was any kind of call to action in the political arena.[4] Indeed, the church's own political involvement had changed drastically in the aftermath of Prop 8, as it sat out four 2012 ballot measures in Maine, Maryland, Minnesota, and Washington State. In an article about the new website, Jim Dabakis said the fact that the church "didn't get involved in any of the four races [gay marriage initiatives] that were on the [November] ballot—not one volunteer, not one dollar—is evidence of this kind of change, and our community has changed dramatically, too."[5]

The most intriguing question raised by MormonsandGays.org was that of the very nature of homosexuality. For decades there had been a consensus within the Mormon hierarchy, largely conforming to expert opinion nationally, that it was simply a voluntary choice that could be unchosen. But a steady stream of scientific evidence pointing to a biological imprint—a combination of genes and the manner in which epigenetic[6] factors influence the behavior of those genes—gradually penetrated the thinking of at least some of the senior church leaders. One who dug deeply into the literature and consulted with medical experts was Dallin Oaks. He cracked opened the door to a biological explanation in his 2006 interview, part of which was posted on the new website, by distancing the church from the behavioral etiology: "The Church does not have a position on the causes of any of these susceptibilities or inclinations, including those related to same-gender attraction." But backing away from a prior position is not the same as moving forward into a new one, and the website took a small step forward.

By saying "individuals do not choose to have such attractions," the church occupied a middle ground that allowed for a biological explanation without directly embracing it, while at the same time holding LGBT Church members accountable for acting out the natural impulses of their not-chosen homosexuality. Such a compromise position is understandable when one considers the conundrum of a full embrace of biological causation: if LGBT people are biologically programmed to be attracted to members of the same sex, is it fair to punish them for engaging in same-sex intimacy within the confines of marriage—the same thing that heterosexuals are encouraged to do? The question is not without precedent within Mormon history: for more than a century, black individuals were denied ordination to the LDS lay priesthood simply because they were black. Responding to the feelings of many members that this was unfair, church leaders devised an after-the-fact justification for the policy that posited that in a premortal state, black people were less valiant than others. That justification was discarded when Spencer W. Kimball extended the priesthood to all worthy black men. This raised the question: How much longer could the unequal treatment of homosexual members of the church survive?

KITCHEN V. HERBERT

In nine years following the ratification of Utah's Amendment 3, which embedded in the state constitution a ban on same-sex marriage, the social fabric of the country changed dramatically. Early in the summer of 2013, the U.S. Supreme Court issued its ruling on *Hollingsworth v. Perry*, the U.S. District Court case that overturned California's Prop 8 as unconstitutional. Although the Supreme Court did not rule on the merits of the case, it found that ProtectMarriage.com, which had pursued the case through the District Court and the Ninth Circuit, lacked standing as a party because it had not suffered a personal and tangible harm. Thus, the Supreme Court allowed Judge Vaughn Walker's ruling that Prop 8 was unconstitutional.

In another case, *United States v. Windsor*, the Supreme Court also ruled unconstitutional the federal Defense of Marriage Act, which had been in effect since 1996. It then became a foregone conclusion among LGBT activists that national legalization of same-sex marriage was inevitable, with the only uncertainties being when and by what route it would occur. While some states had acted legislatively to legalize same-sex marriage, others, particularly the conservative "red states," were unlikely to move in that direction either by legislative action or by voter initiative. That left the courts as the likely route.

Utah, because of its conservative political bent and its majority LDS population, was perhaps the most unexpected place for the next domino to fall. The president of the Utah Senate, Wayne Niederhauser, said, "The Legislature is not going to anytime soon propose a repeal of Amendment 3. It's not perpetual, but it's pretty close.... If any change happens, it's going to happen through a court process, in my opinion."[1]

As Prop 8 and DOMA were being deliberated at the Supreme Court, Mark Lawrence, a gay activist (not related to Gary Lawrence, who played a prominent role in Proposition 8), started a Facebook group called Restore Our Humanity and began to talk to people in Utah. Troy Williams, executive director of Equality Utah, spoke of the pivotal role Lawrence played:

> He is the upstart who came along and filed the lawsuit. He is cranky, not a polished gay who is safe. He is the upstart, more of the Queer Nation type. He was the guy who pulled it all together. He pulled the plaintiffs and the attorneys together. He's kind of a great character, although he is kind of tragic in the sense that he can't get along with people, and so he was falling out with the plaintiffs and falling out with the attorneys, and wasn't able to fully enjoy it. He sabotaged himself as he moved through it, but he was great because he didn't know that what he set out to do was impossible, and so he did it. All the best thinkers were saying, "Don't do it." But it was the right moment, and Mark will always go down in history for seeing what the rest of us could not see.[2]

Lawrence's objective was to assemble a legal team, find ideal plaintiffs, and then challenge Amendment 3 in court. Restore Our Humanity settled on the small Salt Lake City law firm of Magleby & Greenwood, with Peggy Tomsic agreeing to take the lead.[3]

Although the LDS Church played no direct role in the lawsuit, named *Kitchen v. Herbert*, the Mormon overtones were inescapable. Amendment 3 had been proposed and passed by a legislature whose membership was estimated to be up to 90 percent LDS. It was ratified by an overwhelming margin of voters in the only state having a majority LDS population. It was defended, on appeal, by a prominent LDS attorney who gave up a partnership in a prestigious Washington, DC, law firm "so that I can fulfill what I have come to see as a religious and family duty."[4] And three of its six plaintiffs had been model Mormons in their earlier years—until they came out as lesbians.

Kate Call and her wife, Karen Archer, had been legally married in Iowa, but their marriage was not recognized in Utah. Call was raised in an LDS family in Provo, Utah, where her father was a professor at BYU. She served a full-time proselytizing mission in Argentina. Her realization that she was a lesbian came while she was a missionary. She shared the information with her mission president, assuming he would hold it in confidence. "Without my knowledge or consent, my mission president faxed my fourteen-page 'confession' to the General Authorities, my home bishop, and to my parents. In that manner I was outed to my family. They seemed sad and puzzled, but ultimately said they loved me unconditionally. It really wasn't until then that I began to self-identify as a lesbian. Since that time, I have been stigmatized, and suffered discrimination in both the personal and private spheres."[5]

Laurie Wood was raised in the LDS Church and served a full-time proselytizing mission in Southern California. After her mission, she went to Brigham Young University, earned a master's degree in education, and began a career in teaching. While in school at BYU, she met a woman and fell in love.[6]

Kody Partridge was raised in the LDS Church and served a full-time proselytizing mission. "I went on a mission, and I realized that I might be attracted to a woman. I *was* attracted to a woman, and I realized that I might end up spending my life with a woman."[7] After returning from her mission she earned a bachelor's degree at BYU and embarked on a career in teaching.

Wood and Partridge were living together when they were invited to be plaintiffs in a lawsuit challenging Amendment 3.

> They asked us on a Friday, and we had to decide by Sunday night. We had some pretty intense conversation over that weekend, and decided that because of the situation—I was at Utah Valley University and knew I was close to retirement, and if they wanted to fire me I didn't care, and Kody doesn't work in a public school. She works in a private school that is very supportive—so because we could, we knew we had to. So we got with Peggy Tomsic and Jim Magleby, and we met the other plaintiffs. We really didn't know what we were in for; we just knew that it was something that we definitely wanted in our state, and we wanted it for us.[8]

In March 2013, *Kitchen v. Herbert* was filed in the U.S. District Court in Salt Lake City. Judge Robert Shelby, who had been on the federal bench for only six months, was assigned the case. Nominated by Democratic president Barack Obama, Shelby received strong recommendations from Utah's two Republican U.S. senators, Orrin Hatch and Mike Lee—both active Mormons.

Hatch called him "an experienced lawyer 'with an unwavering commitment to the law.'" Lee "said Shelby was 'pre-eminently qualified' and predicted he would be an outstanding judge."[9]

Rather than having a full trial, the two sides agreed to summary judgment, which is a legal remedy in cases where the facts are not contested and the judge rules only on the basis of the law. After the two sides had filed their briefs, Judge Shelby convened a hearing on December 3. Laurie Wood recalled, "They thought it would be an hour, and it ended up being three hours long. He said he would rule sometime after the first of the year, but he came back in seventeen days and caught the world off-guard on a Friday afternoon before Christmas."[10]

As was the case in *Hollingsworth v. Perry*, Judge Shelby applied the legal test of strict scrutiny to the case—that is, if the State of Utah wished to deny to same-sex couples the same right of marriage that it extended to opposite-sex couples, it had to demonstrate in court a compelling state interest for so doing. The essence of his decision was encapsulated in two sentences: "The State of Utah has provided no evidence that opposite-sex marriage will be affected in any way by same-sex marriage. In the absence of such evidence, the State's unsupported fears and speculations are insufficient to justify the State's refusal to dignify the family relationships of its gay and lesbian citizens."[11] He also placed the decision in historical context. "It is not the Constitution that has changed, but the knowledge of what it means to be gay or lesbian. The court cannot ignore the fact that the plaintiffs are able to develop a committed, intimate relationship with a person of the same sex but not with a person of the opposite sex. The court, and the state, must adapt to this changed understanding."[12]

The decision, which was the first federal case to nullify a state ban on same-sex marriage, caught many off-guard. The timing of the decision caught everyone off-guard. Of the decision, Kate Kendell of the National Center for Lesbian Rights said, "Oh, my God, there is no way you could have anticipated [it] six years ago. On the night that Prop 8 passed, if someone would have said to me, 'I know it's bad right now and I know you feel terrible. But let me just tell you that in 2014, same-sex couples will be marrying in Utah,' I would have said, 'There is no way that is going down!' In a way, it's kind of a miracle. It's the whole 'God works in mysterious ways' kind of thing."[13]

Other observers were less than thrilled. The title of an editorial in the *Deseret New*, posted the day of the decision, conveyed as much information as the editorial itself: "In Our Opinion: Judicial Tyranny." It said,

> The essence of judicial tyranny is when a single, unelected federal judge declares the laws and constitution of an entire state null and void with an opinion clothed in the barest of legal precedent. Late on Friday afternoon, U.S. District Judge Robert J. Shelby overstepped judicial bounds, ignored the weight of settled precedent and insulted Utah's electorate by striking down Amendment 3 to Utah's Constitution, the provision that defines marriage as between one man and one woman.... Gays and lesbians are not deprived of any rights they are due in a liberal democracy when a state, like Utah, through open democratic processes insists that marriage is between a man and a woman.[14]

A statement by the church the same day was less vitriolic: "This ruling by a district court will work its way through the judicial process. We continue to believe that voters in Utah did the right thing by providing clear direction in the state constitution that marriage should be between a man and a woman, and we are hopeful that this view will be validated by a higher court."[15]

Completely surprised by the decision and its timing, the Utah attorney general's office was totally unprepared to respond to the fact that same-sex marriage was now the law of the state. Normal protocol would have called for the office to prepare, in advance, a motion for stay pending appeal and have it ready to go if the decision came down against the state. But little was normal in the office, for Attorney General John Swallow had resigned one month prior to Shelby's decision as a result of federal and state investigations of alleged improprieties on his part. In his absence, the office had not prepared motions to stay the decision. Their hastily written motion prepared after the decision was procedurally flawed and was dismissed by the Tenth Circuit Court of Appeals. They appealed the decision to Justice Sonia Sotomayor of the U.S. Supreme Court, who in turn referred the matter to the entire court. On January 6, 2014, the Supreme Court granted a stay pending final disposition of the case, but between December 20 and January 6, same-sex marriage was legal in Utah.

Four days after Justice Sotomayor's action, the church informed local leaders throughout the United States of the implications of *Kitchen v. Herbert*. One of the LDS Articles of Faith states, "We believe in being subject to kings, presidents, rulers, and magistrates, in obeying, honoring, and sustaining the law." Now that same-sex marriage was the law of the state—and likely soon to become the law of the land—they had a delicate balancing act to perform. In a letter to all local church leaders in the United States, the First Presidency and Quorum of the Twelve Apostles wrote, "Changes in the civil law do not, indeed cannot, change the moral law that God has established. God expects us to uphold and keep His commandments regardless of divergent opinions or trends in society. His law of chastity is clear: sexual relations are proper only between a man and a woman who are legally and lawfully wedded as husband and wife." While asking that "those who avail themselves of laws or court rulings authorizing same-sex marriage should not be treated disrespectfully," they directed that no church official perform same-sex marriages (even though such officials receive their authority to conduct marriages from the state, and not the church) and that church properties not be used for "ceremonies, receptions, or other activities associated with same-sex marriages."[16]

Although the church did not waver in its condemnation of same-sex marriage, many of its members did. A poll commissioned by the *Salt Lake Tribune* days after Judge Shelby's decision was announced showed an even split, with 48 percent of respondents in favor of and 48 percent opposed to same-sex marriages being performed in Utah. Seventy-two percent were in favor of same-sex civil unions or domestic partnerships. This was an astounding shift in the decade since 66 percent of voters approved Amendment 3, which banned not only same-sex marriages but also disenfranchised civil unions and domestic partnerships.[17] It was also a dramatic shift even in the shorter run, with support for same-sex marriage being 20 percent higher in 2014 than just two years earlier.[18]

Although there had been several high-profile Mormon and ex-Mormon players throughout the process of the lawsuit at the level of the U.S. District Court, the church itself had no official involvement. Once the case was appealed to the Tenth Circuit Court of Appeals, the church reentered the fray by partnering with the Roman Catholic Church, Southern Baptist Convention, and Lutheran Church–Missouri Synod in submitting an amicus brief, coauthored by attorneys representing the LDS and Roman Catholic Churches.[19]

Oral arguments before the appellate court occurred early in April in Denver. Two months later, the court upheld Judge Shelby's decision. Applying the legal test of strict scrutiny, the appellate judges found that the state's arguments, which largely focused on how same-sex marriage affects child rearing, as well as religious freedom, did not hold up.[20] The church responded with the following statement: "The Church has been consistent in its support of marriage between a man and a woman and teaches that all people should be treated with respect. In anticipation that the case will be brought before the U.S. Supreme Court, it is our hope that the nation's highest court will uphold traditional marriage."[21] The stay on performing same-sex marriages in Utah remained in effect until the case went before the highest court.

When *Kitchen v. Herbert* was appealed to the U.S. Supreme Court, once again the LDS Church weighed in with an amicus brief. Cases from other states, all of which had been decided in favor of same-sex marriage, were simultaneously appealed. At the beginning of its annual session in October 2014, the Supreme Court declined to hear any of the cases.[22] "The unexpected move—a denial of *certiorari*[23] in seven appeals from five states—effectively legalized gay marriage in 11 new states, making same-sex unions legal in most of the country for the first time in history."[24] Although the court gave no explanation for its decision, a *New York Times* article reported, "In recent remarks, Justice Ruth Bader Ginsburg said there was no urgency for the court to act until a split emerged in the federal appeals courts, all of whose recent decisions have been in favor of same-sex marriage." In a terse reply, the LDS Church announced that the ruling would have no effect on its doctrinal position or practices, although "as far as the civil law is concerned, the courts have spoken."[25]

Since the Supreme Court decision affected only eleven states, there was still a glimmer of hope for opponents of same-sex marriage that the highest court would weigh in later and stop more dominoes from falling.

SB 296

The high-profile role of the LDS Church in the passage of Salt Lake City non-discrimination legislation in 2009 was heralded by many as a turn toward a more progressive stance on LGBT issues. The city council's support of nondiscrimination legislation was not surprising, for Salt Lake City is an island of blue in red Utah—among the reddest states in the country. A much more telling test of the church's commitment to LGBT nondiscrimination would be its willingness to endorse statewide legislation. Although legislators sympathetic to LGBT issues continued to introduce antidiscrimination legislation after 2009, the church remained silent and the proposed bills died in committee.

In 2013, however, there was significant behind-the-scenes activity. Early in the legislative session a church official, who spoke on condition of anonymity, said:

> We still haven't worked it through internally, as far as the Church touch-points are concerned, but we are getting a lot closer. I can see possibilities. But once we get it worked through internally, then we have to sit down with the LGBT folks and see if we can all agree on what it is that we can all agree on. It's going to require, on both sides, some give-and-take, and maybe some significant give-and-take. But the possibility of a model where a conservative religious community supports basic nondiscrimination rights within employment and housing, and an LGBT community supports a reasonable protection of religious conscience in the same area could be a very positive and very powerful model.

Word of negotiations that had proceeded quietly for eight months went public early in February. "Attorneys for The Church of Jesus Christ of Latter-day Saints are in quiet discussions with leaders of Utah's gay and lesbian community, trying to hammer out language for a statewide ban on housing and employment discrimination that the church could support.... If the LDS Church, the state's largest faith to which nearly 90 percent of the Utah Legislature belongs, were to endorse the anti-discrimination bill, it would be a major boost for efforts to pass the legislation, which has failed the past several years." An editorial published a week later emphasized the necessity of a nod from the church. "Given the Legislature's antipathy toward the LGBT community, only the LDS Church's imprimatur could wring approval of a statewide ban from a body that is around 90 percent Mormon."[1]

Late in the legislative session a Utah Senate committee approved, for the first time, a statewide nondiscrimination bill on a four-to-three vote but too late in the session to allow floor debate and vote. Absent was the anticipated endorsement of the church in the wake of the months-long negotiations. On the final day of the legislative session, the church issued a tepid statement that it had not taken a position on the legislation. Church spokesman Michael Purdy said, "The church is on the record supporting non-discrimination protections for gay and lesbian citizens related to housing and employment. We also believe that any legislation should protect these rights while also preserving the rights of religious conscience—to act in accordance with deeply held religious beliefs—for individuals and organizations."[2]

Purdy's words suggested that the church's refusal to back the legislation lay in its dissatisfaction with language protecting religious conscience. A report several months later added weight to that premise. "The bill was to be sponsored by a prominent LDS state senator, Curt Bramble. Bramble, historically one of Utah's most conservative Republican legislators, remarked to the media that he would bring the bill forward if the LDS Church approved the final language." As the forty-five-day legislative session proceeded, Brandie Balken, executive director of Equality Utah, received repeated assurances that "they were just working diligently to make sure they 'got it right,' which is Utah political doublespeak for 'Mormon-approved.'" The reason the legislation failed, the report concluded, was "the Church would not approve the language."[3]

Judge Robert Shelby's stunning decision in *Kitchen v. Herbert* at the end of 2013 resulted in an embargo of all LGBT legislation in the 2014 Utah legislative session. The refusal of the U.S. Supreme Court in October 2014 to hear an appeal settled the issue of same-sex marriage in Utah and thus changed the discourse. Clifford Rosky, who provided legal counsel to Equality Utah, said, "Once marriage was finally legalized in Utah—not temporarily, but permanently—then that really opened up a space, because the slippery slope concern was gone now. ... If you are opposed to employment discrimination and opposed to housing discrimination, and your only argument is that you don't want to legalize that because you are worried about marriage, and marriage is here, what's the hold-up? So that created the space."[4]

For a brief time, it appeared that the church was willing to fill that space. One year, to the day, after Judge Shelby announced his decision, and two months after the Supreme Court declined to review it, someone in the Church Office Building leaked to Mormons Building Bridges a beta version of a church website.[5] The paragraph in question appeared to be a full-throated, unprecedented endorsement of statewide antidiscrimination legislation in the areas of LGBT housing and employment: "Church leaders recognize the existence and difficulty of same gender attraction and acknowledge the difference between having same-sex attraction and acting on it. They censure only the latter, and leaders strongly advocate for understanding, inclusion, and kindness toward people of all gender orientations. The Church website mormonsandgays.org details sincere outreach by the Church within the gay community, including support in Utah for nondiscrimination protections of employment and housing."[6]

The apparent endorsement was quickly walked back. "Less than 24 hours after releasing a statement on their website saying the Church of Jesus Christ of Latter Day Saints (Mormon) supported workplace and housing protections for LGBTQ Utahns, church officials have altered that statement to limit the support to a local Salt Lake City ordinance passed in 2009." The phrase "including support in Utah" was changed to "including support in Salt Lake City in 2009." Church spokesman Eric Hawkins said, "The reference to non-discrimination ordinances was meant to reflect the church's support for the 2009 Salt Lake ordinance and is not an announcement of any kind."[7] A parallel statement in the *Deseret News* said that the church "has not changed its position on legislation that protects gays from discrimination in housing and employment."[8]

The rapid about-face was highly unusual for the church and its competent and professional Public Affairs Department. One legislator, who spoke on condition of anonymity, wasn't buying the explanation. "I really believe this is part of a much bigger crisis of leadership. There are factions, and things come and go, and there is a lot of pushing and shoving."

In a meeting in January 2015, the church placed its cards on the table. Troy Williams, executive director of Equality Utah, attended the meeting. "We started talking and it was all very cordial. Then, Alexander Dushku [an attorney representing the church] started talking about individual conscience, saying, 'Why can't you guys budge on the issue of an individual using their conscience, protecting them?' I said, 'I know exactly what that means—that means being able to use your deeply-held religious beliefs to discriminate freely, à la Arizona. Right?'" Rather than argue the fine points of the law, Williams, who is not an attorney, got personal.

"I need to interrupt you gentlemen for a second. I need to tell you about myself. I'm a returned missionary. My entire family is Mormon—my grandparents, my aunts and uncles. My mom died of cancer five years ago, and I had no relationship with her because of this." That stopped Dushku, and it stopped the legal-speak. I said, "For whatever reason, Mormons have lots of gay babies. I don't know why it is, but you do. The people who are hurt the greatest from this culture war are Mormon and Christian families with gay kids, siblings, aunts and uncles. We have to stop this. Our families are being torn apart. We have to stop this, and I need your help to do it. What are we going to do?" That changed the whole tone of the meeting. Dushku was quiet. No more legal talk for the rest of the meeting....

I spoke about my dad and how difficult it was for him to have a gay son—and particularly to have a gay activist son. It's something he can't process and can't talk to me about. Michael [Purdy] was very sensitive to that and wanted to know more about it. And so, we started talking as humans speak to each other. We started dealing with empathy, eyeball-to-eyeball, and heart-to-heart. I thought, "This is how I am going to talk to these guys. It's the only thing I know to do."[9]

On January 26, 2015, the opening day of the Utah legislative session, Troy Williams received an email from Michael Purdy. "[It said] 'I need to talk to you in the morning. We have something to tell you, and I want to give you a heads-up.' I had no idea what this meant. I got on the phone with [State Senator James] Dabakis, and he said, 'They are going to endorse it, we think.'" The following morning, Purdy called Williams and told him that there would be a press conference in one hour. When Williams asked the nature of the event, Purdy responded with a mixed message that was not clarified by the conference: "We are going to endorse the nondiscrimination legislation, and we are going to advocate for religious liberty." When Williams asked, "What do you mean by that, Michael? Do you mean for individuals?" Purdy responded, "Troy, we want fairness for all."

In contrast to the private setting of Williams's comments, those of Senator Steve Urquhart, a strong supporter of antidiscrimination legislation, were quite public. As the legislative session began, he told a reporter, "The fate of this bill is entirely in the hands of the Mormon Church. Most of the legislature is Mormon, and on this issue they are looking to do the bidding of the Mormon God and the Mormon Church. The Mormon Church knows this and knows that the bill will fail without its active participation, because of decades of prior teachings. So if the Mormon Church wants to end employment and housing discrimination in its own state, it will speak up on this issue." Asked if that factored into the church's decision to make a public statement, he responded, "I don't know."[10]

Church leaders organized the press conference on short notice, and Williams and Urquhart received copies of the press release only minutes before it began.

THE PRESS CONFERENCE

Three apostles—Dallin Oaks, Jeffrey Holland, and Todd Christofferson— along with Neill Marriott, a counselor in the general presidency of the Young Women, participated in the conference. Although the lineup was impressive—indeed, arguably unprecedented—the mechanics were awkward and certainly not up to the usual high standards of the Public Affairs Department. The press release gave the appearance of having been hastily written. Senator Urquhart said of it, "The Church doesn't usually put out things with such poor grammar."[11]

In reaching out in advance to Troy Williams, Michael Purdy had indicated that the purpose of the conference was to endorse the proposed nondiscrimination legislation and to advocate for religious liberty. How-ever, the endorsement was almost lost amid impassioned rhetoric stress-ing the need for assurances that churches—and particularly the LDS Church—would be exempted from the same legislation that its leaders were endorsing. Dallin Oaks said, "Those who seek the protection of reli-gious conscience and expression and the free exercise of their religion look with alarm at the steady erosion of treasured freedoms that are guaran-teed in the United States Constitution.... Today we see new examples of attacks on religious freedom with increasing frequency."[12] He gave four examples of such attacks:

- The University of California system—a public institution supported by taxpayer money—denied recognition of several Christian stu-dent groups because they excluded gays and non-Christians from leadership.
- Government lawyers subpoenaed the sermons and notes of Hous-ton pastors who opposed parts of a new law on religious grounds.
- Peter Vidmar, a gold medal–winning Olympic gymnast and active Latter-day Saint, was pressured to resign as the symbolic head of the U.S. Olympic delegation because he had made a $2,000 dona-tion to Yes on 8.
- Brendan Eich was forced to resign as CEO of Mozilla because of his personal beliefs regarding LGBT rights.

Oaks decried these breaches of religious freedom as "every bit as wrong as denying access to employment, housing or public services because of race or gender. Churches should stand on at least as strong a footing as any other entity when they enter the public square to participate in public pol-icy debates.... It is one of today's great ironies that some people who have fought so hard for LGBT rights now try to deny the rights of others to dis-agree with their public policy proposals." While acknowledging that the LDS Church "is on record as favoring such [LGBT nondiscrimination] measures," he stressed the need for "laws that protect faith communities and individ-uals against discrimination and retaliation for claiming the core rights of free expression and religious practice that are at the heart of our identity as a nation and our legacy as citizens." However, the four examples he gave were highly problematic, and none held up to scrutiny.[13]

Jeffrey Holland followed by stressing that "church-owned businesses or entities that are directly related to the purposes and functions of the church must have the same latitude in employment standards and practices as the church itself." He also echoed the call by Oaks for individuals to be exempted from antidiscrimination legislation. "For example, a Latter-day Saint physician who objects to performing abortions or artificial insemination for a lesbian couple should not be forced against his or her conscience to do so, especially when others are readily available to perform that function."[14]

Local reaction to the press conference was lukewarm. One reporter emphasized the positive effect that the church's endorsement might have on proposed legislation. "There was little question that the LDS Church announcement was a game changer. 'It drives a lot of what we do in the session when you have an announcement like that,' said House Speaker Greg Hughes."[15] But another from the same newspaper wrote a more guarded assessment. "Rep. Jacob Anderegg, R–Lehi, who is sponsoring legislation to protect religious individuals' ability to refuse to marry same-sex couples, is not so sure that passage is a sure bet. 'I still think House leadership is going to weigh the church's announcement and make a decision in the best interest of the Senate, the House and all of Utah,' he said."[16]

By contrast, national reaction to the press conference was highly critical. The message of church support for nondiscrimination legislation was lost amid scathing denunciation of what appeared to be an attempt to hold others to a standard that the church rejected for itself. A *New York Times* editorial, posted online the same day, bore the title "Mormon Church Wants Freedom to Discriminate."

> The Mormon Church is now willing, news accounts say, to support anti-discrimination legislation in the realms of housing and employment. In return, all the Mormons want are laws that "protect religious freedom."
>
> We already have that. It's called the Bill of Rights. So what is the church really after? . . .
>
> What they want is legal permission to use their religion as an excuse to discriminate. . . .
>
> Substitute the word "black" or "Jewish" or "Catholic" or, say, "Mormon" for LGBT in these statements, and everyone would be outraged. . . .

Apparently the news conference today was the product of five years' behind-the-scenes negotiations. Five years for this?[17]

The Right Reverend V. Gene Robinson, who years earlier touched off a firestorm within the Episcopal Church in the United States when he became the first openly gay clergyman to be ordained a bishop, called out what he saw as the church's hypocritical stand:

> Anti-discrimination bills, as the adjective would suggest, are meant to protect those named from being discriminated against. The Mormons' "new" stance merely proclaims that they now favor bills which would bar discrimination against lesbian, gay, bisexual and transgender (LGBT) people, as long as those who discriminate against them are given protection for doing so. Such a twisted and distorted approach stretches both the language and the substance of such legislation into an unrecognizable shape and takes us into the realm of the absurd.
>
> Couched in so-called "religious liberty" language, let's call these efforts what they really are: a license to discriminate. The Mormons' support for anti-discrimination is laudable, until you get to the part that begins with "except." It would be unlawful to discriminate, their support says, unless that discrimination comes from one's religious beliefs. Presumably, a restaurant waiter need not serve two men or two women who are quietly holding hands at their table, if the waiter objects to their "lifestyle." Also, presumably, one need not serve an African-American couple at that same restaurant if one's religion says that black people are an inferior race and should not mingle with whites. Or a Jewish couple who is not served by a waiter whose religion teaches her that Jews are not only eternally damned, but are "Christ-killers" to boot! . . .
>
> If the religious exemption is allowed in such legislation, then the Mormons' support is truly a wolf in sheep's clothing. . . . Those who support such a religious exemption to anti-discrimination legislation are trying to sound kind, while clinging to their right to be mean. I, for one, am not buying it![18]

Sarah Warbelow, legal director of the Human Rights Campaign, said, "As a matter of public policy, it appears deeply flawed. Doctors, landlords and business owners would still be allowed to discriminate against gays and lesbians, as long as they cited a religious reason."[19]

An online blog called out the fig leaf of religious liberty. "Based on other remarks made during the press conference, it may be more accurate to conclude the Church supports—or at least turns a blind eye toward—anti-LGBT discrimination as much as it ever has.... 'Religious liberty' is the very language being used by conservatives to advance legislation across the country that would allow individuals and businesses to legally discriminate against LGBT people based on their religious beliefs." In a similar vein, a *Huffington Post* article focused on the "real agenda" of the church. "The new Mormon position is like that candy with a razor blade inside that your mom warned you about on Halloween. While calling for LGBTQ people to be protected from those who hate them for non-religious reasons (and who are those people, anyway?), they have hidden their real agenda, which is to legalize such discrimination by anyone who claims their prejudice is backed by faith.... Don't believe for one second that the LDS church this morning showed compassion or humanity. They're just trying to codify their right to discriminate against LGBTQ people."[20]

A former Mormon had particularly sharp criticism for Dallin Oaks's examples of alleged violations of religious liberty:

[He] managed to work in references to the ousting of Mozilla CEO Brendan Eich, the withdrawal of state funding for Christian clubs at California schools that exclude gay students, and the pressure put on Mormon gymnast Peter Vidmar to decline his place as the U.S. chef de mission in the 2012 Olympics Opening Ceremonies after he participated in anti-same-sex marriage demonstrations.

Not only does the Mormon Church have the gall to present these stories as if they represent the end of "free speech" as we know it—it's clear that they need to spend less time reading their scriptures and more time reading the Constitution—they also go a step further by equating them with the widespread, institutional discrimination of LGBT people. Oaks boldly asserts that "[s]uch tactics are every bit as wrong as denying access to employment, housing, or public services because of race or gender" before adding this petty and fallacious swipe: "It is one of today's great ironies that some people who have fought so hard for LGBT rights now try to deny the rights of others to disagree with their public-policy proposals."

Here's another equation that Mormons should take to heart: Not tolerating intolerance is not the same thing as intolerance itself....

Trading shelter and employment for the right to discriminate on religious grounds is a devil's bargain coming from men who believe they speak for God. This isn't a "fairness for all" approach—it's a mean older sibling drawing a chalk line down the middle of the room. And what we're witnessing now is not a slow step forward but rather Mormon bigotry in its death throes, as the church tries in vain to ride the legal coattails of the very people they have been putting down for so long.[21]

"WE ARE THE VICTIMS"

Rather than adopt a conciliatory posture leading to deeper dialogue in the aftermath of the press conference, Dallin Oaks dug in. In an interview a day later, he "set off a global chain reaction among Mormons this week, when he said he wasn't sure apologizing for the faith's past rhetoric on homosexuality would be advisable. 'I know that the history of the church is not to seek apologies or to give them,' Oaks said in an interview Tuesday. 'We sometimes look back on issues and say, 'Maybe that was counterproductive for what we wish to achieve,' but we look forward and not backward.' The church doesn't 'seek apologies,' he said, 'and we don't give them.'"[22]

Doubling down in an interview broadcast on NPR he said, "We were really the victims of intimidation and retaliation and boycotts in California."[23] One blogger, a gay former Mormon who served a full-time proselytizing mission, immediately called out Oaks:

How dare the white heterosexual male LDS leadership claim they are the victims. How dare they call the very people they have been trying so hard to prevent from obtaining equal status in our society "bullies." I have not seen one suicide of a Mormon person because "those gays" just made living so unbearable for them, they couldn't stand it any longer. I have not heard of one Mormon shaking and crying and praying at night, unable to think of anything but death because "those gays" are getting closer to obtaining full equality. . . .

Them the victims and *us* the bullies?? Not tolerating intolerance is not the same as intolerance itself. I will not bow down and thank LDS leadership for allowing me to work and live without fear of being fired or evicted while they try to ensure I can be denied access to public accommodations because, for some reason, treating me like a regular equal human being goes against their "deeply held religious beliefs." Since when did everyone around you need to accept and follow your beliefs in order for you to treat them fairly? I must have forgotten the rest of that scripture—"Love thy neighbor as thyself. Unless they're a faggot. In that case, feel free to deny them service and send them on their way to find someone who isn't rightfully offended by their very existence."[24]

Troy Williams gave his read of the aftermath: "Any good will that would have come from it was overshadowed by Oak's statements about not giving apologies, and 'we were the victims.'"[25]

Ironically, the bungled press conference and its aftermath may have worked to move the nondiscrimination needle forward. Senator James Dabakis said, "They knew afterwards what an egg they had laid. It kept pressure on them to actually get the nondiscrimination thing done, so in that sense I think it worked for the good."[26]

AN UNLIKELY CHAMPION

Stephen Urquhart, an attorney living in the southwest Utah city of St. George, served in the Utah House of Representatives from 2001 to 2009, when he was elected to the Utah Senate. A staunch Republican in a deeply conservative part of the state, he nonetheless underwent a conversion experience on LGBT issues when his straight teenage daughter raised his consciousness. When she told him that she was going to be the new president of the Gay Straight Alliance at Dixie High School, he responded, "If this is something that you're doing just to do, how about you don't?"

Then I said, "But now, let's talk not politician to daughter. Let's talk father to daughter, because that's the conversation that really matters," he continued. "If this is something that matters to you, then to hell with political concerns."

She responded that it wasn't about her sexuality but about her gay friends. Life was extremely tough for them, and she wanted to offer her support, she told him.

I said, "Great, then this is something we're doing. I'm with you," he recounted.

Urquhart said his thinking began to shift. He stopped seeing sexual orientation as defining a person.[27]

Urquhart's "conversion" came at a fortuitous time. LGBT nondiscrimination legislation—which had been proposed but never passed—had always been sponsored by Democrats, who constitute a vanishingly small caucus within the Utah Legislature.[28] Democrat James Dabakis, who became a state senator in December 2012, saw a problem. "It was *never* going to pass with a Democratic sponsor. So I said to Brandie Balken [executive director of Equality Utah], 'Give it to Urquhart. I'm not going to put my name on it. I'll be a co-sponsor, but let him carry it.' I think that was the genesis of it being viewed as bipartisan."[29] From 2013 forward, Urquhart was the sponsor.

SB 296

As the dust slowly settled from the press conference, the sausage-making process began within the legislature. The proposed bill, SB 296, basically amended existing Utah laws such that "sexual orientation and gender identity" joined other protected classes (such as race and religion) with respect to employment and housing. Those existing laws proved crucial to the success of SB 296. Attorney Clifford Rosky explained:

> Utah's antidiscrimination laws were already unlike any other state's laws, in that the exemptions for religious organizations were very broad. Under Utah law—and we have had antidiscrimination laws since 1969—religious organizations have been exempt from the whole law, so they can discriminate based on race, sex, disability, whatever. That created an opportunity, because all of the things we endorse have to treat LGBT people the same as everyone else. We can't have special rules and burdens for LGBT people.

Inclusion, in our antidiscrimination laws, would mean inclusion with all of the same exemptions that applied to everyone else. So we were not going to pass a law that said churches can't discriminate against gay people, or BYU can't discriminate against gay people. That would be very hard. That would have to get litigated: how does that work? So that problem was already addressed, and that created a huge opportunity.[30]

The devil was in the details.

A SMOKELESS BACK ROOM

A decade earlier, when Amendment 3 moved through the legislative process, the LDS Church was nowhere to be seen. Indeed, a church official, speaking on background, described disappointment on the part of highly placed church leaders who may have foreseen some of the problems that the amendment eventually created, culminating in *Kitchen v. Herbert*. SB 296 was different. Way different. While the basic outline of the legislation had been drawn up in the state senate, the hammering out of details occurred in backroom negotiations that included legislators, LGBT representatives, the American Civil Liberties Union, LDS Church Public Affairs officials, and attorneys representing the church.

Senator James Dabakis was one of the legislators. "It was Hell. It was awful. It was the most difficult thing in history. We were hours and hours and hours and hours."[31] By late February the process had bogged down as attorneys for the two sides argued incessantly over language, with neither side budging. A back-channel appeal to a "high church leader" seemed momentarily to break the logjam, but by the end of the month there was still no agreement on final language.

On Sunday evening, March 1, Senator Urquhart called an emergency meeting that included himself; Senator Dabakis; Michael Purdy of LDS Public Affairs; Alexander Dushku of the law firm Kirton McConkie, representing the church; Robin Wilson, a professor of law from the University of Illinois; Marina Lowe, representing the American Civil Liberties Union; and Clifford Rosky, representing Equality Utah.[32] The primary unresolved issue was religious exemptions. The meeting lasted for three hours, with tempers periodically flaring along the way. Exasperated with the attorneys,

Dabakis finally said, "Guys, this is not about your lofty road of blah, blah; this is about us coming together. You need to get out the way so we can get this thing done. We're not going to get this close again. If this turns out to all blow up, it's going to be on you." Finally, it came down to the Boy Scouts. "It was eight fulltime jobs in Utah that they were worried about. So I said, 'OK, let's make an exemption for the Boy Scouts.' . . . The irony was that that exemption already existed because of the Supreme Court decision in *Boy Scouts of America v. Dale*. It wasn't new ground, but we put 'Boy Scouts of America' in the bill anyway."[33]

Everyone was exhausted, but there was still one hang-up—one word that took the entire matter to the edge of the precipice the following morning. After an eleventh-hour meeting between Senator Stuart Adams, Clifford Rosky, and Marina Lowe, a compromise was reached.[34]

All of the anguish over the meetings, particularly the marathon on Sunday night, served the essential purpose of getting backing from the LDS Church, something that had never happened before on statewide nondiscrimination legislation. The wall between church and state in Utah has always been made of different material than in other states or the federal government, with no better example than the fact that Brigham Young was simultaneously president of the LDS Church *and* governor of the Territory of Utah. However, despite the protests of some at the influence the church can exert in Utah politics, it has the legal right to become involved in political issues so long as it steers clear of endorsing specific candidates for public office. Senator Dabakis explained, "I live in a real world where fifteen votes wins, and there were not going to be fifteen votes in the Senate until we got one big 'Yes.' Why would we spend tens and hundreds of thousands of dollars on lobbyists, lobbying a legislature that was unwinnable until we got that one 'Yes'? So how do we get the one 'Yes'? That became my goal."[35]

THE SECOND PRESS CONFERENCE

Even with the input from the church and its private approval of the final wording of SB 296, passage of the bill was not a foregone conclusion. LDS legislators who for decades had been taught in church that homosexuality was a sin meriting excommunication were not easily motivated to vote in favor of extending rights to a group of "sinners." Senator Dabakis knew what would be necessary to cross the goal line.

I said to the church people, "You have to come up here." They said, "We don't go up there." "You have to come up to the Hill, and you have to have a press conference." That's a tough thing for them to do. We started to talk about what they were going to say, and I said, "You have to endorse 296.... You guys not only have to come, but you have to say, 'We support 296.' You have to say it three or four times. There can be no ambiguity, or we will lose everything." They said, "OK, we will mention 296."

So then they called and said, "We are going to send Elder [Todd] Christofferson and Sister [Neill] Marriott." I said, "No, you have to have a senior apostle! These guys need to be convinced that this isn't some rogue P.R. thing. We have to have [Boyd] Packer or [Tom] Perry. If you send Christofferson, they aren't going to buy it. You have to send a senior guy!"[36]

On March 4, 2015, Apostles Perry and Christofferson, along with Neill Marriott, made a rare, perhaps unprecedented, appearance on Utah's Capitol Hill to endorse SB 296.[37] All three spoke. Christofferson gave an unqualified endorsement: "The Church of Jesus Christ of Latter-day Saints is proud today to support SB 296."[38]

The day after the press conference, SB 296 sailed through the senate committee with a unanimous vote. The following day it passed the full senate by a vote of twenty-three to five. One week later, the house followed suit, approving the bill by a vote of sixty-five to ten. Governor Gary Herbert arranged for a public signing event in the capitol rotunda. In an unscripted moment, Dabakis looked at Perry, who was at the capitol for the second time in two weeks. "I noticed that Elder Perry, who was there, pointed to me and said, 'You are the man!' So I grabbed the microphone, went over to him and said, 'All of this wouldn't have been possible without Elder Perry. I want to thank him.' He didn't appear to want to say anything. But there is a great picture of him saying, 'You're the man!' and me saying, 'You're the man!' Hopefully that sent a message to Mormons everywhere that this wasn't some concocted, coerced, miserable thing. And it sent a message to LGBT people that this was worked two ways."[39]

As SB 296 became law, many people openly acknowledged the crucial role that the LDS Church's support had played. From the legislative point of view, Gregory Hughes, the Republican Speaker of the Utah House of Representatives, quoted in the *New York Times*, said, "The apostles of this faith, which is the predominant faith here in Utah, stepped forward and expressed an earnest and sincere desire to come together. We had not heard that before, and we had not heard that with such specificity, and we took notice." Speaking for the LGBT community, a writer with *Q Salt Lake* stated, "Many in our community are still distrusting of the LDS Church, but they also know that, had the church not stated its support, this bill would not have become law, and may have been decades until it did so."[40]

The legislation was praised nationally not only for what it was but also for where it happened—a stark reversal of the near-universal condemnation of the January press conference. Sarah Warbelow of the Human Rights Campaign, who in the aftermath of the January press conference had been highly critical of the LDS Church position, now gave unqualified approval. "It is a landmark. This is a Republican-controlled Legislature with a Republican governor, and this will be the first time that a Republican-controlled process has led to extension of protections for L.G.B.T. people."[41]

THE LAST DOMINO

In denying certiorari simultaneously to seven appeals of same-sex marriage decisions, including *Kitchen v. Herbert*, the U.S. Supreme Court avoided making a decision with nationwide effect. Since all seven appealed decisions had been in favor of same-sex marriage, there was no conflict between the circuits, which would have been reason for the Supreme Court to grant certiorari. A month after the denial, however, the Sixth Circuit Court of Appeals provided the dissonant voice by upholding same-sex marriage bans in four states—bans that the district courts had overturned.[1] The appellate court ruled that there was no constitutional right to same-sex marriage and that states were free to allow or ban the practice at their discretion, a conclusion that was in direct conflict with the other circuits that had considered the issue. With a single exception, both the winning and the losing sides asked the Supreme Court to grant certiorari and settle the issue during its current term, which would end in late June.[2] The first lawsuit listed carried the title *Obergefell v. Hodges*, the name now universally applied to the landmark decision.

As the year 2015 began, thirty-six states and the District of Columbia—accounting for more than 70 percent of the population—had legalized same-sex marriage, mostly through the courts. Since the majority of the country now approved of marriage equality—and nearly 80 percent of those from eighteen to twenty-nine years of age approved[3]—there was little chance of the Supreme Court turning the clock back in states where same-sex marriage had been legalized; the real question was whether any state would be allowed to continue prohibiting such marriages.

Just one month after the passage of SB 296, the LDS Church joined a diverse coalition of faith traditions in submitting to the Supreme Court, in

Obergefell v. Hodges, an amicus brief in favor of preserving traditional marriage. A formal statement explained LDS participation in the brief, signaling up front a now-shifted emphasis to religious freedom.[4] "Though the case is about the definition of marriage, the focus of the brief is on religious freedom and the many ways the two are connected." Acknowledging that no organization, even a church, can "prohibit same-sex partnerships among the general population," it upheld the rights of churches to "persuasively argue for laws that uphold moral principles based on our understanding of the gospel of Jesus Christ."

The brief sought to make a case that legalization of same-sex marriage, for whatever effects it might have on same-sex couples, would unnecessarily burden others. "By redefining what marriage has been for most of human history, the court will impede the ability of religious people to participate fully as equal citizens in American civic life." A deep concern was the possible effect on speech, association, "public education, employment, public accommodations, and professional certification" if sexual orientation became a protected class—like race. "A pluralistic society that shows true respect and fairness for everyone would not compel or coerce these individuals and entities to betray their religious beliefs and conscience." Fearing that legalization of same-sex marriage would work to marginalize "traditional religious views on sexuality," the church commentary on the brief said, "Essentially, religious beliefs in traditional sexual morality could come to be equated with racism." The writers conveyed no sense of irony in making the comparison to race, which for decades was the basis of discriminatory speech and action justified by a deeply held religious belief that blacks, in particular, were inferior in the eyes of God, and thus could be treated as inferior by whites. The same language used in prior decades to justify religion-based racism was now being used to justify religion-based homophobia.

The church statement quoted from the brief, "The Constitution marks a wiser course by leaving the people free to decide the great marriage debate through their State democratic institutions," and then added commentary. "Having courts resolve these complex social issues is a far more troublesome path than having them resolved by the people themselves through the legislative processes in their own backyards.... By joining in the amicus brief, The Church of Jesus Christ of Latter-day Saints is arguing that 'fairness for all' is much better accomplished in legislatures than in the courts." Not stated was the obvious historical parallel of racism, where the voice of the people, "accomplished in the legislatures," stood as a perpetual barrier to freedom and equality for more than a century and likely would have continued in some parts of the country if the courts had not intervened. Also not stated was the fact that in Utah, where active LDS Church members dominated the legislature, the church would be able to control just what rights and freedoms LGBT individuals would be granted.

In oral arguments on April 28, Justice Stephen Breyer placed opponents of same-sex marriage on the defensive. Noting that marriage was open to "people who both have children, adopt children, don't have children, all over the place," he highlighted one group of people who were barred from marriage: people of the same sex. Why? "The answer we get is, well, people have always done it. You know, you could have answered that one the same way we talk about racial segregation. Or two, because certain religious groups do think it's a sin, and I believe they sincerely think it. There's no question about their sincerity, but is a purely religious reason on the part of some people sufficient? And then when I look for reasons three, four and five, I don't find them."[5]

On June 26, 2015, the Supreme Court issued its decision, ruling that laws prohibiting same-sex marriage were unconstitutional and thus establishing marriage equality as the law of the land. The majority opinion addressed both the strengths of the proequality position and the weaknesses of the opposition:[6]

- Opponents alleged that "it would demean a timeless institution if marriage were extended to same-sex couples." However, the Court found that far from seeking to devalue marriage, same-sex couples "seek it for themselves because of their respect—and need— for its privileges and responsibilities. And their immutable nature dictates that same-sex marriage is their only real path to this profound commitment."
- The notion that "traditional marriage" represented a distinct entity was fallacious. "The history of marriage is one of both continuity and change. Changes, such as the decline of arranged marriages and the abandonment of the law of coverture,[7] have worked deep transformations in the structure of marriage, affecting aspects of marriage once viewed as essential. These new insights have strengthened, not weakened, the institution. Changed understandings of marriage

are characteristic of a Nation where new dimensions of freedom become apparent to new generations."

- Preserving the status quo can work against the essence of the Constitution. "When new insight reveals discord between the Constitution's central protections and a received legal stricture, a claim to liberty must be addressed."

The Court addressed directly an allegation of the amicus brief (and the LDS Church's commentary) that the way to address the issue of same-sex marriage is through the voice of the people—the legislative process. "While the Constitution contemplates that democracy is the appropriate process for change, individuals who are harmed need not await legislative action before asserting a fundamental right.... The idea of the Constitution 'was to withdraw certain subjects from the vicissitudes of political controversy, to place them beyond the reach of majorities and officials and to establish them as legal principles to be applied by the courts.' This is why 'fundamental rights may not be submitted to a vote; they depend on the outcome of no elections.'"

While ruling against the desires of many religious institutions in legalizing same-sex marriage, the Court reached out to calm some of their fears. "It must be emphasized that religions, and those who adhere to religious doctrines, may continue to advocate with utmost, sincere conviction that, by divine precepts, same-sex marriage should not be condoned."

The day the decision was announced, the LDS Church released the following statement: "The Church of Jesus Christ of Latter-day Saints acknowledges that following today's ruling by the Supreme Court, same-sex marriages are now legal in the United States. The Court's decision does not alter the Lord's doctrine that marriage is a union between a man and a woman ordained by God. While showing respect for those who think differently, the Church will continue to teach and promote marriage between a man and a woman as a central part of our doctrine and practice."[8]

Later the same week, the First Presidency and Quorum of the Twelve Apostles clarified church policy in light of the decision. "Changes in the civil law do not, indeed cannot, change the moral law that God has established.... Consistent with our fundamental beliefs, Church officers will not employ their ecclesiastical authority to perform marriages between two people of the same sex, and the Church does not permit its meetinghouses or other properties to be used for ceremonies, receptions, or other activities associated with same-sex marriages."[9]

The battle over legalization of same-sex marriage was over. But the LDS Church had not dropped the subject.

JONAH AND THE DEMISE OF REPARATIVE THERAPY

The klieg light that shone so brightly on *Obergefell v. Hodges* placed into the shadows a simultaneous trial in a New Jersey court that had profound implications for homosexuality. *Ferguson v. JONAH* was a lawsuit alleging that reparative therapy, as practiced by a group first known as Jews Offering New Approaches to Homosexuality, and later changed to Jews Offering New Approaches to Healing, constituted consumer fraud. The case was of interest to Mormonism on three levels. First, one of the plaintiffs, Michael Ferguson, was LDS. Second, several of the witnesses in the trial were LDS. And third, reparative therapy had once been foundational to the LDS Church's response to homosexuality.

In November 2012, the Southern Poverty Law Center, acting on behalf of the plaintiffs, filed the lawsuit under New Jersey's Fraud Act, alleging misrepresentation of reparative therapy costing as much as $10,000 annually, while failing to deliver promised results.[10] In a crucial pretrial action, superior court judge Peter F. Barison Jr. ruled, "It is a misrepresentation in violation of the [New Jersey] Consumer Fraud Act, in advertising or selling conversion-therapy services to describe homosexuality, not as being a normal variation of human sexuality, but as being a mental illness, disease (or) disorder." David Dinielli, deputy legal director for the SPLC, responded, "For the first time, a court has ruled that it is fraudulent as a matter of law for conversion therapists to tell clients that they have a mental disorder that can be cured. This is the principal lie the conversion-therapy industry uses throughout the country to peddle its quackery to vulnerable clients."[11]

The jury phase of the lawsuit included twelve days of testimony whose transcript exceeded three thousand pages. In order to prevail in the lawsuit, JONAH didn't need to prove that its methods consistently worked; it just needed to show success in some cases. Plaintiff Michael Ferguson, commenting on the burden the defendants had of proving efficacy, said, "The defense has had two-and-a-half years to find success witnesses. . . . It got to the point where the judge finally said to the defense, 'Frankly, nobody who you have presented has been a success story. Unless you have somebody who is presenting information that is relevant to the claims of the defense and is a success story, you are wasting the court's time right now.'"[12]

The seven-person jury ruled unanimously that JONAH's claims of sexual-orientation conversion constituted consumer fraud. Sam Wolfe, an attorney with SPLC, explained, "JONAH falsely claimed it had converted hundreds of people from gay to straight. Clients who testified for JONAH about their 'success,' revealed just the opposite: Despite years of effort and expense, the men generally admitted to remaining primarily sexually attracted to other men, despite sometimes marrying women. JONAH could not offer testimony from a single client whose sexual orientation had transformed through its program."[13]

Since the verdict was announced on June 25, one day prior to the Supreme Court's ruling in *Obergefell v. Hodges*, the importance of the ruling was quickly overshadowed. In general, the public was unaware either of the outcome of the JONAH trial or of its implications for reparative therapy. In fact, however, the controversial practice was experiencing death knells.

RELIGIOUS FREEDOM

Shortly after the Proposition 8 election, a writer for the *American Conservative* spotted a subtle shift in the rhetoric of the LDS Church hierarchy. "Shrewdly, Mormon leaders have shifted the debate about marriage to a debate about free exercise of religion. Elder [Quentin] Cook[1] in an address to LDS members warned that the acceptance of gay marriage would inevitably lead to 'legal penalties and social ostracism' for the religious."[2] Indeed, religious freedom soon became a clarion call for church members, with Apostle Dallin Oaks being its principal standard-bearer.

In an address at Brigham Young University–Idaho in October 2009, Oaks said, "The tide of public opinion in favor of religion is receding, and this probably portends public pressures for laws that will impinge on religious freedom."[3] In this and other speeches on the subject, he (and other church leaders) focused on three fears:

- In the event that same-sex marriage became the law of the land, religious denominations might be obliged by the government to perform same-sex marriages, even though such marriages went against church teachings. Particularly threatening to orthodox Mormon sensitivities would be the prospect of same-sex marriages performed in an LDS temple.
- Church entities and church members with strongly held beliefs that homosexuality is morally wrong might be compelled to provide goods or services—"public accommodations"—to LGBT people, including to same-sex couples.

- Churches and their members speaking out in defense of religious principles not aligning with current societal norms might be subjected to public scorn and even legal punishment.

SAME-SEX MARRIAGE CEREMONIES

During the church's first foray into the battle over same-sex marriage, in the early 1990s in Hawaii, a stake president submitted an affidavit to the court stating, "I am reasonably concerned that I will be asked to solemnize such marriages which, under the usages of the LDS Church I am prohibited from doing. If this should occur, I am reasonably fearful that I...could have my license to solemnize marriages revoked, and/or face claims and lawsuits for damages for alleged discrimination based upon sex by same gender couples for whom I, or any of the other Stake Presidents of the LDS Church in the State of Hawaii, refuse to solemnize."[4] The trial judge rejected the argument out of hand, explaining that the Free Exercise Clause of the Constitution would compel the courts to block any such effort.

The same fires of fear were stoked during Prop 8, when the "Six Consequences" document was circulated to local LDS leaders throughout California. One of the alleged consequences was, "Churches may be sued over their tax-exempt status if they refuse to allow same-sex marriage ceremonies in their religious buildings open to the public. Ask whether your pastor, priest, minister, bishop, or rabbi is ready to perform such marriages in your chapels and sanctuaries."[5]

It is difficult to understand why church leaders and spokespersons continued to raise the specter of enforced same-sex marriages, as virtually every court that has ruled in favor of marriage equality has noted that its ruling would not have such an effect. For example, the California Supreme Court decision that led to Prop 8 specifically addressed this point in unambiguous language: "Affording same-sex couples the opportunity to obtain the designation of marriage will not impinge upon the religious freedom of any religious organization, official, or any other person; no religion will be required to change its religious policies or practices with regard to same-sex couples, and no religious officiant will be required to solemnize a marriage in contravention of his or her religious beliefs. Cal. Const., art. I, sect. 4."[6]

Perhaps the continued references to being required to perform same-sex marriages were an attempt to justify the time and enormous expense that went into the church's attempts to thwart marriage equality at the ballot box, efforts that ultimately were for naught. Seen in this light, the policy statement issued by the church in the immediate aftermath of the *Obergefell* decision, of which Oaks was a signatory, was a marker in the ground to delineate the church's right not to be compelled to perform same-sex marriages. "Consistent with our fundamental beliefs, Church officers will not employ their ecclesiastical authority to perform marriages between two people of the same sex, and the Church does not permit its meetinghouses or other properties to be used for ceremonies, receptions, or other activities associated with same-sex marriages."[7] That policy stands unchanged—and unchallenged—today.

Missing from the discussion has been a centuries-long deference to churches in the United States, as noted by a Baptist minister in Salt Lake City in the aftermath of the January 2015 press conference where Oaks made religious freedom the centerpiece. "The measure of religious liberty is whether one can personally practice one's faith, and there is nothing within the new rights being afforded LGBT citizens that interferes with that.... The rights of churches to practice and perform rites as they see fit is locked down and has been since the formation of this country."[8]

Also missing has been an evenhanded discussion of the legal possibility of compulsory performance of same-sex marriages. A recent op-ed column in the *Salt Lake Tribune* by William Eskridge of the Yale Law School, widely regarded as the leading scholar in the United States on the subject of LGBT law, gave such guidance. Citing the Hawaii decision of two decades earlier, he wrote,

> The current Supreme Court certainly agrees with the Hawaii Supreme Court on this precise issue. Indeed, Justice Antonin Scalia raised it at oral argument in Obergefell. He asked Mary Bonauto, counsel for the lesbian and gay couples, whether constitutional marriage rights for those couples would impose a duty upon traditionalist faiths to celebrate those marriages. Speaking for her clients and for the many lesbian, gay, bisexual and transgender rights groups on brief in the case, Bonauto unequivocally answered that the Free Exercise Clause would protect those faith traditions.

Justices Ginsburg and Sotomayor immediately agreed with Bonauto's point. No justice objected to this consensus....

The court's decision in *Obergefell* itself is icing on a cake already well-frosted. While rejecting faith-based arguments supporting the traditional definition of marriage as one man, one woman, Justice Kennedy's opinion for the court went out of its way to agree with Bonauto's, Ginsburg's, and Sotomayor's understanding of the Religion Clauses: "The First Amendment ensures that religious organizations and persons are given proper protection as they seek to teach the principles that are so fulfilling and so central to their lives and faiths, and to their own deep aspirations to continue the family structure they have long revered."[9]

PUBLIC ACCOMMODATIONS

While Utah's SB 296 law protected LGBT persons from discrimination in housing and employment, it steered completely clear of the issue of public accommodations. This has been a particularly vexing area for Dallin Oaks, and he has taken several occasions to cite instances where religious freedom was, in his view, violated in the name of LGBT rights. Two, in particular, bear treatment in some detail.

The first occurred in New Mexico, where a pair of Christians who co-owned Elaine Photography refused to take photographs for a lesbian commitment ceremony. "The lesbian couple filed a complaint with New Mexico's Human Rights Commission, which found the photographers guilty of discrimination and levied a $6,000 fine."[10]

In a speech at Chapman University in California in 2011,[11] Oaks cited this case and condemned the government's action as an infringement of religious freedom. What he failed to explain was that same-sex marriage was forbidden in New Mexico at that time, but "the state has a law specifically banning discrimination on the basis of sexual orientation and the photographer stated she would not photograph a wedding because of the sexual orientation of the persons involved."[12]

The second occurred in New Jersey. "The Ocean Grove Camp Meeting Association, owned by a Methodist church in New Jersey, rented out its beachside pavilion to various groups. The church declined to allow a lesbian couple to use the pavilion for their civil-union ceremony. Local authorities stripped the association of its exemption from *property* taxes and billed it $20,000."[13] Oaks "said it was 'monstrous' to compel a church to allow its property to be used for something that violated its principles."[14] But that was only part of the story.

> What Oaks failed to point out is the simple fact that the church in question was a participant in the New Jersey "Green Acres" program, which provides property tax breaks to participants and requires, in exchange, that the property be open to all, and that New Jersey's anti-discrimination ordinances are followed.
> This wasn't a case of "gay rights" trumping those of a church. This was a case of a church participating in a program, reaping the financial rewards of doing so, and then attempting to violate the basic conditions of that program. Nobody said the United Methodist Church had to participate in Green Acres, but when they chose to do so, and they took the associated tax benefits, they became contractually obligated to honor those anti-discrimination policies. They made a choice, and that choice had consequences.[15]

Also omitted was mention of the fact that when the United Methodist Church sought tax exemption for the building to be used for religious purposes, rather than as a public-use building, the tax exemption was reinstated.[16] These and other examples of which Oaks spoke were problematic, and none withstood scrutiny as examples of LGBT access to public accommodations leading to a harmful violation of religious freedom. One commentator wrote, "[Oaks] cited a few cases (some of the same ones used in scare-tactic ads from the now-discredited National Organization for Marriage) but none of them pertains to the rights of churches or private individuals (acting as private individuals) to create and maintain their own religious beliefs and practices."[17]

And nowhere was there a discussion by Oaks or other LDS leaders of the countless incidents where LGBT people were harmed because access to public accommodations was not protected by law. A Baptist pastor in Salt Lake City spoke of the *real* discrimination suffered by LGBT people for lack of legal protections:

When a couple cannot obtain a marriage license they are legally entitled to based on the religious convictions of the county clerk, then basic rights are being violated. When one is forced to go from pharmacy to pharmacy, trying to get a prescription filled because every pharmacist in town finds the legally prescribed drug to be counter to his/her religious sensibilities, then religious freedom has trumped all other freedoms. When someone is forced to vacate an apartment because the new owner does not agree with the lifestyle of some of the tenants, then religion becomes a façade to mask discrimination.[18]

FREE SPEECH

Freedom of speech works in two directions. On the one hand, people and organizations are free to say what they wish in private and public spaces—at least within very broad limits that do not include shouting "Fire!" in a crowded theater; on the other hand, those with opposing views are equally free to express them, as well as criticize those whose views they oppose. In a speech in 1992, Dallin Oaks acknowledged that part of American life is the give-and-take of public discourse, with all parties having equal status in the public square. "If churches or church leaders choose to oppose or favor a particular piece of legislation, their opinions should be received on the same basis as the opinions offered by other knowledgeable organizations or persons, and they should be considered on their merits." Oaks added that while a church may speak in a different tone of voice, the playing field remains level. "A church can claim access to higher authority on moral questions, but its opinions on the application of those moral questions to specific legislation will inevitably be challenged by and measured against secular-based legislative or political judgments."[19]

Following the scathing criticism leveled at the LDS Church in the aftermath of Proposition 8, Oaks's tone began to change. In a speech on religious freedom a year after the election that was laced with references to Prop 8, he argued that the church—and, by extension, its members when they spoke for their religious beliefs—had a constitutional entitlement to special status. "Surely the First Amendment guarantee of free exercise of *religion* was intended to grant more freedom to religious action than to other kinds of action." With reference to Prop 8, he said, "We must not be deterred or coerced into silence by the kinds of intimidation I have described.... We must also insist on this companion condition of democratic government: when churches and their members or any other group act or speak out on public issues, win or lose, they have a right to expect freedom from retaliation."[20]

Intimidation and *retaliation* are strong words whose use in the context of Prop 8 deserves close examination. Despite the heated rhetoric from both sides during the campaign, there were no credible charges of intimidation—with the possible exception of "threatened boycotts against businesses that failed to donate to their effort during the campaign"—threats made by the Yes on 8 campaign![21]

Oaks's catalog of retaliation included "vandalism of church facilities and harassment of church members by firings and boycotts of member businesses"—boycotts are legally protected exercises of free speech—"and by retaliation against donors."[22]

- Vandalism of church facilities, as noted earlier, was minor, mostly consisting of isolated (and rare) uses of spray paint.
- "Harassment of church members by firings" was a problematic allegation. In the entire state of California, only three church members were reported to have lost their jobs as a result of their support of Prop 8, and in all three instances they resigned and were not fired. In each case, their resignation came in the face of public outcry that included threatened boycotts, yet in each case the employees received votes of confidence from management. Their resignations were voluntary.
- A boycott against a Utah automotive group, triggered by a private donation to Yes on 8 by the wife of the CEO, was resolved amicably within about two weeks. Retaliation against donors is a difficult metric to assess, and anecdotal reports suggested that it largely amounted to ill feelings among coworkers—except within LDS congregations, where those who had *opposed* Prop 8 were often shunned.

That was the fallout from the most expensive, and arguably acrimonious, social-issue campaign in the history of the United States, in which more than thirteen million voters voiced their preferences in a peaceful election. To claim victim status was a stretch, but it was one that Oaks made when, as detailed in an earlier chapter, he likened the church experience to the persecution of blacks during the civil rights era.

The following year Oaks argued, using apocalyptic language, that the legalization of same-sex marriage would be the end of free speech for church members:

> You as believers in God, and keepers of His commandments, would then be regarded as exceptions to the rule. Your conscientious convictions would then be regarded as discriminatory. If you were a Christian school teacher, you could be charged with bigotry for upholding the Lord's law of chastity. In truth dear brothers and sisters, if you lose marriage, you also lose freedom of religion. Atheistic moral bedlam and religious repression go hand in hand. At stake is our ability to transmit to the next generation the life-giving and inseparable culture of marriage and the free exercise of religion.[23]

But within the United States—and the rules regarding public speech certainly differ in other countries—the grim outcome predicted by Oaks had little, if any, legal basis. Indeed, as pointed out earlier, in its decision in *Obergefell v. Hodges*, the Supreme Court addressed specifically the issue raised by him. "Finally, it must be emphasized that religions, and those who adhere to religious doctrines, may continue to advocate with utmost, sincere conviction that, by divine precepts, same-sex marriage should not be condoned."[24]

The real issue for Oaks appeared to be a desire for special rules for churches—a tilted playing field. In a speech at Chapman University in 2011 he argued, "I begin with a truth that is increasingly challenged: Religious teachings and religious organizations are valuable and important to our free society and therefore deserving of special legal protection."[25] The counterargument, precipitated by his comment, cut to the essence of free speech:

> Nobody is attacking Oaks' religion. Nobody. What Oaks, [Boyd] Packer, and the rest of the LDS leadership need to understand is that we all have rights, not just them. And in no way, shape, or form, do their rights take precedence over anyone else's. I don't

care if Oaks wants to stand on a street corner like Fred Phelps[26] and shout anti-gay nonsense at the top of his lungs. He has that right. Packer has that right. The LDS Church has that right. Guess what? I also have the right to say, paraphrasing George Takei, "you sir, are a douchebag."[27]

What Oaks and other LDS authorities also failed to acknowledge was that the playing field they envisioned would tilt only in the direction of their particular brand of religious conservatism. This was highlighted by the Reverend Jim Burklo, senior associate dean of religious life at the University of Southern California. Seeking to solidify alliances with religions leaders from diverse backgrounds, the church invited Burklo and other ministers from Southern California universities to visit the LDS Church headquarters and Brigham Young University in the fall of 2011. In writing about his experience, Burklo gave high praise to the church for how well they were treated and noted a number of positive experiences during his stay in Utah. Inevitably, however, the issue of same-sex marriage came up, and when it did, LDS Church leaders opined that the trend toward such marriages indicated an erosion of the influence of religion. Burklo responded that as a minister in the United Church of Christ, he performed gay marriage ceremonies and advocated for its legalization. Burklo asked:

> "Which of our denominations will prevail in influencing the government's policy? In either case, it seems to me, and to my progressive Christian colleagues, that religious influence and freedom in American society are very alive and well!" This made them sputter a bit. I said that same-sex marriage will be legalized inevitably, no matter what he or I think about it. So we must find other ways for each of our faiths to find acceptance and understanding for our particularities on this issue. They said it's not inevitable for gay marriage to prevail. But then they admitted that was true only for the short term, because young people overwhelmingly support it, so one day it probably will be legalized. This admission greatly surprised me.[28]

THE POLICY

Until the U.S. Supreme Court ruled on *Obergefell v. Hodges*, the ecclesiastical status of LDS-LGBT people living together, whether legally married or not, was a matter for local church leaders to address at their own discretion. Randall Thacker, president of Affirmation: LGBT Mormons, Families & Friends, was an active member of his Washington, DC, congregation while living with his partner. An article in the *Salt Lake Tribune* noted, "His bishop welcomed him back to church last year, saying, 'My role is to bring people to Christ. Please continue to come and I hope you will feel welcome here.'" But Thacker's experience was not the norm. He told the reporter, "There is inconsistency worldwide in the way local leaders view members who support same-sex civil marriage. Some local leaders, including some in Utah, see this as contrary to sustaining the prophet and apostles, which at times has resulted in threats to revoke or actual revocation of a temple recommend and in other instances the release of otherwise-worthy members from ward leadership callings."[1]

Once *Obergefell* was decided and same-sex marriage became the law of the land, church leaders felt obliged to formulate a churchwide policy addressing both legally married same-sex couples and those living together without marriage. On November 5, 2015, news of what is now commonly called "the Policy" exploded on the Internet. The church's Public Affairs Department, which normally is the conduit for announcing church policies through its website, MormonNewsroom.org, was caught flat-footed, having heard nothing of it until that morning.

The Policy had two parts, one that addressed same-sex couples and the other that addressed their children:

- Couples in a same-gender, legal marriage were declared to be in apostasy, and local ecclesiastical leaders were advised that a disciplinary council, which would likely result in excommunication, is mandatory.[2]
- Biological or adopted infants living with same-gender parents, whether legally married or cohabiting, cannot receive "a name and a blessing"—the LDS equivalent of christening. Older children cannot be baptized, and boys cannot be ordained to the priesthood unless they are at least eighteen years of age (the normal age for baptism is eight and for ordination is twelve), do not live with the same-gender couple, and "specifically disavow the practice of same-gender cohabitation and marriage."[3]

GENESIS

Neither the procedure by which the Policy was crafted nor the manner in which it became public knowledge was typical. The church has never disclosed the details of its genesis, but a variety of sources, many speaking on condition of anonymity, allow the construction of a basic outline.

In the aftermath of the *Obergefell* decision in June 2015, local church officials throughout the United States made repeated requests for guidance as to how to deal with church members in same-sex marriages, now that such marriages were legal across the country. Particularly problematic was the church's long-standing one-size-fits-all condemnation of sexual relations outside marriage. The legalization of same-sex marriage suddenly created a conundrum, for homosexual relations could now occur within a legal marriage in all states in the country, as contrasted with only a few states prior to *Obergefell*.

Furthermore, church lawyers and senior ecclesiastical officers were deeply concerned over possible legal liability for the church, whose teachings about the morality of homosexual relations and proscription against same-sex marriage remained unchanged despite the court's decision. One speculation, based on conversations with attorneys, was that "class action was the worst fear, that maybe a group of gay parents could sue the Church and say, 'You have alienated us from our kids.'"[4] The feeling was that a clearly delineated policy would immunize the church against the possibility of such lawsuits. A published report, citing sources felt to be highly reliable, suggested two scenarios for the genesis of the Policy:

> According to an official with routine access to members of the governing councils of the church, the new instructions were the brainchild of two senior apostles who used as a guide the church's policy on baptizing children of parents practicing plural marriage found in the 2010 edition of the [Church] Handbook #1 for regional and local leaders of the church. Although the source did not reveal the names of the apostles involved, it is reasonable to assume that one of them would have been Russell M. Nelson, 91, the president of the Quorum of Twelve Apostles and first in line to succeed Thomas S. Monson, the acutely ailing current president of the church.
>
> A second similarly-connected source insisted that the policy came from Monson himself, with assistance from church attorneys and other staff members.
>
> Both reports maintain that in a fleeting lucid moment the 88-year-old Monson approved the policy.[5]

Several sources stated that the Policy, once formulated within the Office of the First Presidency, did not go through the normal procedure that included discussion within the Quorum of the Twelve Apostles and vetting by the Correlation and Public Affairs Departments—the First Presidency being the only entity in the church that can implement a policy without going through that process.

APPROVAL

The First Presidency and Quorum of the Twelve meet together on a regular basis twice each week. The Thursday meeting in the Salt Lake Temple is more devotional in nature; the Tuesday meeting in the Church Administration Building is more business oriented. On Tuesday, November 3, the new policy was presented to the Quorum for approval, without the usual deliberation process that can extend indefinitely. One Quorum member later commented on background, "Everything we do as the Twelve has to go to the First Presidency, but not everything the First Presidency does has to come through us." Quorum members were simply asked to sustain the First Presidency's policy, without debate. They did so by unanimous vote.

DEPLOYMENT

There are two volumes of the *Church Handbook of Instructions*. The first is intended for stake presidents and bishops and is not available to the general public. The second is intended for a more general audience and may be accessed on the church website by anyone. Both volumes of the *Handbook* exist in two formats: a printed version that is updated every few years and an electronic version that is updated frequently. The day after the new policy was approved by the Quorum of the Twelve, the revised electronic version *Handbook 1* was posted online, accompanied by an email to local church leaders informing them of the change. No public announcement was made by the church.

Local church leaders with access to the online *Church Handbook* include more than three thousand stake presidents and thirty thousand bishops. According to the podcast *Out in Zion*, the text of the new policy was forwarded by one local leader in Utah and another in Seattle to Mormon bloggers on Wednesday night or early Thursday morning.[6] By midday on Thursday, the Policy went viral on the Internet. By Thursday evening church spokesman Eric Hawkins confirmed that the leaked document was accurate.[7] The Public Affairs Department, of which Hawkins was part, had little else to say for the simple reason that it had been unaware of the existence of the Policy until earlier the same morning.

DAMAGE CONTROL

With blog posts and newspaper reports flooding the Internet, Public Affairs quickly began to play catch-up. Several church officials later spoke on the subject, on condition of anonymity. One said, "Public Affairs did not know about this until it hit the news. It was just a total mess." The initial response was a hastily scripted interview, posted on *LDS Newsroom*, that involved Apostle Todd Christofferson, senior advisor to Public Affairs, and Michael Otterson, managing director of Public Affairs. Another official said, "Suddenly a camera crew had to be assembled. They never hold those things in the top floor of the Relief Society Building unless every other space they usually use is completely booked and they can't get people out. Just watch that thing! The body language is just so painful. Neither Michael nor Elder Christofferson wants to be there. They are appalled at the way that they are forced into a terrible situation."

Christofferson began by emphasizing the dark place of same-sex marriage within Mormonism. "We regard same-sex marriage as a particularly grievous or significant, serious kind of sin that requires Church discipline. It means the discipline is mandatory—doesn't dictate outcomes but it dictates that discipline is needed in those cases." He then defended the new policy with respect to its effect on children. "It originates from a desire to protect children in their innocence and in their minority years. When, for example, there is the formal blessing and naming of a child in the Church, which happens when a child has parents who are members of the Church, it triggers a lot of things. First, a membership record for them. It triggers the assignment of visiting and home teachers. It triggers an expectation that they will be in Primary and the other Church organizations." Suggesting that such a relationship between church and child is not likely to be appropriate "in the family setting where they're living as children where their parents are a same-sex couple," he defended the Policy as standing up for the children. "We don't want the child to have to deal with issues that might arise where the parents feel one way and the expectations of the Church are very different."[8]

BLOWBACK

What Todd Christofferson was selling, many weren't buying. Some openly questioned the alignment of the new policy with a church Article of Faith that states, "We believe that men will be punished for their own sins, and not for Adam's transgressions." Why, they queried, would infants and children be denied the blessings of church ordinances and formal acceptance by the community of believers because of the actions of their parents—parents who often wished, themselves, to be part of that community? Randall Thacker said, "I cannot imagine Jesus Christ denying any child a baptism because of the status of their parents. It goes against everything I ever thought the savior and baptism was about."[9] Law professor Edwin Firmage, grandson of deceased apostle Hugh Brown, wrote to the editor of the *Salt Lake Tribune*, "I don't think Jesus gives a tinkers'

damn if I say, 'Oh my hell' when I hit my thumb with a hammer when fix-
ing my roof. But I know he will punish those who invoke his name when
we harm the innocents."[10]

Others contrasted the Policy to the supportive, nonjudgmental words
of Pope Francis I. While still an archbishop in Argentina he said, "The child
has absolutely no responsibility for the state of his parent's marriage," and
earlier in 2015 the *World Religion News* reported, "Pope Francis continues
to urge Catholic priests not to block gay couples from having their children
baptized. Speaking last Sunday during an ordination mass in the Vatican,
Francis reminded that priests should not refuse baptism to anyone who asks
for the sacrament. The pontiff told the priests: 'With baptism, you unite the
new faithful to the people of God. It is never necessary to refuse baptism to
someone who asks for it.'" In the same spirit as the pope's comments were
those of a Jewish rabbi: "Let us imagine that a man and a woman are living together outside of wedlock, as is the case with countless couples in the
United States. Now, one would traditionally have said that they live in sin.
But would anyone, including the Mormon Church, tell them that they are no
longer allowed to come to pray? And if their children are born out of wedlock, are they barred from being members of the Church until they turn 18
and run away from home?"[11]

Yet others wondered why same-sex marriage was now being placed in
a category whose consequences for church members exceeded those of serious crimes. The *New York Times* reported, "Jana Riess, [an LDS] columnist
with Religion News Service, said she was livid that children born to unmarried people, as well as rapists and murderers, can be baptized and blessed,
but not children of monogamous same-sex couples." Indeed, while those in
a same-sex marriage now were to be subjected to mandatory church discipline and their children denied church rites, "sons and daughters of murderers, adulterers, fornicators, drug addicts, unwed mothers, divorced parents
and sometimes non-Mormons can be welcomed into the community with
such special rites, born of the Mormon belief that children are born innocent, rather than carrying the weight of their parents' sins."[12]

Criticism in the abstract was soon joined by personal accounts of the
new policy shredding the fabric of family life. The day it was announced,
Nick Literski, a gay man from Seattle who left the LDS Church after coming
out a decade earlier, told of his daughter's dreams being dashed. "'She now

can't serve a mission unless she 'disavows' her own father's life—basically convinces a stake president that she's sufficiently disgusted by me,' he said, adding that he was physically shaken after reading the policy. 'I'm heartsick,' Literski said. 'It's so incredibly unfair to put her in this position.'"[13] Within the week a woman reported, "I have two moms. I love them. After this new policy was announced, my bishop contacted me to say that if they want to visit me and their grandchildren, they have to stay in separate bedrooms. Or I will face mandatory discipline."[14] The same day, an online blog reported on the son of a lesbian couple: "This time last week, Alyssa Paquette's twelve-year-old stepson was preparing to be ordained to the priesthood in the LDS Church. Now that has all changed.... Paquette expresses shock and grief that on the eve of their son's ordination, he's being rejected. 'It feels like a mourning process, like someone has actually died.'"[15]

LEAVING THE FOLD

For many, the response was to walk away from the church. One high-profile resignation, which occurred within days of the announcement of the Policy, was that of Kate Kendell, executive director of the National Center for Lesbian Rights. Raised a Latter-day Saint, Kendell had distanced herself from church activity years earlier. However, "even at the height of church involvement in the passage of Proposition 8 in California, I never seriously considered removing my name. It just didn't matter that much to me. Spiritually and emotionally, I left the church I grew up in decades ago. And despite being a 'known gay activist' to the church, I was never excommunicated, so my name remained on the church rolls as a member. Not anymore." The Policy pushed her over the edge. "I just did something I thought I would never do. I resigned my membership in the Church of Jesus Christ of Latter-day Saints (the Mormons) and asked that my name be removed from the records."[16]

Wendy Montgomery, cofounder of Mama Dragons, said to a reporter from the *Washington Post*, "I've seen lots of painful things, but nothing so widespread, in terms of the devastation and heartbreak. I personally talked to dozens of people who are walking away. And these aren't people with LGBT ties. These are ardent, faithful, in-the-box believing Mormons who can't abide this."[17] Later, Montgomery reflected on the damage to her own family:

The LDS church's "Exclusion Policy" completely devastated our family. I held my 18-year-old son as he sobbed. He laid his head in my lap and wept for over an hour. He said, "Why does the church hate me so much?" That question seared my heart. To this day, I still don't have an answer for it.

When we attend church now, people who had been friendly before don't make eye contact. Most don't talk to us. Jordan doesn't get invited to activities anymore and we aren't asked to dinner at ward members' homes. We don't have callings, have never spoken in Sacrament Meeting and have never even been asked to give a prayer. Because we love and support our gay son, we make people deeply uncomfortable. Our bishopric hasn't reached out to us in any way. It feels awful. We had a taste of being part of a ward that wanted us, only to have it ripped away three months later.[18]

Nine days after the Policy was announced, a group of the disaffected, estimated to exceed one thousand, gathered in City Creek Park—one block from church headquarters—to sign letters of resignation. The church-owned *Deseret News* reported, "The majority of those who signed letters on or prior to Saturday already had stopped believing or attending worship services years ago for a variety of reasons." One of the departing, Nadine Hansen, posted her letter online. "This policy has not only broken the fingernails I was using to hold onto my membership in the church, it has ripped them out by the roots, and with it a piece of my heart. I simply cannot remain in a place dominated (I will not say 'led') by men who can perpetrate this kind of cruel spiritual abuse on children."[19]

Another woman who resigned during the mass resignation said the attorney who assisted her told her he had processed a total of three thousand letters of resignation.[20] The *New York Times* editorial board, commenting on the exodus, wrote, "In recent days, Mormons have been leaving the church in droves, saying they no longer feel at home in an institution that so resolutely excludes a segment of the population that has become increasingly visible, legally protected and socially accepted in America." A church employee who spoke on condition of anonymity said there had been more resignations during the month of November than the church typically received in an entire year. The president of the Liberty Wells Stake in Salt Lake City went on the record in a priesthood leadership meeting to tell members that as of September 2016, ten months after the Policy was announced, 432 members of the stake—nearly 10 percent—had sent him formal letters resigning their church membership.[21]

For one particularly prominent church member, the Policy was the final straw. Hans Mattsson, a third-generation Swedish Mormon, had served as an Area Seventy in Sweden from 2000 to 2005. His struggles with doctrinal and historical questions regarding the church, exacerbated by the power of the Internet, had nearly caused him to abandon the faith several years earlier. Because he had been the highest-ranking LDS official to describe openly his faith crisis, he was featured in a front-page article in the Sunday New York Times in 2013—an article whose impact was so strong that it broke a logjam within the Quorum of the Twelve and led to the long-delayed online posting of church-commissioned essays on controversial historical issues.[22] Despite his struggles, Mattsson remained active in the church—until the Policy. In response to it he asked rhetorically, "Do you consider that some children are worth less than other children? Apparently!" In the spring of 2016, Mattsson and his wife formally resigned their church membership.[23]

PARTIAL WALK-BACK

A church employee, speaking on background, used the term *not calculated* to refer to the process by which the Policy had been implemented. By circumventing discussion and vetting in the Quorum of the Twelve Apostles, the Correlation Department, the Public Affairs Department, and other church checks, the First Presidency created the atmosphere for a backlash that caught them by surprise. Having boxed themselves into a tight corner with the original announcement, they had little wiggle room. Nonetheless, a week later a small but significant change emerged. Where the original policy had mandated that its provisions applied to children who, at any time, had ever lived with same-sex parents, the revision relaxed conditions slightly. "The provisions of *Handbook 1*, Section 16.13, that restrict priesthood ordinances for minors, apply only to those children whose *primary* residence is with a couple living in a same-gender marriage or similar relationship."[24] The change went by largely unnoticed, and hostility to the Policy continued almost unabated.

LEAKS

By early December, cracks began to appear in the institutional façade. Reports began to surface that there was discontent at a high level. Although there had been a unanimous vote of approval within the Quorum of the Twelve Apostles, messages through surrogates began to portray very mixed feelings. One General Authority told a small group of church members, "The *majority* are unhappy with this policy...and the way the procedure got pushed down on them....I guarantee you that this policy will not last."[25] In a church whose highest echelons of leadership invariably try to give an outward appearance of collegial unanimity, any suggestion of disunity is both unusual and significant.

THE NUCLEAR CARD

In churchspeak, Thomas Monson was "feeling the effects of advancing age."[26] In practical terms, for several years the extent of his participation in public events, most noticeably the semiannual General Conferences, had continually declined.[27] Such decline of function in a church president has been seen periodically over the past half century,[28] and when it occurs, deference shifts to the next-senior apostle, whether serving in the First Presidency or the Quorum of the Twelve Apostles.

In July 2015, with the death of Boyd Packer, Russell Nelson became the president of the Quorum and next in line for the presidency. On January 10, 2016, Nelson delivered an address in Hawaii that was broadcast to young adult church members throughout the world. Entitled "Becoming True Millennials," it effectively plugged the leaks by invoking the one word that immediately demands that all General Authorities fall in line: *revelation.* Referring to the Policy, Nelson said, "When the Lord inspired His prophet, President Thomas S. Monson, to declare the mind of the Lord and the will of the Lord [with regard to The Policy], each of us during that sacred moment felt a spiritual confirmation. It was our privilege as Apostles to sustain what had been revealed to President Monson. Revelation from the Lord to His servants is a sacred process."[29]

Several sources confirmed, on background, that Nelson's speech had not been read in advance or even anticipated by his colleagues in the Quorum of the Twelve Apostles, Public Affairs, or Correlation. Walking back such a high-profile statement by such a high-profile church leader is virtually impossible, yet three lines of evidence suggest that a partial walk-back began to occur almost immediately. One was the headline given to the story in the *Deseret News*, which did not even hint at revelation: "President Russell M. Nelson: 'Becoming True Millennials.'" (The contrasting headline in the *Salt Lake Tribune* emphasized the revelatory nature of Nelson's statement: "Mormon Gay Policy Is 'Will of the Lord' through His Prophet, Senior Apostle Says.")[30]

The second came from what was *not* subsequently said by Nelson's colleagues. In contrast to Spencer Kimball's 1978 revelation on priesthood, where members of the First Presidency and Quorum of the Twelve Apostles bore fervent public witness of divine revelation, this time there was nearly total silence. Nonetheless, the leaks were plugged and remained plugged, as calling the Policy a revelation placed it into a different category that would not easily be changed.

And the third came months later, when Nelson's Hawaii sermon appeared in a new online "Doctrinal Mastery" manual for teachers of LDS youth, in a lesson on "prophets and revelation." A short time thereafter, it was removed from the manual, without explanation.

STATUS QUO

Ten weeks after the Policy was announced, a poll of Utah Mormons showed that 72 percent supported its labeling of legally married same-sex couples as apostates. (Only 18 percent of non-Mormons supported it.)[31] On the one-year anniversary of the Policy's announcement, 72 percent still supported it.[32]

Within one minority demographic, however, the Policy continued to be opposed and continued to have a negative impact on people's lives. As its anniversary approached, Affirmation: LGBT Mormons, Families & Friends conducted an Internet-based survey of its impact. The 791 respondents were nearly equally divided between LGBT and straight. The most significant findings of the survey were:

- Whereas more than half the church-active respondents described their prepolicy trust in the First Presidency and Quorum of the Twelve Apostles to have been "moderately" or "extremely" strong, fewer than 20 percent reported the same level of trust postpolicy.
- Weekly church attendance, maintenance of a current temple recommend, and payment of a full tithing dropped by half.

- The percentage of respondents reporting sadness or depression all or most of the time doubled, from 12 percent to 24 percent.[33]

Another support group, the Mama Dragons, found their hopes similarly dashed. Those hopes had been raised in 2014 by a chance encounter in a Salt Lake City restaurant that involved a dozen Mama Dragons and Apostle Neil Andersen.[34] After a cordial conversation, the women sent letters to Andersen that told heartbreaking stories about their gay children trying to survive in the church—and particularly those who were trying to be celibate. Andersen's brief written response included this sentence: "You will understand why I will not respond to the specific concerns raised in the letters." Yvette Zobell, one of the mothers, commented on her disappointment at the response, which was only heightened with the announcement a few months later of the Policy.

> "You will understand." Really? We will? Really? We're telling you that our kids are suicidal because of the things that you say over the pulpit, and surely we will understand why you can't address our concerns? OK.
>
> We were hoping that the General Conferences would get better, but in 2015, after gay marriage was approved by the Supreme Court, the conferences were terrible, and we had a rash of suicides that we, as Mama Dragons, knew about....
>
> We were hopeful because we got the ear of a General Authority. "Maybe there is a possibility that there can be some change. Maybe they can make life a little better. Maybe they just don't understand, and we can help them." But after The Policy, hope was completely gone. The air was let out. There is no hopeful feeling now. We had been naively hopeful.... Most [of the mothers] have dropped out since the Policy.[35]

TRANS

TRANSGENDER

The Kinsey Scale, first published in 1948,[1] characterized sexual preference—that is, the person to whom one is sexually attracted—as linear, with heterosexuality, bisexuality, and homosexuality positioned on a single line. Subsequent research and experience have shown not only that the scale is far too simplistic but also that it portrays only one side of the coin of human sexuality. The other side is gender identity—that is, how a person self-identifies rather than to whom he or she is attracted. With the disclaimer that gender identity, too, is not strictly linear, it is nonetheless helpful to envision two main clusters: cisgender (someone whose self-identification matches the genitalia) and transgender (the *T* of LGBT).

Within the transgender cluster are such diverse self-identities as transvestite, transsexual, drag king, drag queen, gender fluid, androgynous, genderless, gender-queer, and others. However, some individuals self-identifying with any of the above terms may consider themselves outside the umbrella. Given the number of "flavors" of gender identity, and the range of sexual orientation "flavors" that includes homosexual, heterosexual, bisexual, ambiguous, or absent, the number of possible combinations is enormous.

The LDS Church has said and published very little concerning transgender issues. The word *transgender* does not appear at all in the *Church Handbook of Instructions* or General Conference addresses. In early 2015, in response to a question by Jennifer Napier-Pearce of the *Salt Lake Tribune*, Dallin Oaks acknowledged that the church had not progressed far on a learning curve: "I think we need to acknowledge that while we have been acquainted with lesbians and homosexuals for some time, being acquainted with the unique problems of a transgender situation is something we have not had so much experience with, and we have some unfinished business in teaching on that."[2]

The word *transgender* appears only once in church magazines, in a quotation citing a speech by Dallin Oaks. Even then, Oaks's statement used only the acronym LGBT, to which was added parenthetically "[lesbian, gay, bisexual, and transgender]."[3] Only on the church website Mormonand-Gay.lds.org is there more than a cursory mention of the word *transgender*, and the treatment is curious. In a section titled "Frequently Asked Questions" is the following question: "Why Does the Website Not Discuss Gender Dysphoria or Transgender Issues?" The answer does not closely match the question, for while it acknowledges that a transgender person may also "experience same-sex attraction," it does not explain why the website does not discuss transgender issues:

> Many of the general principles shared on this website (for example, the importance of inclusion and kindness) apply to Latter-day Saints who experience gender dysphoria or identify as transgender. However, same-sex attraction and gender dysphoria are very different. For example, those who experience gender dysphoria may or may not also experience same-sex attraction, and the majority of those who experience same-sex attraction do not desire to change their gender. From a psychological and ministerial perspective, the two are different.[4]

The closest thing to an official church policy came from a statement by church spokesman Eric Hawkins, reported in a *Salt Lake Tribune* article in April 2015:

> An official LDS document, "The Family: A Proclamation to the World," written and approved by the faith's top leaders, states that "'gender is an essential characteristic of individual premortal, mortal, and eternal identity and purpose." . . .
>
> "The church does not ordain transgender people to the priesthood or issue temple recommends to them," Hawkins adds. . . . "We

have faith that ultimately, the emotional pain that many of these people feel will be addressed by a loving God who understands each individual's circumstances and heart."

Hawkins declined to comment about the church standing and prohibitions for those who have had only hormone treatments.[5]

TRANSSEXUAL

Transsexual is a term describing a subset of transgender who choose medical intervention—hormonal therapy, sex-change surgery, or both—to more closely align their physical body with their gender identity. In contrast to the church's silence on transgender, for more than three decades it has included statements and policies on one aspect of transsexuality—transsexual surgery—in the *Church Handbook of Instructions*.[6] Although there is no written explanation for the church's activism with respect to transsexual surgery versus its silence on transgender, it is consistent with its current policy toward homosexuality: *being* homosexual is not sinful, but *acting out* one's homosexuality is. Transsexual surgery "acts out" transgender.

Church policy toward transsexual surgery evolved dramatically over the first decade following the initial statement, and its evolution parallels the pattern first described by Dr. Lester Bush with respect to LDS policies on birth control:[7]

- Until the end of the nineteenth century there were few reliable techniques for birth control. Since the practice was neither widely effective nor widely used, the question rarely came up—not enough to elicit a church policy.
- With the development of the condom, in particular, effective birth control became possible and gradually grew in popularity. If individual church members had concerns about using birth control, they approached ecclesiastical leaders for guidance. Since there were initially few such concerns, guidance was ad hoc and varied from one case to another.
- As the frequency of concerns increased and leaders began to realize that they were sending conflicting signals, they formulated the first churchwide policy, which was draconian. Basically, church

members were told from the pulpit, by apostles, that they would go to hell if they practiced birth control—which was often called by the synonym *race suicide.*

- Over time, reality set in. Sequential policy statements over several decades gradually backed out of the initial hard-line policy. By the 1980s the church abandoned the issue and left the decision entirely to the couple.

The evolution of policy regarding transsexual surgery was nearly an exact replica of birth control. Although transsexual surgery was first performed nearly a century ago, it remained rare until recent decades—rare enough that there was no formal church policy respecting it.

In the late 1970s I witnessed the next step in Bush's progression: individual responses to occasional queries. A recent convert in the ward in which I was Elders Quorum president had undergone transsexual—male-to-female—surgery prior to joining the church in 1977. The baptismal recommend listed both her prior and her current names and noted, "She is a transexual [*sic*]." A year after the baptism, a counselor in the stake presidency, without referencing the woman, said privately that the presidency had consulted with a General Authority (whom he did not name) about the possibility of someone who had undergone transsexual surgery being married in an LDS temple. The answer was yes. The General Authority was likely Hugh Pinnock, who at the time was the executive administrator (the equivalent of today's area president) over the stake in which the woman resided. In a letter to the stake presidency in June 1978, Pinnock wrote, "The answers that you are about to receive are somewhat consensus in nature." He authorized the woman to receive her temple endowment as a woman, "going through with the name she was baptized under and that she uses at the present time." He also preauthorized a temple marriage, with the caveat that the woman "has explained to a *man* the condition of her present physical body."[8]

Pinnock then underscored the fact that his authorization was not a statement of general church policy. "Some of the brethren, as we discussed, still feel that she has an eternal male spirit in a physically mutilated body. All do not feel that way, however, or the letter which I have written you would not be possible." The stake presidency were so surprised at the answer that they contacted another General Authority, Robert Simpson. This time the answer was an emphatic "No!" Notwithstanding Simpson's answer, which did not represent church policy inasmuch as there was not yet *any* church policy on the subject, in February 1980 I attended the woman's temple wedding. Hugh Pinnock performed the ceremony.

Eight months later, in October 1980, Section 8 of the 1976 edition of the *General Handbook of Instructions* was completely rewritten, with the section title being changed from "Church Courts" to "The Church Judicial System." For the first time ever, the word *transsexual* appeared in an official church publication. The stated policy conformed to the third stage of Bush's policy evolution: hard-line.

> The Church counsels against transsexual operations, and members who undergo such procedures require disciplinary action.... Investigators who have already undergone transsexual operations may be baptized if otherwise worthy on condition that an appropriate notation be made on the membership record so as to preclude such individuals from either receiving the priesthood or temple recommends.... Members who have undergone transsexual operations must be excommunicated. After excommunication such a person is not eligible again for baptism.[9]

Three years later, the fourth stage of Bush's evolution began, a gradual softening of the initial hard-line policy. One element of the 1980 policy was modified: while a member excommunicated for having undergone transsexual surgery was not eligible for rebaptism, excommunication was no longer mandatory. "A change in a member's sex *ordinarily* justifies excommunication."[10]

The gradual evolution continued in January 1985, with a revision of the section "The Church Judicial System" in advance of a completely new edition of the *General Handbook* later the same year. Once again there was a subtle but substantive change in the policy: "After excommunication, such a person is not eligible again for baptism *unless approved* by the First Presidency."[11]

In March 1989, a new edition of the *General Handbook* was issued, this time with a completely rewritten policy, one that used the word *elective* for the first time but did not define its meaning. It also placed the policy under a new heading, "When a Disciplinary Council *May* Be Necessary," whereas in the past, transsexual surgery had been grounds for a *mandatory* disciplinary council, although not necessarily one resulting in excommunication. The new policy, in its entirety, was less than half the length of its predecessor: "Church leaders counsel against *elective* transsexual operations. A bishop should inform a member contemplating such an operation of this counsel and should advise the member that the operation *may be cause* for formal Church discipline. In questionable cases, a bishop should obtain the counsel of the First Presidency."[12]

The current *Church Handbook of Instructions* (2017) signals a subtle reverse shift, toward a more hard-line approach: "A person who is considering an elective transsexual operation may not be baptized or confirmed. Baptism and confirmation of a person who has already undergone an elective transsexual operation *require* the approval of the First Presidency. The mission president may request this approval if he has interviewed the person, found him or her to be otherwise worthy, and can recommend baptism. However, such persons may not receive the priesthood or a temple recommend."[13]

It is notable that amid all of the angst over surgery, the other dimension of transsexual change—hormonal therapy—has never been mentioned. One can only speculate over the silence, but a likely explanation is that in the minds of church leaders, hormonal therapy could be considered temporary and even reversible, whereas sex-change surgery is permanent.

TRANS, THE CHURCH, AND THE PUBLIC SQUARE

While the church has consistently kept transgender issues low profile internally, in at least three instances it has stepped into the public square. The first was landmark antidiscrimination legislation in employment and housing (SB 296) passed during the 2015 session of the Utah Legislature, wherein the church assumed a crucial role in signaling to LDS legislators its approval. While SB 296 protected transgender, along with lesbian, gay, and bisexual, similar legislation ran aground several years earlier when church leaders could not accept transgender as part of the package. In private talks, Brandie Balken, executive director of Equality Utah, was told by a church official, "Look, we think we can get this through, but the 'T' part"—transgender—"is going to be a sticking point. There are all these stories about bathrooms and whatever else, and there is a lot of education that needs to go on before we can be at the same point there that we seem to be with 'gay.'" Balken held the line. "For me, that would be closing the door on people that I absolutely love. When we walk through that door, we are going to go together. That's how we are going to get there."[14] Seven months after she made that statement, SB 296 became law and transgender walked through the door.

A second instance—ongoing at the time of this writing, in February 2017—has been a change in policy by the Boy Scouts of America. In late January 2017, following a century-long policy of using "an individual's birth certificate to determine eligibility for our single-gender programs," the group began to allow transgender children to join its boys-only programs, tacit acknowledgment that "communities and state laws are interpreting gender identity differently." A noncommittal response posted on MormonNewsroom.org said, "The Church is studying the announcement made yesterday by Boy Scouts of America. Boy Scouts has assured its religious chartering organizations that, as in the past, they will be able to organize their troops in a way full consistent with their religious beliefs." In May 2017 the church announced it would discontinue its Scouting programs for young men ages fourteen to eighteen, the ages where gender-identity issues would most likely arise.[15] Although LGBT issues were not cited as a reason for doing so, it does not take a great deal of imagination to conclude that they played a role in the decision.

A third instance where the church has publicly confronted transgender issues is a lawsuit currently, in February 2018, before the U.S. Supreme Court, *Gloucester County School Board v. G. G.*, that concerns accommodations for transgender students in schools. The issue before the Court is whether a school or school system receiving federal funds must give transgender students access to sex-separated facilities (such as bathrooms, locker rooms, and open showers) consistent with their gender identity rather than birth certificate.

An amicus brief, filed on behalf of seven major religious organizations but written by attorneys from Kirton McConkie, the LDS Church's outside legal counsel,[16] argued strongly against expanding rights to transgender persons. The underlying rationale of the brief is "the belief that a person's identity as male or female is created by God and immutable." This is consistent with the LDS Church's doctrinal position on sexual attraction, which used to be that attraction to someone of the same birth certificate–assigned gender is chosen (a belief apparently still held by some church leaders) or (in current iteration), if not chosen, is illegitimate to be acted upon and not durable

into a postmortal existence. The brief continues, "Our core beliefs and practical experience hold that gender is a given, consisting of attributes intrin-
sically connected with one's birth sex—not an individual choice.... Major
religions agree that human beings are the creation of God; that He created
them male and female; that to be male or female is an immutable characteristic.... Such identity denotes a divine purpose and cannot be altered
(absent medical necessity) without offending deity.... Denying the intrin-
sic connection between physiology and gender runs counter to the religious
conviction that gender is God-given and immutable."

In a section describing LDS teachings, the brief notes, "Men and women
are not interchangeable. A person's gender is to be embraced, along with the
complementary but distinct paths that God ordains for men and women."
While stating unequivocally that "gender is an essential and eternal attribute of personal identity, the Church acknowledges the reality of gender
dysphoria and related conditions." In other words, "gender dysphoria"—
synonymous with multiple descriptors under the transgender umbrella—
represents lifelong (but not eternal) conditions, not necessarily chosen, that
"impose heavy burdens, and those who bear them deserve compassion and
respect." Although written by attorneys for a legal brief and thus not an official church statement, it is the closest thing currently in the public domain
to resemble LDS doctrine respecting transgender. The brief most certainly
was reviewed by one or more LDS General Authorities before being filed.

THE VIEW FROM THE GROUND

Because there is no official church policy regarding transgender, with the
notable exception of the evolved policy on transsexual surgery, the experiences of transgender church members vary widely, largely on the basis of
the attitudes of local members and ecclesiastical officers. At the one extreme
was a transitioned woman who joined the church several years after I had
attended the aforementioned temple wedding—and after the first enuncia-
tion of the church's hard-line policy (1980) regarding transsexual surgery.
She belonged to a singles congregation in whose leadership I had previously
served, and the Relief Society (the women's auxiliary organization) president brought her to my home seeking advice. I knew the new bishop well and
feared for a bad outcome if the transitioned woman went to him for counsel.
Therefore, I urged that she be redirected to someone more compassionate.

Instead, she went to the bishop. The meeting went very poorly. Not long thereafter, she committed suicide.

At the other extreme are the vignettes of Latter-day Saint transgender individuals who have maintained their church membership and their transgender identity—there are many others who have resigned their church membership—that serve to illustrate the complexity of the issue.

The first is Sarah Jade Woodhouse, who began to transition in 2005 at the age of thirty-nine and is transsexual. She readily acknowledged the dark side of being transgender in the LDS Church. "I've heard so many of my friends go through such horrible things. They don't deserve it." She also spoke to the biology of transgender:

> If we can accept, scientifically, that there are people who are born with a gender identity that matches their genitalia, and that there are people who are born with both genitalia or neither genitalia, then we have to believe that every other variation along that spectrum has to exist as well....People always ask me, "Do you think God made a mistake?" I say, "No!" I don't think God made a mistake at all, but not because I think that I belong in the body I'm in. I think my spirit is perfectly female, and nature makes lots of mistakes. Nature gives us people with cleft palates and missing arms and stuff, and there is no reason that nature couldn't have messed up on my genitalia. I don't see that God made the mistake at all with me.[17]

Then she spoke of her church experiences, which involved several bishops and stake presidents and membership in several congregations within Utah.

> My experience has been awesome. Barring two instances where it was kind of unpleasant, my experience with the church has been amazing. Before I transitioned, when I told my ex and then finally told my bishop, I remember my bishop saying to me in his office, in confidence, "I just don't understand why you can't be the best woman in a man's body that you can be." I said, "Well, that's not exactly how it works." But they gave me a blessing when I left and separated. When I showed up in a new ward, my bishop there said, "I just want you to know that no matter what happens, you will

always have a safe place to come and worship here." Because of those things, I stayed active. They never pushed me away when I started wearing clothes the way I should. I just kept going.

Later, she spoke to several bishops and stake presidents about the possibility of marriage. "I've always been concerned with my ability someday to transition, have the surgery and then get married and have a husband. I just remember asking the question, 'Is that possible?' and having a number of them say they were certain they had heard of instances where that had actually happened." (I assured her that I had witnessed firsthand such an event.)

Following her transition, she spoke with a new bishop in Provo. He acknowledged that he had not previously been presented with the subject. "He said, 'Let's just read the handbook together.'...In his current version it didn't even say excommunication was required. It just said, 'Church discipline may be required.'" That bishop elected to do nothing other than to encourage Sarah to continue participating in church services.

Sarah's encouraging experiences notwithstanding, the lack of a church-wide policy regarding transgender, combined with its low prevalence within Mormonism—she said, "Every ward I have gone to, I'm the first transgender person they have ever seen"—means that individual experiences will likely continue to span a very broad spectrum.

The second example is Emmett Michael Claren.[18] Physically female, he began before puberty to feel like a boy in a female body. Puberty exacerbated the problem. "Where I grew up, in Wisconsin, there was a football field behind my house. I went there almost every day. I'd lay down in the middle of the football field, look up at the sky, and beg God to strike me with a lightning bolt or something. And just change me. Change my body." At night, he would plead with God. "Please, when I wake up in the morning, change me into a boy." At age fourteen, he attempted suicide.

At seventeen, he came out to his parents as gay—that is, physically female and attracted to women. "I also knew that I felt like a boy trapped in a girl's body, but I didn't hear the word 'transgender' until a year later." While coming to terms with being transgender, Emmett served a full-time proselytizing mission as a woman. "I loved my mission and the person I became because of it." Part of the motivation to serve a mission was the hope that "by serving faithfully, my feelings would go away." They did not.

Upon returning from his mission, Emmett enrolled at BYU-Idaho and tried dating men. "I was doing everything right by the book. And I was dying inside....Something wasn't quite matching up. And that's when I really started to realize who I was. I began praying to know who I really was inside. I prayed like I had when I was a child. I was fasting and going to the temple multiple times a week. And I received the confirmation that my spirit is male. And that I am transgender. And it's OK."

Emmett conferred with his bishop. "I told him about my attraction to women. And then I told him that I felt I was transgender." Surprisingly, the bishop suggested that Emmett come to church the following Sunday, dressing and acting according to his own gender identity: male. "I was so happy. For the first time since I could remember, I was truly happy. I went back to my bishop after that week, and told him how I felt and he said that this was between me and the Lord."

In 2016 Emmett had top surgery—removal of female breasts—for which his new stake president, whom he had never met, revoked his temple recommend. "But I have been blessed with a wonderful bishop who is kind and loving and who has welcomed me with open arms....I am as active as I can be right now in my ward. And in eleven days, I will be one year into my physical transition. And I am the happiest I have ever been in my entire life."

The third example is Nick Pratt. He knew something about his self-identity was not right, but as a child in the 1950s he had no name for it. Living the male identity included army service in Vietnam. After returning from Vietnam he suffered post-traumatic stress disorder (PTSD) but didn't seek professional counseling for another four decades.

In the meantime, Nick served faithfully in church callings: Sunday-school president, Elders Quorum president, high councilor, temple ordinance worker, stake presidency counselor, and bishop for six and a half years. But his gender identity remained an enigma.

One day, after he finally began professional counseling to address his PTSD, his counselor asked what he was like before he joined the military. "It was one of the most profound things that I can recall. I said, 'I don't know.' It was just like a black hole, my early life. It just wasn't there. I looked at him and said, 'I don't know.'" Thus began his quest to recapture the memory of his youth and simultaneously define his gender identity. "What I didn't understand when I was younger, what I didn't have a name for when I was younger—I had no concept of gender and sexuality. In our age, you didn't talk about it."

While other church members have expressed themselves as having a mismatch between the gender of their spirit and the gender of their body, Nick does not see the issue so unambiguously. "I shy away from that, the whole spirit thing. Having been a bishop, and sitting across the table from people who have come in to confess something, the thing that came to me was that the Lord just wants us to have the best he can possibly give us. He isn't there to beat us up....What came to me so profoundly during those years was that I had no clue, when we get on the other side, how the Lord is going to sort this all out."

Eventually, Nick spoke with his stake president. "He didn't know where to put me. I'm not attracted to men. 'I'm transgender, but I'm attracted to women. What does that make me? Lesbian.' He about fell off his chair. He just didn't know where to put me, and he was struggling with it. It was the first time he had even talked to anybody who was transgender."

After attempting to transition through hormone therapy, Nick ultimately abandoned the attempt.

> It nearly killed me. But I made the commitment, and I didn't want to lose all those associations with family. I was still working on it day by day, sucking it up, white-knuckling it to deal with the dysphoria. It's not easy. I don't wish it on anybody. The church doesn't get it. How would anybody get it and understand the emotional stress that one feels, day in and day out, twenty-four hours a day? The Lord understands, and I accept that, and that does give me some strength to deal with things. But it is difficult....
>
> I went through my whole life basically thinking, "Where do I belong? I'm bad. I'm evil. I'm sinful." But then I would say, "But why does the Lord keep using me? Why do I get called to these callings and responsibilities, if it's all that bad?" I don't think the Lord cares that much about it. If you are leading the kind of life that you should leave, according to Christ and gospel principles, I don't think he really cares as much as we think he cares about things.

A fourth and recent case, in July 2017, is that of Laurie Lee Hall, which casts a bright light on the conundrum of the ambiguous LDS position on transgender.[19] An architect, biological male, and convert to Mormonism who was married in the Washington, DC, temple, Laurie worked for the church Building Department for two decades. She became the chief architect in the temple construction and design division, working on nearly forty temples. She also moved up the ecclesiastical ladder, being called as a bishop and then serving for eight years as a stake president in Tooele, Utah.

For many years, Laurie kept her gender identity a secret, even from her wife and their four children, but she became increasingly damaged by living as a male. Only the knowledge that "my wife and God loved me" kept her from suicide. As she engaged in prayer in 2011, she "felt heavenly reassurance in her female identity." When she subsequently informed her ecclesiastical leaders of her gender identity, they quietly released her as stake president. Still devoted to her faith, she remained with her wife and declined to resign her church membership.

Laurie gradually changed her hairstyle, dressed in feminine clothing, and started hormone-replacement therapy, none of which violates policies in the *Church Handbook of Instructions*. She never had sex-change surgery, which is the only transgender-associated action that "may be cause for formal church discipline." Nonetheless, the men over whom she had served while stake president excommunicated her in June 2017. A church spokesman, when asked, declined to comment on the case.

And finally, there is the case of Victoria Adam, who reached out to me early in 2018. Responding to a lecture that I gave at the University of Utah in the fall of 2017, entitled "Science and Dogma: Biology Challenges the LDS Paradigm of Homosexuality," she wrote:

> I am a 63-year-old transgendered woman who had an opportunity to "come out," if you will, three years ago. I am attending my local ward but find it very difficult, not so much with members, but with church leaders. It's very difficult in helping others when I am silenced in having a calling and not being able to speak in a Sacrament Meeting. My desire has never been to be an activist. My desire is to be acknowledged as being one who is acceptable. I expressed my gender to my mother at the age of 5. I knew I was different before then. I just wanted to say that you have given me such strength and ability to understand that "I am okay."[20]

WHAT ABOUT THE SPOUSE?

While the stories of openly transgender people are rare in the LDS Church, stories of their spouses are even rarer. One such spouse is Emily Heaton. Several years into her marriage, and with five young children, Emily's husband, Dallas, "out of the blue," informed her that he was transgender. As has so often been the case with sexual orientation, in earlier years Dallas "really believed that going on a mission would fix it, or getting married would fix it—would just make this go away."[21] But a mission did not "fix it," nor did getting married, attending the temple weekly, reading scriptures every night, or reading General Conference talks throughout the year.

Finally, they turned to professional counseling. "We did go through LDS Family Services, and they referred us to an LDS bishop who specialized in sex addiction. It was treated, basically, as a sexual addiction—that Dallas wanting to present as female was just an addiction that she had to give up." That was a nonstarter. "The gospel didn't have any answers. There were no answers for us. The Plan of Salvation worked so well for me," Emily said, "until suddenly it just didn't.... People, including our bishop, would say it's like somebody who lost the use of their legs or is terminally ill. 'You just have to hope that during the resurrection it will all be made whole.' But Dallas's hope was that she would be made whole as a woman, not as a man, and yet the church promised her that she would be a man."

Ultimately, the two of them reevaluated the theology to which they had subscribed all of their lives. "The Plan of Salvation works for most people and makes sense—until it doesn't. It just doesn't work if you are transgender.... The church teaches that our minds and our souls are what are eternal, and that our bodies will be made perfect to fit our minds and our souls; a person who is transgender feels that that their mind and their soul is the thing that is correct, and their body is what is maimed.... There is just no place." And so, they stepped away from the church and with dramatic results:

> Seeing her transition has been amazing, to see the transformation in how she is at peace with herself. She has become a better parent. She could not love because she couldn't love herself. As she has been able to accept herself, she has found peace. Her grandmother, who is still very active in the church, said, "I see a difference, a physical light." That is ironic, because the church would

argue that her light, the light of Christ, has been snuffed out by her transitioning. But it has been the opposite.

Having separated themselves from the church, they also stepped away from their marriage.

Dallas is a lesbian. She is attracted to women.... She is attracted to me, but I am not attracted to women, in general. Seeing her have her confidence and the bravery to say, "It's OK for me to do something I want," also gave me the courage to say, "It's OK for me to not stay. We can be friends and we can co-parent effectively, but the relationship does not meet my needs." But it's hard. Our divorce is ongoing. We haven't finalized anything, but the process is far harder than the transition. It has been more painful. There have been losses. There has been a lot of mourning over the years. You have expectations. I was sure I was going to be the perfect wife, but I couldn't be. Nobody can be.

THE FUTURE

Sarah Jade Woodhouse said that in each ward in which she lived, she was the first trans person in the congregation. But as the societal stigma toward coming out as trans gradually lessens, more people are coming out, and at younger ages than in the past. Encircle is an LGBT support organization founded in Provo, Utah, in mid-2017. Although its founder, Stephenie Larsen, anticipated a daily tally of perhaps a dozen LGBT youth from the surrounding area, the current usage is fivefold higher and extends to distant counties. Larsen said, "This year, we went from having one therapist, to nine. These kids are aching for therapy. They are very open and realize they are breaking. A third of the therapy is now going to gender-variant youth. And a third of the youth who come to Encircle are gender-variant."[22]

INTERSEX

Intersex is the sexuality orphan within Mormonism. The subject is rarely discussed in any church venue, either formally or informally, and the word does not appear at all in the *Church Handbook of Instructions*, any General Conference address, or any of the massive resources within the church web-site, lds.org.[1] Although the term *intersexuality* has been in existence for a century and *intersex* for more than a half century, most Latter-day Saints are oblivious to their technical meaning, much less their doctrinal and pol-icy implications.

Intersex (sometimes known as disorders of sexual development, or DSD) is a blanket term for people "born with sex characteristics (including genitals, gonads and chromosome patterns) that do not fit typical binary notions of male or female bodies."[2] Clinical presentations run the spectrum from ambiguity or absence of genitalia to what used to be termed "true her-maphrodism"—the possession of male *and* female genitalia, along with a mosaic of cells, some of which carry female (XX) chromosomes, while others carry male (XY).

Kimberly Anderson, an LDS intersex person who identifies as female, says of definitions: "There are over thirty diagnosable conditions that fall under the intersex umbrella. That's a nebulous number only because depending on the doctor, they will categorize several of those intersex con-ditions as not falling under the intersex umbrella. So intersex, even of itself, is a tough condition to pin down precisely. There are some that are clearly, unambiguously intersex conditions. Of those, there are probably between twenty-eight and thirty."[3]

Among chromosomal causes of intersex, in some cases there is only one sex chromosome (X), a condition known as Turner syndrome. In others, there are multiple X chromosomes (as many as five have been reported). In Klinefelter syndrome there is a single Y chromosome, with two or more X chromosomes. In XYY syndrome there is one X chromosome and multiple Y chromosomes. And in yet other instances, there are genetic mosaics in which some cells have one abnormal configuration of sex chromosomes, while other cells in the same individual have a different configuration. Visual appearance, gender identity, and sexual preference present a highly variable matrix, with homosexuality being one option. In a word, it's complicated.

On a practical level is the decision of how—or whether—to choose one gender identity over the other. In prior years parents and physician would often assign gender at birth, in the case of ambiguous or bisexual genitalia and proceed with surgery. Given the sometimes-disastrous results, which may not have occurred until after puberty, such intervention is infrequent now. Anderson describes the preferable alternative:

> As a human being, we have the right, we have the duty to ourselves, and we owe it to others to determine the course of our own lives. We are self-determining individuals, we are self-determining beings. I can say that I want to wear blue, I can say that I want to wear a hat, I can say that I want to wear sandals, and no one is going to care. I can say I want to be a doctor. If I'm a man, everyone loves it. If I'm a woman, it's becoming more and more acceptable. As time goes on, the things that we can determine about ourselves are more or less acceptable to the society at large....
>
> I call myself a self-actualized woman. I'm choosing to portray myself as that. I don't care who you see me as, or how you see me; I want the world to know that I am making this choice. No one is making this choice for me. I am making this choice to change how I present myself, change who I allow others to perceive me as. I am making this choice, and I am going with it moving forward.[4]

For the church, a procedural dilemma would occur if a genetically female intersex person was raised as a male and was ordained to the priesthood.

This is not simply a hypothetical situation, as recounted by Dr. David Hatch, a pediatric urologist who is LDS:

> A friend of mine who lives in Salt Lake City emailed me about a situation he came across, where just that kind of thing happened. A genetic female was raised as a male. I don't know how old this person was, but old enough to be married to a woman. Something came up—I never understood what triggered the investigation—and the so-called man came to medical attention, and it was discovered that he was a genetic female and had normal internal female structures. He was a member of the church and had been ordained. His case went to the General Authorities, and the message came back from them that this was no cause for a church court if the person chose to live as a female, consistent with genetics and internal anatomy. But he—or she, in that case—should not function in the priesthood calling. Interestingly enough, they said also that the ordinances performed while the person was living as a male were considered to be intact and need not be repeated. I'm sure there are a number of those stories going around, but they are really hushed. It's an area that hasn't been explored much, and it's fraught with the kind of ramifications that make it feel very dangerous to some people in the church.[5]

Doctrinally, the challenges of intersex are even more daunting, for they reach backward and forward. "The Family: A Proclamation to the World," while not carrying the weight of canon, is nonetheless the de facto doctrinal pronouncement regarding gender, referring to it as "an essential characteristic of individual premortal, mortal, and eternal identity and purpose." If the physical body has the same characteristics as the premortal spirit, do spirits come in more "flavors" than just male and female? Will an intersex person, whose gender is biologically determined, retain an intersex identity in an afterlife existence? Kimberly Anderson believes that the mere existence of intersex poses an irreconcilable dilemma to the LDS Church hierarchy: "The church cannot recognize the intersex individual as a legitimate biological occurrence. It cannot address that in a public fashion at all. The existence of the intersex individual takes the Plan of Salvation and shatters it. It takes the temple doctrines and shatters them. It takes the Proclamation on the Family and shatters it. The intersex individual ruins everything, as far as the church and its gender-binary hierarchy is concerned. So the church will never address the intersex situation openly. Never."[6]

Dr. Hatch similarly addressed the conundrum that intersex poses to church leaders:

> As I've thought about it, the first thing that comes up is the problem with the Proclamation on the Family, where it has a statement about gender being eternal. There have been talks in General Conferences and other places where essentially the authority has said, "This is an area where God makes no mistakes." There is no allowance for these inter-sexuals. In that description, there is clearly a conflict.... We can't include everybody if we say that gender is permanent and eternal, and started in the pre-existence.
>
> That's the reason that DSD is so fascinating to me and many other people. It's a condition in which there is no individual choice. In light of that, it forces us to reconsider some of our assumptions about homosexuals and transsexuals.[7]

SUICIDE

The tragic connection between homosexuality and suicide is well known, as is the dramatic (eightfold) reduction in risk of suicide if LGBT youth are accepted within their families.[1] Yet the incidence of teenage suicide in Utah, the most Mormon state in the country, is rising at the highest rate in the country.

Although suicide draws public attention—Carol Lynn Pearson wrote an entire book about LDS-LGBT suicides[2]—it is the extreme dimension of a far more pervasive disorder that is caused by people and organizations through their disapproving treatment of LGBT people. Laura Skaggs Dulin, a mental health therapist who came out publicly several years ago, spoke of suicide as "just one of many, many potential negative outcomes of sending this persistent message that you must cut yourself off from this part of yourself and not live into it, in all the ways that that plays out....More and more prominently, we are talking about post-traumatic stress disorder."[3]

PTSD has entered the public consciousness largely because it is the most common injury affecting troops who have fought in the long wars in Afghanistan and Iraq. Clinicians at Walter Reed National Military Medical Center, with whom I have consulted, tell me that upwards of half the troops returning from these battle theaters are diagnosed with the disorder—and some say that virtually *all* show signs of it. But PTSD is not restricted to the military. It is diagnosed with increasing frequency among "first responders"—police, fire, emergency medical services—and even among news correspondents deployed to combat zones. It is characterized by permanent damage to the brain and thus is never cured; as is the case with other chronic disorders, though, it can be managed if proper clinical intervention is achieved and maintained.

Laura Dulin went on to elaborate about PTSD among LGBT church members:

> I think a lot of people are misdiagnosed. They may show up as classic depression, but the actual trauma is what it means to be rejected by your family, told by your bishop that you have committed a sin next to murder, and you are integrating some idea about yourself as a sexual deviant who is dangerous. And then the symptoms showing up are more like people having flashbacks and being triggered into fight or flight, or having nightmares about what happened. Or, just by walking into a church or anticipating seeing their families again, their whole body is getting into distress. These are more the symptoms of post-traumatic stress disorder than they would be a classic anxiety disorder or depression.
>
> Initially, the trauma is so severe that thinking about God is synonymous with thinking about rejection from the community, rejection from God's kingdom, and being worthless. The other side of the coin, staying in the church, means I'm cutting myself off from ever having a partner, and it causes all these psychological problems and pain that comes with that. No matter which way you cut it, people who left and people who stayed can still be experiencing the same type of symptoms of post-traumatic stress.

About six months after the Policy was implemented in November 2015, Brian Simmons, a doctoral student at the University of Georgia, initiated his dissertation research into the causes and prevalence of PTSD among LGBT Latter-day Saints. He recruited nearly three hundred participants, with a nearly even mixture of those still active in the church and those who had withdrawn from activity or membership. Nearly three-quarters (73.4 percent) fitted the profile of PTSD based just on their religious experiences—a rate tenfold higher than for the general U.S. adult population.[4]

George Deussen, whose son's story figures prominently later in this chapter, commented on the trauma that he saw inflicted on his son that contributed to his suicide and that continues to be inflicted on other Latter-day

Saint gay youth. "The culture creates such a deep, deep community, a deep reliance on the community, a reliance on the Brethren, a reliance on the leadership—you are just programmed your entire Mormon upbringing to turn into those spaces. When that space, in many ways, rejects you, I think the trauma is so deep that it moves to what we are talking about." Those whose trauma does not lead them to suicide nonetheless suffer permanently. Wendy Montgomery, whose story was told in earlier chapters, spoke of the All Arizona support group to which she and her husband belong. "It's not just the teenagers who are being affected. So many are people divorced from mixed-orientation marriages, some of them still in mixed-orientation marriages. There are people who have been divorced for ten or fifteen years, yet the pain and trauma of it is still front and center. It never entirely leaves them. Those scars run deep."[5]

CLUSTERS OF SUICIDES

The earliest reported cluster of gay LDS suicides involved students at Brigham Young University in 1965—four years before the Stonewall Riots thrust LGBT issues into the public consciousness. Robert McQueen, a gay former Mormon, wrote in the *Advocate* of the irreconcilable conflicts that their religion caused and that he saw as the underlying reason that five young men took their own lives:

> The details were gory and unsettling—a strong, athletic neck snapped by a homemade noose, a beautiful head blown apart, a body smashed like delicate porcelain on the concrete conclusion of a seven-story leap, and two quiet overdoses on begged and borrowed drugs. Homosexuality was, of course, the immediate scapegoat....
>
> But there was something disturbing about these particular deaths, something unnecessary, something these men shared which was as much and possibly more to blame. Risking blasphemy, I concluded, after a long and bitter struggle with my own beliefs, that it was their inability to reconcile in a livable harmony the opposing forces of a rigidly homophobic religion and homosexuality that destroyed them.
>
> Those five young men I met in 1965 were all in their early 20's. They were Mormons. Three of them had recently returned from

missionary service for the Mormon Church.... Months prior to their suicides, four of them had been trapped in the ongoing homosexual witch hunts at BYU and subjected to the Church's disciplinary program. The fifth had sought help on his own by contacting Church authorities and admitting his problem to them. As an initial step in their "counseling," each of them was interviewed by the counselor for homosexual problems at that time, Spencer W. Kimball, now [1975] president and prophet of the Church of Jesus Christ of Latter-day Saints.

The interviews with Kimball reeked of moral blackmail. After all, he was "an apostle of the Lord" and, Mormons believed, spoke with direct authority from God. When he, with uncompromising precision, robbed them of their dignity, their sense of self-worth, their hopes for happiness in this life, and their dream of eternal salvation in the presence of God, they believed him....

Following the interviews, each of these men changed subtly. The smiling faces were seen less frequently and almost always without the smiles. Their expressions grew even more dour as, one by one, each was expelled from BYU, excommunicated from the Church, their families informed through Church channels of the "problem." One by one they discovered their student records contained this sorry piece of information, causing difficulties in attempts to transfer to other schools or gain employment; one by one, they took their lives.

My friends from 1965 were good people. They wanted to be better people, but they believed in their church more than they believed in themselves. When their church rejected them because they were gay, it destroyed them. I doubt the Mormon Church will ever accept even a portion of the blame.[6]

Another cluster of suicides that drew even more public scrutiny occurred at the time of Proposition 22 in California in 2000. The poignant story of Stuart Matis has already been told, but his death was one of at least five, the other four being Clay Whitmer, Steven Wheeler, Clifford Martell, and D. J. Thompson.[7] As related in that chapter, Matis's mother initially denied the link between Prop 22 and her son's suicide but later acknowledged it publicly. Thompson made the linkage in a suicide note: "It is unfortunate that the lives of good people such as Stuart Matis, Matthew Shepard,[8] and many others go unnoticed. I see Proposition 22 as the last straw in my life-long battle to see peace in the world I live in."[9]

The clusters of suicides represent exclamation marks on a continuum over several decades, and the largest exclamation mark occurred in the aftermath of the Policy in November 2015. In less than two months, Wendy Montgomery, whose prominence as a cofounder of Mama Dragons made her a clearinghouse for LGBT-related information, reported that she had been contacted by the families or friends of thirty-two young people who had died by suicide. The report created a sensation within Utah, resulting in headlines in both major Salt Lake City newspapers, but also raising questions as to the accuracy of the number. The *Tribune* article noted, "Trouble is, the number far exceeds the suicide figures collected by the Utah Department of Health. Preliminary figures for November and December show 10 suicides in the Beehive State for people ages 14 to 20, with two more cases 'undetermined.'"[10]

SQUISHY STATISTICS VERSUS GRIM REALITIES

The problem with plunging into statistics is that one easily loses sight of the fact that every suicide is a life unnecessarily lost. Nonetheless, it is important to examine the basis of suicide statistics in order to appreciate how under-reported suicides are, particularly in Utah.

There is a general aversion to declaring suicide as the cause of death, both on societal and on religious grounds. The aversion is particularly strong within Mormonism, in large part because of the residual influence of Bruce McConkie's encyclopedic book *Mormon Doctrine*. McConkie, a General Authority at the time, wrote the book without authorization of higher church leaders—indeed, without even the knowledge of those leaders, including his father-in-law, Joseph Fielding Smith, who at the time was president of the Quorum of the Twelve Apostles. Although it nearly cost McConkie his job,[11] the book achieved quasi-canonical status among many church members. Thus, his jolting description of suicide left a particularly deep imprint on readers: "Suicides. *See* MURDERERS. *Suicide* is murder, pure and simple, and murderers are damned."[12]

When Wendy Montgomery became the focus of intense criticism for her numbers, she spoke to an official at the Utah Department of Health to learn how suicide was defined by the department. "[The official said,] 'The three methods of death that we consider suicide are asphyxiation by hanging, self-inflicted gunshot wound, or poisoning.' And poisoning isn't overdosing on drugs or over-the-counter medications. It's like drinking rat poison or bleach or something. So kids who take a whole bottle of pills? Accidental death. You walk in front of a train, drive your car into a tree, any other method of death is considered accidental. Those are way more common than the three that they consider."[13]

A second challenge in quantifying suicides among LGBT church members is that police officers or medical examiners are not required to note, or even inquire about, the victim's sexual orientation or gender identity. Montgomery said, "A lot of these kids either are not out, or the parents aren't going to own that. I've spoken with policemen in Ogden who were the first on scene at a very obvious suicide. The parents begged them, 'Please write "accidental death."' They didn't want that stigma for their kid. And the policemen did, just to honor the parents' request, even though they knew it was suicide. Whether that kid was gay or not, I don't know."

With those disclaimers, there are some quantitative statements about suicide in which one may have confidence:

- "More adults [per capita] have thought about or attempted suicide [in Utah] than anywhere else in the country" (2014).[14]
- "Utah has one of the highest age-adjusted suicide rates in the U.S. In 2013, it is the leading cause of death for Utahns ages 10 to 17 years old, the second-leading cause of death for ages 18–24 and 25–44, and the fourth-leading cause of death for ages 45–64" (2014).[15]
- "According to a poll conducted by the National Gay and Lesbian Task Force and National Center for Transgender Equality, 41 percent of transgender persons have attempted suicide. That is dramatically more than 'the 4.6 percent of the overall U.S. population who report a lifetime suicide attempt, and is also higher than the 10 percent to 20 percent of lesbian, gay and bisexual adults who report ever attempting suicide,' reported the American Foundation for Suicide Prevention" (2015).[16]
- "The youth suicide rate in Utah has trended upward in recent years, growing at an average rate almost four times faster than the rest of the nation" (2018).[17]

STOCKTON POWERS: THE HUMAN FACE OF LGBT SUICIDE

Stockton Powers grew up in Bountiful, Utah, arguably the most Mormon community in the most Mormon state in the country. While in the seventh grade, he wrote a letter to his sister. "He identified as being gay, and he was worried, and thought that maybe he would be better off if he was gone."[18] The daughter showed the letter to Stockton's parents, Alyson and George. Alyson recalled, "Of course, we talked to him and told him that that wasn't the case, that we loved him no matter what." And they did. Wendy Montgomery, whose son Jordan was one of Stockton's closest friends, said, "Stockton had the fiercest mom. I'm sure Alyson played it all down, but the things that she did and the lengths to which she went to keep him safe and protected and fought for, I've never seen a parent work harder in my life than she. She makes the rest of us Mama Dragons look like little puppy dogs."[19]

At the same time Stockton came out, he was just entering into the Young Men's program. Alyson said, "They gave him the *For the Strength of Youth* pamphlet. In that pamphlet it talks about homosexuality being a sin and that you need to talk to your bishop. At that point he felt like, 'I haven't even done anything that would be sinful, so why am I a sinner?'" When he most needed affirmation from the church whose influence completely surrounded him, the message was derision instead of acceptance. And, despite the parents' best efforts over several years, the same message kept being sent by leaders, by parents, and even by age peers.

Boy Scout camp was one low point. Alyson said, "I was out of town, and George was confronted by the bishop. He said, 'Hey, can you go to scout camp this week?' George said, 'No. I've got a busy week this week. What's up?' He said, 'We've had parents come to us and say that if Stockton goes to scout camp, then their kids won't go to scout camp. Unless you come and sleep in a tent with him alone, he can't go.'" When George conveyed the bishop's message to Stockton, he responded, "Why would I do that? I want to be with my friends." His parents pressed the issue, and the bishop held a meeting with the other parents—but without Alyson and George. His report: "Hey, we had a parent meeting, and we have decided that all the kids are going to sleep out under the stars, and the leaders will sleep under the stars but away, because of the scout rule."

Two years later, Stockton had a similar experience with "pioneer trek," a multiday reenactment of the nineteenth-century cross-country odyssey of

Mormon pioneers, complete with handcarts and outdoor camping. When the stake announced plans for a pioneer trek, Stockton was all-in. "He loved to camp. From the get-go he said, 'I want to go on trek.'... George and I were feeling a little iffy about it, and so George reached out to talk to the stake president because we felt that our Bishop was keeping us at arm's length on the subject." But when they tried to speak to the stake president about the matter, the stake executive secretary blocked them. He said, "No, you are not talking to the stake president. If the stake president talked to every mom about her concerns with her gay child, he wouldn't have time to run the stake.... We don't need you telling us how to administer to our LGBT youth, or anybody else in this stake."

After several heated discussions, local leaders relented and allowed Stockton to go on the trek: "OK, we guess he can come, but you guys better give him a very firm warning. Could he sleep in his own tent?" The leaders' fears notwithstanding, Stockton went on the trek and had a great time. Alyson said, "One of his buddies found a little rabbit that made it home. It was exactly what I predicted. I got this beautiful note from the stake Young Women's president, telling me about how she was doing some activity, and Stockton was the only youth that came over and helped her carry some things, and then walked with her with her handcart for several hours, helping her pull it because she was alone." But even though Stockton enjoyed the trek, he was aware of the undertones. Said Alyson, "As soon as that was over, I think Stockton was pretty much over."

George tried to put the issue in perspective:

For Alyson and me, we just found ourselves in this constant battle where our church leadership was completely unwilling to walk with us, to communicate with us, even though they weren't a resource, but at least to help us through this process. We repeatedly tried to reach out. We knew that Stockton was walking away from the church. We knew the way he was being treated, where it was hurting him deeply and he needed something more safe and more loving. We were desperately seeking an experience for our son, so that even if he walked away, later on in life as he was having experiences, if a couple of Mormon missionaries tracted into his home, that he could say, "You know, the Mormon Church

wasn't really for me, but my goodness, they sure treated me well."
That was our desperation, that we wanted Stockton to have a good
taste and know that that was a possibility. But ultimately, from
our experience in that ward and stake, and in that area, there was
a massive disconnect.

As Stockton moved into his midteen years, the tide of marriage equality swept across the country. In June 2013, the U.S. Supreme Court struck
down the Defense of Marriage Act, which, among other things, had allowed
states to refuse to recognize same-sex marriages granted in other states. In
December of the same year, federal judge Robert Shelby struck down Utah's
Amendment 3, thus legalizing same-sex marriage in the state. And in June
2015, when Stockton was sixteen years old, the U.S. Supreme Court made
same-sex marriage the law of the land.

The legalization of same-sex marriage was met by a backlash among
many church members. George recalled, "There has been so much conversation in the church about [homosexuality] being a sin, and that these
people are apostates—negative dialogue that people want to separate themselves. There is such a conversation in the church about the avoidance of
evil, and they think being gay, or the gay lifestyle, is evil. So they want
to avoid it. They don't want to have anything to do with it. We felt that in
droves." And the attitudes of the parents altered the actions of their children. "The kids who had been very close friends with him would say, 'Stockton, I can't be your friend anymore.' Or they would say, 'I love you and I
want a relationship with you, but outside of school I can't have a relationship with you, because if my parents find out that I am a friend of yours,
they won't approve.' So everywhere he turned, outside of Alyson and me,
and some close friends, he constantly ran into this brick wall that included
our bishop and stake president."

Five months after the verdict in *Obergefell v. Hodges* legalized same-
sex marriage nationally, the church announced the Policy, which labeled
as "apostates" any same-sex couples who lived together, whether legally
married or not. The announcement came as Alyson's mother was dying.
"We were at her side, doing that transition to my mom dying. Stockton
and I briefly talked about it, because we were spending a lot of time with
my mom and I remember him saying, 'Did you hear about that?' 'Yes.' I

asked him how he felt, and he said, 'I'm done.' He asked if he could resign his membership, and we told him that we preferred that he wait until he was eighteen."

Alyson's mother died less than a week after the Policy was announced. "The one thing that stood out to me was that it was almost like Stockton felt that because of the Policy that he was really going to Hell, and that he would never see my mom again.... Stockton came to me that night and he said, 'Mom, I was going to hang myself tonight, but Grandma came to me and told me to come to you and tell you.' And so he told me."

Compounding the situation was a recent battle with substance abuse, a common pitfall for those whose rejection from peers and community leaves them vulnerable to short-term escape strategies with long-term consequences. Seven months after the death of Stockton's grandmother—and the concomitant announcement of the Policy—he spent a weekend with his father from a prior marriage.

> Stockton was fighting to stay clean. He had committed to making changes but found the loneliness to be a silent killer. The night before he took his life we believe he was needing to hear our voices cheering him on. He needed us to wrap him in our arms and recognize the struggle to stay clean, help him navigate these rough waters and help him find his way through it. Unfortunately, he felt like the burden was more than he could bear.
>
> As his mother, I sensed the weight the whole night before, even from afar. I was not able to sleep and was worried that he was on the verge of "using" again. For whatever reason that night I felt his weight and pain, but also felt helpless being 300 miles away.

Stockton's father reached out to Alyson and George on Sunday evening, when they were out of town. He said that he was upset with Stockton. In the middle of the night, Alyson texted Stockton's dad: "I strongly suggest you don't leave him alone in the morning." But his dad left him alone that morning. "When he came back to get him, he had taken his life."

During 2016 Wendy Montgomery attended seven funerals, "all of them teenagers, all of them gay. I watched my son be a pallbearer for Stockton. Our babies should not be burying babies!"[20]

WHO IS TO BLAME?

Stockton Powers's suicide was an event, but it was an event that marked a tragic end to a process that began at least five years earlier. Alyson said, "We in no way can say that the church is 100% liable and culpable for Stockton's death. I believe that with any situation like this, that there are layers." Most LGBT children begin to come to terms with their own sexuality in their early teenage years—years that are fraught with anxiety for *all* teenagers. Yet at a time when they are most in need of peer acceptance, they begin to feel rejection. Alyson said, with pain in her voice, "Our neighborhood is predominantly LDS; and when you lose community in that area, you lose everything. You lose your neighbor friends, you lose your schoolmates, because they are all one-in-the-same. And in a lot of cases, you lose family. It becomes, 'Oh, I have to stay arm's-length from this because I don't want to be connected to something that is contrary to what the community is saying or the culture is doing.'"

Wendy Montgomery expanded Alyson's thoughts on "layering." "You should never attribute suicide to just one issue, because it's very multifaceted. It's never just one thing. People say the church is to blame for all the suicides, but that's false. But the church isn't innocent, either. It has a part to play in the reasons why somebody has decided to attempt suicide."[21]

No church leader would ever knowingly push someone to suicide, yet words sometimes have effects that go contrary to the intent of the speaker. Wendy noted in 2014,

> They don't understand that when they say those things, it is a trackable thing. We work with groups like Affirmation and with the Ogden OUTreach, Marian Edmonds [Allen's] group. It's trackable.... When there is a statement in the Church Newsroom, or a General Conference talk, or an Ensign article, or somewhere the Brethren give a talk on traditional marriage—and there have been many of these statements given since the Amendment 3 decision last year—even if they think they are being very loving and inclusive, those numbers that Marian gets almost quadruple. The week of General Conference in October, when [Dallin] Oaks gave that horrible talk—we had the [Dieter] Uchtdorf talk that said, "There is a place for you; please come, we want you here"—and then the next morning there was the Oaks talk that was horrible: "God's

laws will never be trumped by man's laws"—that week there were fourteen suicides! These numbers are trackable. Every time they say something like this, these numbers skyrocket.[22]

Similarly, the following year, in the aftermath of a memorable General Conference address by a prominent LDS General Authority, Carol Quinn, a non-Mormon professor at Metropolitan State University of Denver, wrote the following:

> My student, Melissa, a married lesbian mother, visited my office on Wednesday, a mixture of anger, frustration, and sadness visible on her face. Four gay Mormon youth had taken their lives since L. Tom Perry, a senior member of the Quorum of the Twelve Apostles of the Church of Jesus Christ of Latter-day Saints (LDS), told LGBTQ people that their relationships were counterfeit. He was speaking at the Saturday, April 4, 2015 General Conference about the sanctity of marriage as between one man and one woman. Sitting in my office, Melissa was exhausted and heartbroken. Tuesday night she had stayed up until 3:30 in the morning talking with a terrified, suicidal young man, reassuring him that he was not alone. He survived that night, though Melissa fears that he's still not out of the woods.[23]

What was most hurtful about Perry's sermon was not so much the words that he used, although they were problematic to those in committed, same-sex relationships, but rather the juxtaposition with his pivotal role in the passage of SB 296 just weeks earlier. The photograph of Perry and openly gay state senator James Dabakis, smiling in exultation at the passage of the bill, drew national attention and raised hopes that church leaders were softening their positions on some crucial LGBT issues. Wendy Montgomery lamented, "So to have him give such a condemnatory talk only weeks after seeming to offer a hand of fellowship and friendship to the LGBTQ community felt like a slap in the face."[24]

The sustaining of Russell M. Nelson as the new church president in January 2018 became another catalytic event for some LGBT youth, doubtless because of his role in giving quasi-canonical status to the Policy early in 2016. Wendy Montgomery reported, "Since Nelson has become the prophet, just in the Mama Dragon group alone—because there are probably so many more that we don't know—we have had twenty or thirty kids that have been in hospitals for suicide attempts, that are our children—children of Mama Dragons that are so supportive and loving of their kids. These aren't homophobic families. Just the thought of him being prophet is sending people over the edge."[25]

Recently, an employee of the church's Public Affairs Department met with Stephenie Larsen, founder of Encircle. "He said, 'You and I both understand that suicide is complicated. The church is getting blamed for these suicides. That's the narrative. What do you think?' I said, 'Do you want me to tell you the truth?' 'Yes.' I said, 'It is the church's fault. You can spend five minutes with me in a support group, and it becomes very evident how these kids view themselves because of what they have been told in church. They don't think God loves them, because of who they are.'"[26] Indeed, a letter that Stockton Powers wrote to his seminary teacher, which she forwarded to his parents shortly after his death, said, "God must hate me, because his people hate me."[27]

WHAT CAN WE DO?

At the conclusion of Stephenie Larsen's conversation, she was invited to suggest a way forward. "All I could really say to him was, 'You need to make parents know that they never need to choose between their child and the church. These kids are born this way. It is not their choice.'"[28] Thus far, good intentions notwithstanding, too many parents have not received that message. One good intention was the creation of a website, MormonandGay.lds.org, but it wasn't sufficient. Laura Dulin said,

> I haven't seen a single client yet who said to me, "I was really thinking about hurting myself, and then there was this church website that I sought out." It's not happening. Or, "We had this lesson in Sunday School where we referenced this church website." I don't think it's doing anything, other than having them sort of cover their butt. . . . Nothing ultimately keeps people from having to make the decision of either cutting themselves off from the church, or cutting themselves off from a partner. Those two things, having a life partner or having a community in your faith, are both essential

human needs. Until we actually change that, we will continue to cause people trauma.[29]

Some who are outside the church hierarchy are making a difference, and they do so by giving unqualified love and acceptance. Stephenie Larsen said, "I have had at least fifty kids—and I'm not exaggerating—say to me, 'Thank you for doing Encircle. This saved my life.' That is in less than a year." But the essential change needs to come from within the church hierarchy. Wendy Montgomery said, "I feel like whatever good Affirmation does, or Mama Dragons, or All Arizona, it's like a drop of water in the bucket. We can't stem the tide until they change the message from the top." And, concluded George Deussen, "The blood of my son is begging for change. There will be continued blood spilt, the lives of these precious youth, until that happens."[30]

THE SCARLET LETTER

In the 1963 edition of the *General Handbook of Instructions*, church leaders formalized the means by which bishops of one congregation could alert bishops of another congregation regarding "problems that may exist with newly-arrived members of their ward." The nature of the problems was not specified. A new form that would be attached to a person's membership record, WD-8, "a small red sticker, . . . will preclude the calling of unworthy persons to positions of responsibility." Follow-up conversations would be between the two bishops. A later edition of the *Handbook*, in 1976, clarified that once the bishop-to-bishop contact had been made, "the bishop should remove the [red] tag from the membership record."[1]

In 1998 the policy changed significantly. For the first time, transgressions warranting annotation were enumerated: "incest, sexual offense against or serious physical abuse of a child, plural marriage, an elective transsexual operation, repeated homosexual activities (by adults) or embezzlement of Church funds or property." Perhaps more significant was a change in the duration of the annotation. Whereas in the past it was removed once the new bishop conferred with the prior one, "In all cases, annotation of membership records is removed only with First Presidency approval upon request of the stake president."[2]

While the intent of the annotation has been to protect church members, misuse of it can lead to lasting trauma to the annotated. Too often it has become—and remains—Mormonism's Scarlet Letter. Three vignettes illustrate the damage that this policy can inflict on church members and their families.

CHRISTOPHER LEE—RELITIGATING REPENTANCE

Christopher Lee served a full-time proselytizing mission in Portugal and Cape Verde. After his mission, he attended BYU "and had a very typical Mormon story. I taught at the Missionary Training Center, went to BYU, did a graduate degree at BYU. While I was finishing my undergraduate degree, I met my wife and we were married." They eventually had six children, but early in the marriage Christopher began to realize there was a problem. "I knew that I was attracted to men, but I just believed the church's line that we are all tempted by something, and you just have to overcome it and you'll become normal if you live a normal life."[3]

Living a normal life turned out to be problematic. "It wasn't very long after that that I started to really struggle with depression and a lot of self-doubt and self-loathing. During that period at BYU, on a couple of different occasions I engaged in mutual masturbation with a couple of other people. Eventually, I felt so guilty about that that I confessed. I told my wife, I told my bishop. I was disfellowshipped, and that was the source of the annotation." Christopher repented, returned to full fellowship, and assumed his religious life would proceed as before.

Several years later, in a new congregation, his bishop asked him into his office one day and said, "Hey, we're thinking about a calling for you, but I need to ask you something." He had a printed copy of Christopher's membership, at the bottom of which was an asterisk and an annotation saying, "Call Salt Lake for more information." Until then, Christopher did not know that his record had been annotated. "I didn't know there was this process of marking you. The guy that's the plumber and sits down the bench from you one Sunday is the bishop the next, and they are going to tell him this shameful secret about you."

A decade later, Christopher and his family moved to Singapore. In the intervening years, he engaged in "all kinds of professional and non-professional reparative and conversation therapy efforts," spending about $100,000 in the process. Living now in an expatriate congregation, he was quickly called as president of the Young Men.

Several months after receiving his calling, his bishop, Scott Quinton, said to him, "Hey, I had my personal priesthood interview today with President Lai, and he told me about the annotation on your record, and said that you cannot be the Young Men's president, that there is a restriction." Bishop

Quinton's response was unusual. "It said, 'Before making any callings for the youth, call this number in Salt Lake City.' But it did not say anything about Christopher being gay, homosexual. That's not anywhere in the annotation. I ignored all that. The annotation was there. He was my Young Men's president. He was doing wonderful, wonderful things as Young Men's president. So I didn't call the number. I was not intending to call the number."[4]

In a subsequent meeting with President Lai, Bishop Quinton suggested that they work together to remove the annotation. However, Christopher was not inclined to go down that road. He told them, "I've made my peace with it. This is their deal, and I think it has to do more with the Catholics and their sex abuse scandals, and the church wanting to cover themselves from a legal perspective than it really has to do with repentance and my eternal salvation. So I really don't want to dig this up." But they persisted, and he acquiesced. He regretted it. "It just brought up a lot of negative, dark things"—things of which he had repented and been forgiven, or at least assumed so—a decade earlier.[5]

The most painful part of the annotation-removal process was responding in writing to a series of questions from the office of the church's general counsel—the same questions he had answered a decade earlier to everyone's satisfaction:

- What dates did Lee engage in homosexual activities?
- How many partners did he have?
- What was the nature of his relationship with them? Were any of them long-term?
- When did his last incident occur?
- Does Lee recall any of their names? Were any of them LDS? If so, please identify them.
- Has he had any relapses since coming back into full fellowship?
- Has he ever attended counseling for same-sex attraction? If so, when did this occur and how long did therapy last?
- Has he ever experienced legal difficulties in relationship to his same-sex attraction issues? If so, please explain the legal consequences.[6]

Christopher explained,

It was just a litany of questions that said, "Let's just peel back the scabs and dig into everything," years and years later. That threw me into a tailspin. After a day or two, I wrote a letter back to Scott so that he could forward it to the stake president and legal counsel. I said, "I am not participating in this. I have repented of this. It has been closed for a decade or more. It's been years and years. I'm done. I didn't ask for this process. I didn't want to participate in this. I am not OK with this. I thought that when you are forgiven, that meant you are forgiven. I'm done. I'm not participating in this any further. I'm out. I'm done."[7]

Christopher moved back to the United States, but his former bishop and stake president persisted in their effort to have the annotation removed from his membership record. Not long after he resettled in Idaho, he received word that the annotation had been removed. But by then, it was too late. "It was the catalyst for me really going through that trauma and ever being open to the thought that Mormonism wasn't anything but absolutely perfect. That annotation process absolutely was the catalyst that drove me to insanity. My anxiety was so high, and it finally just cracked."

The Policy, announced in November 2015, was the final straw. By that time Christopher was a church member in name only. "When I read it, it was like, 'I can't even be associated with this in name.' I looked up, right then, the form letter, cut and pasted it into an email, and sent it to the church records and formally resigned, right then, that day."

JAKE BERNHARDT—WHEREIN WAS THE SIN?

Jake Bernhardt is a gay man in a mixed-orientation marriage that has lasted twenty years. He and his wife are raising seven children. They plan to stay together despite the challenges that Jake's sexual orientation brings into the marriage.

Several years ago, Jake went to his bishop to seek counsel regarding his thoughts and feelings about men. "I couldn't stop these thoughts. I couldn't change my feelings. I was getting more and more scared that it was only a matter of time and opportunity, that sooner or later I was going to be in a situation with a man who was giving indications that maybe something could happen, and I would not be strong enough to resist. And then, I would lose my salvation." He was not prepared for the response from the bishop, which took the form of intense inquisition. "You say you have these feelings, you have these thoughts. Have you *ever* acted on them in any way? What have you done? Who have you done things with? Can you tell me the names of those individuals?"[8]

As a result of the interview, whose purpose Jake thought to have been therapeutic, his bishop immediately released him from his calling as Young Men's president. "He told me that I should not communicate with any of the young men. I should not communicate with any of the other leaders. He would contact the other leaders for me and cancel any meetings that I had scheduled. And, I was to stop exercising my priesthood, that I should not give my children a blessing or offer anything related to the priesthood, that I should anticipate not taking the sacrament." And the reason for punitive action? "I had touched guys in ways that weren't appropriate, but I had never engaged in sex with a man. I had never given or received a blowjob. I hadn't engaged in oral sex. I had never engaged in mutual masturbation. I hadn't done any of those things, but I had had thoughts that scared me to death, about all of those things."

What Jake did not realize for many months was that as a result of his seeking out the bishop for advice and assistance, the bishop had annotated his membership record. But it did not stop there. "I think that he was having a hard time believing that I was telling him everything. I think that he was expecting that maybe I would break down further, and finally confess that I had been hooking up with guys, or that I had had outright elicit affairs, something like that." But none of that had happened. Nonetheless, the bishop convened a disciplinary council, and as a result Jake was disfellowshipped for a minimum of twelve months.

Then the bishop required that Jake meet with him monthly. Part of his therapy was to read Spencer Kimball's *The Miracle of Forgiveness*.

Because I wanted so desperately to make things right, I didn't just read those chapters, I read the entire book from front cover to back, including the chapter that addresses homosexuality. That just confirmed for me how awful I was for the weakness that I had already demonstrated. When President Kimball says that it would be better that you tie a millstone around your neck and sink to the depths of the Great Salt Lake, rather than commit an act of homosexuality, that was absolute confirmation that I was doing the right thing in getting help and subjecting myself to discipline so that I could be strong, so that I could have the assistance that I clearly needed, so that I wouldn't make those horrible mistakes, so that I wouldn't fall further.

The toll on Jake was immense. He was doing everything requested of him by his bishop, yet his life was deteriorating. "There was a time when I was suicidal—not actively, but I had absolutely no desire to live. I felt no value in my own life. In fact, I viewed myself as a substantial burden on those I loved, and the source of incredible pain for the people that I loved most."

As the date for his daughter's baptism approached, Jake asked the bishop if there was any way he could participate in the important rite of passage. Being disfellowshipped, he knew he could not perform either the baptism or the confirmation. Perhaps something else? Could he speak at the baptismal service? No. "Can we sing a song as a family? Something to show support and be involved in our daughter's baptism." No. "I'm so sorry, but you absolutely cannot participate in any fashion in your daughter's baptism, because it is an official church meeting and you have been disfellowshipped."

At the end of the year of disfellowshipment, Jake asked if he could be restored to full fellowship. Had there been any infractions during that time? No. Sorry, not yet. They waited another six months, again with monthly meetings with his bishop. Then another convening of the disciplinary council. This time, a favorable outcome—or so it seemed. "Brother Bernhardt, we know that the Lord has accepted your offering of a broken and a contrite spirit, and that you have repented fully. The Lord accepts that offering."

But first, the bishop had to confer with the stake president, who in turn asked to meet with Jake. At the end of that meeting, the stake president said, "I will be communicating with Salt Lake City to get clearance to re-fellowship you." Why? "All matters of church discipline, worldwide, ultimately pass through Salt Lake City, and the Brethren reserve the right, in any case, to take an interest. Brother Bernhardt, they have taken an interest in yours." Why had they taken interest in Jake's case, when countless church members commit moral infractions with the opposite sex that Jake never committed with someone of the same sex? Because of the annotation the bishop had placed in his membership record.

The stake president conferred with church headquarters, and after a considerable delay he read to Jake the letter that he received: "In no less than twelve months from the date on this letter, Brother Bernhardt can, if he chooses, request that we reconsider his standing with the church." The response threw Jake into a deep depression. Nonetheless, "we just kept slogging along. We went to church every Sunday. I passed the sacrament by, and I sat outside of the temple for one of my closest friend's wedding, for my brother-in-law's wedding, for another very close friend's wedding, and we continued not explaining to anyone. We carried on."

The process dragged on for another eighteen months—a full three years after Jake voluntarily reached out to his bishop for help. Finally, the news from headquarters that he had been awaiting. His stake president said, "I have the privilege of letting you know that not only have you been forgiven by the Lord, but you have been forgiven by his church. You are now officially returned to full fellowship with the saints, to enjoy all of the blessings and privileges of your membership in the church. . . . It's as if nothing ever happened. Your sins have been wiped away." However, there was one caveat:

> I do want to make sure that you remember the discussions that we have had previously about the annotation on your records, which will be permanent. For your lifetime, there is a mark. Anytime you move to a new ward, of course, the leadership will be aware of that annotation. Remember that I did clarify for you that this means that you will never be in a calling that would put you in a position to interact with children or with minors. But you can be in the Elders Quorum presidency, and you can teach adult Sunday School. There's so much that you can do. But I want to make sure that you remembered that that mark is there.

What should have been a joyful process of reentering full fellowship within the church turned out to be anything but that for Jake, as well as for his wife. "I was waiting for that rush of the Spirit. I was waiting to feel relieved and to feel loved; but I just felt broken. I just felt hurt." The following Sunday, for the first time in three years, Jake took the sacrament. "It felt absolutely empty." He and his wife went to the temple together for the first time in three years. "It was a miserable experience. It was awful, and it just got worse. It reached the point where I recognized that there was a very clear connection between my path of suicidality and my church attendance. When I went to church, I felt awful about myself."

The Policy of November 2015 was the final straw for Jake's wife. He continued to go to church for about four months thereafter, but there had been too much pain for too long. He told his bishop, "We can't pretend. We can't carry on." The response: "Well, that brings up some concerns for your temple recommend." I said, "It's OK. You can have it. I don't need it."

Jake's epitaph for his church membership is poignant. "We believed. We did not doubt. We put our full trust in the leaders of the church, and we were hurt incredibly for having done so." The Scarlet Letter was never removed from his membership record.

JORDAN MONTGOMERY—A SCARLET LETTER CHILD

Jordan Montgomery was ten years old when his parents, active LDS, were enthusiastic supporters of Proposition 8. What they did not realize at the time was that he was in the process of sorting through his own sexual orientation. In January 2012, Jordan came out to his parents. His mother, Wendy, recalled,

> He was 13 years old. My brother, who was a bishop at the time, counseled us to visit with our own bishop and tell him about Jordan. So we met with our bishop in March of 2012 to tell him Jordan was gay (with Jordan's permission). We scheduled regular meetings with him and our stake president each month for the next 2 years because we wanted to keep this topic in front of them, hoping they would be kind, accommodating and inclusive of our son when complex issues arose—like scout camp, youth conference and his Boy Scout Eagle Project (the BSA was in the midst of the "gay debate" around this time and whether they would let gay scouts participate).[9]

Usually, Wendy and her husband, Tom, attended the meetings together, but on a few occasions the bishop pulled Wendy aside during the three-hour meeting block on Sundays. "Each of these one-on-one meetings with the bishop was awful. He said harsh and belittling things to me that he never said in front of Tom.... I felt shamed, small, and very alone during these impromptu interviews. After it happened a few times, I refused to meet with him alone."

During one of those meetings, her bishop told Wendy that he "had put an asterisk in Jordan's church records." She had never heard of such a thing. When she inquired of the bishop what it meant, "He said it meant that since Jordan had 'same sex attraction,' it was unlikely that he'd be able to work with youth.... I dismissed it in that moment since I just wanted to get out of that really uncomfortable meeting." Not until months later, upon researching the subject of the annotation on Jordan's membership record, did Wendy begin to understand the gravity of the situation.

> The more I learned, the more sick to my stomach and furious I felt. For those with an asterisk, it is their own lifelong scarlet letter. It ensures that they will never be able to work in the nursery, in the primary, in the young men's/women's, or hold any high-level calling. (The other people in the church that have asterisks in their church records are convicted felons, child molesters, etc.) This was put in my son's permanent church records at thirteen years old. He was a deacon and worthy of the Aaronic Priesthood which he held. He had never even held a boy's hand. He had been interviewed by this same bishop and found worthy to pass the Sacrament. This archaic policy feeds into that damaging and untrue myth that homosexual equals pedophile. To make matters worse, a ward bishop can put the asterisk in someone's church records, but ONLY a member of the First Presidency can remove it.
>
> The following year, we had the opportunity to meet with Elder [D. Todd] Christofferson. While in our meeting with him, I asked him if he could remove the asterisk from our son's church records. He said that he couldn't, unfortunately. It could only be removed by one of the First Presidency.
>
> So it appears that a lowly bishop has the power to ecclesiastically abuse a child and forever brand him a danger to others, and not even an Apostle has the power to heal it.

WHY?

Three questions relating to annotated records continue to resonate. First, given that the policy in the *Church Handbook of Instructions* clearly states that the annotation is for "repeated homosexual activities (by adults)," how is it that a thirteen-year-old boy who had never held hands with another boy now has a blemished permanent record that not even an apostle is empowered to cleanse?

Second, why is there a double standard? Heterosexual activity among adults, whether consenting or not, does not elicit an annotation on the membership record—activity that might include fornication, adultery, and even sexual assault, including serial transgression. Pedophilia is not equivalent to homosexuality, and there are no convincing data that LGBT people represent any greater threat to children than do straight people.

Furthermore, why is there no annotation for one of the most pervasive threats to church members, fraud? A report in a Provo, Utah, newspaper in 2010 spoke to the issue: "Keith Woodwell, director of the Utah Division of Securities, said Utah has a lingering reputation as the fraud capital of the country. While he said that reputation is no longer accurate, Utah County's reputation as fraud capital of the state may be." Woodwell's judgment on Utah's "lingering reputation" appears to have been overly optimistic, for an article six years thereafter in the *Deseret News*, which described a particularly egregious case of intrafamily fraud, noted, "This story isn't unusual in Utah. It happens all too often, fueling the state's reputation as the fraud capital of the United States. People will exploit their close personal relationships, whether it's in business or more likely through neighborhood or religious associations."[10] Yet there is no provision in the *Church Handbook* for annotations on membership records of those who have committed fraud.

And third, how seriously do church leaders view repentance? One of the church's canonical books, Doctrine and Covenants, quotes the Lord in the first person: "Behold, he who has repented of his sins, the same is forgiven, and I, the Lord, remember them no more."[11] Yet, as Christopher Lee learned, the church remembered, and relitigated, his case more than a decade after he had satisfied himself and his local church leaders that his repentance had been genuine and complete. The pain of being compelled to relive his prior actions proved to be a tipping point for him, and his response was to resign his church membership.

Mormonism's Scarlet Letter.

WHAT'S NEXT?

Although church doctrine and policy on LGBT issues remain static since the November 2015 policy announcement, the half-century view of history reveals enormous changes. In the dark days of the administration of Spencer Kimball, when gay men were often tracked down and excommunicated for *being* gay, no one would have imagined a time when openly gay men and lesbian women would serve full-time proselytizing missions. If past is prologue, there will be evolutionary steps in the future, just as there have been with every significant point of LDS doctrine. What those steps will be and when they will occur cannot be predicted with surety, but it is my hope that an accurate rendering of how we got to where we are now will serve to inform the church leaders who eventually take those steps. I conclude with some observations that may sharpen the focus of future thought and action.

"I WANT TO COME BACK"

In 2011 my wife and I hosted in our home a "Mormon Stories Conference." The convener of the meeting, John Dehlin, had earlier given up a career with Microsoft in order to pursue doctorate studies in psychology, with a goal of understanding and helping Latter-day Saints struggling with their faith. In 2005 John pioneered the genre of the "Mormon podcast," for which I was the first interviewee. At the time of this writing, John had conducted and posted more than nine hundred podcasts in the *Mormon Stories* series.

The conference in our home attracted a wide spectrum of current and former LDS Church members. At the end, during an open-microphone session, a man who lived in the Washington, DC, area (where we live) stood and spoke from the heart. His story was later captured online. "Jon Burlison was excommunicated in 1981 after he proclaimed at a Mormon priesthood meeting that LDS forefather Joseph Smith was not a prophet. Yet after three decades away, one Sunday last year he found himself at a ward in Kensington, Md. 'I am apostate, excommunicated, gay and atheist,' he said. 'I am welcome in the Kensington Ward.'"[1] Six years later, he remains excommunicated and living with his husband—and he sings regularly in the Kensington Ward choir. He has returned to his spiritual home, assisted by a welcoming bishop and congregation.

While many—perhaps most—LGBT Mormons have either withdrawn informally from church activity or resigned their memberships, in the past decade there has been a counterintuitive trend of some returning to activity—counterintuitive because during the same decade the LDS Church has been one of the least LGBT-welcoming denominations in the country. Writer Andrew Sullivan commented in 2012, "I have to say that in my visits to Salt Lake City to talk to huge PFLAG [formerly known as Parents, Families and Friends of Lesbians and Gays] groups, I saw an emerging generation of parents and siblings of gay Mormons who are insistent that Mormon family values extend to gay family members as well."[2] The following year, Sharon Groves, then the director of the Religion and Faith Program of the Human Rights Campaign, said:

> This year I saw something I hadn't seen before among the Mormons who attended [the annual Affirmation conference]—an unapologetic desire for reconciliation with their LDS roots. Everyone who attends Affirmation is not a practicing Mormon and many have had deeply painful experiences inside the church including being excommunicated for being LGBT or LGBT supportive. Yet despite these experiences, the Mormons I met share a desire for reconciliation. . . .
>
> These Mormons were ready for reengagement and their meeting in Salt Lake City demonstrated such a commitment. They worshipped at Temple Square, they held testimony meetings, and they brought some of the most prominent Mormon leaders in the LDS community, including football legend Steve Young and his wife Barb Young to the conference.[3]

When I interviewed John Gustav-Wrathall, the current president of Affirmation: LGBT Mormons, Families & Friends, he got specific about the timing of the trend.

My spiritual experience happened in Salt Lake in August of 2005. It completely took me by surprise. At that point in my life I anticipated that I had been done with Mormonism for a very long time and I was never going to be involved in Mormonism....

I had a very powerful, spiritual experience in which I felt the Lord very clearly telling me, "It's time for you to come back." It was very upsetting to me at the time that I had this experience, partly because I had no idea what it meant. At that time the only way I envisioned coming back was leaving my husband. At that point also, my sense was that nobody in the Church would want me back. So I actually was very upset. I wept at the time. My response to God was, "I don't understand why. How does this make any sense?"

At that time I didn't tell anybody about this spiritual experience that I had had. I certainly didn't tell my husband; I certainly didn't tell my parents. I kept it completely to myself. But over the following month or so I continued to feel this prompting that I needed to come back to the Church. At one point the prompting that came to me was, "All I am asking you to do is go to church. I'm not telling you to leave your husband, I'm not telling you to do anything but just come back."...

Up until that moment, I would have described myself as an agnostic or maybe even an atheist. I felt this presence of the Spirit in such a way that I knew that God was real and that this was coming from God. Even though the content of the prompting was deeply disturbing to me, the presence of the Spirit was such a peaceful, powerful thing for me. I realized that I wanted that presence of the Spirit in my life. I never wanted to be without it again. When the Spirit said to me, "All I'm asking you to do is go to church," I said, "OK, I can do that. I can handle that."[4]

Over the subsequent years, Gustav-Wrathall started to encounter other people who "were in the same boat." He worked within Affirmation to start the "Prepare Group," consisting of people who wanted to return. It started small, but by the time of this writing it includes more than four hundred people. "When we have asked questions about their journey, large numbers of these individuals were talking about spiritual experiences that they had had, independent of each other, and all of them were since 2005." He then related a conversation with a gay man who was a friend of William Bradshaw, a retired BYU professor of biology and father of a gay son. "He told me about a spiritual experience that he had recently, in which the word that he got from the Spirit was, 'A key has been turned.' It was his sense that the Lord had done something."

Coming back to a church that demands celibacy is enormously difficult for most LGBT members. For many it may be impossible. But a recent study that looked at psychosocial health among LGBT Mormons found that of all possibilities—which included celibacy, mixed-orientation marriage, or committed same-sex relationship, with or without church activity—the best outcome occurred among those who were both openly LGBT (whether celibate or not) and active in the church.[5] It should be noted that this was the smallest group within the study and that the effect size between it and the group composed of openly LGBT who did not affiliate with the church—the second-best outcome—was small. The common denominator in both groups was their authenticity regarding their sexuality.

AFTERLIFE THEOLOGY

Mormon afterlife theology began in 1829 where many Christian denominations of the era stood: universal salvation. A verse in the Book of Mormon states, "And he also testified unto the people that all mankind should be saved at the last day, and that they need not fear nor tremble, but that they might lift up their heads and rejoice; for the Lord had created all men, and had also redeemed all men; and, in the end, all men should have eternal life."[6]

The theology soon began to evolve, driven initially by an 1832 vision, to a hierarchical, merit-based heaven with three kingdoms, the highest of which would be populated by those who received LDS baptism while living.[7] Another vision four years thereafter presented Joseph Smith with a conundrum: his deceased brother Alvin, who died before the church was established and thus did not receive baptism, was in the highest—Celestial—kingdom. "[I] marveled how it was that he had obtained an inheritance in that kingdom, seeing that he had departed this life before the Lord had set his hand to gather Israel the second time, and had not been baptized for the remission of sins."[8] In 1840 Smith began to address the conundrum by initiating the unique LDS theology of proxy salvation, wherein church members perform baptism and other salvific rites on behalf of the deceased.[9] The final step in Smith's evolutionary journey occurred in 1843 with a revelation that subdivided the Celestial Kingdom into three heavens. "In order to obtain the highest, a man must enter into this order of the priesthood (meaning the new and everlasting covenant of marriage)."[10]

In essence, current LDS policy concerning homosexuality represents "reverse engineering" of the church's current afterlife theology—that is, if there is no provision for LGBT in Mormon heaven (and there is no mention of homosexuality in any of the uniquely LDS canonical works), then homosexuality in this life must be a temporary condition. Some church leaders have boldly taught this theology, as described in earlier chapters. To recap, James Mason, who had served as a General Authority until 2000, told an audience at the 2005 annual conference of Evergreen, "In the day of resurrection you will have normal affections and be attracted to the opposite sex." Lance Wickman, who with Dallin Oaks did an extensive interview in 2006 that was published on the church website Mormon Newsroom, spoke with apparent assuredness on the subject: "Same-gender attraction did not exist in the pre-earth life and neither will it exist in the next life. It is a circumstance that for whatever reason or reasons seems to apply right now in mortality, in this nano-second of our eternal existence." Bruce Hafen, an active-duty General Authority at the time, said in a speech at the 2009 Evergreen conference, "If you are faithful, on resurrection morning—and maybe even before then—you will rise with normal attractions for the opposite sex. Some of you may wonder if that doctrine is too good to be true. But Elder Dallin H. Oaks has said it MUST be true, because 'there is no fullness of joy in the next life without a family unit, including a husband and wife, and posterity.'"[11]

The church's previous experiences with "reverse engineering," however, have not always been favorable. When the church began to deny the priesthood to any member with black ancestry, the initial justification was that they were the seed of Cain through Noah's son Ham.[12] This assertion, however, was entirely without scientific support, and, more important, it raised the question of why all black members of the church should be punished because of something a presumed ancestor did. Since a key Article of Faith asserted that men would be "punished for their own sins, and not for Adam's transgressions," a new justification needed to be reverse engineered. Church leaders therefore concluded that black people merited their lower station in life and their exclusion from priesthood and temple blessings because they had been less valiant in the preexistence.[13]

Less than thirty years after these principles were confidently asserted by the First Presidency at the time (George Albert Smith, J. Reuben Clark, and David O. McKay), another First Presidency (Spencer W. Kimball, N. Eldon Tanner, and Marion G. Romney) extended priesthood and temple blessings to all worthy black members. The previous reverse-engineered explanations for the priesthood bans have since been relegated to the status of "folklore," which "must never be perpetuated."[14]

Will the claim that homosexuality is merely a temporal condition also be rethought at some future time? At least one church leader, Dieter Uchtdorf of the First Presidency, has walked back such bold assertions.[15]

Uchtdorf's disclaimer notwithstanding, there simply is no room in current LDS theology for homosexuality in the afterlife. One church member, writing days after the announcement of the Policy, summarized the dilemma: "As a gay Mormon, I make my home in the borderlands. In a theology that says every man must be married to a woman in order to be with God and progress in heaven, gay Mormons are anomalies. No one quite knows what to do with us."[16]

Reverend Harry Knox, founding director of the Human Rights Campaign's Religion and Faith Program, spoke extensively with Latter-day Saints about their afterlife theology and its implications for LGBT people. He summarized the response of many:

> "Look, I've spent a good portion of my time in this organization talking about marriage and how important it is, and how it's important for everyone and how children need to be supported, and how this is the core of our belief system. And now you are telling me that it's an exclusive business. We're the same people who learn about our ancestors so we can pray them into heaven—and yet, do I bother to pray for my gay ancestors or not?" This really raised some deep existential, and also theological questions for people. It made them think about their faith. It was no longer a matter of training and recitation, as religion is for most people; it became a

matter for them all of faith. "What do I really believe in?" That's just good for a faith organization from time to time.[17]

MIXED MESSAGES

With one of the most highly centralized and disciplined bureaucracies among organized religions, Mormonism's hierarchy generally speaks with one voice. The fact that mixed messages continue to emanate from its highest levels suggests deep divisions behind the façade of unity. While some General Authorities are more and more allowing of a biological underpinning of homosexuality, others continue to view it as a choice, the contrary declaration on the church website MormonandGay.lds.org notwithstanding.

Recently, in March and April 2017, three back-to-back events underscored the continuing theme of mixed messages. On March 16, the church posted on its website MormonandGay.lds.org a video entitled *The Mackintoshes' Story*.[18] The video includes footage of Xian Mackintosh, a gay returned LDS missionary who is no longer active in the church, and his parents, Scott and Becky. Although Becky notes that Xian's relationship with his partner is "not in harmony" with church teachings (and the partner is never shown), the video recounts the parents' journey from anger and denial to loving acceptance of their son. Scott recounts, "I put my arms around my son and just loved him. I can't help but feel that the Savior loves him deeply."[19]

Yet within days of the posting of the Mackintosh video, a speech by General Authority Seventy Larry Lawrence appeared in the church magazine the *Ensign*:

> One of Satan's counterfeits for faith is superstition. His counterfeit for love is lust. He counterfeits the priesthood by introducing priestcraft, and he imitates God's miracles by means of sorcery.
>
> Marriage between a man and a woman is ordained of God, but same-sex marriage is only a counterfeit. It brings neither posterity nor exaltation. Although his imitations deceive many people, they are not the real thing. They cannot bring lasting happiness.[20]

Days after the printing of Lawrence's article, Apostle Jeffrey Holland held out a nonjudgmental olive branch to the outliers within Mormonism, including LGBT persons. Speaking in the church's annual General Conference and building on the theme of the song "All God's Critters Got a Place in the Choir," Holland said, "The loss of even one voice diminishes every other singer in this great mortal choir of ours, including the loss of those who feel they are on the margins of society or the margins of the Church.... There is room for the single, for the married, for large families, and for the childless. There is room for those who once had questions regarding their faith and room for those who still do. There is room for those with differing sexual attractions."[21]

While the church has maintained a consistent opposition to same-sex marriage, its vacillation between homophobic and hemophilic rhetoric serves to preserve an unhealthy tension that is evidenced by continual hemorrhage of LGBT persons, their families, and their allies.

BIOLOGY: THE ELEPHANT IN THE ROOM

At the time of the LDS Church's entry into the LGBT arena, science had little to say in the 1970s about the nature of homosexuality. The field of molecular biology, which has been the key to the scientific understanding of homosexuality, was in its infancy. But as science has moved forward and constructed an increasingly strong foundation for understanding the biological basis of homosexuality, the church has largely turned a blind eye. As noted earlier, a strong consensus, backed by an increasingly persuasive scientific literature, is that homosexuality is a matter of biology, rather than choice. Homosexuality is an indelible, unchangeable imprint, deep within the anatomical brain, that can result from an increasing variety of known causes—some genetic, some epigenetic—none of which is a conscious choice. The church's failure to embrace fully the findings of science continues to foster a culture of homophobia that was demonstrated boldly by its decisive role in promoting California's Proposition 8 in 2008 and reinforced in November 2015 with the Policy.

Science matters. If we embrace the findings of science that sexual orientation and gender identity are biologically and indelibly imprinted during fetal development and that they are varieties of normal, then we become a more just society—as well as recipients of the enormous gifts that LGBT people bring to the table. But if we reject the findings of science and insist that homosexuality is just a bad choice that can be unchosen, all of society suffers.

THE MORE DIFFICULT PLEASURE

Andrew Solomon, a gay man whose outrage at the LDS Church for its support of Proposition 8 was the initial spark that led me to write this book, spoke hopefully for the future of the church. It is fitting, since he provided the first word for my journey, that I allow him the last word:

> There is a line that I always loved from Lucretius. He said, "The sublime is the art of exchanging easier for more difficult pleasures." The presumption of that formulation is that the more difficult pleasures are actually better than the easier pleasures. That is why one does that. Being in a marriage and having children is the greatest pleasure, but it is certainly not the easiest pleasure. It is not like eating ice cream. It takes a lot of effort and work, and I feel like that is where, to me, the Mormon Church is missing its point. Though I don't expect that that epigram from Lucretius would be the basis of church policy, I think what the Church should ideally do, and does appear to do in the context of straight relationships, is to support people in crossing from the easier pleasure of momentary carnal satisfaction, into the more difficult pleasure of love and family and relationship.[22]

NOTES

PREFACE

1. Hereafter, the abbreviation LDS and the word Mormon are used interchangeably.
2. Gregory A. Prince, "'An Exquisite and Profound Love': An Interview with Andrew Solomon."
3. Michael Purdy to the author, August 14, 2015.

INTRODUCTION

1. Bruce R. McConkie, *Mormon Doctrine*, 129.
2. Andrew Rosenthal, "Mormon Church Wants Freedom to Discriminate," *New York Times*, January 27, 2015.

CHAPTER 2. GENESIS

1. For a history of the gay rights movement and its many organizations that existed prior to Stonewall, see John D'Emilio and Estelle B. Freedman, *Intimate Matters: A History of Sexuality in America*.
2. Psychologist Marybeth Raynes said of the asymmetrical treatment, "One of the reasons we don't really access women is that for some reason parents of gay and lesbian children don't advocate for their daughters the same way they do for their sons. Lesbian women in the Church whom I've talked to sort of think the Church is irrelevant. 'We're second-class citizens to start with, since we don't have the priesthood, so this is sort of two-for-two. It doesn't mean spirituality or a connection to God is irrelevant; it's just that the structure doesn't work, so I'm out of here.' And nobody goes after trying to get their stories. So most of what has come about, in my mind, has been from the grassroots up, to people such as yourself. They self-formed in some ways. But women don't do that. I can name any number of lesbian LDS women, whether they have stayed or left, but nobody takes the time or interest to seek them out." Marybeth Raynes interview, April 7, 2013.
3. The first edition of the *Church Handbook* was titled *Instructions to Presidents of Stakes, Bishops of Wards and Stake Tithing Clerks*, and its title changed several times over the decades. In order to minimize confusion over changing titles, I will refer to it as *Church Handbook of Instructions*—or

simply *Church Handbook*—in the text, and give the actual title of the cited edition in the footnote.

4. For a comprehensive treatment of the history of homosexuality in the United States from the mid-nineteenth century forward, see William N. Eskridge Jr., *Dishonorable Passions: Sodomy Laws in America, 1861–2003*.

5. Caitlin Ryan interview, March 15, 2015.

6. "Relief Society Leader Hails Anita Bryant's Homosexuality Stand," *Salt Lake Tribune*, June 11, 1977, B3; "Unnatural, without Excuse," *Church News*, July 9, 1977, 16.

7. "LDS Leader Hails Anti-gay Stand," *Salt Lake Tribune*, November 5, 1977, D3.

8. Russell M. Nelson, "Where Is Wisdom?," General Conference address, October 1992, https://www.lds.org/general-conference/1992/10/where-is-wisdom?lang=eng.

9. Allan Berube, *Coming Out under Fire: The History of Gay Men and Women in World War Two*.

10. Erin Alberty, "Longtime Utah LGBT Advocates Recount Brutal History," *Salt Lake Tribune*, October 8, 2014.

11. "A Bleak Beginning for Gay Rights," *Q Salt Lake*, January 24, 2013.

12. Connell O'Donovan, "'The Abominable and Detestable Crime against Nature': A Revised History of Homosexuality & Mormonism, 1840–1980," 2004, http://www.connellodonovan.com/lgbtmormons.html.

13. Douglas A. Winkler, "Lavender Sons of Zion: A History of Gay Men in Salt Lake City, 1950–79," 220.

14. J. Reuben Clark Jr., "Home, and the Building of Home Life," *Relief Society Magazine* 39 (December 1952): 793–94; J. Reuben Clark Jr., *Conference Report*, October 2, 1954, 79.

15. Ernest L. Wilkinson diary, May 21, 1959.

16. McConkie published the book without the prior knowledge of his colleagues in the LDS hierarchy. The backlash caused by its publication in 1958 resulted in a stern rebuke from church president David O. McKay, who confided to his inner circle of associates that he had contemplated releasing McConkie from his church calling because of the problems the book was causing the church. See my book written with Wm. Robert Wright, *David O. McKay and the Rise of Modern Mormonism*, chap. 3.

17. McConkie, *Mormon Doctrine*, 639. Although some of the harshest language of the first edition of the book was softened in the second edition, published in 1966, the language condemning homosexuality was reprinted verbatim.

18. "Unnatural, without Excuse," 16. The LDS Church was hardly alone in this kind of characterization of homosexuality. At the time, nearly all major Judeo-Christian denominations condemned it in language that would have fitted comfortably within LDS discourse.

19. *General Handbook of Instructions*, 1968, 122.

20. *General Handbook of Instructions*, 1976, 71.

21. *General Handbook of Instructions*, 1983, 51; 1985, 8-1.
22. *General Handbook of Instructions*, 1989, 10-4; First Presidency circular letter, November 14, 1991.
23. *Church Handbook of Instruction. Handbook 1: Stake Presidents and Bishops*, 2010, 28. In spite of the current policy, however, there continue to be isolated reports of LGBT members being denied missionary service despite being celibate. John Gustav-Wrathall to the author, December 12, 2016.
24. Mitch Mayne, "A Way Out of Danger for Mormon Youth," *Advocate*, June 14, 2012.
25. D. Michael Quinn, *Same-Sex Dynamics among Nineteenth-Century Americans: A Mormon Example.*
26. David O. McKay diary, March 4, 1965.
27. *General Handbook of Instructions*, 1983, 51 (emphasis in the original).
28. *Church Handbook of Instructions. Book 1: Stake Presidencies and Bishoprics*, 2006, 110.
29. In common LDS usage there is only one "sacrament," which is the equivalent of communion, or sacrament of the Lord's Supper in other Christian traditions.
30. "Oakland Presentations: Mitch Mayne Statement," *Salt Lake Tribune*, September 6, 2009.
31. *Homosexuality*, 1973, 4; Boyd K. Packer, General Conference address, October 2, 1976, *Conference Report*, October 1976, 101; Boyd K. Packer, *To the One*, 2; *Understanding and Helping Those Who Have Homosexual Problems: Suggestions for Ecclesiastical Leaders*, 3.
32. Connell O'Donovan, "The Etiology of Homosexuality from Authoritative Latter-day Saint Perspectives, 1879–2006," November 2006, http://www.connellodonovan.com/etiology.htm.
33. *Homosexuality*, 1973, 5.
34. *Homosexuality*, 1981, 1. "Published by the First Presidency and the Council of the Twelve Apostles of The Church of Jesus Christ of Latter-day Saints."
35. Packer, *To the One*, 10, 18.
36. Many religious traditions have similarly employed a highly selective reading of the Bible to defend racism. See William N. Eskridge Jr., "Noah's Curse: How Religion Often Conflates Status, Belief, and Conduct to Resist Antidiscrimination Norms."
37. Packer, *To the One*, 4–5; *Homosexuality*, 1981, 2.
38. Boyd K. Packer, General Conference address, October 2, 1976, *Conference Report*, October 1976, 101.
39. Boyd K. Packer to Dallin H. Oaks, March 16, 1978.
40. Boyd K. Packer, "The Fountain of Life," BYU devotional address, March 29, 1992, https://www.lds.org/manual/eternal-marriage-student-manual/intimacy-in-marriage?lang=eng.

41. Bruce Bagemihl, *Biological Exuberance: Animal Homosexuality and Natural Diversity*.

42. J. Balthazart, *The Biology of Homosexuality*, 17.

CHAPTER 3. THE CURE, 1.0

1. *Bishop's Training Course and Self-Help Guide*; Spencer W. Kimball and Mark E. Petersen, *Hope for Transgressors*, 7; Spencer W. Kimball, *New Horizons for Homosexuals*, 10–11.

2. *Homosexuality*, 1973, 18; First Presidency circular letter, May 30, 1975; *Understanding and Helping Those Who Have Homosexual Problems*, 4.

3. Winkler, "Lavender Sons of Zion," 44.

4. S. Kimball and Petersen, *Hope for Transgressors*, 4.

5. Winkler, "Lavender Sons of Zion," 211.

6. *Homosexuality*, 1973, 18.

7. First Presidency circular letter, May 30, 1975.

8. "Beliefs vs. Gay Mormons," *Phoenix Gazette*, October 10, 1987, Religion section, 1.

9. Tom Christofferson, "Out in Zion," podcast #8, September 28, 2015, "Reparative Therapy in the LDS Community, Part 1"; "Ministering Resources—Same-Sex Attraction," March 2015; Robert Rees to the author, December 12, 2016.

10. S. Kimball and Petersen, *Hope for Transgressors*, 5; Marvin and Geneva Peterson interview, March 3, 2015; Christofferson, "Out in Zion."

11. John P. Dehlin, "Sexual Orientation Change Efforts, Identity Conflict, and Psychosocial Health amongst Same-Sex Attracted Mormons."

12. John P. Dehlin et al., "Psychosocial Correlates of Religious Approaches to Same-Sex Attraction: A Mormon Perspective."

13. Claudia Bradshaw interview, March 4, 2012.

14. T. J. O'Brien, "You Are Not Alone: A Plea for Understanding the Homosexual Condition," 125.

15. Gordon B. Hinckley, "Reverence and Morality," General Conference address, April 1987, *Ensign*, May 1987; *Understanding and Helping Those Who Have Homosexual Problems*, 4.

16. Ronald Schow interview, March 18, 2013.

17. Peggy Fletcher Stack, "Yearning for a 'Romantic Attachment' They Never Had—Gay Mormon Josh Weed and His Wife of 15 Years Are Divorcing," *Salt Lake Tribune*, January 30, 2018; Josh Weed and Lolly Weed, "Turning a Unicorn into a Bat: The Post in Which We Announce the End of Our Marriage," *The Weed: All Kinds of Real*, January 25, 2018, http://joshweed.com/2018/01/turning-unicorn-bat-post-announce-end-marriage/.

18. Weed and Weed, "Turning a Unicorn into a Bat."

19. Ibid.

CHAPTER 4. SPENCER KIMBALL AND *THE MIRACLE OF FORGIVENESS*

1. Leonard J. Arrington diary, December 30, 1973.
2. First Presidency circular letter, signed by Spencer W. Kimball, N. Eldon Tanner, Marion G. Romney, and Gordon B. Hinckley, to "All Stake, Mission, and District Presidents; Bishops; and Branch Presidents," January 5, 1982. The letter caused such a stir, particularly in congregations where the bishop read it from the pulpit, that nine months later the issue of oral sex was quietly shelved by a follow-up First Presidency letter. "We have received a number of letters from members of the Church which indicate clearly that some local leaders have been delving into private, sensitive matters beyond the scope of what is appropriate.... You should never inquire into personal, intimate matters involving marital relations between a man and his wife." First Presidency circular letter, October 15, 1982.
3. *The Church and the Proposed Equal Rights Amendment: A Moral Issue*, a pamphlet inserted into the February 1980 issue of the *Ensign*, the church's monthly magazine for adults.
4. Edward L. Kimball and Andrew E. Kimball Jr., *Spencer W. Kimball: Twelfth President of the Church of Jesus Christ of Latter-day Saints*, 271, 381.
5. Spencer W. Kimball, "A Counselling Problem in the Church," Brigham Young University, July 10, 1964. Typescript of address.
6. Edward L. Kimball, *Lengthen Your Stride: The Presidency of Spencer W. Kimball, Working Draft*, 87n30.
7. David O. McKay diary, December 11, 1968.
8. E. Kimball, *Lengthen Your Stride*, 79.
9. While much of the book focused on transgressions related to sex, it is silent on topics that are of great concern in today's society: rape, sexual abuse of spouses, and sexual abuse of children.
10. Spencer W. Kimball, *The Miracle of Forgiveness*, 78–86.
11. Peggy Fletcher Stack, "LDS Classic 'Miracle of Forgiveness' Fading Away, and Some Mormons Say It's Time," *Salt Lake Tribune*, July 25, 2015.
12. John Gustav-Wrathall interview, October 18, 2015.
13. Stack, "LDS Classic 'Miracle of Forgiveness' Fading Away."
14. Gustav-Wrathall interview, October 18, 2015.
15. David Malstrom, "A Son's Story," *Reunion: The Family Fellowship Newsletter* (Winter 1997): 3.
16. Allen Bergin interview, September 27, 2015.
17. S. Kimball and Petersen, *Hope for Transgressors*, 5–6.
18. First Presidency circular letter, March 19, 1970.
19. S. Kimball, *New Horizons for Homosexuals*, 20; Spencer W. Kimball, *A Letter to a Friend*, 9.
20. Spencer W. Kimball, "God Will Not Be Mocked," General Conference address, October 4, 1974, https://www.lds.org/ensign/1974/11/god-will-not-be-mocked?lang=eng.

21. Joshua Kors, "Oscar Winner Dustin Lance Black on Mormonism, Prop 8, Sarah Palin and the Challenges of Being Gay," *HuffPost Politics*, August 26, 2010.

CHAPTER 5. THE MEMORANDUM

1. Dallin H. Oaks, "Principles to Govern Possible Public Statement on Legislation Affecting Rights of Homosexuals," August 7, 1984, 1.
2. Ibid., 7.
3. Ibid., 9–10.
4. Ibid., 11.
5. Ibid., 12.
6. Ibid., 13.
7. Ibid.
8. Ibid., 14.
9. Ibid., 15; "Transcript of News Conference on Religious Freedom and Nondiscrimination," www.mormonnewsroom.org, January 27, 2015.
10. Oaks, "Principles to Govern Possible Public Statement," 15–17.
11. Ibid., 18.
12. Ibid., 18–19.
13. Ibid., 20; amicus brief, *Baehr v. Miike*, on behalf of Hawaii's Future Today, March 17, 1997.
14. Oaks, "Principles to Govern Possible Public Statement," 5.

CHAPTER 6. HAWAII

1. William N. Eskridge Jr., "The First Marriage Cases, 1970–74," in *Love Unites Us: Winning the Freedom to Marry in America*, ed. Kevin M. Cathcart and Leslie J. Gabel-Brett.
2. Although the movement began in Minnesota, attorneys in Kentucky, taking the lead from Minnesota, moved more quickly and actually began their lawsuit first. I am indebted to William Eskridge for this information.
3. William Eskridge to the author, July 14, 2016.
4. Erin Alberty, "Longtime Utah LGBT Advocates Recount Brutal History," *Salt Lake Tribune*, October 8, 2014.
5. Andrew Sullivan, "Here Comes the Groom: A (Conservative) Case for Gay Marriage," *New Republic*, August 28, 1989.
6. Paul M. Barrett, "I Do/No You Don't: How Hawaii Became Ground Zero in Battle over Gay Marriages," *Wall Street Journal*, June 17, 1996, A1.
7. Kate Kendell interview, December 3, 2014.
8. Barrett, "I Do/No You Don't," A4.
9. In 1996 Lawrence H. Miike replaced John Lewin as state director of health, and his name was substituted for Lewin's as the defendant. To avoid confusion, the original name of the case, *Baehr v. Lewin*, is used throughout this chapter.

10. Barrett, "I Do/No You Don't," A4.

11. *McGivern et al. v. Waihee et al.*, Civ. No. 94-00843 HMF; Order Granting in Part Plaintiff's Motion for Temporary Restraining Order, December 23, 1994.

12. "Affirmation Member Testifies on Marriage before Hawaii Senate," 1, 11; First Presidency circular letter, signed by Ezra Taft Benson, Gordon B. Hinckley, and Thomas S. Monson, February 1, 1994.

13. "LDS Church Opposing Gay Marriages," *Deseret News*, March 30, 1994.

14. Defendant-Appellee Director of Health's Answering Brief, July 5, 1995.

15. Affidavit of Charles W. H. Goo, President, BYU-Hawaii 1st Stake, February 16, 1995; *Baehr v. Lewin*, Docket Item 39.

16. Answer of Defendant-Intervenors to Complaint for Injunctive and Declaratory Relief Filed May 1, 1991; signed by James M. Sattler, attorney for Defendant-Intervenors Charles W. H. Goo, Harry Haleakala Brown Jr., Delbert F. Kim, and the Church of Jesus Christ of Latter-day Saints; *Baehr v. Lewin*, Docket Item 39, February 23, 1995.

17. "Church Joins Hawaii Fight over Same-Sex Marriages," *Deseret News*, February 24, 1995; Eskridge to the author, April 27, 2017.

18. Transcript of an audiotaped proceeding had before the Honorable Herbert K. Shimabukuro, presiding judge, on March 15, 1995. Motion to Intervene as Defendants, in the Circuit Court of the First Circuit, State of Hawaii.

19. Notice of Appeal, April 12, 1995, *Baehr v. Lewin*, Docket Item 47.

20. See Prince and Wright, *McKay and the Rise of Modern Mormonism*, chap. 5.

21. "Church Opposes Same-Sex Marriages," *Church News*, March 4, 1995.

22. Decision of Hawaii Supreme Court, January 23, 1996, *Baehr v. Miike*, 910 P.2d 112 (Haw. 1996) (emphasis in the original); Eskridge to the author, April 27, 2017.

23. Boyd K. Packer, interviewed by Helen G. Whitney for her PBS documentary *The Mormons*, broadcast in 2007. Interview conducted February 25, 2006, Salt Lake City. Transcript from Helen Whitney, "Boyd Packer, Part 3—Tape #3220."

24. "LDS Church Leaders Speak about Congress of Families," *Deseret News*, November 28, 1998.

25. Gregory A. Prince, "'There Is Always a Struggle': An Interview with Chieko N. Okazaki."

26. Gordon B. Hinckley, "Stand Strong against the Wiles of the World," address in Relief Society General Conference, September 23, 1995, *Ensign*, November 1995, 98–101.

27. M. Russell Ballard, "The Sacred Responsibilities of Parenthood," BYU devotional address, August 19, 2003.

28. Amicus Curiae Brief of the Church of Jesus Christ of Latter-day Saints, April 14, 1997. Extracts of the Proclamation were cited in the introductory section of the brief; the entire proclamation was included as Appendix A.

29. A later chapter will describe the unsuccessful attempt by Apostle Boyd Packer to canonize the proclamation with an unscripted statement from the pulpit in the October 2010 General Conference. Notwithstanding the lack of formal canonization to date, there is no doubt that the average church member considers it on the same level as canonized scripture. Anecdotal evidence suggests that no passage of scripture has been framed and hung on as many walls of LDS homes as has the proclamation.

30. Amicus Curiae Brief of the Church of Jesus Christ of Latter-day Saints, April 14, 1997.

31. Loren C. Dunn to Neal A. Maxwell, October 24, 1995.

32. Loren C. Dunn, "Report to the Public Affairs Committee on Same-Gender Marriage Issue in Hawaii," November 21, 1995.

33. Donald L. Hallstrom to Loren C. Dunn, November 28, 1995.

34. Loren C. Dunn, "Report to the Public Affairs Committee on Same-Gender Marriage Issue in Hawaii," November 29, 1995.

35. Loren C. Dunn, "Report to the Public Affairs Committee on Same-Gender Marriage Issue in Hawaii," December 5, 1995.

36. Dunn, who was not an attorney, misspoke in assuming the case would go to the U.S. Supreme Court. The decision by Daniel Foley to file the case in a Hawaii court rather than a federal court served two functions. One was that the Hawaii Constitution, because of its unique sex-discrimination clause, was felt to be friendlier to the plaintiffs than the U.S. Constitution. The other was that by keeping the case out of the federal court system, an appeal to the U.S. Supreme Court was rendered extremely unlikely.

37. Tom Ramsey, Hawaii Equal Rights Marriage Project (HERMP) press release, December 8, 1995.

38. Loren C. Dunn to Neal A. Maxwell, December 20, 1995.

39. See Prince and Wright, *McKay and the Rise of Modern Mormonism*, chap. 4.

40. "Church Joins Hawaii Fight over Same-Sex Marriages."

41. Loren C. Dunn to Neal A. Maxwell, January 16, 1996; Rex E. Lee, "Same-Sex Unions: Let Voters Decide," *Honolulu Advertiser*, March 3, 1996.

42. Donald L. Hallstrom to Loren C. Dunn, February 23, 1996; Loren C. Dunn to Neal A. Maxwell, March 11, 1996.

43. "LDS and Catholic Coalition Opposes Hawaii Legislation," *Deseret News*, February 21, 1996; Loren C. Dunn to Neal A. Maxwell, March 6, 1996.

44. Donald L. Hallstrom to Loren C. Dunn, November 28, 1995.

45. Loren C. Dunn to Neal A. Maxwell, March 21, 25, 1996.

46. "Religions Political Extremists Increase the Pressure on Hawaii's Senators," tripod.com, March 27, 1996.

47. Loren C. Dunn to Neal A. Maxwell, April 24, 1996.

48. Donald L. Hallstrom to Loren C. Dunn, April 29, 1996.

49. David Orgon Coolidge, "The Hawai'i Marriage Amendment: Its Origins, Meaning and Fate." The Defense of Marriage Act will be treated in a subsequent chapter.

50. Loren C. Dunn to Henry B. Eyring, November 19, 1996.

51. Findings of Fact and Conclusions of Law, *Baehr v. Miike*, First Circuit Court, Hawaii, December 3, 1996.

52. Press statement, *Hawaii's Future Today*, December 3, 1996.

53. J. Stevens Keali'iwahamana Hoag to Von Keetch, Esq., Kirton & McConkie, December 10, 1996; Lance B. Wickman to Neal A. Maxwell, December 17, 1996.

54. Ronald T. Y. Moon, "Address at the Hawai'i State Legislature, State of the Judiciary Address 2," January 22, 1997; Angela Miller, "Justice Speaks Up for Courts," *Honolulu Advertiser*, January 23, 1997; Loren C. Dunn to Neal A. Maxwell, January 24, 1997.

55. Dallin H. Oaks to Loren C. Dunn, October 31, 1995.

56. Loren C. Dunn to M. Russell Ballard, March 4, 1997, "H.L.M. Strategy for California and Hawaii."

57. David Orgon Coolidge (d. 2002) was the founder of the Marriage Law Project. Not LDS, he coauthored with Lynn Wardle the book *Revitalizing Marriage in the Twenty-First Century: An Agenda for Strengthening Marriage*.

58. Loren C. Dunn to M. Russell Ballard, April 10, 1997.

59. Loren C. Dunn to M. Russell Ballard, April 17, 1997.

60. Loren C. Dunn to M. Russell Ballard, April 30, 1997.

61. Loren C. Dunn to Robert D. Hales, "The Success of the Coalition, *Hawaii's Future Today* in Hawaii and What Lies Ahead," July 18, 1997.

62. Marlin K. Jensen, Loren C. Dunn, and Richard B. Wirthlin to Public Affairs Committee, "Same Gender Marriage Initiatives: Hawaii and California," July 1, 1997.

63. Marlin K. Jensen to the Public Affairs Committee, "SGM Update," October 9, 1997.

64. Mike Yuen, "New Isle PAC Hopes to Derail Gay Marriages," *Honolulu Star-Bulletin*, November 11, 1997.

65. Mike Yuen, "Group Plans Ad Campaign against Gay Marriages," *Honolulu Star-Bulletin*, July 21, 1998.

66. Mike Yuen, "Same-Sex Marriage Already an Election Hot Button," *Honolulu Star-Bulletin*, August 3, 1998.

67. Coolidge, "Hawai'i Marriage Amendment."

68. John Cloud, "For Better or Worse: In Hawaii, a Showdown over Marriage Tests the Limits of Gay Activism."

69. Mary Adamski, "Christian Groups at Odds over Ads against Same-Sex," *Honolulu Star-Bulletin*, October 1, 1998.

70. Mike Yuen, "Linking of Marriage Debate, Abortion Called 'Outrageous,'" *Honolulu Star-Bulletin*, October 6, 1998.

71. Mike Yuen, "55% Favor Ban on Same-Sex," *Honolulu Star-Bulletin*, October 31, 1998.

72. Mike Yuen, "Same-Sex Marriage: The Entire Nation Is Watching Hawaii," *Honolulu Star-Bulletin*, October 29, 1998.

73. Mike Yuen, "'Yes' Won with Focus, Clear Message," *Honolulu Star-Bulletin*, November 5, 1998.

74. Coolidge, "Hawai'i Marriage Amendment."

CHAPTER 7. BACKLASH, 1.0

1. David W. Dunlap, "Some States Trying to Stop Gay Marriages before They Start," *New York Times*, March 15, 1995, A18.

2. First Presidency circular letter, signed by Ezra Taft Benson, Gordon B. Hinckley, and Thomas S. Monson, February 1, 1994.

3. "3 LDS Officials Seek to Join Hawaii Suit," *Deseret News*, April 14, 1995.

4. "Defense of Marriage Act," 104th Cong., 2nd sess., House of Representatives, Report 104-664 (Washington, DC: US Government Printing Office).

5. Morris Thurston interview, January 17, 2014. In spite of Reid being a devout Latter-day Saint ever since converting to the faith during college, some of his harshest critics have been coreligionists.

6. Sam Francis, "A Mormon Paradox: Fellowship in the Shadow of Intolerance," *Advocate*, April 28, 1998; Arthur S. Anderson to Marlin Jensen, Loren Dunn, Lance Wickman, Richard Wirthlin, and Lynn Wardle, "Design and Content of Coalition Organizing Instruction Book," June 1, 1998.

7. In the Superior Court for the State of Alaska, Third Judicial District at Anchorage, *Jay Brause and Gene Dugan, Plaintiffs, vs. Bureau of Vital Statistics, Alaska Department of Health & Social Services, and the Alaska Court System, Defendants*, case no. 3AN-95-6562 CI, Memorandum and Order, February 27, 1998.

8. "SGM Report," March 12, 1998.

9. "Gay Marriage Advocates Slam Mormon Contribution," JuneauEmpire.com, October 4, 1998.

10. "SGM Report," February 12, 1998.

11. Pam Belluck, "Nebraskans to Vote on Most Sweeping Ban on Gay Unions," *New York Times*, October 21, 2000, A9.

12. Carrie A. Moore, "Church Backing Helps Measures in 2 States," *Deseret News*, November 8, 2000.

13. Stacy J. Willis, "Anti–Gay Marriage Petition Nears Filing," *Las Vegas Sun*, June 8, 2000.

14. Jere Keys, "Saints & Sinners: Can the Gay Community and the Mormon Faith Understand Each Other?," *Out Las Vegas Bugle*, August 30–September 13, 2002, 18.

15. North America West Area Presidency, Loren C. Dunn, C. Max Caldwell, and Cree-L Kofford, to "Dear Brothers and Sisters," January 26, 1996.

16. Loren C. Dunn to Neal A. Maxwell, August 20, 1996.

17. Marlin K. Jensen to Loren C. Dunn, February 6, 1997; Marlin K. Jensen to domestic area presidents, "Status of Anti-HLM Legislation in Ten Targeted States, February 7, 1997."

18. Loren C. Dunn to M. Russell Ballard, February 11, 1997; Loren C. Dunn to M. Russell Ballard, "H.L.M. Strategy for California and Hawaii," March 4, 1997.

19. Lynn D. Wardle to Marlin K. Jensen, Stuart Reid, Loren C. Dunn, and Richard B. Wirthlin, "Field Poll of California," March 10, 1997; Don Lattin, "Mormon Leader Pledges to Fight Same-Sex Marriages," *San Francisco Chronicle*, March 20, 1997, A8; Loren C. Dunn to M. Russell Ballard, March 25, 1997.

20. Lynn D. Wardle to Loren C. Dunn, April 24, 1997.

21. Gary Lawrence to California Defense of Marriage Leadership Group, May 12, 1997. This memo was transmitted from Loren C. Dunn to Marlin K. Jensen on May 13, 1997.

22. Robert D. Hales to M. Russell Ballard, June 20, 1997.

23. Marlin K. Jensen, Loren C. Dunn, and Richard B. Wirthlin to Public Affairs Committee, "Same Gender Marriage Initiatives: Hawaii and California," July 1, 1997.

24. Faust served in the First Presidency from 1995 until his death in 2007.

25. Loren C. Dunn to Robert D. Hales, July 18, 1997; Loren C. Dunn to Marlin K. Jensen, October 9, 1997.

CHAPTER 8. PROPOSITION 22

1. Lynn D. Wardle to SGM committee members: Marlin K. Jensen, Loren C. Dunn, David E. Sorensen, Lance B. Wickman, Richard B. Wirthlin, Arthur S. and Jan Anderson, and Von Keetch, March 26, 1998. The ultimate decision to change state law with the initiative, rather than amend the state constitution, had far-reaching consequences, which will be examined in a subsequent chapter.

2. Marlin K. Jensen to the California SGM Referendum File, "California Definition of Marriage Initiative," December 17, 1998.

3. Marlin K. Jensen, Cecil O. Samuelson, and Richard B. Wirthlin to the Public Affairs Committee, "California Definition of Marriage," February 25, 1999.

4. North America West Area Presidency, John B. Dickson, John M. Madsen, and Cecil O. Samuelson, to Area Authority Seventies, stake presidents, mission presidents, bishops, branch presidents, and all church members in California, May 11, 1999.

5. Douglas L. Callister to stake presidents in California, May 20, 1999.

6. Maria Titze, "Mormon Letter vs. Letter of the Law," *Salt Lake Observer*, July 30–August 12, 1999.

7. "Utah, the Mormon Church and Same-Sex Marriage: Proof That California Mormons Have Been Raising Funds for the Knight Initiative," *Pillar of the Gay and Lesbian Community*, August 1999.

8. "Mormon Money," *Newsweek*, August 9, 1999, 6.

9. Gary Watts to Cecil O. Samuelson, June 2, 1999.

10. Carol Oldham interview, January 14, 2015.

11. "Mormons Now Target California," SFGate.com, July 4, 1999.

12. Don Lattin, "Mormon Church: The Powerful Force behind Proposition 22," SFGate.com, February 6, 2000.

13. Gordon B. Hinckley, General Conference address, October 2, 1999.

14. Doug Ireland, "California's Knightmare," *Nation*, January 27, 2000; Kathy Worthington, "California's Knight Initiative Vote Is March 7," *Pillar of the Gay and Lesbian Community*, February 2000, 6.

15. Kendell interview.

16. Jeffrey Bohn interview, September 1, 2015.

17. Robert Rees interview, August 10, 2014; Bruce Fey, "Stuart Matis: A Friend, an Example," brucefey.blogspot.com, November 27, 2012.

18. Fey, "Stuart Matis."

19. Stuart Matis, "Don't Stereotype Gay People," letter to the editor, *BYU NewsNet*, February 21, 2000.

20. Carol Lynn Pearson, *No More Goodbyes: Circling the Wagons around Our Gay Loved Ones*.

21. Matis, "Don't Stereotype Gay People."

22. Stuart Matis, letter to his cousin Clay, https://hfarg.wordpress.com/index-2/chapter-3-doctrines-and-policies/stuart-matis-letter-to-his-cousin/.

23. Carol Ness, "Gay Mormon Hoped Suicide Would Help Change Church," SFGate.com, March 2, 2000.

24. Carrie A. Moore, "Alone in the Fold: Many LDS Gays Struggle to Cling to Faith Despite Their Yearnings," *Deseret News*, December 3, 2005.

25. Nick Literski to Joe Geisner, August 17, 2014.

26. Marilyn Matis, interviewed by Doug Wright on *Everyday Lives, Everyday Values*, KSL Radio, October 17, 2004.

CHAPTER 9. AMENDMENT 3

1. Carey Goldberg, "Vermont Panel Shies from Gay Marriage," *New York Times*, February 10, 2000.

2. Troy Williams interview, March 30, 2015; Rebecca Walsh, "Amendment to Ban Gay Marriage Hits Opposition," *Salt Lake Tribune*, May 13, 2004.

3. "The Proposed Anti-gay Amendment to the Utah State Constitution," *Pillar of the Gay and Lesbian Community*, June 2004, 24.

4. Deborah Bulkeley, "Most Back Marriage Amendment," *Deseret News*, June 27, 2004.

5. "First Presidency Issues Statement on Marriage," Newsroom.LDS.org, July 7, 2004.

6. Brooke Adams, "LDS Backs Amendment against Gay Marriages," *Salt Lake Tribune*, July 8, 2004.

7. Rebecca Walsh, "LDS Church Shuns Political Fight over Utah's Marriage Amendment," *Salt Lake Tribune*, August 30, 2004.

8. Kevin Davis, "Mormons Endorse Gay Marriage Ban," PlanetOut.com, July 8, 2004.

9. Rebecca Walsh, "A.G. Candidates Unite against Gay Marriage Amendment," *Salt Lake Tribune*, August 7, 2004.

10. Walsh, "LDS Church Shuns Political Fight."

11. http://www.mormonnewsroom.org/article/first-presidency-statement-on-same-gender-marriage, October 20, 2004; Deborah Bulkeley, "Same-Sex: LDS Stand," *Deseret News*, October 20, 2004.

12. Rebecca Walsh, "LDS Church Issues Edict on Marriage," *Salt Lake Tribune*, October 20, 2004.

13. Robert Gehrke, "Buttars Retires," *Salt Lake Tribune*, March 10, 2011.

14. Buckley Jeppson interview, October 5, 2015.

15. In the all-male lay Mormon priesthood there are several ordained offices for adult males, the two most common being elder and high priest, with the latter being the more senior.

16. Buckley Jeppson to Lavina Fielding Anderson and Hellmut Lotz, November 4, 2005.

17. The Mormon Alliance (Mormon-alliance.org) was founded in 1992 "to identify and document ecclesiastical/spiritual abuse in the Church of Jesus Christ of Latter-day Saints." It was discontinued in December 2016.

18. Jeppson interview.

19. Jennifer Dobner, "Mormon in Legal Gay Marriage Faces Cutoff," Associated Press, March 15, 2006.

20. I had been called to the Washington, DC, stake high council only weeks before Dobner's article was published and remained in that assignment for the following five years.

21. Jeppson interview; Peggy Fletcher Stack, "Gay Mormon Describes Life on Brink of Excommunication," *Salt Lake Tribune*, August 13, 2006.

CHAPTER 10. THE CURE, 2.0

1. The term *electrical shock* should not be confused with *electroshock* or *electroconvulsive therapy*, which terms generally are used to refer to a medical procedure used to treat profound depression.

2. Merrill J. Bateman, BYU president, to Connell O'Donovan, April 9, 1997.

3. Max Ford McBride, "Effect of Visual Stimuli in Electric Aversion Therapy."

4. "Head of Mormon Church: 'Gays Have a Problem,'" *Daily Kos*, December 29, 2004.

5. *Legacies*, a documentary by Sean Weakland, 1996, http://www.lds-mormon.com/legacies.shtml; Connell O'Donovan, "'The Abominable and Detestable Crime against Nature': A Revised History of Homosexuality & Mormonism, 1840–1980"; Ellen Fagg, "Plays about Gay Mormons Attracting Audiences

Nationally," *Salt Lake Tribune*, March 15, 2008; "Mo's vs. 'Mos: The battle between Mormons and Gays," *Q Salt Lake*, September 14, 2009.

6. M. P. Feldman and M. J. MacCulloch, "Application of Anticipatory Avoidance Learning to the Treatment of Homosexuality"; McBride, "Effect of Visual Stimuli."

7. One student who had taken course work from Thorne dated a woman in 1971, five years before McBride's dissertation. "She said, 'Oh, you're in psychology. Do you know Dr. Thorne?' I said, 'Yes, he was my teacher.' She said, 'I work for him.' 'Oh, are you a secretary?' 'Oh, no.' 'Well, how do you know him?' 'Well, I work in his private practice.' 'What do you do?' Then she got squeamish and didn't want to talk. She said, 'Well, we don't like to talk about it.' I said, 'Well now, you have me interested.' Well, she was a model for his aversive therapy. She would dress up in a short dress and act sexy, and if they were able to get aroused they would remove the shock. I was just appalled to think something like that would be going on." Jake Zollinger interview, September 8, 2015.

8. Michelangelo Signorile, "The Secret History of Mormons," *Out*, August 1996, 26.

9. Fagg, "Plays about Gay Mormons."

10. John Clarence Cameron, interviewed by Jodi Mardesich, "Archive of *14*," theatre.uIowa.edu, January 2008.

11. O'Donovan, "'Abominable and Detestable Crime against Nature.'"

12. Rob Killian, www.facebook.com/groups/Affirmation, March 31, 2015.

13. Lee Olsen, "A Personal History," *Reunion: The Family Fellowship Newsletter*, no. 14 (Winter 1998): 3.

14. *Legacies*, documentary by Weakland.

15. Rob Killian, MD, MPH, Sunstone Symposium paper, August 1996.

16. Zollinger interview.

17. Evergreen International, "About Us," website last modified December 6, 2004.

18. Eric Gottfrid Swedin, "'You Are Healing Souls': A History of Psychotherapy within the Modern Latter-day Saint Community."

19. Kristopher Albert Goodwill, "Religion and the Spiritual Needs of Gay Mormon Men."

20. Harold C. Brown to Gary Watts, April 20, 1993; Ron Schow, "Homosexual Attraction and LDS Marriage Decisions," 134.

21. Evergreen International, "About Us"; Larry Richman, sixteenth annual Evergreen International Conference, September 16, 2006. Transcript.

22. "Evergreen Conference Attracts Hundreds," *Q Salt Lake*, September 27, 2011; Peggy Fletcher Stack, "LDS Official to Address Group for Gay Mormons," *Salt Lake Tribune*, September 14, 2006; James O. Mason, "The Worth of a Soul Is Great," fifteenth annual Evergreen International Conference, September 17, 2005; "Evergreen International Conference Attracts Hundreds."

23. Boyd K. Packer, General Conference address, October 2, 1976, *Conference Report,* October 1976, 101; Richman, sixteenth annual Evergreen International Conference; Rosemary Winters, "Is LDS Church Taking a Step Back on Gay Issues?," *Salt Lake Tribune,* September 25, 2009.

24. Mason, "Worth of a Soul Is Great"; Bruce C. Hafen, address at Evergreen International annual conference, September 19, 2009; *LDS Newsroom.*

25. Winters, "Is LDS Church Taking a Step Back?"

26. Ron Schow to Larry Crenshaw, commissioner, LDS Family Services, October 7, 2011.

27. David Eccles Hardy to Boyd K. Packer, October 7, 1999.

28. Katherine Rosman, "Mormon Family Values," *Nation,* February 25, 2002.

29. http://www.apa.org/pi/lgbt/resources/sexual-orientation.aspx.

30. Arvel Lee Beckstead, "The Process toward Self-Acceptance and Self-Identity of Individuals Who Underwent Sexual Reorientation Therapy."

31. "Ex–Gay Movement Leader A. Dean Byrd Dies," *Q Salt Lake,* April 8, 2012.

32. "Psychiatry Giant Sorry for Backing Gay 'Cure,' *New York Times,* May 18, 2012; Robert Spitzer, MD, ExGayWatch.com, April 26, 2012.

33. Josh Levs, "California Governor OKs Ban on Gay Conversion Therapy, Calling It 'Quackery,'" CNN.com, October 2, 2012; Richard Ferré interview, March 29, 2015.

34. James Kirchick, "'I Am Sorry'—Alan Chambers' Apology and the End of Exodus International," June 24, 2013, http://www.thedailybeast.com/articles/2013/06/24/i-am-sorry-alan-chambers-apology-and-the-end-of-exodus-international.

35. Peggy Fletcher Stack, "Longtime Support Group for Gay Mormons Shuts Down," *Salt Lake Tribune,* January 2, 2014; Schow interview, January 15, 2015.

36. Gary Watts, speech at B. H. Roberts Society meeting, May 18, 1995.

37. Dehlin, "Sexual Orientation Change Efforts."

38. J. P. Dehlin et al., "Sexual Orientation Change Efforts among Current or Former LDS Church Members."

39. K. Bradshaw et al., "Sexual Orientation Change Efforts through Psychotherapy for LGBQ Individuals Affiliated with the Church of Jesus Christ of Latter-day Saints."

40. "Ending Conversion Therapy: Supporting and Affirming LGBTQ Youth," *Substance Abuse and Mental Health Services Administration,* October 2015.

41. Alfred C. Kinsey, Wardell B. Pomeroy, and Clyde E. Martin, *Sexual Behavior in the Human Male.*

42. Elizabeth C. James, "Treatment of Homosexuality: A Reanalysis and Synthesis of Outcome Studies"; Victor Brown Jr. to Robert K. Thomas, academic vice president, BYU, November 14, 1978.

43. William Bradshaw interview, December 28, 2015.

44. Allen Bergin to the author, August 3, 2017.

CHAPTER 11. A CONSTITUTIONAL AMENDMENT

1. Michael McCurry interview, December 19, 2014. The following quotes also come from this interview.
2. Michael O'Neill interview, November 7, 2017.
3. Ronnie Shows et al., "H.J. RES. 93 Proposing an amendment to the Constitution of the United States relating to marriage (http://thomas.loc. gov/cgi-bin/bdquery/z?d107:h.j.res.00093:), U.S. House of Representatives, Library of Congress, May 15, 2002.
4. Charlie Savage, "Frank Sees Referendum for Ruling in Gay Marriage," *Boston Globe*, November 24, 2003.
5. Christopher Smith, "Amendment Fails to Make It to a Vote; Backers Vow to Keep Pushing," *Salt Lake Tribune*, July 15, 2004.
6. Marilyn Musgrave et al., "H.J. RES. 106 Proposing an amendment to the Constitution of the United States relating to marriage" (http://thomas.loc. gov/cgi-bin/bdquery/z?d108:h.j.res.00106:), U.S. House of Representatives, Library of Congress, September 23, 2004.
7. O'Neill interview.
8. "Church Support Calls for Constitutional Amendment," LDS Newsroom, April 24, 2006.
9. David D. Kirkpatrick, "A Religious Push against Gay Unions," *New York Times*, April 24, 2006.
10. First Presidency to General Authorities, Area Seventies, and Stake Presidents in the United States, May 25, 2006.
11. For example, in the Washington, DC, area, Dan Romney, executive secretary of the Washington, DC, Stake, sent such a directive to bishops, branch presidents, high council, and the stake presidency within the stake on May 27, 2006.
12. Harry Reid interview, October 31, 2017.
13. Reid was Senate minority leader from January 3, 2005, through January 3, 2007, and again from January 3, 2015, through January 3, 2017. He was Senate majority leader from January 3, 2007, through January 3, 2015. In both positions, he was the highest-ranking Latter-day Saint of either political party ever to serve in the U.S. Congress.
14. David Kihara, "Reid, His Church Agree to Disagree on Amendment," *Las Vegas Review-Journal*, June 4, 2006.
15. R. B. Scott, "Mixing Religion and Politics: Oh, What a Tangled . . . ," *Salt Lake Tribune* editorial, June 4, 2006.
16. Robert Gehrke, "Bush, LDS Church United on Marriages," *Salt Lake Tribune*, June 6, 2006.
17. Deborah Bulkeley and Suzanne Struglinski, "Senators Reject Ban on Gay Marriage," *Deseret News*, June 8, 2006.
18. Holly Mullen, "Unusual Role for the LDS Church," *Salt Lake Tribune*, June 8, 2006.

19. Gary Watts to Jeffrey R. Holland, Quentin L. Cook, Cecil O. Samuelson, and Rolfe Kerr, July 23, 2006.

20. Jane Ann Morrison, "Letter from Member of Reid's Church Illustrates Wide Rift on Gay Marriage," *Las Vegas Review-Journal*, August 19, 2006.

21. "Same-Gender Attraction," Newsroom.LDS.org, August 2006.

CHAPTER 12. DALLIN OAKS AND THE INTERVIEW

1. Dallin H. Oaks, "Principles to Govern Possible Public Statement on Legislation Affecting Rights of Homosexuals," August 7, 1984 (emphasis in the original).

2. Packer, *To the One*; Dallin H. Oaks, "Same-Gender Attraction," *Ensign*, October 1995.

3. Schow interview, January 15, 2015.

4. "Same-Gender Attraction," Newsroom.LDS.org, August 2006.

5. "Family Fellowship Response to an Interview with Elder Oaks and Elder Wickman on Same Gender Attraction as Conducted by the Church's Public Affairs Staff in August, 2006," http://www.theldsfamilyfellowship.org/wp-content/uploads/2013/01/Oaks_Wickman_Aug_2006.pdf.

CHAPTER 13. *GOD LOVETH HIS CHILDREN*

1. Peggy Fletcher Stack, "LDS Church Revises Pamphlet on Gays," *Salt Lake Tribune*, July 28, 2007; *Homosexuality*, 1973; *Homosexuality*, 1981; *Understanding and Helping Those Who Have Homosexual Problems*.

2. Schow interview, March 21, 2013. Schow suggested that Packer had asked that Byrd, who was not originally on the committee, be added to it.

3. Richard Ferré interview, March 1, 2015.

4. Dallin H. Oaks, "Same-Gender Attraction," *Ensign*, October 1995, 6–14; W. Byne and B. Parsons, "Human Sexual Orientation: The Biologic Theories Reappraised," 228.

5. R. Ferré interview, March 1, 2015; Schow interview, March 21, 2013.

6. Schow interview, March 23, 2013.

7. *God Loveth His Children*.

8. "Same-Gender Attraction," Newsroom.LDS.org, August 2006.

9. Mike Green, "Letter to the Editor," *Q Salt Lake*, August 16, 2007, 12.

10. Richard Ferré to the author, January 2, 2017.

11. Elaine Jarvik, "Criticism, Praise for LDS Pamphlet," *Deseret News*, July 28, 2007.

12. Stack, "LDS Church Revises Pamphlet on Gays."

CHAPTER 14. WHAT ABOUT LESBIANS?

1. *Homosexuality*, 1973.

2. *Homosexuality*, 1981.

3. *Understanding and Helping Those Who Have Homosexual Problems*.

4. Raynes interview.

5. Peggy Fletcher Stack, "Many May Be Called, but Few Women Are Chosen to Speak at Mormon General Conference," *Salt Lake Tribune*, April 7, 2017. In addition to the male bias of church publications and general conferences, it is noteworthy that Max McBride's BYU dissertation project that used electrical shock reparative therapy recruited only male students.

6. Lesbian, gay, bisexual, transgender, queer, intersex, asexual/same-sex attracted.

7. Hermia Lyly, "The Case of the Missing Lesbians," May 2013, http://affirmation.org/case-missing-lesbians-queer-women-lds-lgbtqiasga-world/.

8. Judith Mehr to the author, February 8, 2017.

9. Maureen Davies, "Resisting Erasure," 2017.

10. Ellen, December 2013, http://affirmation.org/ellen/.

11. Melissa Malcolm King, "Finding Hope," December 2016, http://affirmation.org/finding-hope/.

12. Laura Root, "Being Mormon, Lesbian, and in Love," January 2017, http://affirmation.org/being-mormon-lesbian-and-in-love.

13. Ellen Koester, "Journey to Gay (and God Gives an Answer)," July 2013, http://affirmation.org/journey-gay-god-gives-answer/.

14. Barbara Graziano interview, February 5, 2017. The following quotes also come from this interview.

15. Jacey Fortin, "A 12-Year-Old Came Out to Her Mormon Church. Then Her Mike Was Cut Off," *New York Times*, June 22, 2017.

CHAPTER 15. PROPOSITION 8

1. "In the Supreme Court of California," S147999, May 15, 2008, 11 (emphasis in the original).

2. Jansson interview, November 16, 2015. The following quotes also come from this interview.

3. Peggy Fletcher Stack, "LDS Church Wades into California Traditional Marriage Case," *Salt Lake Tribune*, February 23, 2008; Jansson interview.

4. Elaine Jarvik, "Niederauer Named San Francisco Archbishop," *Deseret News*, December 16, 2005.

5. "Archbishop Niederauer Explains Catholic Involvement in Prop. 8," Catholic News Agency, December 4, 2008.

6. Jansson interview.

7. Fred Karger interview, July 8, 2014.

8. Matthai Kuruvila, "S.F. Archbishop Defends Role in Prop. 8 Passage," *San Francisco Chronicle*, December 4, 2008.

9. Matthai Kuruvila, "Catholics, Mormons Allied to Pass Prop. 8," *San Francisco Chronicle*, November 10, 2008.

10. Circular letter to General Authorities, Area Seventies, and the following in California: Stake and Mission Presidents, Bishops, and Branch Presidents, June 20, 2008.

11. Dean Criddle interview, September 4, 2016.

12. Lance Wickman and Patricia Wickman, interviewed by Heidi Swinton, published December 19, 2012, https://www.youtube.com/watch?v=bA6oGH9khL8; Thurston interview.

13. "LDS Church Proposition 8 Broadcast Transcript, 8 Oct 2008," WikiLeaks, release date October 15, 2008.

14. "The Divine Institution of Marriage," LDS Newsroom, August 13, 2008 (emphasis in the original).

15. "LDS Church Proposition 8 Broadcast Transcript."

16. Katharine K. Baker, "The Stories of Marriage."

17. "The Divine Institution of Marriage."

18. A recent review by the Columbia Law School of seventy-eight scholar studies about the well-being of children with gay or lesbian parents concluded, "Taken together, this research forms an overwhelming scholarly consensus, based on over three decades of peer-reviewed research, that having a gay or lesbian parent does not harm children." http://whatweknow.law.columbia.edu/topics/lgbt-equality/what-does-the-scholarly-research-say-about-the-wellbeing-of-children-with-gay-or-lesbian-parents/.

19. "The Divine Institution of Marriage."

20. Ibid.

21. Andrew Rosenthal, "Mormon Church Wants Freedom to Discriminate," *New York Times*, January 27, 2015. Six weeks after Rosenthal's editorial, the LDS Church worked with the Utah Legislature to pass a landmark LGBT nondiscrimination law, SB 296, the first in the country from a "red state" legislature.

22. "LDS Church Proposition 8 Broadcast Transcript"; Decision of Hawaii Supreme Court, January 23, 1996, *Baehr v. Miike*, 910 P.2d 112 (Haw. 1996). See also William N. Eskridge Jr., "Churches Need Not Fear That Same-Sex Marriage Will Be Forced on Them," op-ed, *Salt Lake Tribune*, October 8, 2016.

23. *In re Marriage Cases*, 43 Cal. 4th 757 (Cal. 2008).

24. "LDS Church Proposition 8 Broadcast Transcript"; California Education Code, Section 51933.

25. "LDS Church Proposition 8 Broadcast Transcript."

26. Matthai Kuruvila, "Mormons Face Flak for Backing Prop. 8," *San Francisco Chronicle*, October 27, 2008.

27. Gary Lawrence, State LDS Grassroots Director, to All Area Directors, Regional Coordinators, and Zip Code Supervisors, August 7, 2008.

28. Thurston interview.

29. "Proposition 8 Volunteer Outline (Western Yolo & Northern Solano Counties)," August 2008.

30. Gary Lawrence, State LDS Grassroots Director, to All Area Directors, Regional Coordinators, and Zip Code Supervisors, August 7, 2008.

31. Lisa Leff, "Same-Sex Marriage Ban Nets Big Bucks," *Salt Lake Tribune*, October 27, 2008.

32. John Wildermuth, "Prop. 8 among Costliest Measures in History," *San Francisco Chronicle*, February 3, 2009.
33. "Proposition 8 Volunteer Outline."
34. "Proposition 8: Who Gave in the Gay Marriage Battle?," *Los Angeles Times*, http://projects.latimes.com/prop8/.
35. Stephen Prince interview, August 21, 2015; Criddle interview.
36. Mark Schoofs, "Mormons Boost Antigay Marriage Effort," *Wall Street Journal*, September 20, 2008.
37. Carol Lynn Pearson interview, January 12, 2014.
38. "Mormons Lead the Way in Financing Yes on Prop. 8 Efforts," *Sacramento Bee*, October 13, 2008.
39. Monica Youn, "Proposition 8 and the Mormon Church: A Case Study in Donor Disclosure."
40. Nadine Hansen interview, October 22, 2013.
41. Jessica Garrison, "Prop. 9 Leads in New Poll, Opponents Say," *Los Angeles Times*, October 8, 2008; Andrew Sullivan, "The Mormon Church vs. Civil Marriage Equality," *Daily Dish*, October 22, 2008; Kuruvila, "Mormons Face Flak for Backing Prop. 8."
42. Mary Barron, "Christian Vote Key in Prop 8," *National Catholic Reporter*, November 28, 2008.
43. Joanna Brooks, "When Mormons Mobilize: Anti–Gay Marriage Prop. 8 Effort 'Outed'?," *Religion Dispatches*, February 2, 2010.
44. Carina Mifuel interview, July 30, 2014.
45. Brooks, "When Mormons Mobilize."
46. Sherod Waite interview, July 18, 2014.
47. "LDS Church Proposition 8 Broadcast Transcript."
48. Waite interview.
49. Carol Lynn Pearson diary, October 29, 2008; Cosette Blanchard interview, June 11, 2015.
50. Criddle interview.
51. Name withheld, from Carol Lynn Pearson diary, August 10, 2008.
52. "Prop-8-imonies," ByCommonConsent.com, September 7, 2008.
53. Vesper Holly, "Prop-8-imonies," ByCommonConsent.com, September 7, 2008.
54. "Granddad," "Prop-8-imonies," ByCommonConsent.com, September 7, 2008.
55. Barbara Young to Marlin K. Jensen, April 24, 2008.
56. Ibid.
57. Julie Ogden to the author, July 15, 2014.
58. Lee Oldham interview, January 14, 2015.
59. Carol Oldham, "Proposition Eight," January 14, 2015.
60. In a video clip that was posted online, Lawrence said, "The idiot who wrote the 'Six Consequences, is me.' "Mormon Pollster Gary Lawrence: I'm the

Idiot Who Wrote 'Six Consequences,'" LatterDayMainStreet.com, February 1, 2010.

61. Criddle interview; Jennette Yates interview, January 16, 2015.

62. Thurston interview; Morris A. Thurston, "A Commentary on the Document 'Six Consequences'... If Proposition 8 Fails," posted September 12, 2008.

63. "Leading Legal Scholars Reject Prop 8 Arguments," published October 29, 2008, *YubaNet.com*, downloaded October 30, 2008, http://yubanet. com/california/Leading-Legal-Scholars-Reject-Prop-8-Arguments.php#. UI6uzLT6ofE; "No on Proposition 8: Debunking the Myths Used to Promote the Ban on Same-Sex Marriage," *Los Angeles Times*, November 2, 2008, http://www.latimes.com/news/opinion/la-ed-prop8-2-2008nov02,0,5926932. story.

64. Richard Jacobs interview, January 19, 2014.

65. Clifford Rosky interview, March 31, 2015.

66. Guy Adams, "The Honeymoon's Over for Gay Newlyweds as Mormons Lead Revolt," *Independent* (London), October 18, 2008; Bruce Bastian interview, July 30, 2014.

67. Jacobs interview, January 19, 2014.

68. Richard Jacobs, "Do Mormons Deserve Equal Protection under the Law?," *Huffington Post,* October 20, 2008.

69. Jim Carlton, "Gay Marriage in Peril in California," *Wall Street Journal*, October 22, 2008.

70. Dan Aiello, "Memo Links Mass. Couple to Prop 22, Mormon Strategy," *Bay Area Reporter*, November 27, 2008.

71. Dan Aiello, "Mass. Couple Pushes Prop 8," *Bay Area Reporter*, October 23, 2008.

72. Aiello, "Memo Links Mass. Couple to Prop 22."

73. Jansson interview.

74. Kilian Melloy, "Mormons' $22M Backing of Prop. 8 Incites Critics," EdgeBoston.com, November 4, 2008.

75. Maggie Gallagher, "Marriage Wins in California," RealClearPolitics.com, November 6, 2008; Jacobs interview, January 19, 2014.

76. Jacobs interview, January 19, 2014.

77. Peggy Fletcher Stack, "LDS Church's Stance against Gay Marriage Its Most Vigorous since 1970s," *Salt Lake Tribune*, October 26, 2008. LDS doctrine holds that in a premortal existence, one-third of all spirits sided with Lucifer and were thus denied the privilege of being born into a physical body.

78. Morris Thurston to Joseph Bentley, Director, Orange County Public Affairs [LDS], August 17, 2008.

79. Pearson diary, July 20, 2008.

80. BYU *Daily Universe* editorial, July 8, 2008.

81. Barbara Young to "Bishop Branson," June 24, 2008.

82. Barbara Young, remarks at the San Francisco Human Rights Campaign Gala, October 11, 2014.

83. Carol Lynn Pearson to the author, April 28, 2015.

84. Robert Rees, "Church Should Let People 'Govern Themselves,'" op-ed, *Salt Lake Tribune*, July 5, 2008; Rees interview; Pearson diary, January 28, 2009.

85. Email to Carol Lynn Pearson, November 2, 2008. Name of sender withheld.

86. Andrew Callahan interview, March 25, 2015.

87. LDS Public Affairs Department to General Authorities and the following leaders in the United States: Area Seventies; Stake, Mission, and District Presidents; Bishops and Branch Presidents, August 18, 2008.

88. Callahan interview.

89. Kilian Melloy, "Mormon Priest Threatened with Excommunication in Marriage Row," EdgeBoston.com, September 22, 2008; Weldon Sleight, Stake President, to Andrew Callahan, September 25, 2008.

90. Kendell interview.

91. Kuruvila, "Catholics, Mormons Allied to Pass Prop. 8."

92. This point was highlighted by a 2010 documentary film entitled *8: The Mormon Proposition*.

93. "Equality's Winding Path," *New York Times*, November 6, 2008.

94. Jesse McKinley and Kirk Johnson, "Mormons Tipped Scale in Ban on Gay Marriage," *New York Times*, November 15, 2008, A1.

95. Chris Johnson, "Calif. Officials Investigate Mormon Role in Prop 8," *Washington Blade*, December 5, 2008.

96. Doe Daughtrey, "The Mormon Proposition," *Religion in the News* (Winter 2009).

97. Frank Schubert and Jeff Flint, "Passing Prop 8: Smart Timing and Messaging Convinced California Voters to Support Traditional Marriage," *Politics*, February 2009.

98. Tim Rutten, "Both Sides in the Same-Sex Marriage Controversy Need to Cool Down," *Los Angeles Times*, November 15, 2008.

99. Schubert and Flint, "Passing Prop 8."

100. William Eskridge to the author, April 27, 2017.

101. Tim Dickinson, "Same-Sex Setback," *Rolling Stone*, December 11, 2008.

102. Lillian B. Rubin, *Dissent Magazine*, November 14, 2008.

103. Jacobs interview, January 19, 2014.

CHAPTER 16. BACKLASH, 2.0

1. Williams interview; Bastian interview.

2. Jacobs interview, January 19, 2014.

3. Guy Adams, "'No More Mr. Nice Gay' as Mormons Face Vote Backlash," *Independent* (London), November 8, 2008; Peter Danzig, MormonsforMarriage.com, November 7, 2008; Tami Abdollah, "L.A. Mormon

Temple Closed after Suspicious Envelope Arrives in Mail," *Los Angeles Times*, November 13, 2008.

4. "Thousands of Prop. 8 Opponents Protest LDS Church at Temple Square," KSL.com, November 7, 2008; Williams interview.

5. Brock Vergakis, "Utah Faces Potential Boycott after LDS Push for Prop 8," *Deseret News*, November 10, 2008.

6. Bill Marriott, "The Facts about Marriott and California's Proposition 8," www.blogs.marriott.com, November 11, 2008.

7. Fred Karger, "Help Fine the Missing Mormon Money," RightsEqualRights.com, February 10, 2009.

8. Jennifer Dobner, "Gay Rights Group Filing Complaint in Prop 8 Battle," Associated Press, February 11, 2009.

9. Laura Compton, MormonsforMarriage.com, November 21, 2009.

10. Pearson diary, July 19, 2008.

11. Emily Rampton interview.

12. Wendy Montgomery interview, July 16, 2014.

13. Ibid., March 14, 2015.

14. Brandie Balken interview, April 11, 2013.

15. Michael Chipman interview, April 9, 2015.

16. Stephanie Pappas interview, April 9, 2015.

17. Andrew Callahan, "Son of Prominent Yes on 8 Leader Quits Mormon Church over Prop 8," *Daily Kos*, November 14, 2008.

18. Nikki Boyer interview, July 25, 2015; Montgomery interview, March 14, 2015.

19. Tami Abdollah and Cara Mia DiMassa, "Prop. 8 Foes Shift Attention," *Los Angeles Times*, November 14, 2008.

20. "El Coyote Boycott? Mormon Manager's Faith Overrides 'Love' for Customers," fdlactionfiredoglake.com, November 13, 2008.

21. "L.A. Restaurant Manager Who Donated to Prop. 8 Resigns," *Advocate*, December 9, 2008.

22. Jesse McKinley, "Theater Director Resigns amid Gay-Rights Ire," *New York Times*, November 13, 2008.

23. "Gay, Lesbian Artists Sought Boycott against Venue," KCRA.com, November 12, 2008.

24. Jessica Garrison and Joanna Lin, "Mormons' Prop 8 Aid Protested," *Los Angeles Times*, November 7, 2008.

25. "Catholic Bishop Decries Religious Bigotry against Mormons," LDS Newsroom, November 7, 2008.

26. Sarah Pulliam, "A Latter-day Alliance," *Christianity Today*, December 2, 2008.

27. "Prop 8 Backlash Is 'An Outrage That Must Stop,' Group Says in Support of Church," LDS Newsroom, December 5, 2008.

28. Kerry Kinsey and Brent Hunsaker, "Same-Sex Marriage Protest Held near LDS Temple Square," ABC4News.com, November 7, 2008.

29. Rosky interview.
30. Andrew Solomon interview, March 28, 2011.
31. "Now It's Gays versus the Mormons," *Salt Lake Tribune*, May 29, 2009.
32. Fred Sainz interview, August 15, 2014; Kendell interview, December 3, 2014.
33. Ashley Surdin, "Protesters Target Supporters of Gay Marriage Ban," *Washington Post*, November 15, 2008.
34. Joe Solmonese interview, January 12, 2016; Bruce Bastian, "Prop 8, a Campaign Based on Fears and Lies," *Huffington Post*, December 16, 2008.
35. "Prop. 8 Supporters Must Be Identified," *Deseret News*, January 31, 2009; Rick Jacobs, "Why We're Mad at the Mormon Church," op-ed, *Los Angeles Times*, December 8, 2008.
36. Eric Gorski, "Mormon Leader: Religious Freedom at Risk as Church Faces Backlash for Funding Anti-Gay-Marriage Vote," Associated Press, October 13, 2009.
37. Stephen Hunt and Brian Maffly, "Utah Gay Marriage Supporters Predict Surge of Activism," *Salt Lake Tribune*, November 15, 2008.
38. Pearson diary, December 27 2008.
39. Peter Henderson, "Insight: Silent or Supportive, Conservatives Give Gay Marriage Momentum," Reuters, March 25, 2013.
40. Balken interview.
41. Jacobs interview, January 19, 2014.
42. Jennifer Dobner, "Utah Prime Location for Gay-Rights Movement," Associated Press, May 3, 2009.
43. Susan Donaldson James, "California Upholds Gay Marriage Ban," ABCNews.go.com, May 26, 2009.
44. Balken interview; "Person of the Year Thomas S. Monson," *Q Salt Lake*, December 15, 2008.
45. Sharon Groves interview, November 19, 2014.

CHAPTER 17. THE KISS

1. "Church Responds to Same-Sex Marriage Votes," *Mormon Newsroom*, November 5, 2008; Rosky interview; Pappas interview.
2. "Equality Utah Takes LDS Church at Its Word," Equality Utah press release, November 10, 2008.
3. Balken interview.
4. Rosemary Winters, "Gay-Rights Push Suffers Setback," *Salt Lake Tribune*, January 27, 2009.
5. "Common Ground Bills Pass Rules Committee," *Q Salt Lake*, February 13, 2009.
6. LaVar Christensen, "A Principled Understanding of Same-Sex Politics," *Sutherland Institute*, February 5, 2009; "Buttars Compares Gays with Radical Muslims, Will Take Down America," *Q Salt Lake*, February 18, 2009. Buttars's comments were so offensive that he was stripped of his membership and

chairmanship of two Senate committees for his antigay comments. Robert Gehrke, "Buttars: 'I Don't Have Anything to Apologize For,'" *Salt Lake Tribune*, February 20, 2009.

7. Rosky interview.

8. Pappas interview.

9. Deeda Seed interview, December 30, 2016.

10. Eric S. Peterson, "Kiss Off: A Gay Couple Cited for Holding Hands on Main Street Plaza," *City Weekly*, July 10, 2009.

11. Jared Page, "'Love Advocates' Plan 'Kiss-In' at Main Street Plaza," *Deseret News*, July 11, 2009.

12. Seed interview.

13. Lindsay Whitehurst, "'Kiss-In' to Show Support for Gay Couple in LDS Trespassing Controversy," *Salt Lake Tribune*, July 12, 2009.

14. "Couple Cuffed and Ticketed for a Kiss on LDS Church Main Street Plaza," *Q Salt Lake*, July 12, 2009.

15. Lindsay Whitehurst, "Protestors Gather to Smooch near LDS Temple," *Salt Lake Tribune*, July 12, 2009.

16. Scott Taylor, "LDS Church Defends Actions in Plaza 'Kissing' Incident," *Deseret News*, July 18, 2009.

17. Ben Fulton, "Salt Lake City Kissing Protest Brings Cheers, Jeers (with Multimedia)," *Salt Lake Tribune*, July 20, 2009.

18. Rosemary Winters and Malinda Rogers, "Prosecutor Drops Case against Gay Couple Accused of Trespassing on LDS Property," *Salt Lake Tribune*, July 29, 2009.

19. Aaron Falk, "No Charges in Main Street Plaza Trespassing Case," *Deseret News*, July 29, 2009.

20. Seed interview.

21. James Dabakis interview, August 2, 2013.

22. Seed interview.

23. Dabakis interview, August 2, 2013.

24. Jesse Fruhwirth, "Secret Gay/LDS Meetings," *City Weekly*, November 18, 2009.

25. Balken interview.

26. Dabakis interview, August 2, 2013.

27. Dabakis interview, April 8, 2015.

28. Balken interview.

29. Ibid.

30. Dabakis interview, August 2, 2013.

31. Ibid.; Pappas interview.

32. Williams interview, March 30, 2015.

33. Solmonese interview.

34. Aaron Falk, "Salt Lake City Seeks Input on Gay-Resident Protections," *Deseret News*, November 10, 2009.

35. "Legislators, Gov. Disapprove of Gay and Transgender-Friendly Ordinance," *Q Salt Lake*, August 31, 2009.

36. Derek P. Jensen and Rosemary Winters, "Salt Lake Nondiscrimination Effort under Fire," *Salt Lake Tribune*, August 26, 2009.

37. Dabakis interview, August 2, 2013.

38. Balken interview.

39. Rosky interview.

40. Kirk Johnson, "Mormon Support of Gay Rights Statute Draws Praise," *New York Times*, November 12, 2009.

41. "Sutherland Statement on SLC Nondiscrimination Ordinances and LDS Support," October 12, 2009.

42. "Utah Lawmakers Won't Take Up a Ban on Discrimination against Gays," *New York Times*, January 31, 2010.

43. Rosky interview.

44. William Eskridge to the author, November 20, 2016.

45. Dabakis interview, August 2, 2013.

46. Ibid.

47. Dabakis interview, April 8, 2015.

CHAPTER 18. *HOLLINGSWORTH V. PERRY*

1. Jacobs interview, June 12, 2010.

2. Jo Becker, "A Conservative's Road to Same-Sex Marriage Advocacy," *New York Times*, August 18, 2009, http://www.nytimes.com/2009/08/19/us/19olson.html?_r=1&hp=&pagewanted=all.

3. Jacobs interview, June 12, 2010.

4. Julia Rosen, "An Explosive Afternoon: LDS Church," www.EqualityonTrial.com, January 20, 2010; Brian Leubitz, "Your Right Hand Is My Left Hand: The LDS Church and the Prop 8 Campaign," www.EqualityonTrial.com, January 20, 2010.

5. American Foundation for Equal Rights, "Closing Arguments—Video Clip Transcripts," http://www.afer.org/wp-content/uploads/2010/06/Perry-Trial-Closing-Arguments-Video-Clip-Transcript1.pdf.

6. In the U.S. District Court for the Northern District of California, no. C 09-2292 VRW, August 4, 2010.

7. "Church Statement on Proposition 8 Ruling," *LDS Newsroom*, August 4, 2010.

8. Joanna Brooks, "LDS Church Response to Prop. 8 Begs Question of Polygamy," *Religion Dispatches*, February 8, 2012.

9. In the Supreme Court of the United States, no. 12-144, March 26, 2013.

CHAPTER 19. THREE MEN, TWO MESSAGES

1. Boyd K. Packer, General Conference address, October 2, 1976; *Conference Report*, October 1976, 100–101.

2. Ibid.

3. Peggy Fletcher Stack, "LDS Church 'Retires' Mormon Apostle's 'Little Factory' Pamphlet," *Salt Lake Tribune*, November 14, 2016.

4. E. Kimball, *Lengthen Your Stride*.

5. Packer, *To the One*.

6. Martha Sonntag Bradley, *Pedestals and Podiums: Utah Women, Religious Authority, and Equal Rights*.

7. Gregory A. Prince, *Leonard Arrington and the Writing of Mormon History*.

8. Boyd K. Packer, "Talk to the All-Church Coordinating Council," May 18, 1993.

9. Boyd K. Packer, "Ye Are the Temple of God," General Conference talk, October 2000, *Ensign*, November 2000; Boyd K. Packer, "On the Shoulders of Giants," BYU J. Reuben Clark Law Society Devotional, February 28, 2004; Boyd K. Packer, interviewed by Helen G. Whitney for the PBS documentary *The Mormons*, broadcast in 2007. Interview conducted February 25, 2006, Salt Lake City. Transcript from Helen Whitney, "Boyd Packer Part 3—Tape #3220.

10. Criddle interview.

11. Ibid.

12. Carol Lynn Pearson, "Elder Marlin K. Jensen Listens to Pain Caused by Prop 8," CLPearson.com, September 27, 2010; Joanna Brooks, "Mormon Leader: 'I'm Sorry' for Hurtful Legacy of Prop. 8," *Religion Dispatches*, October 4, 2010.

13. Peggy Fletcher Stack, "Apostle: Same-Sex Attraction Can Change," *Salt Lake Tribune*, October 4, 2010.

14. Boyd K. Packer, General Conference address, October 3, 2010. The transcript was made by the author from the audio recording of the address that is posted on lds.org.

15. Julie Bolcer, "Mormon Leader Reaffirms Prop. 8 Support," *Advocate*, October 4, 2010.

16. Peggy Fletcher Stack, "Mormons Divided on LDS Apostle's Speech on Gays," *Salt Lake Tribune*, October 5, 2010.

17. Human Rights Campaign, "HRC to Mormon Apostle: Your Statements Are Inaccurate and Dangerous," October 4, 2010.

18. https://www.lds.org/general-conference/2010/10/ cleansing-the-inner-vessel?lang=eng.

19. "Mormon Church Clarifies Intent of President Boyd K. Packer's Talk," *Deseret News*, October 8, 2010.

20. "2,000–3,000 Protest for Gay Rights Outside Mormon Church Offices in Salt Lake City," *Deseret News*, October 7, 2010; "Thousands Surround LDS Temple Square in Protest of Packer Speech," *Q Salt Lake*, October 7, 2010.

21. Rosemary Winters, "Petition against Packer's Speech Draws 100,000 Signatures," *Salt Lake Tribune*, October 8, 2010.

22. Peggy Fletcher Stack, "Packer Talk Jibes with LDS Stance after Tweak," *Salt Lake Tribune*, October 11, 2010.

23. "LDS Church Condemns Bullying of Gay Community," KSL.com, October 12, 2010.

24. Jennifer Dobner, Associated Press, "Mormon Church Says Cruelty toward Gays Is Wrong," *San Jose Mercury News*, October 12, 2010.

25. Peggy Fletcher Stack, "High-Ranking LDS Leader Weighs in on Same-Sex Attraction," *Salt Lake Tribune*, October 25, 2010.

26. Ibid.

CHAPTER 20. BRIDGES TO SOMEWHERE

1. Solmonese interview.

2. Joe Solmonese, *The Gift of Anger: Use Passion to Build Not Destroy*, 56.

3. Solmonese interview.

4. "Mormons Building Bridges by Marching in Utah Pride Parade," Mormons Building Bridges press release, May 29, 2012.

5. Williams interview.

6. "Mormons Building Bridges by Marching in Utah Pride Parade."

7. Joanna Brooks, "400 Churchgoing Mormons March in SLC Pride Parade," *Religion Dispatches*, June 4, 2012; Williams interview.

8. Jennifer Dobner, "Mormon Group Shows Its Support in Salt Lake City Gay Parade," *New York Times*, June 3, 2012.

9. Neil J. Young, "Equal Rights, Gay Rights and the Mormon Church," *New York Times*, June 13, 2012.

10. Peggy Fletcher Stack, "Tribune's Utahns of the Year: Mormons Building Bridges," *Salt Lake Tribune*, December 25, 2012.

11. "New Pamphlet Seeks to Help Mormon Parents with Gay Kids," *Q Salt Lake*, June 15, 2012.

12. Ryan interview.

13. Joseph Walker, "New Booklet Targets LDS Families of Homosexual Youth," *Deseret News*, June 15, 2012.

14. Montgomery interview, March 14, 2015.

15. Ibid.

16. "Gay Mormons Organize," *Advocate*, November 2, 1977.

17. *Affirmation/G.M.U. Newsletter*, December 11, 1977; Jeppson interview.

18. "LDS Homosexuals Featured in National Gay Magazine," *Sunstone Review* 2, no. 11 (1982): 8.

19. "Gay Mormons Try to Meet New Leader," *Los Angeles Times*, February 11, 2008.

20. Affirmation Executive Committee to Thomas S. Monson, February 6, 2008.

21. Jennifer Dobner, "LDS Officials to Meet with Gay Group," Associated Press, April 7, 2008.

22. "LDS Church Responds to Gay Mormons Group," MormonTimes.com, produced by *Deseret News*, August 12, 2008.

23. John Gustav-Wrathall to the author, December 12, 2016.

24. Alan Blodgett to the author, December 2, 2014.

25. Gustav-Wrathall to the author, December 12, 2016.

26. Peggy Fletcher Stack, "Mama Dragons Lead the Fight for Their Gay Mormon Kids," *Salt Lake Tribune*, May 4, 2015; Wendy Montgomery, "Mormon Mother Fighting for LGBTQ Inclusion in Her Church," *Huffington Post*, May 21, 2015.

CHAPTER 21. MORMONSANDGAYS.ORG

1. Randall Thacker to Affirmation Board of Directors, December 21, 2012.

2. "New Church Website on Same-Sex Attraction Offers Love, Understanding and Hope," *LDS Newsroom*, December 6, 2012. In 2016 a replacement site, MormonandGay.lds.org, was launched by the church, at which time MormonsandGays.org was taken down.

3. Spencer W. Kimball, "A Counselling Problem in the Church," Brigham Young University, July 10, 1964. Typescript of address.

4. The backing out from political activism on the part of church members preceded the website. The 2006 edition of the *Church Handbook of Instructions* contained the following sentences that were deleted from the 2010 edition: "Church members are encouraged 'to appeal to legislators, judges, and other government officials to preserve the purposes and sanctity of marriage between a man and a woman, and to reject all efforts to give legal authorization or other official approval or support to marriages between persons of the same gender.'"

5. Peggy Fletcher Stack, "New Mormon Church Website Has Softer Tone on Gays," *Salt Lake Tribune*, December 6, 2012.

6. Epigenetic factors are those that control the expression of genes. They are sometimes of greater importance than the nucleic acid sequences of the genes themselves.

CHAPTER 22. *KITCHEN V. HERBERT*

1. Dennis Romboy, "Gay Marriage: What's Next for Utah?," *Deseret News*, July 3, 2013.

2. Williams interview.

3. "Restore Our Humanity Founder Mark Lawrence," *Q Salt Lake*, January 16, 2014.

4. Erin Fuchs, "Lawyer's Religious Memo Reveals Why He Quit to Fight Gay Marriage Full-Time," *Business Insider*, January 23, 2014.

5. Kate Call Declaration, filed October 10, 2013.

6. Laurie Wood interview, May 16, 2016.

7. Kody Partridge interview, May 16, 2016.

8. Wood interview.

9. "Who Is Judge Shelby?," *Q Salt Lake*, January 9, 2014.

10. Wood interview.

11. *Kitchen v. Herbert*, Memorandum Decision and Order, December 20, 2013.

12. Robert Barnes, "Decades of Battles Converged for Momentous Decision: From Hawaii to White House, Gays' Right to Marry Seemed Far from Inevitable," *Washington Post*, June 27, 2015.

13. Kendell interview, December 3, 2014.

14. Scott G. Winterton, "In Our Opinion: Judicial Tyranny," editorial, *Deseret News*, December 20, 2013.

15. "Church Statement on Court Ruling Regarding Same-Sex Marriage in Utah," *LDS Newsroom*, December 20, 2013.

16. "Church Instructs Leaders on Same-Sex Marriage," *LDS Newsroom*, January 10, 2014.

17. Brooke Adams, "Poll: Utahns Evenly Split on Same-Sex Marriage," *Salt Lake Tribune*, January 15, 2014.

18. Matthew Breen, "Mormons, God and Gays," *Advocate*, March 5, 2014.

19. Brady McCombs, "LDS Church Weighs in on Gay Marriage," *Provo Daily Herald*, February 11, 2014.

20. Jessica Miller, "10th Circuit Court: Utah's Same-Sex Marriage Ban Is Unconstitutional," *Salt Lake Tribune*, June 26, 2014.

21. Emily Eyring, "LDS Church Issues Statement Regarding Overturned Utah Marriage Amendment," *Deseret News*, June 25, 2014.

22. "Mormon Church, Other Faiths Urge U.S. Supreme Court to Intervene in Gay Marriage Issue," *USA Today*, September 6, 2014; Robert Barnes, "Supreme Court Declines to Review Same-Sex Marriage Cases," *Washington Post*, October 6, 2014.

23. Certiorari is a writ seeking judicial review. The U.S. Supreme Court receives thousands of such appeals each session but accepts only a small fraction for review.

24. Marissa Lang, "Utah Clerks Issuing Marriage Licenses to Same-Sex Couples," *Salt Lake Tribune*, October 6, 2014.

25. Adam Liptak, "Denying Review, Justices Clear Way for Gay Marriage in 5 States," *New York Times*, October 6, 2014; "Church Responds to Supreme Court Announcement," *LDS Newsroom*, October 6, 2014.

CHAPTER 23. SB 296

1. Robert Gehrke, "Mormon Church in Talks on Statewide Law to Protect Gays from Bias," *Salt Lake Tribune*, February 7, 2013; Editorial Board, "A Helping Hand: LDS Should Support Equal Rights," *Salt Lake Tribune*, February 18, 2013.

2. Dennis Romboy, "Proposed Non-discrimination Law Won't Be Heard on Senate Floor," *Deseret News*, March 11, 2013.

3. "Empowering Our Persecution," *Q Salt Lake*, June 21, 2013.

4. Rosky interview.

5. Williams interview.

6. Eric Ethington, "Breaking: Mormon Church Announces Endorsement of Housing, Employment Protections for LGBT People," www.TheNewCivilRightsMovement.com, December 20, 2014.

7. Eric Ethington, "Mormon Church Walks Back Statement Of Support for Non-discrimination Laws," www.TheNewCivilRightsMovement.com, December 21, 2014.

8. Tad Walch, "LDS Church Clarifies Position on Nondiscrimination Legislation," *Deseret News*, December 21, 2014.

9. Williams interview. In February 2014 the Arizona Legislature passed a bill that would have allowed "business owners to turn away gay and lesbian customers, employers to deny equal pay to women, or individuals to renege on contract obligations—as long as they claim to be doing so in the name of religion." "Arizona Passes Law Allowing Discrimination," MSNBC.com, February 21, 2014. Public outcry was so intense that Republican governor Jan Brewer vetoed the bill.

10. Stephen Urquhart interview, January 27, 2015.

11. Ibid.

12. "Transcript of News Conference on Religious Freedom and Nondiscrimination," *LDS Newsroom*, January 27, 2015.

13. Geoff Nelson, "Erosion of Religious Liberty?," RationalFaiths.com, January 29, 2015.

14. "Transcript of News Conference." Given the church's long-standing condemnation of abortion, and overt threat to discipline LDS physicians who conducted therapeutic abortions, Holland's statement was breathtaking.

15. Robert Gehrke, "With LDS Announcement, Is Anti-discrimination Bill Now a Slam-Dunk?," *Salt Lake Tribune*, January 27, 2015.

16. Peggy Fletcher Stack, "In Major Move, Mormon Apostles Call for Statewide LGBT Protections," *Salt Lake Tribune*, January 27, 2015.

17. Andrew Rosenthal, "Mormon Church Wants Freedom to Discriminate," *New York Times*, January 27, 2015.

18. Rt. Rev. V. Gene Robinson, "Dear Mormons: Thanks but No Thanks," *Huffington Post*, January 30, 2015.

19. Daniel Burke, "Mormon Church Backs LGBT Rights—with One Condition," CNN.com, January 27, 2015.

20. Zack Ford, "Despite Its Announcement, the Mormon Church Hasn't Actually Done Anything for LGBT Equality," ThinkProgress.org, January 28, 2015; Brooke P. Hunter, "How the Mormons Punked the Press," *Huffington Post*, January 28, 2015.

21. Samantha Allen, "The Mormon Church's Gay Rights Charade," TheDailyBeast.com, January 28, 2015.

22. Peggy Fletcher Stack, "No Apology? Really? Mormons Question Leader Dallin H. Oaks' Stance," *Salt Lake Tribune*, January 30, 2015.

23. "Mormon LGBT Announcement Met with Cheers, Skepticism," *All Things Considered*, January 29, 2015.

24. Jonathan Adamson, "LDS Leadership Calls for Right to Discriminate under Guise of 'Religious Freedom,'" RideTheWindsBack.blogspot.com, January 29, 2915.

25. Williams interview.

26. Dabakis interview, March 30, 2015.

27. Niraj Chokshi, "Gay Rights, Religious Rights and a Compromise in an Unlikely Place: Utah," *Washington Post*, April 12, 2015.

28. As of November 2016, only five of twenty-nine state senators were Democrats and only twelve of seventy-five state representatives.

29. Dabakis interview, March 30, 2015.

30. Rosky interview.

31. Dabakis interview, March 30, 2015.

32. Senator Urquhart related this information to the author in a conversation in the Utah Senate lounge the following day, March 2, 2015.

33. Dabakis interview, March 30, 2015.

34. Ibid.

35. Dabakis interview, April 8, 2015.

36. Dabakis interview, March 30, 2015.

37. Robert Gehrke, "Mormon Leaders, LGBT Groups Trumpet New Anti-bias Bill as a 'Model,'" *Salt Lake Tribune*, March 5, 2015.

38. "Utah Gay Leaders Stand Side-by-Side with Mormon Apostles to Endorse Nondiscrimination/Religious Freedom Bill," *Q Salt Lake*, March 4, 2015.

39. Dabakis interview, March 30, 2015.

40. Laurie Goodstein, "Utah Passes Antidiscrimination Bill Backed by Mormon Leaders, *New York Times*, March 12, 2015; Michael Aaron, "Nondiscrimination Laws Years in the Making Signed into Law," *Q Salt Lake*, April 2015.

41. Goodstein, "Utah Passes Antidiscrimination Bill."

CHAPTER 24. THE LAST DOMINO

1. Robert Barnes, "Appeals Court Upholds Ban on Same-Sex Marriage in Four States," *Washington Post*, November 6, 2014.

2. Robert Barnes, "As Gay Marriages Begin in Florida, Supreme Court Is Set to Meet on Issue," *Washington Post*, January 5, 2015.

3. Editorial Board, "The Supreme Court and Gay Marriage," *New York Times*, January 16, 2015.

4. "Religious Freedom and Fairness for All," MormonNewsroom.org, April 13, 2015.

5. *Obergefell v. Hodges*, oral arguments to the Supreme Court, 14-556, April 28, 2015.

6. *Obergefell et al. v. Hodges, Director, Ohio Department of Health, et al.*, Supreme Court of the United States, no. 14-556, Decided June 26, 2015.

7. Coverture was a legal principle wherein women forfeited their rights and property to their husbands upon marriage. Some elements of coverture

persisted within parts of the United States until the middle of the twentieth century.

8. "Supreme Court Decision Will Not Change Doctrine on Marriage," *LDS Church News*, June 26, 2015.

9. "Church Leaders Counsel Members after Supreme Court Same-Sex Marriage Decision," *LDS Newsroom*, June 30, 2015.

10. "Utah Student Files Lawsuit against So-Called 'Reparative Therapy,'" *Q Salt Lake*, November 27, 2012.

11. Susan K. Livio, "Judge: Therapists Who Say Gays Can Be 'Cured' Are Committing Fraud," *Salt Lake Tribune*, February 17, 2015.

12. Michael Ferguson, interviewed July 15, 2015, by John P. Dehlin.

13. Sam Wolfe, "Gay-Conversion Therapy Should Be Exposed for What It Is, Consumer Fraud," op-ed, *Salt Lake Tribune*, August 29, 2015.

CHAPTER 25. RELIGIOUS FREEDOM

1. Quentin L. Cook was a practicing attorney until he was called to be a member of the Quorum of the Twelve Apostles on October 6, 2007.

2. Michael Brendan Dougherty, "Mormons at the Door," *American Conservative*, February 23, 2009.

3. "Transcript of Elder Dallin H. Oaks Speech on Religious Freedom," *LDS Newsroom*, October 13, 2009.

4. Affidavit of Charles W. H. Goo, President, BYU-Hawaii 1st Stake, February 16, 1995, *Baehr v. Lewin*, Docket Item 39.

5. Morris A. Thurston, "A Commentary on the Document 'Six Consequences...If Proposition 8 Fails," originally posted September 12, 2008.

6. *In re Marriage Cases*, 43 Cal. 4th 757, p. 117.

7. "Church Leaders Counsel Members after Supreme Court Same-Sex Marriage Decision," *LDS Newsroom*, June 30, 2015.

8. Curtis L. Price, pastor, First Baptist Church, Salt Lake City, "Religious Freedom Is Not under Attack in This Country," op-ed, *Salt Lake Tribune*, February 7, 2015.

9. William N. Eskridge Jr., "Churches Need Not Fear That Same-Sex Marriage Will Be Forced on Them," op-ed, *Salt Lake Tribune*, October 8, 2016.

10. "Religious Liberty and Gay Marriage: Is Oaks Right? Yes and No," *Salt Lake Tribune*, October 24, 2009.

11. Mitchell Landsberg, "Religious Freedom under Siege, Mormon Leader Says," *Los Angeles Times*, February 5, 2011.

12. Glenden Brown, "Dallin Oaks Demands Special Rights: He Doth Protest Too Much," OneUtah.org, February 7, 2011.

13. "Religious Liberty and Gay Marriage."

14. Landsberg, "Religious Freedom under Siege."

15. Bob Henline, "Perverting Religious Freedom," *Q Salt Lake*, February 17, 2011.

16. James Peron, "There They Go Again: Mormon Paper Distorts Facts to Bash Marriage Equality," *Huffington Post*, February 12, 2012.

17. Joanna Brooks, "Mormon Leader: Religious Freedom under Attack by Gay Rights," *Religion Dispatches*, February 9, 2011.

18. Price, "Religious Freedom Is Not under Attack in This Country."

19. "Religious Values and Public Policy," address given February 29, 1992, BYU Management Society, Washington, DC, *Ensign* 22, no. 10 (1992): 60–64.

20. "Transcript of Elder Dallin H. Oaks Speech on Religious Freedom," *LDS Newsroom*, October 13, 2009.

21. "Prop. 8 Supporters Must Be Identified," *Deseret News*, January 31, 2009.

22. "Transcript of Elder Dallin H. Oaks Speech on Religious Freedom," *LDS Newsroom*, October 13, 2009.

23. "Apostle Talks Religious Freedom to Boston Youth," *LDS Newsroom*, June 17, 2010.

24. *Obergefell et al. v. Hodges, Director, Ohio Department of Health, et al.*, Supreme Court of the United States, no. 14-556, Decided June 26, 2015.

25. "Transcript of Elder Dallin H. Oaks' Speech Given at Chapman University School of Law," *LDS Newsroom*, February 4, 2011.

26. Phelps (1929–2014) was a Baptist minister and senior pastor of the Westboro Baptist Church in Topeka, Kansas. He and his congregation gained national notoriety for their public demonstrations against LGBT people. The group's website, GodHatesFags.com, is indicative of the general tone of their speech—speech that continues to be protected by the First Amendment despite its hateful content.

27. Henline, "Perverting Religious Freedom."

28. "Questioning General Authority," posted in *Musings by Jim Burklo*, November 8, 2011, http://tcpc.blogs.com/musings/2011/11/questioning-general-authority.html.

CHAPTER 26. THE POLICY

1. Peggy Fletcher Stack, "Can Mormons Back Same-Sex Marriage and Still Get in the Temple?," *Salt Lake Tribune*, January 17, 2014.

2. While the outcome of a disciplinary council is nominally within the discretion of local leaders, rather than General Authorities, it seems unlikely that the result of a council hearing could be anything other than excommunication. The only way a married couple could "repent" of their apostasy would be to divorce each other. It seems odd for a family-centered church to require the breakup of a family as a prerequisite to membership, particularly in the case of a same-sex couple with children, but that would seem to be the result of the Policy.

3. *Church Handbook of Instructions*, electronic version, sections 6.7.3 (apostasy) and 16.13 (children).

4. Bryce Cook interview, January 31, 2016.

5. R. B. Scott, "Mormon LGBT Policy Prompts Anger, Resignations and Fresh Concerns about Aged Leaders," TheMuss.net, December 16, 2015.

6. "Faithful Questioning and the Policy Changes," February 2, 2016, http://www.outinzion.org/25-seeking-a-better-understanding-of-the-policy-changes/.

7. Jennifer Dobner, "New Mormon Policy Makes Apostates of Married Same-Sex Couples, Bars Children from Rites," *Salt Lake Tribune*, November 5, 2015.

8. D. Todd Christofferson, "Church Provides Context on Handbook Changes Affecting Same-Sex Marriage," *LDS Newsroom*, November 6, 2015.

9. Dobner, "New Mormon Policy Makes Apostates."

10. Ed Firmage, "Denying Sacraments to Children Is Sinful," letter to the editor, *Salt Lake Tribune*, January 14, 2016.

11. Alison Lesley, "Pope Francis Tells Priests Do Not Deny Baptisms," *World Religion News*, April 30, 2015; Rabbi Shmuley Boteach, "Why Is the Mormon Church Punishing Children of Gay Marriage?," Observer.com, November 10, 2015.

12. Laurie Goodstein, "Mormons Sharpen Stand against Same-Sex Marriage," *New York Times*, November 6, 2015; Peggy Fletcher Stack, "Mormons' Biggest Fear about New Gay Policy: Children Paying for Parents' Sins," *Salt Lake Tribune*, November 10, 2015.

13. Dobner, "New Mormon Policy Makes Apostates."

14. Jerilyn Hassell Pool, "Suffer the Little Children" Facebook group, November 10, 2015.

15. Jana Riess, "Mormon Boy Denied Priesthood Ordination Because His Mom Is Living with a Woman," November 10, 2015, janariess.religionnews.com.

16. Kate Kendell, "Leaving Mormon Church over 'Cruel' Policy on Gays' Kids," ReligionNews.com, November 10, 2015.

17. Michelle Boorstein, "Mormons Plan to Quit over Church's New Policy Banning Baptism in Gay Families," *Washington Post*, November 12, 2015.

18. Wendy Montgomery to the author, February 12, 2017.

19. Tad Walch, "Activists, Mostly Inactive Mormons, Resign from LDS Church at SLC Event," *Deseret News*, November 14, 2015; Nadine Hansen, letter of resignation from the LDS Church, November 15, 2015.

20. Lavina Fielding Anderson to the author, January 7, 2016.

21. Editorial Board, "Stung by Edict on Gays, Mormons Leave Church," *New York Times*, November 19, 2015; Abraham Taylor to the author, March 15, 2017.

22. Laurie Goodstein, "Some Mormons Search the Web and Find Doubt," *New York Times*, July 20, 2013.

23. Travis Stratford to the author, February 6, 2017. Stratford, a former missionary to Sweden, had been influential in assisting Mattsson to cope with his earlier faith crisis.

24. First Presidency circular letter, November 13, 2015 (emphasis added).

25. Cook interview.

26. Tad Walch, "Elder Scott Unable to Attend Meetings of the Twelve, but Elder Perry Returns," *Deseret News*, May 8, 2015.

27. Thomas S. Monson died on January 2, 2018. Twelve days later, Russell M. Nelson became the seventeenth president of the church.

28. Gregory A. Prince, Lester E. Bush Jr., and Brent N. Rushforth, "Gerontocracy and the Future of Mormonism."

29. Russell M. Nelson, "Becoming True Millennials," Worldwide Devotional for Young Adults, BYU-Hawaii, January 10, 2016.

30. "President Russell M. Nelson: 'Becoming True Millennials,'" *Deseret News*, January 10, 2016; "Mormon Gay Policy Is 'Will of the Lord' through His Prophet, Senior Apostle Says," *Salt Lake Tribune*, January 10, 2016.

31. Peggy Fletcher Stack, "Split Surfaces in LDS Policy on Same-Sex Couples: Mormons Back It; Other Utahns Don't," *Salt Lake Tribune*, January 23, 2016.

32. Jana Riess, "Commentary: Most U.S. Mormons Approve of Church's Policy on Gay Couples, Study Shows," *Salt Lake Tribune*, November 1, 2016.

33. "Affirmation Survey on the Impact of the LDS Church's November 2015 Policy Change on LGBT Mormons, Families and Friends," October 15, 2016.

34. The restaurant was Market Street Grille, one of more than a dozen Salt Lake City restaurants founded by John Williams, who was gay.

35. Yvette Zobell interview, February 4, 2017.

CHAPTER 27. TRANS

1. Kinsey, Pomeroy, and Martin, *Sexual Behavior in the Human Male*.

2. "Tribtalk" interview, https://www.youtube.com/watch?v=UIJ6gL_xc-M.

3. Ronald A. Rasband, "Faith, Fairness, and Religious Freedom," address at Brigham Young University, September 15, 2015, *Ensign*, September 2016.

4. https://mormonandgay.lds.org/articles/frequently-asked-questions.

5. Peggy Fletcher Stack, "Transgender Mormons Struggle to Feel at Home in Their Bodies and Their Religion," *Salt Lake Tribune*, April 2, 2015.

6. In 1998 the title of the manual, which is the LDS equivalent of canon law, was changed from *General Handbook of Instructions* to *Church Handbook of Instructions*.

7. Lester E. Bush Jr., *Health and Medicine among the Latter-day Saints*.

8. Hugh W. Pinnock to [stake president], June 30, 1978 (emphasis in the original).

9. "The Church Judicial System," October 1980, 2 (emphasis added).

10. *General Handbook of Instructions*, 1983, 53 (emphasis added).

11. "Section 8: The Church Judicial System," January 31, 1985, 52 (emphasis added).

12. *General Handbook of Instructions*, 1989, 10-4 (emphasis added).

13. *Church Handbook of Instructions, Book 1*, 2017, section 16.3.16 (emphasis added).

14. Balken interview.

15. David Noyce, "Will Mormon Church Embrace Scouting's New Transgender Policy? It's Assessing the Issue," *Salt Lake Tribune*, January 31, 2017; "Church Responds to BSA Policy Announcement," MormonsNewsroom.org, January 31, 2017; "Church Replacing Varsity and Venturing Scouting with New Activities Program," *LDS Church News*, May 11, 2017, https://www.lds.org/church/news/church-replacing-varsity-and-venturing-scouting-with-new-activities-program?lang=eng. The effective date of the change was January 1, 2018.

16. United States Conference of Catholic Bishops, Union of Orthodox Jewish Congregations of America, National Association of Evangelicals, Ethics and Religious Liberty Commission of the Southern Baptist Convention, the Church of Jesus Christ of Latter-day Saints, the Lutheran Church–Missouri Synod, and the Christian Legal Society. The petition, "Brief of Major Religious Organizations as *Amici Curiae* Supporting Petitioner," was written by Alexander Dushku, R. Shawn Gunnarson, and Joshua D. K. Figueira of Kirton McConkie, Salt Lake City, and filed on January 10, 2017.

17. Sarah Jade Woodhouse interview, February 6, 2017.

18. Emmett Michael Claren, "Finding Spiritual Peace through Transition," November 2016, http://affirmation.org finding-spiritual-peace-through-transition/.

19. Peggy Fletcher Stack, "After Leading LDS Congregations and Designing Mormon Temples, This Utah Dad Is Building a New Life—as a Woman," *Salt Lake Tribune*, July 21, 2017.

20. Victoria Adam to the author, February 26, 2018.

21. Emily Heaton interview, October 16, 2017.

22. Larsen interview, February 22, 2018.

CHAPTER 28. INTERSEX

1. Duane Jeffery's "Intersexes in Humans: An Introductory Exploration," although published nearly four decades ago, remains a useful introduction to the subject from an LDS perspective.

2. "Free & Equal Campaign Fact Sheet: Intersex," United Nations Office of the High Commissioner for Human Rights, 2015, https://unfe.org/system/unfe-65-Intersex_Factsheet_ENGLISH.pdf.

3. Kimberly Anderson interview, February 13, 2017.

4. Ibid.

5. David Hatch interview, April 29, 2017.

6. Anderson interview.

7. Hatch interview.

CHAPTER 29. SUICIDE

1. Caitlin Ryan and Robert A. Rees, *Supportive Families, Healthy Children: Helping Latter-day Saint Families with Lesbian, Gay, Bisexual and Transgender Children.*

2. Pearson, *No More Goodbyes*.

3. Laura Skaggs Dulin interview, February 12, 2018.

4. Brian Williams Simmons, "Coming Out Mormon: An Examination of Religious Orientation, Spiritual Trauma, and PTSD among Mormons and Ex-Mormon LGBTQQA Adults."

5. George Deussen interview, February 20, 2018; Wendy Montgomery to the author, March 4, 2018.

6. Robert I. McQueen, "Outside the Temple Gates—the Gay Mormon," *Advocate*, August 13, 1975, 14.

7. Pearson diary, November 10, 2008.

8. Matthew Shepard, who was not LDS, was brutally beaten by two men and left in the cold of an October night in Wyoming in 1998. He died several days later. Outrage over the hateful nature of his murder led to the Matthew Shepard and James Byrd Jr. Hate Crimes Prevention Act of 2009.

9. Hugo Salinas, "A Witness Sealed with Blood: Gay Mormon Suicides and the Politics of Silence," 3–5.

10. Tad Walch and Lois M. Collins, "LDS Church Leaders Mourn Reported Deaths in Mormon LGBT Community," *Deseret News*, January 28, 2016; Peggy Fletcher Stack, "Suicide Fears, If Not Actual Suicides, Rise in Wake of Mormon Same-Sex Policy," *Salt Lake Tribune*, January 28, 2016.

11. See chapter 3 of Prince and Wright, *David O. McKay and the Rise of Modern Mormonism*, for a detailed account of the scandal caused by the publication of *Mormon Doctrine*.

12. McConkie, *Mormon Doctrine*, 696. In a second edition of the book, published eight years later, he walked back his harsh judgment: "Obviously, persons subject to great stresses may lose control of themselves and become mentally clouded to the point that they are no longer accountable for their acts. Such are not to be condemned for taking their own lives." I have heard from multiple sources that in the eight years between the two editions of the book, one of McConkie's close friends committed suicide, thus causing him to rethink the issue.

13. Montgomery interview, February 21, 2018.

14. "Facts/Data," Utah Suicide Prevention Coalition, September 2014.

15. "Indicator Report—Suicide," Violence and Injury Prevention Program, Bureau of Health Promotion, Division of Disease Control and Prevention, Utah Department of Health, December 9, 2014.

16. Peggy Fletcher Stack, "Transgender Mormons Struggle to Feel at Home in Their Bodies and Their Religion," *Salt Lake Tribune*, April 2, 2015.

17. Luke Ramseth, "Utah's Governor Launches Youth Suicide Task Force as State Reveals 44 Suicide Deaths among 10-to-17-Year-Olds in 2017," *Salt Lake Tribune*, January 17, 2018.

18. This and other quotes from Stockton's parents, Alyson and George Deussen, are from an interview conducted on February 20, 2018.

19. Montgomery interview, February 21, 2018.
20. Ibid.
21. Ibid.
22. Ibid., July 16, 2014.
23. Carol V. A. Quinn, "LGBTQ Mormons Take a Courageous Stand against Church Leadership," conveyed April 12, 2015, by email from Yvette Zobell.
24. Montgomery to the author, March 4, 2018.
25. Montgomery interview, February 21, 2018.
26. Larsen interview.
27. G. Deussen interview.
28. Larsen interview.
29. Dulin interview.
30. Larsen interview; Montgomery interview; G. Deussen interview.

CHAPTER 30. THE SCARLET LETTER

1. *General Handbook of Instructions, No. 19*, 1963, 54; *General Handbook of Instructions, No. 21*, 1976, 86.
2. *Church Handbook of Instructions, Book 1*, 1998, 129.
3. Christopher Lee interview, April 4, 2018. The following quotes also come from this interview.
4. Scott Quinton interview, April 8, 2018.
5. Lee interview.
6. Email to Bishop Scott Quinton, January 15, 2014.
7. Lee interview.
8. Jake Bernhardt interview, March 29, 2018. The following quotes also come from this interview.
9. Wendy Montgomery to the author, March 30, 2018.
10. Janice Peterson, "Investment Fraud Rampant in Utah County," *Provo Daily Herald*, February 28, 2010; Dennis Romboy, "Utah's Fraud 'Epidemic': Victims Share Anger, Embarrassment, Hurt," *Deseret News*, October 27, 2016.
11. Doctrine and Covenants 58:42.

CHAPTER 31. WHAT'S NEXT?

1. Naomi Zeveloff, "Gay Mormons Challenge Church," Salon.com, June 11, 2012.
2. Andrew Sullivan, "Will the Mormon Church Ever Accept Gays?," TheDailyBeast.com, June 15, 2012.
3. Sharon Groves, director, Religion and Faith Program, Human Rights Campaign, "LGBT Mormons Claim Their Faith," www.hrc.org/blog, September 17, 2013.
4. Gustav-Wrathall interview, October 17, 2015.
5. Dehlin et al., "Psychosocial Correlates."
6. Alma 1:4.
7. Doctrine and Covenants, 76:51.

8.   Doctrine and Covenants, 137:6.

9.   Gregory A. Prince, *Power from on High: The Development of Mormon Priesthood*, chap. 3.

10. Doctrine and Covenants, 131:2 (parentheses in the original).

11. James O. Mason, "The Worth of a Soul is Great," Evergreen International Fifteenth Annual Conference, September 17, 2005; Lance B. Wickman, "Interview with Elder Dallin H. Oaks and Elder Lance B. Wickman: 'Same-Gender Attraction,'" 2006, http://www.mormonnewsroom.org/article/interview-oaks-wickman-same-gender-attraction; "Elder Bruce C. Hafen Speaks on Same-Sex Attraction," www.mormonnewsroom.org, September 19, 2009.

12. "Why are so many of the inhabitants of the earth cursed with a skin of blackness? It comes in consequence of their fathers rejecting the power of the holy priesthood, and the law of God. They will go down to death. And when all the rest of the children have received their blessings in the holy priesthood, then that curse will be removed from the seed of Cain, and they will then come up and possess the priesthood, and receive all the blessings which we now are entitled to." First Presidency statement, August 17, 1949, quoting Brigham Young.

13. "The position of the Church regarding the Negro may be understood when another doctrine of the Church is kept in mind, namely, that the conduct of spirits in the premortal existence has some determining effect upon the conditions and circumstances under which these spirits take on mortality and that while the details of this principle have not been made known, the mortality is a privilege that is given to those who maintain their first estate; and that the worth of the privilege is so great that spirits are willing to come to earth and take on bodies no matter what the handicap may be as to the kind of bodies they are to secure; and that among the handicaps, failure of the right to enjoy in mortality the blessings of the priesthood is a handicap which spirits are willing to assume in order that they might come to earth. Under this principle there is no injustice whatsoever involved in this deprivation as to the holding of the priesthood by the Negroes." Ibid.

14. Interview of Jeffrey Holland by Helen Whitney on March 4, 2006, for the PBS documentary television program *The Mormons*, http://www.pbs.org/mormons/interviews/holland.html.

15. Peggy Fletcher Stack, "High-Ranking LDS Leader Weighs in on Same-Sex Attraction," *Salt Lake Tribune*, October 25, 2010.

16. Kent Blake, "Burning the Borderlands: A Personal Reaction to the Mormon Church's Policy Changes on Same-Sex Couples," *Huffington Post*, November 10, 2015. Taylor G. Petrey explored the implications of a gay-friendly LDS afterlife: "Toward a Post-heterosexual Mormon Theology," *Dialogue: A Journal of Mormon Thought* 44, no. 4 (2011): 106–41.

17. Harry Knox interview, October 27, 2015.

18. https://mormonandgay.lds.org/videos?id=11549365994538963301.

19. Bob Mims and Peggy Fletcher Stack, "Mormon Church Releases Video of Family Accepting Gay Son Who Leaves the Faith," *Salt Lake Tribune*, March 21, 2017.

20. Larry R. Lawrence, "The War Goes On," *Ensign*, April 2017, 32–39.

21. Jeffrey R. Holland, April 1, 2017, https://www.lds.org/general-conference/2017/04/songs-sung-and-unsung?lang=eng.

22. Solomon interview.

BIBLIOGRAPHY

I am indebted to many people who shared with me unpublished documents. In each instance, I have a photocopy of the document in my personal archive. I also have photocopies of the newspaper and Internet articles referenced throughout this book. All other sources are referenced only in the endnotes throughout the book. Copies of all of my notes, with the exception of the full-length transcriptions of the interviews, will be deposited in my papers at the Marriott Library of the University of Utah following publication of the book.

PUBLISHED SOURCES

"Affirmation Member Testifies on Marriage before Hawaii Senate." *Affinity* 16, no. 1 (1994).

Bagemihl, Bruce. *Biological Exuberance: Animal Homosexuality and Natural Diversity.* New York: St. Martin's Press, 1999.

Baker, Katharine K. "The Stories of Marriage." *Journal of Law & Family Studies* 12 (January 1, 2010): 1–55.

Balthazart, J. *The Biology of Homosexuality.* New York: Oxford University Press, 2012.

Becker, Jo. *Forcing the Spring: Inside the Fight for Marriage Equality.* New York: The Penguin Press, 2014.

Beckstead, Arvel Lee. "The Process toward Self-Acceptance and Self-Identity of Individuals Who Underwent Sexual Reorientation Therapy." PhD diss., University of Utah, 2001.

Berube, Allan. *Coming Out under Fire: The History of Gay Men and Women in World War Two.* New York: Free Press, 1990.

Bishop's Training Course and Self-Help Guide. Salt Lake City: Church of Jesus Christ of Latter-day Saints, 1970.

Boies, David, and Theodore B. Olson. *Redeeming the Dream: The Case for Marriage Equality.* New York: Viking, 2014.

Bradley, Martha Sonntag. *Pedestals and Podiums: Utah Women, Religious Authority, and Equal Rights.* Salt Lake City: Signature Books, 2005.

Bradshaw, K., J. P. Dehlin, K. A. Crowell, R. V. Galliher, and W. S. Bradshaw. "Sexual Orientation Change Efforts through Psychotherapy for LGBQ

Individuals Affiliated with the Church of Jesus Christ of Latter-day Saints."
   Journal of Sex and Marital Therapy 41 (2014): 391–412.

Bush, Lester E., Jr. *Health and Medicine among the Latter-day Saints*. New York:
   Crossroad, 1993.

Byne, W., and B. Parsons. "Human Sexual Orientation: The Biologic Theories
   Reappraised." *Archives of General Psychiatry* 50 (1993): 228–39.

Cathcart, Kevin M., and Leslie J. Gabel-Brett, eds. *Love Unites Us: Winning the
   Freedom to Marry in America*. New York: New Press, 2016.

The Church and the Proposed Equal Rights Amendment: A Moral Issue. Salt Lake
   City: Church of Jesus Christ of Latter-day Saints, 1980.

Cloud, John. "For Better or Worse: In Hawaii, a Showdown over Marriage Tests the
   Limits of Gay Activism." *Time*, October 19, 1998.

Coolidge, David Orgon. "The Hawai'i Marriage Amendment: Its Origins, Meaning
   and Fate." *University of Hawai'i Law Review* 19 (2000): 20–119.

Dehlin, John P. "Sexual Orientation Change Efforts, Identity Conflict, and
   Psychosocial Health amongst Same-Sex Attracted Mormons." PhD diss.,
   Utah State University, 2015.

Dehlin, John P., Renee V. Galliher, William S. Bradshaw, and Katherine A.
   Crowell. "Psychosocial Correlates of Religious Approaches to Same-Sex
   Attraction: A Mormon Perspective." *Journal of Gay & Lesbian Mental Health*
   18 (2014): 284–311.

Dehlin, J. P., R. V. Galliher, W. S. Bradshaw, D. C. Hyde, and K. A. Crowell. "Sexual
   Orientation Change Efforts among Current or Former LDS Church Members."
   Journal of Counseling Psychology 62, no. 2 (2014): 95–105.

D'Emilio, John, and Estelle B. Freedman. *Intimate Matters: A History of Sexuality
   in America*. New York: Harper and Row, 1988.

Eskridge, William N., Jr. *Dishonorable Passions: Sodomy Laws in America, 1861–
   2003*. New York: Viking, 2008.

———. "Noah's Curse: How Religion Often Conflates Status, Belief, and Conduct to
   Resist Antidiscrimination Norms." *Georgia Law Review* 45 (2011): 665–720.

Feldman, M. P., and M. J. MacCulloch. "Application of Anticipatory Avoidance
   Learning to the Treatment of Homosexuality." *Behavior Research and
   Therapy* 2 (1964): 165–83.

God Loveth His Children. Salt Lake City: Church of Jesus Christ of Latter-day
   Saints, 2007.

Goodwill, Kristopher Albert. "Religion and the Spiritual Needs of Gay Mormon
   Men." Master's thesis, California State University, Long Beach, 1999.

Hinckley, Gordon B. *Standing for Something: 10 Neglected Virtues That Heal Our
   Hearts and Homes*. New York: Times Books, 2000.

Homosexuality. Welfare Services Packet 1, 1973. Salt Lake City: Church of Jesus
   Christ of Latter-day Saints, 1973.

Homosexuality. 2nd ed. Salt Lake City: Church of Jesus Christ of Latter-day Saints,
   1981.

James, Elizabeth C. "Treatment of Homosexuality: A Reanalysis and Synthesis of Outcome Studies." PhD diss., Brigham Young University, 1978.

Jeffery, Duane. "Intersexes in Humans: An Introductory Exploration." *Dialogue: A Journal of Mormon Thought* 12, no. 3 (1979): 107–13.

Kimball, Edward L. *Lengthen Your Stride: The Presidency of Spencer W. Kimball, Working Draft.* Salt Lake City: Benchmark Books, 2009.

Kimball, Edward L., and Andrew E. Kimball, Jr. *Spencer W. Kimball: Twelfth President of the Church of Jesus Christ of Latter-day Saints.* Salt Lake City: Bookcraft, 1977.

Kimball, Spencer W. *A Letter to a Friend.* Salt Lake City: Church of Jesus Christ of Latter-day Saints, 1978.

——. *The Miracle of Forgiveness.* Salt Lake City: Bookcraft, 1969.

——. *New Horizons for Homosexuals.* Salt Lake City: Church of Jesus Christ of Latter-day Saints, 1971.

Kimball, Spencer W., and Mark E. Petersen. *Hope for Transgressors.* Salt Lake City: Church of Jesus Christ of Latter-day Saints, 1970.

Kinsey, Alfred C., Wardell B. Pomeroy, and Clyde E. Martin. *Sexual Behavior in the Human Male.* Philadelphia: W. B. Saunders, 1948.

McBride, Max Ford. "Effect of Visual Stimuli in Electric Aversion Therapy." PhD diss., Brigham Young University, 1976.

McConkie, Bruce R. *Mormon Doctrine.* Salt Lake City: Bookcraft, 1958.

O'Brien, T. J. "You Are Not Alone: A Plea for Understanding the Homosexual Condition." *Dialogue: A Journal of Mormon Thought* 26, no. 3 (1993): 119–40.

O'Donovan, Connell. "'The Abominable and Detestable Crime Against Nature': A Brief History of Homosexuality and Mormonism, 1840–1980." In *Multiply and Replenish: Essays on Mormon Sex and Family,* edited by Brent Corcoran. Salt Lake City: Signature Books, 1994.

Packer, Boyd K. *To the One.* Address given to the Twelve Stake Fireside, Brigham Young University, March 5, 1978. Salt Lake City: Church of Jesus Christ of Latter-day Saints, 1978.

Pearson, Carol Lynn. *No More Goodbyes: Circling the Wagons around Our Gay Loved Ones.* Walnut Creek, CA: Pivot Point Books, 2007.

Prince, Gregory A. "'An Exquisite and Profound Love': An Interview with Andrew Solomon." *Dialogue: A Journal of Mormon Thought* 46, no. 1 (2013): 160–89.

——. *Leonard Arrington and the Writing of Mormon History.* Salt Lake City: University of Utah Press, 2016.

——. *Power from on High: The Development of Mormon Priesthood.* Salt Lake City: Signature Books, 1995.

——. "'There Is Always a Struggle': An Interview with Chieko N. Okazaki." *Dialogue: A Journal of Mormon Thought* 45, no. 1 (2012): 112–40.

Prince, Gregory A., Lester E. Bush Jr., and Brent N. Rushforth. "Gerontocracy and the Future of Mormonism." *Dialogue: A Journal of Mormon Thought* 49, no. 3 (2016): 89–108.

Prince, Gregory A., and Wm. Robert Wright. *David O. McKay and the Rise of Modern Mormonism*. Salt Lake City: University of Utah Press, 2005.

Quinn, D. Michael. *Same-Sex Dynamics among Nineteenth-Century Americans: A Mormon Example*. Urbana: University of Illinois Press, 1996.

Ryan, Caitlin, and Robert A. Rees. *Supportive Families, Healthy Children: Helping Latter-day Saint Families with Lesbian, Gay, Bisexual and Transgender Children*. San Francisco: Family Acceptance Project, 2012.

Salinas, Hugo. "A Witness Sealed with Blood: Gay Mormon Suicides and the Politics of Silence." *Affinity* 22, no. 11 (2001).

Schow, Ronald. "Homosexual Attraction and LDS Marriage Decisions." *Dialogue: A Journal of Mormon Thought,* 38, no. 3 (2005): 133–42.

Simmons, Brian Williams. "Coming Out Mormon: An Examination of Religious Orientation, Spiritual Trauma, and PTSD among Mormons and Ex-Mormon LGBTQQA Adults." PhD diss., University of Georgia, 2017.

Solmonese, Joe. *The Gift of Anger: Use Passion to Build Not Destroy*. Oakland, CA: Berrett-Koehler, 2016.

Swedin, Eric Gottfrid. "'You Are Healing Souls': A History of Psychotherapy within the Modern Latter-day Saint Community." PhD diss., Case Western Reserve University, 1996.

Understanding and Helping Those Who Have Homosexual Problems. Suggestions for Ecclesiastical Leaders. Salt Lake City: Church of Jesus Christ of Latter-day Saints, 1992.

Winkler, Douglas A. "Lavender Sons of Zion: A History of Gay Men in Salt Lake City, 1950–79." PhD diss., University of Utah, 2008.

Youn, Monica. "Proposition 8 and the Mormon Church: A Case Study in Donor Disclosure." *George Washington Law Review* 81 (November 2013): 2108–54.

INTERVIEWS

Anderson, Kimberly. February 13, 2017.

Balken, Brandie, former executive director, Equality Utah. April 11, 2013.

Bastian, Bruce. July 30, 2014.

Bergin, Allen, psychologist. September 27, 2015.

Bernhardt, Jake. March 29, 2018.

Blanchard, Cosette. June 11, 2015.

Bohn, Jeffrey. September 1, 2015.

Boyer, Nikki. July 25, 2015.

Bradshaw, Claudia. March 4, 2015.

Bradshaw, William, professor emeritus of biology, Brigham Young University. December 28, 2015.

Callahan, Andrew. March 25, 2015.

Chipman, Michael. April 9, 2015.

Cook, Bryce. January 31, 2016.

Criddle, Dean, former president, California Oakland Stake. September 4, 2016.

Dabakis, James, Utah state senator. August 2, 2013; March 30 and April 8, 2015.

Deussen, Alyson. February 20, 2018.

Deussen, George. February 20, 2018.

Dulin, Laura Skaggs, mental health therapist. February 12, 2018.

Ferré, Jann. March 29, 2015.

Ferré, Richard, psychiatrist. March 1 and 29, 2015.

Graziano, Barbara. February 5, 2017.

Groves, Sharon, former director of religion and faith program, Human Rights Campaign. November 19, 2014.

Gustav-Wrathall, John, president, Affirmation. October 17 and 18, 2015.

Hansen, Nadine. October 22, 2013.

Hatch, David, physician. April 29, 2017.

Heaton, Emily. October 16, 2017.

Jacobs, Richard, founder, Courage Campaign. June 12, 2010; January 19, 2014.

Jansson, Mark. November 16, 2015.

Jeppson, Buckley. October 5, 2015.

Karger, Fred. July 8, 2014.

Kendell, Kate, executive director, National Center for Lesbian Rights. December 3, 2014.

Knox, Harry, former director of religion and faith program , Human Rights Campaign. October 27, 2015.

Larsen, Stephenie, founder, Encircle. February 22, 2018.

Lee, Christopher. April 4, 2018.

McCurry, Michael, former press secretary, White House. December 19, 2014.

Mifuel, Carina. July 30, 2014.

Montgomery, Wendy. July 16, 2014; March 14, 2015; February 21, 2018.

Oldham, Carol. January 14, 2015.

Oldham, Lee. January 15, 2015.

O'Neill, Michael, former staffer, Senate Judiciary Committee. November 7, 2017.

Pappas, Stephanie, former chair, Equality Utah. April 9, 2015.

Partridge, Kody, plaintiff in *Kitchen v. Herbert*. May 16, 2016.

Pearson, Carol Lynn, author of LGBT books. January 12, 2014.

Peterson, Geneva. March 3, 2015.

Peterson, Marvin. March 3, 2015.

Prince, Stephen. August 21, 2015; September 4, 2016.

Quinton, Scott. April 8, 2018.

Rampton, Emily. October 4, 2017.

Raynes, Marybeth, psychologist. April 7, 2013.

Rees, Robert. August 10, 2014.

Reid, Harry, former U.S. senator. October 31, 2017.

Rosky, Clifford, professor of law, University of Utah. March 31, 2015.

Ryan, Caitlin, clinical social worker. March 15, 2015.

Sainz, Fred, vice president, Human Rights Campaign. August 15, 2014.

Schow, Ronald, LGBT activist. March 18, 21, and 23, 2013; January 15, 2015.

Seed, Deeda. December 30, 2016.

Solmonese, Joseph, former president, Human Rights Campaign. January 12, 2016.

Solomon, Andrew, National Action Council, National LGBTQ Task Force. March 28, 2011.

Thurston, Morris. January 17, 2014.

Urquhart, Stephen, former Utah state senator. January 27, 2015.

Waite, Sherod. July 18, 2014.

Williams, Troy, executive director, Equality Utah. March 30, 2015.

Wood, Laurie, plaintiff in *Kitchen v. Herbert*. May 16, 2016.

Woodhouse, Sarah Jade. February 6, 2017.

Yates, Jennette. January 16, 2015.

Zobell, Yvette. February 4, 2017.

Zollinger, Jake. September 8, 2015.

INDEX